GIFTS OF THE DESERT

DOUBLEDAY

New York   London   Toronto   Sydney   Auckland

KYRIACOS C. MARKIDES

GIFTS

OF THE

DESERT

THE FORGOTTEN PATH OF
CHRISTIAN SPIRITUALITY

PUBLISHED BY DOUBLEDAY
a division of Random House, Inc.

DOUBLEDAY and the portrayal of an anchor with a dolphin are registered
trademarks of Random House, Inc.

Book design by Judith Stagnitto Abbate / Abbate Design

Library of Congress Cataloging-in-Publication Data

Markides, Kyriacos C.
Gifts of the desert : the forgotten path of Christian spirituality / Kyriacos C.
Markides.—1st ed.
p. cm.
Includes bibliographical references
1. Desert Fathers. 2. Spiritual life—Christianity. 3. Monastic and religious
life—Middle East. I. Title.

BR60.A65M27 2005
248.4'819—dc22
2005041438

ISBN 0-385-50663-5

PRINTED IN THE UNITED STATES OF AMERICA

November 2005

5 7 9 10 8 6 4

FOR MAROULLA AND VASSOS

CONTENTS

CONTENTS

VIII

AUTHOR'S NOTE

I am grateful to a number of people for the present volume. First and foremost, I am indebted to Father Maximos, the central character of this work, for his generosity in guiding my adventures into Eastern Orthodox mystical spirituality. Needless to say, I alone am responsible for whatever shortcomings or inaccuracies may be found in the pages that follow.

I am also very grateful to Bishop Kallistos Ware for carefully reading the first draft of this manuscript and for offering me his invaluable and constructive critique. Most significantly, I am thankful for his willingness to be interviewed at Oxford University, allowing his wisdom and profound knowledge of Eastern Orthodoxy to shine through the pages of a key chapter in this book.

I am, of course, always deeply thankful to my colleagues in the sociology department of the University of Maine for their continuous support in my research endeavors over the years and for a sabbatical leave in the spring of 2003. I am also grateful to sociologist Peter Berger, director of the Institute on Culture, Religion and World Affairs at Boston University, and to Elizabeth Prodromou, the associate director, for offering me a visiting professorship at their institute during the spring semester of 2004 that allowed me to focus on completing the writing of this manuscript.

My gratitude extends also to the following friends for the role they played directly or indirectly in the making of this work: Nikos and Dora Aivaliotis, Akis and Rodoulla Lordos, and Dafnis Panayides, as well as all others who appear in this book. I am deeply grateful to my literary agent of over twenty years, Ashala Gabriel, for her exemplary professional expertise and belief in the value of my work as well as for the title of this book. I would also like to extend my heartfelt appreciation to former editor of Doubleday Eric Major, for his encouragement to write *Gifts of the Desert*, as well as to his successor, Michelle Rapkin, and to associate editor Andrew Corbin. Their personal warmth and enthusiastic support of this project were invaluable.

My colleague and friend Mike Lewis, professor of art at the University of Maine, was the first to read each chapter as I completed it, and he offered me priceless feedback. Most important, his deep appreciation of the content of the book sustained me over the years. I feel particularly blessed to have my office right below his studio. Such a providential arrangement allowed me to have frequent contact with him and be a beneficiary of his wisdom during frequent peripatetic dialogues through the university woods.

Much love and thanks go to my friends and relatives in Cyprus, particularly my sister Maroulla and my brother-in-law Vassos for their love and for making our stay on the island always such a rich experience. To them I dedicate this work.

Without the love, sustained support, encouragement, and lively presence of my wife, Emily, our son Constantine and daughter Vasia, I could not have pursued this intellectual and spiritual Odyssey. They have been the foundation of my sanity and sense of well-being. As in my previous book, the last reading before sending the manuscript to the editor was done by our novelist son Constantine. I am the proud beneficiary of his superb mastery of the English language. Lastly and most important, this book, like all the others I have written, is a far superior work thanks to Emily. In addition to being my lifelong companion, intellectual partner, and best friend and confidante, she has also been my informal and most critical editor in chief of everything I have written.

I have followed the same policy that I applied in my previous books regarding the forms of male Greek names used for direct address in the dialogues. For example, "Father Maxim*os*" is addressed as "Father Maxim*e*."

A person named "Kyriacos" is addressed as "Kyriaco," "Andreas" is addressed as "Andrea," "Lavros" as "Lavro" and so on. Female Greek names do not pose such a problem.

In most cases I have used pseudonyms to safeguard the anonymity of the subjects as much as that is possible. For the same reason, and on occasion, I made minor alterations in terms of time, and of the venue where episodes have taken place. This does not apply to historical events and personalities. *Gifts of the Desert,* like its predecessor, is not fiction. Rather it is based on personal experiences and encounters. The reader may wish to consult the glossary at the end of the book when needed.

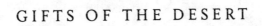

GIFTS OF THE DESERT

ONE

JOURNEY
TO
SEDONA

t was dark when we entered Sedona, named after the wife of the nineteenth-century postmaster who helped keep the settlers in contact with the rest of the world. The relatively few neon lights testified to Sedona's reputation as a "New Age mecca," a center for alternative health practitioners and a mosaic of new religious movements. As we drove slowly through the downtown area to get a first glimpse of the place, I felt for a moment as if I had just entered Corinth during Saint Paul's time.

All the street lights were unusually dim, offering minimal illumination for pedestrians. Our friend Pat, who, together with her husband, Philip, had picked us up at the airport explained that the city council, wisely, had passed ordinances to protect the night from artificial light pollution. People could still look up and gaze at the Milky Way and experience the massive presence of the mountains, mute and silent, surrounding the desert town.

"Too much luminosity at night obstructs our capacity to reflect and contemplate our relationship to God and our place in the universe," Philip announced as he pressed the brakes at a stoplight.

His comment brought to my mind an experience I shared with my wife Emily during a visit to the Sivananda Yoga Retreat on Paradise Island, Nassau. I had been invited there to give a presentation on the lives and teachings of Eastern Orthodox saints and sages. Among the speakers was an astronomer who showed slides of outer space taken by the Hubble telescope. We were profoundly moved by what we saw, awed by the magnificence and beauty of the physical universe. One stunning photo showed an endless expanse of galaxies, billions of them, that the Hubble telescope managed to capture on film.

"You cannot see the colors now, but tomorrow, before your workshop, we will take you for a long hike," Pat promised. "You will then understand why we decided to settle here."

When Mary and Joan, two former Catholic nuns who had recently migrated to Sedona from the Northwest, invited me to offer a workshop "The Forgotten Path of Mystical Christianity" I accepted at once. Colleagues and friends familiar with that region of the Southwest assured me that Sedona is a dream place and that the beauty of the land is indescribable and "beyond this world."

There was another reason for accepting their invitation to fly from our home in Maine to Arizona. Southeast of Phoenix, at the heart of the Arizona desert, lay a recently established Greek Orthodox monastery named after Saint Anthony, the first Christian hermit, who spearheaded the monastic movement during the fourth century. I had heard unusual and controversial stories about the circumstances that led to the creation of the monastery, and being somewhat of a connoisseur and collector of extraordinary tales, I decided to go see it for myself. The monastery was set up during the mid-nineties. It was the creation of a venerated elder from Mount

Athos, the inaccessible monastic republic in northern Greece and the subject matter of my research and writing during the previous ten years.[1] A remnant of the Byzantine Empire, Mount Athos has served since the ninth century as a refuge for monks and hermits who, in that remote peninsula, preserved what many consider to be the mystical, holy tradition of early Christianity.

It was, therefore, a unique opportunity for Emily and me to combine our journey to Sedona with a six-day retreat at Saint Anthony's monastery. Frequent visits to monasteries have not only been necessary for my research but also have served as a source of spiritual renewal and rejuvenation, a balancing act to an otherwise cerebral, academic lifestyle. We had contemplated for some time the possibility of visiting the Arizona monastery to hear firsthand the details of how such an unlikely institution popped up in the heart of an American desert. Most important, after hearing legends about his charisma and extraordinary "gifts of the Spirit," we wished to meet the Athonite elder responsible for setting it up.

A further bonus of the Sedona trip was the opportunity to reconnect with our friends Philip and Pat, who volunteered to give us a lift from the Phoenix airport to Sedona, a two-hour drive. Thanks to our mutual interests in spiritual matters and in Cyprus, where they lived for a while on a Fulbright scholarship, we remained in touch.

"Keep in mind that while in Arizona, you must drink lots of liquids," Pat warned us after Philip, sighing with relief, got us out of the airport maze and onto the right interstate. "The air is extremely dry and your body needs water, plenty of it. You will soon find out that Arizona is very different from Maine, or Cyprus for that matter."

"Sedona," Philip said, pointing with his hand in the direction where we were heading, "is more conducive to spiritual work than any other place we have been to. It is really charged with healing energy. You will soon find out for yourself." After a pause, he continued, "We feel comfortable in Sedona because it is a center of diverse religious currents." Pat added that in fact the whole of Arizona offers itself for spiritual work: "One feels it in the very fabric of its landscape." Our friends were deeply spiritual, but not "religious" in the conventional sense.[2] They represented the type of people I expected to encounter during my upcoming workshop.

3

"At this stage in our lives we needed a place where we can focus more on our spiritual growth and less on career and worldly achievements," Philip said. Over the years he had heroically managed to fight off melanoma through a combination of organic nutrition, alternative therapies, and systematic, deep meditation. "After all, as you know," he continued, "deserts offer themselves for spiritual work. Right? When we get there you will see what I mean. Sedona is vibrant with spiritual energy."

With such an introduction there was a heightened sense of anticipation about what awaited us ahead. When I mentioned the name of the monastery of Saint Anthony, it was all news to them. However, Philip quickly added that it did not surprise him that the Arizona desert was chosen as a fitting location for a monastery: "Whoever created it must have known that this area is a vortex of spiritual energy," he added with a smile as they dropped us off at a cozy inn built several miles above Sedona at the base of a lush and cool canyon.

Early the next morning, Pat and Philip took us on a two-hour hike through the canyons. As predicted by my friends, the outdoor excursion, instead of tiring me, filled me with energy. After a couple of hours' rest I felt ready to lead the workshop and face the 180 people who had flown in from around the country. Among the participants were a few mainstream Protestants, a number of disenchanted Catholics, former churchgoers of all denominations, New Age enthusiasts, holistic health practitioners, spiritualists, acolytes of Native American shamanism, liberal Jews, and aficionados of Eastern religions such as Hinduism, Tibetan Buddhism, and Zen. In addition to Emily and myself, there were two more Greek Orthodox, a father and his songwriter son, who appeared excited that I was to explore with all these diverse seekers the mystical tradition of Eastern Christianity.

With the exception of atheists, agnostics, and doctrinaire skeptics, much of the modern American multiethnic and multireligious landscape seemed to be represented. I was fascinated and slightly intimidated. Here was a gathering of mostly professional people, many of them disenchanted with the prevailing materialist worldview as well as with organized religion, who were in search of "authentic spirituality." In spite of all of America's enormous problems, domestic and international, I was not aware of any other society in the history of the world, I thought to myself as I faced my audience, to have provided such hospitable parameters for the free exploration of spirituality as contemporary America has done. Compared to the more religiously homogeneous societies of the past, in today's multicultural America one may belong to whatever religion one chooses without the fear of ostracism or the risk of being anathematized as a heretic. I shared these thoughts with my receptive audience in my opening remarks. It was a good start.

The presence of Philip, Pat, and Emily sitting in the front row, along with my two good friends Joan and Mary, the former Catholic nuns who organized the event, eased the mild nervousness I always feel when I first face a new audience. Before the formal introductions began, and until everybody found their seat, a local musician played a couple of her own mesmerizing and soothing compositions on a harp.

After a few jokes and before getting into the substance of the workshop, I asked the participants to reflect on a simple idea. I asked them to contemplate for a few seconds the myriad of coincidences that had brought us all together in a precise and perfect manner in that auditorium during that particular time. A seemingly minor change in our lives, I brought to their attention, would have drastically altered all the probabilities that had made our gathering a reality.

The moment I noticed a degree of receptivity in the participants' faces I engaged them in a simple exercise: "For five minutes write down on a piece of paper all the coincidences that you consider turning points in your life. Imagine how your life might have developed without those coincidences and experiences. You might then arrive at some interesting conclusions not only about your life but also about the nature and fabric of reality."

With the exception of one elderly lady, everybody showed readiness to participate in that brief and simple exercise of self-exploration. When the time was up I asked them, if they felt comfortable, to share what they wrote down with two strangers in the room for twenty minutes.

There was much commotion as people moved their chairs around in search of strangers. After the initial introductions they began to talk about their lives feverishly. I joined the group nearest to me. A buzzing energy swept the conference room, melting away barriers of anonymity and impersonality. When the twenty minutes were over it required an extra effort on my part to bring the group to order. I then proceeded to ask what the underlying meaning of this exercise might be beyond their getting to know one another. A woman volunteered an answer, that all the coincidences in our lives cannot be just random events but rather form part of a meaningful nexus of interconnectedness that defies any rational comprehension. Given the selective nature of the audience, it was not surprising to get similar responses from the other participants. As one put it: "It is important to remind ourselves that our lives are neither accidental nor coincidental."

"Yes. This is a spiritual axiom shared by most of the great teachers of humanity," I responded. "It is an antidote to contemporary feelings of alienation, self-estrangement, and meaninglessness. It is this primordial question of human destiny that we will explore today through the spiritual tradition and teachings of the holy elders of Eastern Christianity." I then went further to suggest that what may be true about our lives may also be true about the universe at large and mentioned the well-known aphorism "as above so it is below."

A Vietnam veteran (a fighter pilot, I learned later) asked me to elaborate on what I meant by that statement. "Today," I responded, "the majority of astrophysicists agree that our universe came into existence as a result of an original explosion that took place about fifteen billion years ago. It is what they call the Big Bang theory of the creation of the universe. They also agree that, had there been an infinitesimal alteration in temperature during the explosion, our universe as we have known it could not have come into existence. Any thinking human being, therefore, who reflects on creation must wonder that perhaps nothing in the cosmos is the arbitrary result of randomness. The probability that the universe is the product of such randomness is equal to the probability that, as British cosmologist Fred Hoyle once put it, a tornado sweeps through a junkyard and causes the creation of a fully operating jet plane.[3] I am also reminded of what the leading contemporary philosopher of consciousness, Ken Wilber, once said—that any rational human being who contemplates the creation of the universe cannot but become an idealist. He implied by such a statement that an intelligent reality must be behind the creation of the world. Otherwise, he reasoned, how could the dust particles that came into existence at the moment of the cosmic explosion, presumably ex nihilo, have found each other and created such an intricate and infinitely complex universe? Wilber concluded that the mathematical formulas and the natural laws must have predated creation, a notion that would have found Plato in full accord. We must always keep in mind, therefore, that materialist science has the authority to tell us how things are only from the moment of the explosion until today. It has no legitimacy, no power to tell us anything of what happened or who was there prior to the explosion. It cannot tell us why the explosion took place in the first place. That is in the province of religion and spirituality, and the legitimate authorities on that subject are the great saints and prophets and not specialized scientists who may know next to nothing about spiritual realities.

"Therefore, what seems to be true about the universe," I concluded, "must also be true about our own lives. After all, we are an integral part of this wondrous universe. Based on this premise, our life cannot be accidental, but, as the Eastern Orthodox Christian elders insist, it is governed by spiritual laws set down by Providence within eternity. We will try to explore some of these laws today by studying the lives and teachings of sages and saints."

With the brief exercise behind us, I shared with my audience some of the key coincidences in my own life that set the stage for my involvement in and exploration of the Christian mystical tradition that we were about to examine.

"It all began on a trip to Mount Athos during the spring of 1991. As some of you might know, Mount Athos is a peninsula in northern Greece, thirty miles long by ten miles wide. For the last thousand years it has been a monastic republic and a refuge of Eastern Orthodox monks and hermits who have been practicing in silence an ancient, ascetic way of life that has as its primary goal union with God. I never could have imagined that a journey to one of these monasteries would have changed my life so decisively and so profoundly."

I then recounted my "accidental" encounter with Father Maximos, a young monk I met outside the gate of the first monastery I visited: "Like most people living in the modern world, I was suspicious of monasticism and considered it an institutional anachronism, a relic of the medieval Dark Ages. I originally traveled to Mount Athos out of curiosity and at the insistence of a friend who challenged me to overcome my prejudices and join him on a pilgrimage to the Holy Mountain to meet, as he put it, real spiritual elders whose luminous faces radiated the love of Christ.

"Meeting Father Maximos," I went on, "was in fact the empirical confirmation of what Antonis, my friend, had promised. I soon realized that the then thirty-three-year-old Athonite monk possessed uncommon wisdom, which it seemed to me he acquired not only from books but also, and primarily, from direct experience. I was immediately attracted to Father Maximos, who has become since then my key mentor and informant in my explorations of Eastern Christianity's mystical tradition.

"I found out soon after our initial meeting that in spite of his relatively young age Father Maximos had a reputation as a *pneumatikos*, a spiritual elder and guide for laypeople as well as Orthodox priests and monks. I was profoundly impressed not only by his deep knowledge of the spiritual tradition he represented but also by his life, which embodied that tradition. I came to know him as a loving and compassionate spiritual guide, a confessor, endowed with a highly developed and disarming sense of humor.

"After that initial visit to Mount Athos I decided to shift my writing from the investigation of the worldview of lay mystics, which had preoccupied me for the previous ten years,[4] to the spiritual tradition that Father Maximos represented. This shift became possible for me as a result of a series of unusual coincidences, and after Father Maximos was asked by his own elders to return to his native Cyprus in order to help revive Christian monasticism on the island. Since the early nineties I have been visiting him there during summers and sabbatical leaves, and with his help I have embarked on a lifelong exploration of the mystical tradition of Eastern Orthodox spirituality."

I went on to say that my association with Father Maximos had helped me to overcome my totally negative outlook on and predisposition against organized religion. This negativity had been the legacy of my academic training, which had been, on the whole, hostile to religion. Soon after my exposure to Mount Athos and Father Maximos I realized that there was profound knowledge and wisdom embedded in the very structure of the

Church itself. This knowledge and this wisdom has been preserved since the early years of Christianity within its monasteries and within the very liturgy and services of the Church, or the *Ecclesia*. And I mean by that term not only the structure of the Church but the sum total of its practices, methods, and sacred texts, the testimony of saints, and their teachings on how to experientially know God.

"Imagine my own fascination," I continued, "when I discovered that within my own cultural tradition there existed a system of 'eldership' that I thought was a characteristic only of Buddhism and Hinduism."

I explained that what I meant by eldership was a system of discipleship, or mentorship, whereby an elder, ideally one graced by the Holy Spirit, supervises the spiritual development of his followers. The aim of this mentoring is to guide them toward direct experience of the divine and union with God, what in the Eastern Church is called *Theosis*. I paused to answer a number of questions. It was clear that the spiritual tradition I was presenting was entirely new and unfamiliar to my audience.

"The foundation of the teachings of the holy elders of the Christian East," I went on, "can be summarized as the 'Threefold Way,' the soul's journey toward union with God. It proceeds in three identifiable stages."

Using a black marker, I wrote down three words on a flip chart: *Catharsis, Fotisis, Theosis.* "Let me explain what they mean. According to the Eastern Christian elders all human beings live in *amartia*, or sin, which does not mean the violation of some moral injunction, as it is popularly understood, but a life cut off from God. Based on the story in Genesis, the original humans lived in paradise in a state of blissful oneness with God. Their primary preoccupation was the contemplation of their maker. The Fall heralds the shattering of that unity, plunging humanity into a state of alienation and estrangement from God. Our exit from Eden implies that we have lost sight of our origins. As a result, we turned our attention exclusively toward the created world while completely forgetting our heavenly origins. As we were caught up in a daily struggle for survival, our hearts got hardened and blinded to the fact of our divine inheritance. We don't know who we truly are, nor do we know the joy associated with the state of attunement and continuous communion with the divine. The holy elders teach that this ignorance and forgetfulness is our fundamental 'illness of

9

the heart,' the paramount problem of our existence and the source of all our psychological and spiritual malaise. Consequently, we are obsessed with and exclusively focused on the ephemeral pleasures of this world: food, sex, material possessions, power, fame, and so on. In short, we have become prodigal sons and daughters wasting our lives away. The more passionate we are in the pursuit of these goals, the greater the distance between us and God, the real source of our fulfillment and ultimate salvation.

"This state of existence is one of pain and suffering. At a certain point, however, an exhausted prodigal son becomes aware of his misery and longs for the palace of the loving father, where even the servants, according to the parable, are better off than him. The prodigal son then decides to return home in total humility, trusting his father's infinite compassion and forgiveness. This is the moment when the soul undergoes *metanoia*, repentance, a radical transformation of heart and mind. As a contemporary religious writer puts it, 'To repent is to awaken from the sleep of ignorance, to rediscover our soul, to gain the meaning and purpose of our lives by responding to the incomparable love of the One who is "not of this world."'[5] The arduous and difficult process of the return journey begins at this turning point of *metanoia*.

"Catharsis is the stage when, after realizing their predicament, people begin to systematically struggle to purify their hearts to make them vessels of the Holy Spirit so they will be in a position to see and experience God. This purification implies the rejection of all negative desires and destructive passions. This is the meaning of Christ's beatitude 'Blessed be the pure in heart for they shall see God.' The elders of Eastern Christianity teach that for as long as our hearts are hostage to worldly passions and desires we can never be visited by divine grace. This grace, they believe, resides deep within us but in our blindness we are unaware of its presence.

"Within the context of the Eastern Orthodox spiritual tradition a methodology has been devised by the holy elders on how to purify the heart so that it may begin to become aware of God's presence. It is called *askesis*, which literally means a set of spiritual exercises and practices for the overcoming of egotism and the 'acquisition of the Holy Spirit.' It is, incidentally, from this word that the word *ascetic* derives, implying the full-time practitioner of *askesis*. The aim of *askesis* is the overcoming of the material world's enchantment and the replacement of egotistical passions with only one all-consuming passion, the passion to become one with God. In Eastern Orthodox spirituality *askesis* presupposes fasting, confession, holy communion, self-observation, alignment of thought and action with Christ's commandments, ongoing study of sacred texts including the lives of saints, regular attendance at communal worship, and ceaseless prayer, which is often accompanied by prostrations in front of holy icons. Most important, parallel to this work on oneself, the catharsis of the heart through *askesis* implies the systematic cultivation of loving compassion for one's neighbor, expressed through practical acts of charitable service. Inner work must be balanced by outer action for the good of others.

"Ideally, *askesis* implies establishing a relationship with an elder who can put us on a special program and oversee our spiritual development as teachers oversee the education of their students.

"At first, these practices reminded me of the various yoga methods of Eastern religions, a reality that contemporary philosophers like Ken Wilber assumed existed only in those religions. For him the West lacked a method of experientially reaching God and relied exclusively on the intellect for that purpose. It is this practice of purifying the heart that I believe the Christian East can offer to the modern West, where such practices have been driven from sight as a result of the increasing secularization of contemporary life along with its exclusive focus on worldly pursuits. I was tremendously excited by this realization. It is a 'Christian yoga' of *hesychia*, or silence, that has also been discovered by an increasing number of western practitioners such as Thomas Merton, the celebrated American Catholic monk.[6]

"The word 'Fotisis,' the second stage in the evolution of the soul, literally means "illumination." It is the enlightenment of the soul. Once the soul has undergone its catharsis and has been cleansed of its negative passions, then it may be endowed with *charismata*, or gifts of the Spirit. Foremost among these gifts, the holy elders say, is the experience of the 'Uncreated Light.' The purified heart can see God directly in a state of mystic ecstasy and inner illumination."

After reading to my audience some reports on how elders have described that state, I proceeded to explain how in addition to the direct experience of God the soul may be endowed with further gifts like prophetic vision and healing powers, as well as unusual abilities, which today we call "paranormal." These include clairvoyance, telepathy, teleportation, out-of-body travel, and the like. All these so-called paranormal phenomena are part of the culture and lore of the Holy Mountain.

"I was told by eyewitnesses of elders who levitated in a state of mystic ecstasy in front of the altar or while praying in front of the icon of the Holy Virgin. I have heard extraordinary stories of how contemporary elders like Paisios and Porphyrios[7] were seen in two places at the same time. These are tales that one usually reads or hears about in the life of Indian yogis.[8] It was a revelation for me that what I thought existed only in India and Tibet was very much part of the Christian spiritual tradition.

"I should point out that all these charismatic gifts are offered to the soul only after its purification. They are, literally, gifts of the Spirit that naturally emerge at a certain point in the spiritual development of the self. The elders warn, however, that such gifts must not be ends in themselves since such powers may lead the individual astray. The temptations are great to misuse such gifts. That is why authentic elders never demonstrate their spiritual powers for personal gain but employ them only sparingly in order to help others toward their God realization. At the same time these elders routinely deny that they are graced with such spiritual gifts. To pursue gifts of the Spirit directly without prior catharsis from egotistical passions is like stealing from God."

Several questions were raised by the audience concerning this point, particularly whether the pursuit of such abilities as extrasensory perception (ESP) or out-of-body travel is advisable or not. I reminded them that as far as the holy elders are concerned the primary goal must be to work on the stage of Catharsis. "That's where we must put all our efforts and engage our will. The seeking of gifts before a person matures does not help the individual advance spiritually. It may be counterproductive. Instead of helping the person progress toward union with God it may stimulate narcissism that may lead to further alienation from our divine source.

"Finally, the third stage in the spiritual development of the self is the attainment of *Theosis,* the ultimate destination of the human soul. Like the previous stage of Fotisis, it is totally in the hands of Providence. We cannot reunite with God strictly on our own accord. To repeat, our will must be employed only at the first stage, the stage of Catharsis. The other two stages follow naturally as God's rewards, so to speak, for our struggles to purify our hearts.

"When *Theosis* is reached, the original split between the self and God is finally overcome. It is like the return of Adam and Eve back into the garden of Eden, or the prodigal son back to the palace. This oneness with God is beyond all human description or comprehension."

A young woman at the back of the room, who had earlier mentioned she was a practitioner of Zen Buddhism, wondered whether the holy elders understood oneness with God as the annihilation of the separate self within the totality of the Godhead.

"In Christian spirituality," I replied, after thanking her for having raised such an important question, "the soul upon deification maintains its autonomy within the oneness of God. The self does not get diluted into the All. What is annihilated is the sum total of our egotistical passions and desires, not our uniqueness as persons created in the image of God for eternity. There is a big difference from certain notions stipulating that the final end of spiritual development is the total obliteration of individual personhood. Saints like Seraphim of Sarov or Maria the Egyptian, and every person who attains that stage of *Theosis* will retain their uniqueness within God while continuing as saints to work for the salvation of others. Incidentally, *Theosis* is not something that one can attain only after one's departure from the earth, it is possible while one is still alive. The paradisiacal state is possible from this side of the divide."

There was a lively discussion of this issue for a while. We then had a ninety-minute lunch break. Most of the participants drove to nearby restaurants where, unavoidably, the conversations continued. I had several participants ask me during lunch why the Threefold Way has not been part of Western Christianity and why it is found only in the Christian East, in such isolated places as Mount Athos. "Actually," I replied, "I am not certain that it is only found in the East. But it is perhaps true that it has been better preserved and institutionalized there. Answering your question, will require a history lesson."

Realizing that the issue was of interest to the rest of the participants I

13

postponed any further discussion until after we returned from lunch. I then put on my mantle as a sociologist and began by briefly going over the key historical events responsible for the preservation of the Threefold Way in the Christian East and the reasons for its relative marginalization in the West.

My brief foray into the history of Christianity provoked a lively discussion that lasted for more than an hour. My audience was alert and well read. We then had a coffee break and listened to recorded chants by Athonite monks as well as nuns living in monasteries adjacent to Mount Athos. Once we had reassembled for the last part of the workshop I elaborated further on the basic teachings of Eastern Christianity as related to me primarily by Father Maximos. We covered a wide scope of topics, ranging from the inner laws that govern our lives to the role of icons in spiritual practices to the importance of thought in promoting or undermining our return journey to God. After showing slides from Mount Athos and further discussing the spiritual wisdom preserved in those monasteries we listened in silence to more hymns and chants of the Christian East.

Just as I was about to thank the participants for their attentiveness and end the workshop, a woman who had earlier identified herself as a "born-again Christian" raised her hand with marked intensity.

"Christ taught that only through him can one go to the Father. How should we understand this statement?" she asked. Given my audience, it was the most challenging question I faced.

I had a feeling that she needed affirmation for her beliefs and consciously or unconsciously wished to prompt me into declaring that only Christians will inherit heaven. Feeling somewhat uneasy, I reflected for a few seconds. I knew that, whatever answer I could possibly come up with, someone might feel offended or excluded. I began by admitting that it was the first time I faced such a question and that I was not certain whether I could give a satisfactory answer. "Furthermore," I added, "I am not a biblical scholar who can offer an authoritative exegesis of scripture. I am certainly not a theologian." Inwardly I asked for guidance as I placed my left hand in my pocket and fiddled with a *komboschini* [a string of black knots made out of wool that the Athonite monks use for ceaseless prayer]. Father

Maximos had given it to me after pulling it off his own hand. It offered me a sense of security at that moment.

"Look," I replied finally. "There are two possible ways to answer your question. The first is to interpret that passage in the New Testament literally, the way many Christians today would interpret it. In this sense, nobody who is not a baptized Christian can be saved. Some denominations would even make the claim that only through their specific community can a human being find salvation. This is, let us say, an 'exoteric' belief shared widely among fundamentalist Christians. It is a belief, however, that divides people, raising serious questions about God's fairness and love for all his creatures. The typical objection is this: Does it mean that the billions of people who are not born Christian and who may have never even heard of Christ will be lost for eternity? From a more esoteric, 'inner Christian' perspective such a conclusion seems misguided, to put it mildly. It denies the possibility of salvation to the overwhelming majority of the human race. Surely this could not have been Christ's intention when he made that statement."

I was encouraged by the facial expressions of the participants and continued. "Why then don't we make an attempt to interpret that statement in a more inclusive way? Why don't we try to look at it in terms of its possible inner meaning? I believe the Gospel of John offers us guidelines to answer questions like yours. Christ, according to the Gospel, is 'the true Light, which lighteth every man that cometh into the world' [John 1:9]. Do you agree?" After she nodded I continued. "Well, that says it all. Every human being has the Christ within his or her very nature. Furthermore, we are told that Christ is total and unconditional Love. Is it not, therefore, reasonable to conclude that whoever wishes to go to the Father, i.e., God, must attain the state of absolute and selfless love that Jesus embodied? If Christ is Love, then anyone who reaches that state of purification reaches the Father. No one can go to the Father, therefore, outside of total and selfless love. It must be so by definition. Such an understanding would embrace the world, leaving no one outside. This is, I believe, the true spirit of the Christian message and this is what I understand the great saints of Christianity have taught either explicitly or implicitly."

15

Someone in the back of the room raised his hand. "Is it necessary," he said, "to identify love only by the name 'Christ?' Can we call Christ by other names?"

"I don't know. I believe names have power and they carry specific meanings. But I suppose it would depend to a great extent on the culture we happen to find ourselves in and the language we use. What is important, I believe, is what meaning we attach to whatever word we use. If the word encompasses the absolute love of God I personally have no problem calling Christ whatever name suits different peoples in different historical periods or cultural settings, or in different galaxies for that matter. After all, history, culture, and language are temporal and relative realities, as galaxies are. Christ is the Absolute God and Logos that transcends all humanly constructed realities. Christ is beyond time and space. That is why, I believe, the mystical experiences of the great saints throughout history provide the most powerful, experiential verification of the reality of the timeless nature of the *Christos Logos* residing in the innermost center of every human being. Perhaps it was Jesus as the historically manifested Christ who did not allow Paul to meet him in the flesh precisely because Paul was being groomed by Providence for his special historic mission. Paul's experience underscores the reality of the cosmic Christ residing in the heart of every human being, demonstrating the fact that every human being can meet the Christ Logos at all places and at all times."

I noticed widespread consensus and affirmation regarding what I had said and felt gratified. I was not certain, however, that my answer satisfied the woman who raised the question. Nevertheless, I ended the workshop feeling rejuvenated with the ideas I had explored with that very alert audience. Along with our hosts and friends, Emily and I spent the rest of the evening at a Mexican restaurant where we continued our conversation. When our symposium ended we promised to keep in touch and report back on our upcoming pilgrimage to the monastery of Saint Anthony.

TWO

GIFT

OF THE

DESERT

 was pleased to learn that a shuttle taxi service connected the Phoenix airport with the newly established monastery of Saint Anthony's. "What a relief," I said to Emily as I replaced the receiver. Neither of us was in the mood to venture driving into the desert on our own. In less than half an hour after my call the shuttle arrived. For sixty-five dollars we were to be dropped off outside the gate of the desert retreat for our weeklong stay.

The driver, an affable gentleman in his sixties, had a pronounced fondness for ceaseless chatter. During the ninety-minute ride we learned more than we were eager to know about his life in Arizona, his wife of forty years, his grandchildren, his hobbies, and his former employer. A retired salesman from Connecticut, he had migrated to Arizona chiefly to satisfy his passion for golf. Driving pilgrims to Saint Anthony's was a part-time distraction to make his retirement more comfortable and affordable.

"I play golf three hundred and sixty-five days a year," he announced with an air of supreme satisfaction at his good fortune. "There is constant sunshine here, great for golf." After a few rare moments of silence he began shaking his head.

"They are really strange people out there," he said, referring to the fifty monks of the monastery.

"Oh yes?" I said vaguely. I assumed that a Greek Orthodox monastery in the heart of the Arizona desert must have seemed like an incongruous oddity to an Anglo-Saxon golf-playing retiree from the Northeast. I presumed that in his mind a monastery must have looked suspiciously like some sort of a New Age cult, one of many found in abundance all across America.

But our good man had something else in mind. "Their food is abominable," he said with disgust as if to warn us of the culinary horrors that awaited us. "I can't fathom how human beings can live without meat." He shook his head for emphasis. "No Sir, I've got to have my daily meat. Otherwise I feel as if I haven't eaten anything.

"By the way," he hastened to add, "there is a McDonald's not far from here. I could stop by for you to get something before we get there." Our gregarious driver glanced at us inquisitively through his rearview mirror, waiting for our response to his generous offer.

"No thank you, we have just eaten," I replied.

There was a minute of silence as we rested our eyes on the vastness of the desert while zooming by an isolated cluster of run-down houses with a rusty pickup truck by the side of the road. "Do you see these cacti?" our taxi driver and self-appointed tourist guide said, pointing at scores of bushes with innumerable menacing white needles. "Don't get near them. They're not called 'Jumping Joyous' for nothing. Those suckers shoot out their needles the moment they feel you close to them. It's true. There are millions of them all around this desert. Let me tell you, people unfamiliar with this area get into very serious trouble."

"Thanks for the warning," I said. "What else must we know about the desert?"

"Don't go on a hike unprepared, especially if you don't know the terrain. There are dangers out there. Every year we hear of people dying from dehydration. They don't carry enough water. So they get disoriented and die."

I raised my eyebrows as I looked at the vast, lunar landscape of barren plains. All around the horizon were vegetation-free, rugged-looking, inhospitable mountains. I wondered why a group of Orthodox monks would make their home in the middle of such a desolate land.

"We're getting close to the monastery," our driver informed us as he pointed at some barely visible buildings in the distance. The closer we came, the greater our amazement.

"This is extraordinary," we said to each other as we got out of the minivan and collected our luggage. I had heard of how unusual the monastery was, but never did I imagine it to be of such magnitude. It stuck out like an oasis at the heart of the Sahara. Inside the extensive perimeter of the monastery's grounds we found a great diversity of flora: palm trees, orange groves, an orchard of olive trees (unusual for that part of America), vegetable gardens, vineyards, and a great variety of flowers ranging from jasmine to every different kind of rose. The grounds were well groomed and carefully looked after. Scattered about the flower gardens were kiosks, ideal places for reading and contemplation. Marveling at the earthly Eden, I thought of Isaiah's words "and the desert shall bloom." The contrast between the grounds inside the monastery and the surrounding landscape could not have been sharper. "Keep hitting that golf ball," I said to our meat-eating taxi driver as I handed him the fare. "It's good for longevity."

At the office next to the entrance gate we were given a warm welcome by Father Athanasios. A black-bearded, amiable monk in his late thirties, he was in charge of making arrangements for incoming pilgrims as well as hosting curious tourists who would often arrive by the busload.

"I came to the monastery as a visitor, just like any other tourist," he said with a broad smile while writing down our names and addresses in his registry. "But as you can see, God had other plans for me. The moment I stepped inside that gate I said to myself, 'Here is where I belong, here is where I want to spend the rest of my life.'"

We learned that, besides becoming a magnet for pilgrims, the monastery of Saint Anthony was also gaining a reputation as an Arizona landmark. In addition to his spiritual work Father Athanasios was assigned the task of gatekeeper in order to monitor the growing tourist traffic. He was responsible for enforcing the rules of the monastery and protecting the privacy of the other monks by instructing both tourists and pilgrims as to what parts of the monastery were off limits. We could visit the various chapels and the main church as well as stroll freely around the gardens but neither pilgrims nor tourists were allowed to take pictures of the monks or loiter around their living quarters.

Father Athanasios offered us and the group of tourists who had just arrived a glass of cool water and a piece of Turkish delight, a tradition imported from Mount Athos. Following strict traditional rules and in order to impress upon visitors the fact that they were entering sacred ground, neither men nor women were allowed to walk beyond the gate of the monastery without proper attire. No one dressed in shorts could get in. To accommodate visitors, however, Father Athanasios distributed to those who needed it a wide piece of colorful cloth that they could wrap around their waists. In addition, women had to cover their heads with scarves that he readily handed out. This was not required in other monasteries that we had visited and so we were, at first, a bit put off.

After these preliminary preparations, Father Athanasios escorted us around the buildings and gardens while describing how this desert miracle had begun taking shape only six years ago. He avoided, however, elaborating on the details of how such a feat was accomplished. A key value of monastic life is discernment, which in this case meant avoiding information that could scandalize the uninitiated. Father Athanasios simply talked in generalities, mentioning that the creation of the monastery was made possible by "the generous contributions of devout pilgrims and by the grace of God who constantly works miracles."

This "miracle," however, was the result, I was later told, of extraordinary coincidences. The monastery was the creation of Father E——, a charismatic monk from Mount Athos. Elder E——, my informants explained, was called by Providence on a special mission to spread Athonite monasticism to America. During the early nineties, after prolonged suffering from health problems, the elder was sent to America for treatment. That was his first contact with the West. Upon his return to Mount Athos and while in a state of deep prayer, he heard God speak in his heart, informing him that he must return to America and create monasteries. According to the story, the elder resisted as he was already advanced in age and had no knowledge of English. In fact he felt dismayed with the prospect of abandoning his beloved Mount Athos, where he had spent most of his life. Moving to a faraway land that he hardly knew or understood was a deeply disagreeable prospect. The message, however, was persistent and in spite of his own wishes, circumstances eventually landed him in Canada, where he set up a women's monastery. He was eventually forced out of Canada by the Orthodox ecclesiastical authorities because they found his brand of Christianity too cultlike and too austere and fundamentalist. It was then that he crossed the border to the United States.

Elder E—— and a group of his local sponsors drove around the deserts of the Southwest to find an appropriate location, buy land, and build an Athonite monastery in America. It had to be away from the cities, deep enough in the desert to safeguard the conditions of silence for systematic spiritual work. One day during their search they heard church bells ringing. The elder considered it a sign that they had located the divinely ordained spot. He asked his companions and supporters to buy the land at that very spot. They, however, had serious reservations. The area was without a drop of water. Elder E——, nonetheless, insisted, and his financial patrons and disciples finally agreed to buy the land, a large area of desert whose purchase they feared was tantamount to throwing their money away. Human habitation of any sort appeared virtually impossible. Besides, they knew that the authorities would never issue a permit to set up such an installation in a place where there was no water source nearby.

As expected, the state of Arizona rejected their request. A proposal to import water was not an option that might persuade the officials to change their minds. Then the elder inquired whether they could get permission to begin construction in the event that they did find water. The answer was yes. Elder E—— then retreated into the desert for three days, abstaining from all food and water and doing nothing except praying. At the end of the third day the elder announced that there was water deep under their desert property. He then identified the exact spot where they should dig. Immediately his sponsors hired a company to begin the drilling. When they reached a thousand feet, lo and behold, water gushed out in great force. They had hit upon a large underground lake.

The discovery, which they attributed to a miracle, not only made possible the creation of the monastery of Saint Anthony's but also led to plans for further expansion, including the creation of a women's monastery nearby. In addition there was enough surplus water to sell to nearby towns.

These events reinforced Elder E——'s reputation in the eyes of his devotees as an exceptionally gifted elder. Several people who visited him assured me that when they went for confession they didn't even need to utter a word about themselves, since "he could read our soul like an open book." I even met pilgrims who claimed, with utmost sincerity, that they saw the elder levitating in a state of deep prayer, something he himself would deny. He attributed their stories to fantasies and delusions. To his followers and disciples this attitude of humility was further confirmation of his holiness. To critics, however, such miracle stories were the hallmarks of a cult made up of gullible people, creating further problems for Elder E——.

Irrespective of the authenticity of the miracle stories, what seemed to be clear was that Elder E——'s coming to America started a process of establishing ancient-type Christian monasteries on this side of the Atlantic. Not only did he create the monastery of Saint Anthony's, but during his first six years in the United States he was also the force behind the creation of sixteen other such institutions, seven for men and nine for women. One of my informants pointed out that even Saint Pachomios, considered along with Saint Anthony as the father of Christian monasticism, had created only five monasteries during his lifetime. Elder E——'s ambition was to create a total of twenty monasteries in North America, as many as there are on Mount Athos. In the meantime, the elder routinely visited the other monasteries from his base at Saint Anthony's, offering counseling to monks and nuns as well as to an increasing crowd of pilgrims who sought him out. "Elder E——," Father Maximos once told me, "is the apostle of Orthodoxy to America. Make sure to visit him." A large picture of the septuagenarian elder had decorated Father Maximos's office at the Panagia monastery in Cyprus while he was still the abbot there.

I had Elder E—— in my mind, wondering when we would get a chance to meet him, when Father Athanasios ended his tour with the visitors. He let the tourists visit the several chapels dedicated to various saints, one of which was the impressive Russian-style church dedicated to Saint Seraphim of Sarov, a favorite saint of Emily's.

Father Athanasios escorted Emily and me to our assigned cells. She had to stay with the women pilgrims in special quarters away from the men. That was the protocol of monastic accommodation for visitors. During our six-day stay we would talk to each other only on occasion. At services we stood silently for hours on opposite sides of the *katholike* (central church for common worship). Similar arrangements prevailed at the communal meals.

"Supper will be after vespers," Father Athanasios informed me as he escorted me into a clean Spartan room with two simple beds. I shut the door and lay down to rest and reflect. After a few minutes, I noticed a printed statement on the inside of the door. I stood up and went over to it. It was written both in Greek and in English. The Greek version was more elaborate than the English and read as follows:

Beloved pilgrims of the Monastery of Saint Anthony:

In the name of our Christ we welcome you with an abundance of Love. We pray that here you will find bodily and emotional comfort away from the troubles and tensions of the world. We fervently hope that when you return to your homes you will feel freer from worldly concerns and that you will be filled with divine grace. Please forgive us if, because of our own possible oversight, you may find something disagreeable to you. Be certain that we are always very happy to see you here at our monastery time and again. We consider you our brothers, sisters, and parents in Christ and consider you as part of ourselves. Do not hesitate to request from us whatever you might need. We are ready to serve you for the love of our Christ, always.

This holy monastery was created by God to serve you, His overburdened children that He loves so much. The appearance of a monastery like this one is a clear indication of God's presence and love for all human beings. You may comfortably and blissfully stay in our humble monastery for up to ten days. In

23

case you need to extend your visit beyond this period of blessedness you must ask for permission and the blessing of either the Abbot or of our Elder. Please note that without their consent you cannot extend your stay. Again we welcome you with open and love-filled hearts.

The Brotherhood of the Holy Monastery of Saint Anthony.

The first thing I wished to accomplish after I settled in was to meet with Elder E——. Following Father Maximos's injunction was, after all, my primary reason for visiting the monastery. I mentioned my wish to the first pilgrim that I befriended, Stephen from Toronto. His cell happened to be next to mine and we quickly established a friendly relationship. We first met in the small kitchen/living room next to our cells when I went for a glass of water. He informed me that the way to get to the elder was to speak first to the abbot. Stephen then told me some stories about Elder E——, whom he had met several times during previous visits.

"You've got to see him," Stephen stressed. "It will be a life-changing experience. One day someone had an audience with the elder for confession. After it was over that very person called another monastery and learned that in fact Elder E—— was there at the very same time. Such stories abound about the elder." Stephen was not concerned about the incredulity that such a tale could generate in someone unfamiliar with Athonite lore. He then went on to talk about other unusual phenomena that were attributed to the elder.

I felt as if I were on Mount Athos, where such miracle stories are standard daily news among pilgrims and monks, as regular as the evening news monitoring the ups and downs of the stock market. I thanked him for the information and advice and went out in search of Emily in hopes that we might meet the abbot together that very night. My intention was to have the abbot arrange for us to meet with Elder E—— the following day. I was aware that the elder was particularly fond of Father Maximos and wished to convey greetings to him. Having heard stories by his followers about his charismatic abilities and criticisms by opponents of the elder, I wished to get a chance to see for myself.

Luckily I bumped into Emily right away. She was admiring the flower gardens with another pilgrim, a mother of one of the monks. Emily was also keen on meeting the abbot so we hurried to the hallway outside the confessional, where the abbot was seeing pilgrims on a first-come-first-serve basis. We sat outside waiting our turn. We were fourth in line. The abbot had been counseling pilgrims and offering confession all day long. I was reminded of similar scenes during my many years of association with Father Maximos on Mount Athos and in Cyprus. It was part of the Athonite spiritual tradition for a hieromonk (a monk ordained as a priest to administer the sacraments) to freely and tirelessly offer his spiritual services to the faithful. I knew from experience that authentic psychotherapy often took place during those encounters. In contrast to Catholic practice, the confessor and the "confessee" sit in front of each other without any barrier to assure anonymity. And unlike secular psychiatric sessions, such encounters are offered free of charge and without a specified time limit. The needs of the pilgrim determine the amount of time the confession lasts. Our visit, however, was for a different purpose.

By the time our turn came it was almost nine. The overburdened abbot in his red stole looked exhausted. Born in America of Greek parents, Father P—— spent years on Mount Athos and returned to America only after Elder E—— asked the abbot to join him on his apostolic venture. It turned out that Father P—— had been a friend of Father Maximos from the time they were novices together on the Holy Mountain. That helped us establish an immediate rapport with the abbot.

"Father, who was the landscaper who designed the gardens?" asked Emily, a passionate connoisseur of gardens and flowers.

The abbot shrugged his shoulders. "There was no professional landscaper," he replied enigmatically. After a pause he continued. "Elder E—— simply guided us step by step on how to construct them, where to build the various structures, where to plant the trees, everything."

"But how did he know?"

"The elder simply downloaded paradise," the abbot said with a smile.

"Downloaded paradise?" Emily wondered.

"That's right. Through the grace of the Holy Spirit the elder experienced paradise on the other side and simply instructed us in minute detail how to replicate and reconstruct it on this side."

25

"Simple," I blurted. Then in a serious tone I asked, "Father, when can we meet the elder?"

"But didn't Father Athanasios tell you?" the abbot said, surprised.

"Tell us what, Father?" My face dropped in anticipation of bad news.

"The elder left this morning for San Antonio."

I looked at Emily in dismay. "It happened unexpectedly," the abbot rushed to explain. "There will be a festival at the new monastery related to the consecration of the main church. He will preside over the ceremonies."

The forty-five-year-old abbot told us that in fact he too was leaving in three hours. At midnight he planned to start driving with another father so that they would arrive at San Antonio before ten in the morning to assist Elder E—— with the consecration. I knew that such a ritual was demanding and lasted for hours. The abbot had three hours to rest before the long journey. We began feeling guilty for chipping away at his sleep time.

"Nan evlogimeno [May it be blessed]," I said with a sigh. It was a customary monastic saying for when things go awry and contrary to our wishes. It means that God must have his reasons.

The abbot went on to further inform us that he and the elder were to return to the monastery on Sunday evening and we could perhaps see him then. "Alas, it's the day when we are returning to Maine," I said. I explained that we could not afford to stay a single day longer due to our teaching responsibilities. We would have to return another time to meet the elder. "Providence must have its reasons," I murmured and shrugged in resignation.

"If it is a consolation," Father P—— said, "you may be able to enjoy a more quiet period at the monastery. When Elder E—— is here the word spreads quickly and the place gets packed with pilgrims from all over, particularly Los Angeles and the Bay Area." On that note we wished the abbot a safe journey for his nocturnal ten-hour drive to San Antonio and walked to our respective cells for sleep before the bells would begin ringing for the morning service at three thirty.

Having no other choice, we took the abbot's advice to enjoy the peacefulness of the place. The bells rang at exactly three thirty. The monks had already been up since midnight praying alone in their cells as they followed the program assigned to them individually by the elder. They gathered at the main church for the start of the *Orthros*, the morning service that ended with the Eucharistic liturgy.

Overcoming my desire to stay in bed for a little longer I hurriedly put on my clothes and walked outside. Before entering the church I stood outside for a few minutes, looking up at the sky. A myriad of stars shone brilliantly through the clear night. Only the occasional howling of a coyote broke the silence. I realized why the early fathers of the Church chose the desert as their favorite place of residence. It is easier, I thought, to connect with God, undistracted by the noise and concerns of the world.

There were no lights in the church except for a few candles in front of the icons. It was a familiar sight in Athonite monasteries. "Darkness," Father Maximos once told me, "is more conducive to deep prayer." That is why monks pray most of the night and sleep and work during the day. I could hardly see any faces. The black-clad monks moved about like shadows. I wasn't even able to recognize Emily standing on the left side of the church among the other women pilgrims.

The service and the chanting were exactly as I had known them in other monasteries in Greece and Cyprus. For a second I forgot I was in Arizona and fancied myself in some remote monastery of Mount Athos. Except for the presence of women and the visits by tourists, Saint Anthony's was an exact replica of an Athonite monastery. Only Greek was used during services and the same *typikon* (program) was followed in minute detail. For the moment, at least, it was clear that at Saint Anthony's there was little interest in assimilation into the surrounding culture. Perhaps that was one of the criticisms levied against the elder by his detractors. The monks had to go through rigorous training in Greek so that they could follow the services, read the New Testament in the original Greek, study the sacred texts, and read biographies of saints and the homilies they left behind them.

I wondered how long such a state of affairs could last given the power of American culture to assimilate ethnic enclaves. I remembered what Father Maximos once told me: "When the Orthodox spiritual tradition enters a new society it is important that it eventually adjusts to that culture by adopting the local language and customs, assuming that they do not conflict with the core teachings of the *Ecclesia*. Otherwise it will not take root." This is how Orthodoxy spread among the Russians and the Slavs.

Two Byzantine monks, Cyril and Methodios, translated the Greek texts into the "Cyrillic" alphabet, created by Cyril himself, so that the Slavs, who at the time had no written language, would be able to read the scriptures and the written spiritual tradition of Orthodoxy in their own Slavonic language. "American society," Father Maximos told me when I raised the issue of Orthodox spirituality in America, "will have to produce its own home-grown saints so that they may provide spiritual guidance to their people."

I had the feeling that Elder E—— intended to prepare the ground for such a possibility. Perhaps he was planting the seeds in the Arizona desert so that American Orthodox saints might be produced in due time. They could then translate the texts and the chants into a spiritually meaningful English in the same way that the Orthodox missionaries in Africa whom I had met in Cyprus had translated the liturgical texts into several African languages. They adopted Orthodoxy to local customs, so much so that a bishop would join the congregation in an African dance during the Eucharist.

As the hours progressed and the darkness receded I began to recognize faces and was able to spot Emily on the other side of the church. Beautiful newly painted icons in vivid colors appeared all around us, including a large icon, the *Panagia Arizonitissa*, the Most Holy Mother of Arizona, already famous for its miraculous and healing properties. It was only then that I realized the leading chanter, who had impressed me with his baritone voice, was a young African-American monk. Besides Greek-American and Greek monks there were also a number of monks and novices from other ethnic groups. In fact I was told that the third in authority of the monastery, a forty-year-old black-bearded hieromonk, speaking impeccable Greek, was a Jewish philosophy graduate from Harvard. He was in charge of the monastery during the absence of both the abbot and Elder E——. In addition, he provided his services as a confessor to pilgrims, conversing with them either in Greek or in English. While a student at Harvard he made the dramatic decision to become an Eastern Orthodox monk after his encounter with the elder. When I expressed my surprise about his case to Father Athanasios he promptly reminded me that Jesus was Jewish as were all of his apostles and early disciples.

The service ended at seven. The monks went to their cells to sleep until eleven while we the pilgrims walked to the dining hall for breakfast. Upon waking, the monks would work until one. Then after a short service a common meal was served when monks and pilgrims ate together. The monks then would return to work for the rest of the day until vespers in the early evening. Then they would eat a light dinner and retreat to their cells at eight for another four-hour rest. At midnight they would wake up for the new cycle of prayer and work. Their calendar and sense of time was radically different from the academic calendar, or any other calendar for that matter. I knew from my sociological training that our membership in society determines to a great degree our experience and conception of time and space. A miner has a different sense of time than an academic or a monk, and a food gatherer of the Ituri forest of Africa who has never left the rain forest has a different sense of space than a camel driver in the Sahara or a taxi driver in New York.

After breakfast I wandered around the grounds, exploring the area with an undiminished sense of amazement. In a unique and unobtrusive way the buildings synthesized Byzantine and Native American construction styles of the Southwest.

I found a bench hidden in a corner of the garden and sat down to write my impressions of the desert paradise in my notebook: "The phenomenon of an Athonite monastery within the vastness of the Arizona desert could not have emerged and taken root at any other period in American history. The uniqueness of contemporary America may very well lie in its considerable tolerance, diversity, and openness. The ease with which new religions can crop up with relatively little fear of persecution is not a phenomenon that we should take for granted." While I was jotting down my thoughts Father Athanasios passed by escorting a new group of tourists. A monk watering the garden was reciting the Jesus Prayer, "Lord Jesus Christ have mercy on me," "Lord Jesus Christ have mercy on me," over and over to himself, without paying attention to anything around him.

"The strict separation of church and state that the founding fathers of the American republic so wisely set down as the law of the land," I went on to write, "provided the parameters for the preservation of religious freedom in America. Their intentions were spiritual: to preserve the dignity and freedom of the individual to worship according to each person's understanding of God. Their intention was not to banish God from public life, as it has been so misinterpreted in our contemporary political life.[1] It is this constitutional foundation for the protection of religious freedom, combined with the increasingly multiethnic nature of American society, that created the conditions for Elder E—— to build his monasteries. It is the same religious freedom that made it possible for Transcendental Meditation to spread like brushfire, that permitted the creation of Buddhist centers, Hindu ashrams, and Baha'i temples all over North America. Such developments were not likely to appear in more homogeneous societies that are more often than not intolerant toward the presence of other religions." My inner conversation came to an end when another wandering pilgrim came and sat opposite me on another bench.

"Oh man, I can't believe all this, I really can't." After a few more expressions of amazement he introduced himself as Andrew, a Greek-American businessman in his middle thirties who wondered how it was possible to have such an establishment in such a location. It was his first visit to a monastery. Andrew explained that he came to Saint Anthony's after hearing so much about it. "But I never could have imagined it would be on such a grand scale." Being an experienced and successful businessman he guessed that the entire monastery with its modern facilities and elaborate landscaping, "must be worth over thirty million bucks."

"Where did they find all that money?" he wondered.

"I don't know. The monks claim the monastery is a gift from God," I replied.

"It has to be," Andrew said in a tone that left me uncertain whether he literally meant it.

"In fact I asked the abbot that very question. He said that it was made possible by the contributions of 'devout pilgrims.' Obviously, Elder E—— as a monk did not have a penny."

Andrew was easy to relate to and we became confidants to each other during our weeklong stay. He was devoutly religious but not in a fundamentalist way. I appreciated his critical and practical mind as he explored his own spirituality during his stay there. He complained about the lack of spirituality found among the churches back in his hometown but repeatedly voiced his enchantment with Saint Anthony's monastery and the deep spirituality he encountered there. So great was his awe of the monastery that for the first time he decided to go to confession. His confessor was the Jewish hieromonk from Harvard.

While we chatted, monks would pass by for their errands, always reciting the Jesus Prayer. For an outsider who was unfamiliar with Athonite spiritual practices it must have been quite a novelty to hear people praying like this while watering the plants, washing dishes, peeling potatoes, or planting trees. But for the monk and the serious spiritual seeker any moment should not be wasted in idleness but filled with prayer.

During my chat with Andrew another pilgrim came by. It was Stephen, the fellow from Toronto that I met earlier. He looked haggard and upset to the point of desperation. Stephen's shoes, pants, and shirt were covered with hundreds of tiny pointed needles. Unfamiliar with the prevailing conditions in the desert, he had walked beyond the boundaries of the monastery to befriend the six German shepherds kept on long leashes at the edge of the monastery to keep the coyotes away. But he foolishly ventured a little further into the desert and was attacked by a cactus, a Jumping Joyous.

We spent the next hour helping poor Stephen free himself of the needles. In the process we learned about his life. He came to the monastery with the intention of becoming a monk. He wished to escape from a bad marriage. But the elder refused to accept him as a novice and counseled instead that he should return to the world and fix his relationship with his Catholic wife of twenty-five years.

"The elder told me that I should stop trying to change her and instead redirect my focus on changing myself by becoming a better person. He advised me to become a servant to my wife and leave the rest to God."

Stephen decided to follow the elder's advice. To maintain his attention on that task he visited the monastery regularly and hoped that his wife would also join him at some point. We were told that the relationship with his wife was already beginning to improve.

Over the years that I had known him, Father Maximos would repeatedly say to me that choosing the monastic life should not be the result of an urge to escape from the world and its problems. Novices who come with such intentions tend to make bad monks and are routinely sent back.

The only acceptable reason for becoming a monk or a nun is the prompting of an inner calling and an irresistible desire to unite with God. Otherwise, the person would be following the wrong path with possible psychologically damaging consequences.

That afternoon I went for exercise on a fast-paced walk with Andrew. We ventured beyond the gates of the monastery but remained on the straight, endless asphalt road that connected the desert paradise with the rest of the world. We were not tempted to veer off on some dirt trail. We knew better after witnessing what happened to Stephen. Neither of us was anxious for any close encounters with a Jumping Joyous.

Andrew was eager to hear about my work and showed great interest in Orthodox monasticism. Though religious, he was of the liberal, critical variety and therefore a good conversationalist with whom to bounce around thoughts without any reservations or concerns about being misunderstood. Often, religious people are notoriously intolerant of others bearing ideas that do not reinforce their own beliefs. Such attitudes create barriers of communication.

Somewhat on the heavy side, Andrew lamented his sedentary life as a computer whiz. It was a skill that had made him a fortune in the stock market, so that by his mid-thirties he did not need to work any further. He now turned his attention from computers to issues of everlasting value. The pursuit of money, he confided to me, took a toll on him to such a degree that he had come close to a breakdown. When he contemplated psychiatric assistance a friend suggested he instead visit the monastery of Saint Anthony's as a healing retreat. The move was the best decision he had ever made in his life, he assured me.

Carried away with our conversation, we found ourselves several miles from the monastery. Without realizing it we had been walking away from the monastery for over an hour. "Strange," Andrew said as he pointed at some suspicious piles of animal excrement in the middle of the road. "Are there dogs around here?"

"Dogs? These fresh piles couldn't be those of dogs. My friend, there are no dogs around here. Let's head back quickly before the coyotes sniff us out."

Like two clumsy buffoons in an Italian comedy we reached the monastery's gate panting and sweating. An elderly woman standing and leaning on her cane looked at us with curiosity. "You fellows, where have you been?" When we told her she shook her head disapprovingly. "The other night I couldn't sleep from the howling of the coyotes and the barking of the dogs. It was a real pandemonium. Didn't you hear them?"

"No, I didn't hear a thing," I said.

She told us how unwise it was for us to go into the desert without knowledge of the place and without the *Evlogia* (blessing) of the fathers. "Not only are there coyotes and rattlesnakes around here, but there are also some mountain lions."

The grandmother apparently was a frequent patron of the monastery and went on to tell us further tales of the lurking dangers. "The last time I came here there was a mountain lion seen roaming in the gardens."

"No kidding!" Andrew exclaimed.

"Oh, yeah! It's very rare to see mountain lions in these deserts but it did happen. The monks began ringing the church bells and banging pots and pans from the kitchen. It finally ran away when the dogs started barking."

Andrew looked concerned. "Thank you. We'll keep it in mind," he said to the grandmother and we walked toward our cells for a quick shower before vespers began.

"Isn't it interesting," I said. "On Mount Athos the monasteries were built like impenetrable fortresses on top of remote cliffs and mountains to protect the monks from enemies. In earlier centuries someone sat in a tower keeping watch for approaching pirate ships, invading armies, or marauding troops. Time and again monks in these monasteries were massacred by such invaders." I paused. "Do you see what I am driving at?"

"What do you mean?"

"Well, here the only problems the monks may face are from coyotes and an occasional stray mountain lion that they can chase away with noise. Look, even the outer gate is permanently open, day and night. The American West today may be a safer place for an Athonite monastery than Mount Athos ever was for most of the centuries of its existence."

"I see your point." Andrew grinned as we walked into our cells. "But can it protect itself from the tourists?"

"That remains to be seen."

After vespers we had a light dinner. Andrew and I volunteered to work in the kitchen helping the monks clean the dishes. We then enjoyed the rest of the evening at a bench in the garden while the monks entered their cells to continue with their spiritual practices and prayers and get some needed sleep.

A tall, athletic-looking man in his early forties with a bushy black mustache and a broad smile joined us. He introduced himself as Stavros, a Greek-American and a former monk. He had just returned to America from Mount Athos.

Stavros was the first ex-monk I had met and I was keen on hearing his story. He had spent four years on Mount Athos as a novice at a leading monastery. However, he finally concluded that he was not made for the monastic life. "I was happy that my elder offered me his blessings to return to the world. So here I am."

Stavros, who looked easygoing and well grounded, experienced reentry problems upon his return to the States so he ended up seeking professional help. His recovery from the culture shock had been gradual, and he expected that he would probably need another couple of years to reach a new equilibrium in his life. He told us how relieved and happy he felt when he discovered the monastery of Saint Anthony. So great was his need to maintain his connection with Athonite monasticism that he decided to move from New Jersey to Tucson, Arizona, where he would be near the monastery for frequent visits, with Elder E—— as his spiritual guide.

For the next hour Stavros told us of his life on Mount Athos and the difficulties he faced there. "The main problem as far as I was concerned," he said, "was the fact that I was a Greek-American and therefore my knowledge of the Greek *Katharevousa* [the more archaic, Byzantine Greek used in church services and prayers] was not very good. I felt that it would have taken me another ten years as a novice before I could become a fully integrated monk. That was very frustrating."

He paused as Stephen joined us. "You see, life is tough on Mount Athos. It requires extraordinary stamina. I realized I was not made for such a rough existence. But those who are called for that lifestyle and make it develop an extraordinary capacity to focus. They live in a radically different world and their prayers are extremely powerful. They can really heal people. I have witnessed this time and again."

"Why didn't you leave earlier instead of staying there for such a long time?" Andrew wondered.

Stavros smiled and replied that his *diakonia* (divinely assigned task) was to look after three very elderly monks with whom he had established a very strong connection. "They showered me with their blessings day and night. How could I abandon them? I decided to leave the Mountain only after they passed away. Had it not been for them I would have returned to the world much earlier.

"The toughest part of becoming a monk is not what people usually assume to be the main problem, which is the celibate way of life. No. The toughest part is when you have to give up your old self. Over time you see yourself being cleansed of everything that cluttered your mind: movies, television, hobbies, material comforts, your self-definition, and so on. All these are washed away. Some people, like myself, cannot face such a challenge and leave. If you do make it, you are given a completely new identity. You are no longer the person you used to be. That person is dead. You are now in a different world.

"I have to say," Stavros continued, "that the monks here in Arizona have it much tougher than those on Mount Athos."

"How so?" I said in surprise. "I thought it would be much easier here."

"No, no. It is much more difficult. There are too many temptations here. The presence of women is one. The comings and goings of tourists is another. Physically speaking, they are really not outside the world. It is much more demanding to struggle to remove yourself from the world while you are in it. Mount Athos is helpful because it is so remote and isolated."

"Yet even Mount Athos is being discovered by thousands of pilgrims," I said. "Of course, without this discovery there wouldn't perhaps be the type of revival that has been taking place there during the last thirty years."

"This place," Stavros said, "in spite of worldly distractions and temptations is a true *philokalia* [embodiment of spiritual beauty] that can lead people to real union with God. But it's not easy to get there."

Our conversation with Stavros turned toward the pope's efforts to bring unity among the Christian churches and the role Mount Athos could

35

play in that direction. The patriarch of Constantinople has also worked tirelessly toward healing the rift that split Christianity during the eleventh century. He too has encouraged the ongoing East–West dialogue for reconciliation. But despite the fact that during services Athonite monks eulogize the patriarch of Constantinople as their spiritual overseer and presiding bishop, they themselves remain aloof and often suspicious of these overtures. I knew from past contacts with Athonite monks that the ecumenical movement did not stir any excitement among their ranks. So I asked Stavros, who was part of that community and seemed to have an intimate understanding of the way his former fellow monks thought, of his opinion on the matter.

"Look," he replied after a few moments of reflection. "I personally think that this pope is a good person and very sincere about his desire for reconciliation, in spite of suspicions among many Athonite monks. My concern is who will succeed him. To be honest with you, I can't see how Mount Athos will ever be willing to compromise for the sake of unity either with Catholicism or with Protestantism for that matter. The Athonite monks' primary concern is to preserve the inner spirituality of the Christian religion. They feel that they are its custodians. So they are not interested in public relations or in getting involved in a process of give and take for the sake of reconciliation. They understand, of course, that the external church, as represented by the patriarch, has to make such overtures by necessity. However, it is unthinkable for them to accept a union of the churches under the pope. Any attempt in that direction will lead to another schism within the Eastern Church itself. As far as the monks are concerned, the Western Church should return to the original church from which it cut itself off in 1054 C.E. They are confident and certain that their path is the one charted by Christ and they feel it is their responsibility to do everything they can to preserve it for future generations and for the good of the world.

"When I first went to Mount Athos," Stavros continued, "I was perplexed about such rigid attitudes. But later I came to understand the position of the fathers. Athos is the leading saint-creating mountain. By living outside of this world Athonite monks are in no mood to compromise with the world. I have seen this with many elders. They are ready to talk to anybody about Orthodoxy if they are genuinely interested in the subject, but they are not interested in engaging in idle networking. They are definitely not interested in proselytizing anyone. They just don't have the time for it."

"Now that you are back in the world, Stavro, what do you plan to do?" Stephen asked. "Will you start a family of your own?"

"That is the least of my concerns," Stavros replied. "I have to first adjust to the world and then figure out what to do with my life. I was married for seventeen years, you know. It was after my divorce that I went to Mount Athos."

When we retreated to our rooms I spent some time taking notes about the conversations we had at the kiosk. Obviously, I wrote, Stavros was not "made" for the monastic life. The need to escape from the world is not a durable foundation for such a lifestyle. Sooner or later the person will find that out and eventually return to the world. Only an overwhelming passion to find God, as Father Maximos insisted, can make monasticism an attractive way of living.

While reflecting about Stavros's case, I thought of a conversation (reported in a new book on Mount Athos I was reading) between a hermit and Dr. Constantine Cavarnos while the latter was on a journey to the Holy Mountain in the late fifties.

"Why did I come here? You will ask me," said the hermit, whose name was John. "*For the sake of eternity.* Our life here on earth, whether we are plain folks, scientists or professors, princes or kings, will inevitably come to an end. When we die, these titles and capacities will mean nothing, absolutely nothing. The only thing that will matter then will be the quality of our soul, whether it is good or bad, whether we have saved it or lost it. Heaven and hell are everlasting, whereas our earthly life is insignificantly brief."[2]

The hermit's answer was similar to answers that I received when I would raise the same question with monks I had met over the years. Yet the decision to become a monk may come suddenly and unexpectedly as in the case of the Jewish Harvard graduate who met Elder E——. I heard of others who traveled to Mount Athos as curious tourists and ended up putting on the cassock. The elders of the Holy Mountain emphasize the irrelevance of one's motives upon entering their community. As an elder once put it to me, "A person may have his reasons for visiting Mount Athos but God may have his." For example, Father Maximos once told me of a German minister who visited Mount Athos during the period of the Great Lent. After spending an all-night vigil that lasted for eighteen hours, he announced during *trapeza* (the communal meal) that he had decided to become Orthodox. The reason he offered was that only a miracle could keep him standing in church for so many hours without being bored or tired. That visitor eventually became a monk and stayed on Mount Athos in one of the monasteries.

I placed my notebook by the side of my bed and before turning the light off I pulled from my bag a book on hermits and randomly opened it. The page involved a story related to the life of a desert father:

> A brother came to Abbas Macarius one day and asked how he could be saved and the Abbas told him to go to the burial ground and insult the dead. So he did so, hurling insults and stones at the graves. When he got back, Macarius asked him if they had responded and the brother said they had said nothing, so Macarius told him to go and praise the dead. He went to the burial ground and sang the praises of the men buried there. When he reported back, Macarius asked how the dead had taken his congratulations and the brother replied that they had said nothing. So the Abbas said: "You know all those insults you hurled at them and they said nothing; you also if you want to be saved—be a dead man, taking no notice either of the injustice of men or of their praises. Behave like the dead and you will be saved."[3]

When Emily and I said farewell to our new friends on Sunday morning we promised that we would be back someday. During our return journey to Maine we exchanged notes about our separate but equally profound experiences at the monastery of Saint Anthony. For Emily the experience helped her sharpen her understanding of "eco-peace" communities, a concept and a phenomenon she has been trying to promote in her teaching and social activism.

THREE

AEGEAN PILGRIMAGE

n early May, the end of the academic year, I turned my grades in with great relief. I was now free to think and to plan my upcoming journey to Cyprus, where I would reconnect with Father Maximos. With his assistance I was to further my explorations into the spiritual tradition of Eastern Christianity, which he had so penetratingly mastered after many years as a monk on Mount Athos. It was clear to me that I had much to learn from him.

Many changes had occurred since I last saw Father Maximos. At the time he was still abbot of the Panagia monastery up on the pine-covered Troodos Mountains situated at the center of the island. In a most surprising and unexpected way he was now an elected bishop of the Church of Cyprus. I knew that neither Father Maximos's return to Cyprus from Mount Athos in 1993 nor his ascent to the bishop's throne were part of his life's ambitions. His heart's desire was to remain on Mount Athos with his elders, working in silence toward his salvation, focusing exclusively on otherworldly pursuits. But his elders had other designs for him. They requested that he leave the Holy Mountain because, as I was told, they foresaw that he was destined for a special mission in the world outside. In spite of his relatively young age, forty-four, Father Maximos was already considered an elder, a person who, being gifted with the grace of the Holy Spirit, could guide others toward their spiritual perfection and realization of God.

It was late in the afternoon when I arrived in Cyprus on June 20, 2001, after a seven-thousand-mile journey from Bangor, Maine, via Boston and London. I felt exhausted from the long trip, but due to a seven-hour jet lag I was unable to sleep. After calling Emily back in Maine to let her know of my arrival, I sat at the balcony of our fourth-floor apartment in Limassol, which overlooked the sea and was adjacent to the zoological garden. I cherished the evening breezes coming from the sea, always a welcoming relief from the day's heat, which soars to uncomfortable heights during the summer.

While staring in a semidazed state at the moon as it rose out of the Mediterranean, I heard noises and commotion in the street below. I looked down and noticed throngs of pedestrians entering the open-air theater of Limassol's public park, located just fifty meters to the right of where I was sitting. Carefully groomed and filled with a variety of trees, including a lush breed of pine, the park was a small oasis surrounded by the once picturesque but now overdeveloped and overpaved city. My arrival apparently coincided with some major cultural event, a common affair during the summer months.

The music of *La Traviata* began. My fatigue disappeared instantly. Forgetting about sleep, I remained glued to the balcony, humming along with the familiar stanzas that were as loud and clear as if I were sitting in the front row of the packed theater.

Once the performance was over, I reflected upon my plans for the coming day. Though eager to contact Father Maximos at the bishopric, I decided I would first visit my old friend and confidant Stephanos, who was recovering from open-heart surgery. I was anxious to find out about his health. Just before I left Maine, Erato, Stephanos's wife, had explained over the phone how they had almost lost him. The nine-hour emergency operation had been extremely delicate. Because of its novelty and complexity, the American-trained surgeons had to be in continuous telephone consultation with specialists in New York while the operation was in progress in Cyprus. Erato confided that the surgeons estimated Stephanos's chances of survival as negligible. Fortunately, the sixty-six-year-old Stephanos survived the ordeal and was gradually on his way to recovery.

I felt great relief. Stephanos and Erato had been my closest confidants and advisors during my twenty years of adventures with mystics, hermits, and monks. Stephanos had also been like an older brother to me, an intimate friend. In a remarkable coincidence, he had also been a close associate and confidant of Father Maximos. That was enormously helpful for my work.

"I attribute my survival to a miracle," the exhausted-looking Stephanos told me when we sat in their living room drinking iced tea at mid-morning. "My doctors were great," he said, "but had it not been for Father Maximos, I don't think I would have made it."

Erato added that Father Maximos had organized an all-night emergency prayer vigil the night that the ambulance rushed the almost unconscious Stephanos to the hospital. He was at her husband's side praying, during and after the operation. "The energy of his prayer was so intense," Stephanos claimed, "that I literally felt it penetrating every cell of my body. This was particularly so," he went on to say, "when Father Maximos, soon after the operation, placed his stole and right hand over my head and murmured special healing prayers."

Stephanos said that Father Maximos had warned him on the Monday before the operation that he should prepare himself emotionally and spiritually because, regardless of the fact that the doctors had scheduled the operation two weeks later, he was to have it on Friday. And so it happened. On Friday Stephanos collapsed and had to be whisked sixty miles north of Limassol to the Nicosia general hospital. For Stephanos and Erato it was another sign and validation that Father Maximos, whom they had adopted as their elder and spiritual guide, was endowed with gifts of the Spirit. "I am certain," Stephanos stressed in his tired voice, "that the extension of my life is the result of an act of grace thanks to the intercession of Father Maximos.

"You know," he continued after a deep breath, "I have been reflecting on this and came to the conclusion that I can't afford to lose any more time. It has become abundantly clear to me that I must use every second that I have left on this earth for spiritual work. Every other preoccupation is trivial for me at this point."

I spent the rest of the day with my friends. At one point I escorted Stephanos on a careful and slow walk around the block, an activity prescribed by the doctors. While Stephanos was taking cautious steps, we talked about our favorite subject, Father Maximos. No one in Cyprus had a more intimate knowledge of the former monk from Mount Athos than Stephanos, who played a key role in his election as a new bishop of the troubled Church of Cyprus. In order not to tire my friend, however, I did not press for details on that development. I preferred our conversation to remain focused on his recovery.

"Were you afraid of dying?" I asked casually as we walked.

"With Father Maximos's help I felt liberated from that fear." With effort Stephanos inhaled deeply.

"How?" I asked.

"Do you know what he whispered in my ear just before the operation? 'Don't wish for anything. Don't wish to get well. Don't wish to live. Don't wish to die. Surrender totally to the will of God.' That advice really freed me from all fear and anxiety. I relaxed and abandoned myself into the hands of Providence." Stephanos paused. "In retrospect what he told me in my ear was very Zenlike, don't you think?"

"Yes. It is a paradoxical admonition," I agreed. "It is also very good psychology."

What I loved about Stephanos was his exposure to and familiarity with spiritual traditions outside of Eastern Orthodoxy. This diverse exposure on his part made our association and friendship special, since we could understand each other well. I too had been exposed to other traditions of the Far

East, like Transcendental Meditation, which I practiced diligently for seven years prior to my encounter with Mount Athos.

We returned from our afternoon walk and Stephanos sank into an armchair. "Did you know," Erato said, "that in three days Father Maximos will lead a pilgrimage to the Aegean Islands? They chartered a boat and as far as I know there is still room. Would you like to join them?"

"Join them?" I mumbled clumsily. I did not know what to say. I had, of course, come to Cyprus to be with Father Maximos. Yet I hesitated to suddenly make plans for more travel when I had hardly recovered from my long trip.

"I wouldn't miss such an opportunity, Kyriaco," Stephanos said somberly, noticing my reticence. "It is important for your work. I just wish I was in a position to join you myself."

I could not ignore his advice. Before I even had a chance to meet with Father Maximos to congratulate him on his ascendancy to the bishopric I began making plans to join him and five hundred other pilgrims for a seven-day Aegean cruise. The itinerary included visits to holy shrines at several Greek islands, including Patmos, the island of John's Apocalypse, a place I had always wished to visit. We would also steam around Mount Athos itself.

Erato, who knew the organizers, immediately made a few phone calls, and in a matter of minutes I had reserved a cabin that was conveniently located on the same level of the boat as that of Father Maximos. Once I made my decision, I began looking forward to the possibility of casual contact with him during the pilgrimage.

Given Father Maximos's change of status I realized that I had to take every opportunity to be with him. I could no longer take for granted the luxury of daily contact with the Athonite elder. During a sabbatical leave from the university in the spring of 1997 I was a guest resident and researcher at the Panagia monastery. My cell had been next to his. Father Maximos's altered status drastically changed the parameters of my association with him.

This unforeseen development had taken place when one of the local bishops was forced to resign because of a series of alleged scandals that included financial fraud on a grand scale. It even triggered the interest of

43

Interpol, which dispatched its sleuths to Cyprus in order to unravel the controversial financial dealings of the former bishop, which had cost international investors millions.

The vacant bishopric throne had to be filled with a new bishop. In accord with the unique manner of selecting bishops in Cyprus, the entire body of the faithful had to vote and draft a successor. Father Maximos, who by that time had become popular on the island as a charismatic abbot and a spiritual advisor to thousands, was at the top of the list of possible successors. His supporters demanded he agree to be considered as a candidate. A key role in that direction was played by my friends Stephanos and Antonis, the businessman who first introduced me to Father Maximos on a visit to Mount Athos. Working together, they managed to persuade their elder to accept the burdensome task "for the good of the church," plagued as it was by a string of sexual, financial, and political scandals. They saw Father Maximos as a potentially revitalizing force within the higher echelons of the church hierarchy. The contested elections led to a landslide victory by the forces that supported Father Maximos, causing an outpouring of public enthusiasm as thousands took to the streets to celebrate when the results were announced.

But his victory created sharp discord within the church itself. Some bishops and archimandrites considered his election a tragedy. He was bringing to the island an ascetic model of the church that was apparently at odds with the status quo, which was characterized by a lavish display of wealth and chronic corruption reminiscent of the Catholic Church during the declining decades of the Middle Ages. Consequently, I was informed, from day one of his ascendancy to the bishopric throne, some of his colleagues in Christ allegedly began conspiring against Bishop Maximos, waging a relentless form of guerrilla warfare to force him to resign and return to Mount Athos. For a period of time one of the bishops refused to even participate in common worship with him, so great was his aversion toward his fellow bishop.

Soon after his election Father Maximos was accused by the same group of clergy of being "an agent of Mount Athos" who was plotting to subjugate the autocephalous Church of Cyprus by seducing young men and women into monasticism and by creating "followers" and "devotees."

Furthermore, he was accused of not being enough of a nationalist patriot, as bishops were supposed to be. They even alleged that somehow he was importing to the island the seeds of religious fanaticism. One of the bishops became particularly incensed when he found out that Father Maximos refused to eat meat in a society where lamb on the skewer was an entrenched cultural tradition. Such culinary preferences on the part of the Athonite monk were unacceptable eccentricities.

When these ploys did not work another accusation popped up—that one of Father Maximos's elders was a philanderer, habitually fornicating with nuns. Father Maximos was deemed guilty by association. It was an accusation that brought only hilarity for it was publicly perceived as totally groundless. The accused elder was in his late eighties.

Then, as Antonis put it, "they played their last card." The same people accused Father Maximos of being a homosexual. For a homophobic society, that was the ultimate stigma. It was clear to those close to Father Maximos that this accusation too was only a maneuver to force the elder out of the island. His detractors went as far as to recruit two false witnesses who were ready to testify in front of a clerical tribunal that Father Maximos had had sexual escapades with them. "The machinations against Father Maximos could make for a much more fascinating novel about church corruption than Umberto Eco's *The Name of the Rose*," Father Nikodemos, a friend of Father Maximos who joined him in the bishopric, told me jokingly when I met him in his office.

The aging archbishop, who believed in Father Maximos's innocence, ordered an open inquiry and convened a *Mezon* (Greater) synod of the Orthodox Church, composed not only of the local bishops but also of bishops from other Orthodox churches, a move that enraged Father Maximos's enemies as their influence and power was now diluted. In a dramatic inquiry that lasted several days Father Maximos was exonerated and two of his accusers were forced to resign. One of the high points of the trial was reached when the two impostors brought over from Greece were asked to identify Father Maximos among the bishops who were seated during the inquiry. Both of them separately failed the test by pointing at the wrong bearded hierarch. Father Maximos was not in the room.

When word got out that the synod had proclaimed Father Maximos innocent, church bells began ringing in his diocese and thousands of his followers flooded the streets of Limassol to await his arrival from Nicosia, where the trial took place. The monk from Mount Athos turned bishop of the worldly church was given a hero's welcome, and his position was solidified to such an extent that rumors began circulating that he was now the most likely successor to the aging archbishop. What impressed the devout was his supreme serenity during his ordeal and his refusal to counterattack or make public statements against his accusers. He preferred instead to engage in intensified forms of fasting and prayer. The humble monk from Mount Athos whom I had met only ten years earlier during my pilgrimage there was now a hair's breadth away from the archbishopric throne.

The following morning, after my contact with Stephanos and Erato, I went straight to the bishopric to meet with Father Maximos, whom I hadn't seen since January. As usual, the warmth of his friendship and hospitality made me feel very much at home and he was pleased to hear that I was to join the Aegean pilgrimage. However, carrying on a conversation was not easy that day. There was much commotion as a number of police entered the office for an urgent meeting regarding traffic arrangements during the upcoming official visit of the patriarch of Georgia and his entourage. The Georgians were on a special visit to the island as guests of the Church of Cyprus. Expecting crowds, the police planned to block the streets to motorized traffic around the main cathedral in downtown Limassol where the ceremonies were to take place. Presiding over formal events and religious rituals was now part of Father Maximos's new responsibilities. The official visit was to take place the following morning and even though the two hierarchs did not speak each other's language they were to conduct a common liturgy.

"When I was at the monastery, Kyriaco, I knew exactly when to sleep, when to work, and when to pray," Father Isaac, a monk who accompanied him from the Panagia monastery, lamented. "Not anymore. Everything changed."

I sat outside of Father Maximos's office as Father Isaac dealt with a stream of visitors requesting an audience with the new bishop, who was consulting with the policemen. The two telephones never stopped ringing.

On several occasions Father Isaac answered both lines at the same time. What a radical change from life in the monastery, I thought, as I watched him handle his new role. The need for a more rational management of appointments was evident.

Father Isaac confided to me how rocky the transition had been for him from the monastery to his new position as the gatekeeper to Father Maximos's office. In addition, he was now an ordained priest who, along with Father Nikodemos, served in the cathedral adjacent to the bishopric. "I hardly get any sleep and as you can see I am always on the phone," he complained as he put the receiver down before another call came in.

"I am impressed with how well you manage, Father Isaac," I said.

"Fortunately, I spend two days of the week at the monastery. That's how I replenish my energy. Otherwise I would have really gone crazy."

Father Isaac spoke with such comic gusto that in spite of my sympathy for his predicament I had to restrain myself from laughing. At the same time he seemed to cherish the privilege of being so close to his spiritual elder. I was certain that such an opportunity must have made his peers back at the monastery envious.

"Why don't you join us for lunch, Kyriaco?" Father Maximos suggested after the police left and we had a chance to chat for a few minutes in his office.

"I'd love to!" I said and gladly followed him and Father Isaac into the dining hall of the bishopric for a tasty vegetarian Cypriot meal of stuffed peppers, tomatoes, and squash. Overworked, Father Maximos was struggling to recover from a head cold, an uncomfortable condition in the midst of the summer. He had to get well since we were only days away from the Aegean pilgrimage. Yet, overburdened with so many responsibilities, spiritual and administrative, he refused to give his body the necessary rest. "I have to be a good host to the patriarch," he explained. "This man endured unspeakable persecution by the Communists for decades. It is not right for me to stay in bed."

Father Maximos wiped his mouth with a white towel as we stood up for the blessing of the leftovers. I noticed that his beard was getting a little gray and that he had put on some weight. He no longer had the luxury of walking in the mountains as he did during his life on Mount Athos and at the Panagia monastery. When I brought up his ordeals with the church he sighed with a smile.

"When I was on Mount Athos as a young monk," he said, "I puzzled over a passage in the Gospel and went to my elder for clarification. I asked him, 'Father, the Gospel urges us to love our enemies, but how can I do that since I don't have any enemies?' Do you know what he told me? 'Don't be in a hurry. You will have plenty of them in time.' " I was pleased to see that in spite of his new formal status Father Maximos had not lost his sense of humor.

We finished lunch close to two, the start of the afternoon siesta, a necessity in Cyprus during the summer. I knew that Father Maximos needed that time to rest so I was ready to leave when he asked me to join him the next day for a visit to the Panagia monastery. I immediately accepted. "Be here tomorrow at seven in the evening. By that time we'll be done with the formalities with the patriarch and we can take off for the mountains," he said. "I have some errands to do at the monastery and I need to do them before we leave for Greece. Can you stay there for the night?"

"Wonderful," I responded, looking forward to revisiting, even for a brief period, the time I spent with him in the spring of 1997 as his unofficial chauffeur at the Panagia monastery. Father Maximos never learned how to drive. Being his driver was a role I cherished since it offered me the opportunity to spend time alone with him and engage in informal conversations on Christian spirituality. I was to drive him to the monastery, just as I used to do, which would give us a couple of hours together without the intrusion of outsiders.

"How is it that you have never learned how to drive, Father Maxime?" I asked as we headed off for the monastery. "There is no person on this island who does not know how to drive," I continued, deliberately exaggerating. "Why not you?"

"It is Providence that prevented me, Kyriaco, Providence!" Father Maximos replied with a grin. "My ignorance in that area may have saved me from being defrocked."

"What's the connection?"

"During last year's *Mezon* synod one of the two witnesses they brought over from Greece claimed in front of the ecclesiastical tribunal that he and I would, among other things, visit a nudist camp together. They asked him 'Did you go there by car?' 'Yes,' he replied. Then they asked him, further, 'Did he drive his own car?' Again he replied, 'Yes' and then elaborated on how I used to pick him up from his apartment and how we would drive to remote beaches where no one could spot us."

It was known that Father Maximos could not drive but the witness was not properly coached. That fiasco, plus the inability of other witnesses to identify Father Maximos, was the final straw that led to his acquittal, to the chagrin of his opponents.

I mentioned that many people were amazed at how it is possible that men of God would do such a thing. How could they as agents of the Holy Spirit act in such a blatantly evil way? Father Maximos explained that they were not aware their actions were evil. They may have been misguided, thinking that they were working for the good of the church. Then he reminded me that the history of the church is full of such incidents. He stressed, however, that we must never be scandalized by such developments. The *Ecclesia* transcends the members of the clerical hierarchy.

As a sociologist I had no trouble, of course, explaining why such phenomena do take place. Institutionalized religion unavoidably has within itself the seeds of discord and competition for power and status just like any other organization. Institutionalization in a religious movement is an unavoidable and necessary development if a religion is to survive over decades and centuries. During this process, however, people who may not be motivated by purely spiritual considerations can join and climb up the church hierarchy. Sociologists have a special term for this development: the "dilemma of mixed motivations."[1]

Father Maximos was not interested in sociological theorizing and pointed out that throughout the history of the church many Christian saints were persecuted by fellow clerics. He gave as an example the life of Saint Nektarios, a twentieth-century Greek Orthodox saint who was accused by his enemies within the church of debauchery and of fathering a score of illegitimate children. Saint Nektarios, a charismatic priest and ordained bishop from the island of Aegina known as a healer of people's souls and bodies, withstood the humiliation of such allegations with patience

49

and ceaseless prayer. He never defended himself and died with the stigma of the philanderer. Only after his death did his innocence get established. When healing miracles attributed to Elder Nektarios began happening, the Orthodox Church canonized him as a saint. I had the impression that Father Maximos, given what he had gone through, identified with Saint Nektarios. It was not surprising that the itinerary of the upcoming pilgrimage included a stopover at the island of Aegina to pay homage to its patron saint.

"I am really looking forward to the upcoming journey," I said, changing the subject as we reached Platres, a touristy mountain village just below the summit of Troodos. "I'm sure it will be very enjoyable."

"That's not the reason for going on a pilgrimage," Father Maximos reminded me in a playful, teasing tone as I turned a sharp curve.

"Oh, yes, right. But I should hope that being on a boat sailing around the Aegean at the end of June would not exactly be torture." Then in a more serious tone I asked what he thought would be the spiritual benefits of such a pilgrimage. Father Maximos paused as he considered my question.

"Do you remember," Father Maximos said, "the description in the Old Testament of how Moses appeared to his people after he received the Ten Commandments and walked down Mount Sinai?"

"He looked radiant?" I replied, unsure what he was alluding to.

"That's right. The people could not rest their eyes on him. Moses' face shone with such intensity that he had to cover his head in order to communicate with his people."

"How does the *Ecclesia* explain such a phenomenon?" I asked, thinking of similar stories I'd heard on Mount Athos of saints' auras shining with brilliance even in the darkness of night.

"You see, Kyriaco, every time a human being comes in contact with God there is an immediate influx of God's energy into that person. That's what causes it."

"But not everybody has a chance to climb Mount Sinai and find God."

"Well, you can contact God in a variety of ways. Obviously, you don't need to travel to Egypt."

"Such as?" I asked.

"We contact God through the divine liturgy, through prayer, through pilgrimages, through study, through whatever."

"God is infinite and there are infinite ways of contacting him."

"Exactly. Therefore, we should know that every time we make an effort to reach God, in whatever way, there is an immediate energy on the part of God that rushes our way. God is the light that lightens every human being that comes to this earth."

"Yet not everyone who tries to contact God radiates like Moses."

"Not all objects have the same receptivity to the light," Father Maximos said "One stone may accept abundant amounts of radiance, another less or even none, and another may reflect the light with great brilliance. It is the same with human beings. Some are graced with a greater capacity to reflect God's light than others. But it is a fact of spiritual life that every time we make an effort to reach God in whatever manner, we are the beneficiaries of the energy of the Holy Spirit. The amount of radiance we reflect depends on the intensity and sincerity of our effort, the state of our spiritual growth, and our capacity to receive the light. So to answer your question, the purpose of pilgrimages is primarily to create conditions within ourselves that will make us receptive to the light, to the energies of the Holy Spirit."

I mentioned the stories I had heard while growing up in Cyprus of how people in the old days were highly esteemed after their return from a pilgrimage to Jerusalem. In my grandparents' time it was considered a major undertaking to venture on a boat and travel two hundred miles southeast to get to the Holy Land. Upon their return the pilgrims were often welcomed in special processions by the entire community, which would chant hymns while the priests, carrying crosses and icons, would bless them with incense. From that day on the pilgrims would be addressed by the honorific title of *Hadji* or "Pilgrim."

"This is a tradition that goes back to the early years of Christianity," Father Maximos added. "In the biographies of saints, for example, we learn that even though they lived secluded lives and avoided external activities, they often subjected themselves to all kinds of tribulations by traveling on foot over vast distances for months and even years in order to pay their respects to holy places where Jesus had lived. They considered such pilgrimages a necessity in their spiritual life."

"By contrast, today's pilgrimages are quite easy," I said. "It is possible for us to reach the other side of the world in a matter of hours. Look at me. Where is Maine and where is Cyprus? Only two days ago I was mowing the grass in our backyard. Now I am traveling with you toward the Panagia monastery."

After a few minutes I mentioned that people who are unfamiliar with the culture of the *Ecclesia* may not easily understand the meaning of these pilgrimages. "Outsiders may consider pilgrimages as excuses for a vacation," I said, deliberately trying to provoke Father Maximos into a spirited response.

He waved his hand dismissively. "Our pilgrimage will have very little of the worldly comforts of a tourist cruise. There will be no entertainment on the boat, no radio or television, no nightclub activity. The central gathering where cabaret shows are usually being performed will be turned into a place of worship and liturgy. There will be no singing other than chants and certainly no ballroom dancing."

"Wonderful! It sounds like a perfect holiday," I said in jest.

"Not everybody will see it that way," Father Maximos said, laughing. "But such measures are necessary if we are to take full advantage of the pilgrimage. After all, we have to prepare ourselves spiritually if we are to become receptive to the grace embedded in the sacred shrines that we plan to visit. It is very important that we don't allow our hearts and minds to get distracted by external events and by the temptations of the outer world. You see, in order to spiritually benefit from such a venture we must become as inwardly focused as possible." He paused for a few seconds and then continued. "This brings to my mind a pilgrimage we undertook many years back when we traveled with our elder to the island of Tinos [famous for the miraculous icon of the Holy Virgin]. We steamed the eight hours from Piraeus to that holy island in total silence. During the journey our elder would not allow us to eat anything, drink anything, or even talk to anybody. It was a journey of fasting and silence."

"An outsider would find such austerities difficult to comprehend."

"We followed this regimen not because we didn't want to eat, drink, or talk to one another but because we understood the value of this practice as a way of protecting and preserving the heart's dynamism so that it could commune with the grace residing in the holy place we were about to visit. It was important that we maintained an inner focus."

"Please, don't tell me we will follow such a regimen on this pilgrimage," I joked, glancing sharply at Father Maximos.

"Relax, Kyriaco!" Father Maximos said in a teasing voice, "such exercises are for monks and nuns. But whether we are monks or laypeople, what is important to keep in mind is the principle of going on a pilgrimage prepared, so as to maximize its spiritual value."

"Is that why you have inaugurated the practice of having vespers every Saturday night in your diocese?"

"Yes. To receive full benefit from the Sunday mass you must prepare yourself the night before. It means to place yourself in a proper spiritual frame of mind for the Sunday Eucharist. You see, if we don't prepare ourselves we will not be in as good a position to commune with the holy energies that emanate during the Sunday liturgy.

"Of course," Father Maximos said thoughtfully, "our lives should be a continuous preparation for an ongoing dialogue with God."

"So if we go on this pilgrimage without preparation we will not get any spiritual benefit."

Father Maximos nodded. "It will just be a pleasant vacation, not a pilgrimage." To illustrate his point he narrated a story from the *Gerontikon* (a compilation of several volumes of stories about the lives of holy elders) related to the life of an elder known as Abba Isaiah, the spiritual guide to a group of monks. "One of his disciples had difficulties relating to the other monks. He was irritable, constantly grumbling and angry. At the same time he recognized that he had a problem and wished to overcome it. One day he went to his elder and said: 'I am convinced that if I go on a pilgrimage to the Holy Land I will be able to absorb the grace that emanates from the holy shrines. It will help me free myself from my anger and become a good monk.' The elder urged him to stay put and carry on with his personal struggle and told him that there was no need to travel all the way to the Holy Land. The elder advised that conditions at the monastery were more conducive to helping him overcome his shortcomings. 'If you genuinely struggle to overcome your problems,' the elder said, 'then I believe God will help you. What you need is not pilgrimages but to struggle against your passions.'

"But that monk insisted on getting his elder's blessing to go on this pilgrimage," Father Maximos continued. "Finally the elder gave his permission. 'Okay,' he conceded. 'Since you are so insistent then by all means go ahead.' Exuberant, the disciple began preparing for the long journey, which at that time was done on foot with pack animals and lasted for months. Before he left the monastery he went to his elder and, as was the custom, performed a prostration in front of him in order to receive his blessing. The elder then gave him a small tight bundle to take along on his journey. Inside he placed a head of garlic, an onion, and a piece of dried hot pepper. 'Please,' he told that disciple, 'do me a favor. Everywhere you go, after making the sign of the cross, rub this bundle over all the holy shrines you visit. Then bring it back. I want to have it absorb as much grace as possible so that I can use it as a talisman. The monk was delighted. He thought he was doing his elder a great favor.

"Several months later this monk returned from his pilgrimage feeling fully charged with divine grace. He appeared humble and peaceful. But this condition lasted for no more than two months. With the slightest provocation he regressed to his old ways and again created problems in the community. At a certain point the elder asked him to hand over the bundle and asked all the monks to gather. Then the elder opened it up. He raised the head of garlic and said, 'You went garlic and came back garlic.' He picked up the onion and said, 'You went an onion and came back an onion.' He pointed at the pepper and said, 'You went as a pepper and came back as a pepper.' Jerusalem had no effect on them," Father Maximos said and laughed.

"I'll keep that in mind during our journey," I said and lowered the window a bit to let the mountain air in.

I did not ask any further questions for several minutes as I focused on the road ahead. Father Maximos, exhausted from the head cold and the day's activities, had dozed off. I tried not to disturb him until I turned the engine off outside the gate of the Panagia monastery. It was past nine and most of the fathers were either asleep or carrying on with their individual prayer practices. At three thirty the bells would be ringing for the morning service.

Several monks waited for our arrival, including Father Arsenios, the new abbot. There was joy in their faces as they welcomed Father Maximos, who continued to be their elder and confessor. Once an elder undertakes the spiritual development of a disciple, a sacred covenant is forged that must never be broken. It is mainly for this reason that Father Maximos would be spending two days a week at the Panagia monastery. It was to fulfill the spiritual obligation he undertook when he agreed to play the role of elder for the thirty or so monks who lived there. Furthermore, he continued to be, in spite of his new status as bishop, the unofficial abbot, overseeing not only the spiritual progress of his monks but also the overall development of the monastic community. It was clear to me that hardly anything of importance was undertaken without prior consultations with him. The inner spiritual bond that was forged between the monks at the Panagia monastery and their elder remained unbroken in spite of the external changes of status and social circumstances.

We returned to Limassol at eight the following evening. As I stopped the car in front of the bishopric Father Maximos asked me to be back there at nine the following morning so that we could drive together, along with Father Isaac and Father Nikodemos, to the harbor to board the chartered liner *Calypso*, our temporary home for our weeklong Aegean adventure. Already Father Isaac and Nikodemos made the necessary preparations for the journey. They had assembled a number of icons and filled two suitcases with religious artifacts necessary for the services that were to take place aboard the ship. In addition there were ten gallons of Commandaria wine (sweet port wine, a Cyprus specialty) as a gift to the Vatopedi monastery for communion purposes. Our itinerary included a brief stopover at Vatopedi, the thriving Athonite monastery where Father Maximos began his monastic career.

Monks, pilgrims, and nuns mingled together as we boarded the *Calypso* around ten the following morning. There were no tourists on board except the pilgrims, the few nuns, and the monks accompanying Father Maximos. The captain and the officers of the Greek-owned luxury liner were all Greek. But the sailors who oiled the engine, painted the railings, scrubbed the decks, and tied off the docking lines were mostly Asians, men from the Philippines, Sri Lanka, and Bangladesh. The cleaning personnel, on the other hand, were all Eastern Europeans (mostly women), and the dancing girls, who had a break for the course of that particular voyage, were tall Russian and Romanian women spending their time smoking and socializing among themselves as they enjoyed their time off. The world's stratification system, I mused to myself as I entered my cabin, was reflected in the makeup of the boat's crew.

The wind picked up as we left the Limassol harbor and some pilgrims, unused to sea travel, looked distraught. Their anxiety was lessened somewhat when Father Maximos, helped by his assistants, conducted a short *deisis* (communal prayer) for good weather at the central hall. During the *deisis* the icon of Saint Nicholas, patron saint of seafarers, was placed next to Christ and the Holy Virgin. An hour later, by the time we passed near the Rock of Romios (the legendary birthplace of Aphrodite) at the southwestern part of Cyprus, the winds subsided, as did the anxieties of the inexperienced travelers.

Right after the *deisis*, Father Maximos spoke briefly on the purpose of the journey. He reminded us that we were on a pilgrimage, not a pleasure cruise, and because of that there wouldn't be any worldly entertainment. It would have defeated the objective of the pilgrimage. "I implore you," Father Maximos added, "to be accommodating. If there are difficulties, consider them as a form of *askesis*.

"The devil," he said playfully, "is bent on coming aboard uninvited, free of charge and without a ticket. He will do his best to create mischief. He will tempt us to create a fuss for minor reasons. 'I don't like the food,' or 'I don't like my cabin,' or 'I don't like the person I share the cabin with,' and on and on."

I had a feeling, as I listened to Father Maximos, that he had faced such problems on previous pilgrimages. By giving his pep talk he cleverly inhibited the emergence of possible trouble as the journey progressed. Saint Nicholas helped with his little miracle, making everybody happy and contented. The seas quieted down completely as we lost sight of Cyprus and headed to Aegean waters.

Taking advantage of the calm seas, pilgrims sat around on the deck cherishing the freshness of the open sea. After jotting down a few notes, I took a stroll around the boat with Antonis and Father Nikodemos, enjoying the setting sun.

"Just imagine," Father Nikodemos said as he shook his head, "one of the bishops was fuming because Father Maximos was not a meat eater. Can you believe that? Another one was overheard complaining, 'How is it that when I give a talk barely twenty people attend whereas when Maximos gives a talk over a thousand people show up?' "

"Jealousy is a very human weakness, Father Nikodeme," Antonis said, as we rested our arms at the bow of the boat watching the sun disappear in the horizon.

"It sure is!" said Father Nikodemos. "Do you know what is the most difficult challenge for us monks to overcome?" he asked and proceeded to answer his own question. "It is not sex or gluttony or money, but ambition, particularly ambition for spiritual development. That's where the devil finds entrance into our hearts. The greatest danger for a monk is jealousy. 'Why him and not me?' "

Jealous is the greatest danger for a monk.

FOUR

ANGER
WITHOUT
SIN

he Aegean shone in the brightness of the full moon as we passed one island after another. Sitting alone outside my cabin, I gazed at the whiteness of the foam generated by the boat's propeller plowing steadily through the still sea. I reflected on the events of the past few days and wrote down some of my impressions. Dinner, followed by vespers and a short talk by Father Maximos, had taken place an hour ago, and most of the pilgrims were in their cabins. The following afternoon we would arrive at the island of Tinos to pay homage to the miraculous icon of the Holy Virgin, the Orthodox equivalent of the Madonna of Guadalupe and the Virgin of Lourdes.

Already we had left the island of Patmos where we spent the day visiting two monasteries, one for men and the other for women. Most important for our pilgrimage, we paid homage and lit candles at the legendary cave where John the Beloved is believed to have dictated to a faithful disciple the Apocalypse, the final book of the New Testament, while in a state of ecstasy. With those powerful impressions still vivid in my mind I hurried off to a quiet spot in order to take notes before new episodes and events would push them deep into the back alleys of my memory.

Father Maximos had a particular fondness for Patmos, not only because of John's awesome vision at the famous cave but because of the island's simplicity and serenity, something not found in more commercial and tourist-dominated Greek islands. It is the serenity of the place that strikes visitors the moment they set foot on the island. That fact, however, did not detract me from my uneasiness as I contemplated John's ecstatic vision. In past conversations with Father Maximos I had expressed my ambivalent feelings toward the Apocalypse with its images of wholesale slaughter and torment. Unlike the other texts of the New Testament, the Apocalypse is open to bizarre interpretations that often cause irrational reactions and mass hysteria among the faithful of a less critical disposition. I once ventured to tell him that I wish the fathers of the Church did not include the book as part of the New Testament canon.

For Father Maximos, however, the meaning of the Apocalypse is to serve as a reminder of the need for *metanoia*, the radical shift of our individual and collective consciousness in the direction of God. Inevitably, he said, we will experience our own "apocalypse" the moment we exit this world, which could come at any time.

I was preoccupied with these thoughts when I heard Father Maximos's soothing voice. "Enjoying the evening, Kyriaco?" He stepped out of his cabin and leaned over the boat's railing scanning the horizon while taking in a few deep breaths.

"Absolutely," I replied, pleased with his unexpected appearance. These were the special moments I had looked forward to when I decided to join the pilgrimage. Considering that most of the passengers were Father Maximos's spiritual followers, it was a rare opportunity to have private moments

59

and conversations with him. On board he was almost always surrounded by pilgrims and fellow monks and nuns.

"I hope this trip gives you some needed rest," I said casually. He sat down on a reclining chair next to me.

"Real rest for me, Kyriaco, is to be alone in a hermitage," he replied, in a tone that sounded more like a complaint. His new status as a spiritual celebrity came with a heavy price considering his personal ambition went no further than being a monk on Mount Athos.

"I see what you mean." Ever since he was elected bishop there were few opportunities to be solitary, an essential part in a monk's life.

We had exchanged only a few more sentences when Antonis appeared along with his wife Frosoula and two cousins, Maria and Eleni. We urged them to join us, an invitation they gladly accepted. Father Maximos was like a human magnet, with his casual and informal ways. To be totally alone with him was only possible in the context of a confession.

"Father Maxime," I said, "during your talk this evening you mentioned in passing that it is possible for a person to be angry without committing a sin. What did you mean exactly? How is this possible? I always assumed that authentic spiritual life means inner peace and freedom from anger."

"You are of course right. But when I said anger without sin what I had in mind was a reference from the Fourth Psalm when the prophet David speaks in the voice of God requesting that we rid our anger of sin."

"Isn't this a paradox, a contradiction?"

"It sounds like double-talk," Antonis quipped.

"Not quite," Father Maximos replied. "Look. The holy elders are very clear about this. Anger is an integral part of our human nature, a gift from God."

"A gift from God?" Maria exclaimed with a puzzled look. "I thought anger is what gets us into trouble."

"I will explain. God gave us the capacity for anger, right? It is one of the powers of the soul, just like justice, wisdom, courage. However, these God-given powers are more often than not misused by us. They don't function in us the way God intended them to function."

"But how do we misuse anger?" I asked.

"Simple. We misuse it when we direct it against fellow human beings, when, for example, we become filled with resentment every time we assume that we are treated unjustly. We misuse it when we are consumed by feelings of rejection, causing us to lash out at people around us. We also misuse it when we marshal our anger in the pursuit of what we consider to be our rights, according to the worldly meaning of that term, that is."

"Some will say that what you are suggesting, Father Maxime, is a recipe for passivity that invites abuse by others," I suggested. "Modern counselors train people to stand up for their rights."

"Don't be in a hurry, Kyriaco," Father Maximos replied and with his right hand signaled patience. "Anger does not work properly in us when it is mixed up with our egotism, that's all. The holy elders teach that if you wish to find out whether you are dominated by egotism you can ask yourself whether you get angry or not, and why. If you do, then there is no need to speculate whether you are an egotistical person. The presence of anger in your heart is a sign that you lack humility."

"This is the normal state that we all find ourselves in," I pointed out. "When our desires are blocked we get angry. You might say it is natural."

"It is not natural," Father Maximos replied. "It is natural in our fallen state, yes. But it is not natural in our essence. Our natural, essential state is the state that the saints attain."

"It is the state beyond desires and worldly preoccupations," Antonis said. He had read extensively on the teachings of the holy elders, routinely passing on to me "must-read" books.

"Exactly. The angry, quarrelsome individual who loses his inner peace for this or that reason or this or that cause is someone who has a spiritual problem. He is dominated by a destructive passion, whether we call it egotism, self-centeredness, narcissism, or pride. So let us not find personal excuses. We get angry because we feel someone committed an injustice against us, or tried to cheat us, or said something nasty about us, or slandered us, or tried to steal from us, or whatever."

Father Maximos smiled enigmatically and added, "There will always be people who will try to commit some injustice against us. Does this mean that we should be permanently angry? Does it mean that we must never find peace within ourselves but always blame others for our anger?"

"That is the state many of us find ourselves in. Have you ever been to

Athens?" I asked rhetorically, alluding to the proverbial impatient and volatile Athenian pedestrian.

"Then what must we do?" asked Eleni, in her first personal encounter and interchange with Father Maximos.

"We must realize that we can confront all these problems in a state of inner tranquility. The angry individual suffers from egotism, no matter what the cause of his anger.

"I am reminded of a story in the *Gerontikon*," Father Maximos continued after a short interruption when another pilgrim joined us. "There was this monk who was always angry, always finding fault with others and blaming them for his shortcomings and problems. He attributed his anger to the communal way of living. He reasoned that in the monastery there were too many people with diverse interests and different personality traits. Based on that belief, he decided to retreat into the desert and live alone as a hermit. He was calm and peaceful there for the first three days. On the fourth day, while trying to fill his cup with water (a precious commodity in a desert), he accidentally spilled it on the ground. He tried for a second time and again he knocked over his cup. He burst with anger, kicking and smashing the stool upon which he was sitting. At that moment he saw the devil laughing in front of him. He then realized that the problem was inside him and he had only himself to blame for his outbursts. This monk understood that he had to work on himself to fight against the passion of anger that dominated him and quit blaming others for his own shortcomings. The desert was no help to him."

As Father Maximos continued to speak, energized by our conversation, two nuns, Athanasia and Ioanna, appeared on the deck near us. Father Maximos signaled to them to join our circle, which was beginning to expand. He then went on to tell another story as the radiant-looking nuns pulled up two chairs and shyly joined us. "I would like you to compare the behavior of that monk with that of an Athonite elder I knew who was considered to be a *Salos* [a fool in Christ]. We used to call him the *Jacobaki* (Jacob was his real name). *Jacobaki* roamed barefoot all over the Holy Mountain, during summer and winter. He had no permanent hermitage or home and was almost naked. He would just stay for the night wherever others would give him food and offer him hospitality and then move on. His cassock had become gray from the many years of wear and tear, and you couldn't even tell which was the original cloth, so full was it of patches. One day, a couple of brothers decided to dress him with a new cassock, but he adamantly refused to take off the old one. The brothers grabbed him and forced it upon him. While they did that he kept saying to them, 'Now I am going to get angry at you. I am really going to get angry.' But he could not get angry, no matter how much he was provoked and no matter how much he tried to get angry.

"Do you see what happened? Someone like *Jacobaki*, who reached such depths of humility, had no room in his heart for anger, no matter how much he tried."

"On the other hand, we who live in the world get angry even in our sleep!" Antonis said.

"That's because we don't have peace within us. We have wishes and desires and a personal will but we have no real peace," Father Maximos lamented. He then stood up to stretch his legs and watch the reflection of the moon on the unusually calm waters. "To return to my original question," I said, "when can one be angry and not sin?"

"God has given us the power of anger," Father Maximos said returning to his seat, "to use in accordance with our true nature."

"But when? Why? In what way must we use it?"

"We should use it when we get angry at our passions, against the demons that do their best to keep us away from God, against sin. Quite often the pressure of our passions is so intense that we must muster all our power to resist it. Anger is the energy that enables us to confront our passions, to resist the circumstances and temptations that we may find ourselves in. If we are soft and weak we may surrender to all sorts of temptations."

"I assume you mean that we should have enough strength within ourselves to keep from compromising our conscience. This is what you mean, I suppose, by natural anger."

"Right. Isn't it admirable that the holy fathers, who were paragons of meekness, demonstrated such power of resistance against evil? Saint

Chrysostom exhorts us to make the whole world our friends but also to be ready to make enemies for the love of Christ. This is unavoidable, you know."

"I am not sure I understand," Maria said.

"Suppose a friend comes to you and asks you to be part of a scheme that goes contrary to your conscience. That's when you must marshal the power of your anger and say no. And you must do that even if this would cost you a friendship."

"I suppose it is a question of how we rank our values and the kind of values we espouse," I said.

"This is true in everything we do. Just the other day someone came for confession and told me that he had had an extramarital affair in order to help a woman friend come out of her depression because she was so unhappy with her marriage. Her husband was indifferent to her and was not satisfying her sexually. Let me ask you, is this the way to help another human being?" Father Maximos crossed his arms and leaned back on his chair.

Once we quieted down I mentioned the case of a psychiatrist whose "therapeutic" interventions for treating depressed female clients included sleeping with them in order to help them overcome their difficulties. Father Maximos shook his head in disbelief as the rest laughed.

"The man of God is neither gullible nor suggestible. He knows when to retreat in the face of provocation and when to resist. With full consciousness and knowledge he allows himself to become humbled, to remain silent. But there will be times when he will have to gather his anger and fight."

"Just like Jesus lashing out at the merchants and chasing them out of the temple," Antonis said.

"Very good. That's when Jesus demonstrated his anger—"

"Father Maxime, I must confess I have some difficulty with that particular episode in the New Testament," I interjected. "It has been used as an excuse throughout history for religiously motivated violence, like that of anti-abortion activists blowing up clinics in the U.S. or that of holy warriors fighting in the name of Christ. It is the same problem with Islam when extreme fundamentalists excuse their jihads as sanctioned by Allah. Mohammed, after all, took up the sword and led his army against his enemies."

"Obviously we mean something different here," Father Maximos replied. "Jesus' anger sprang out of his deepest nature. He had used this natural power of anger to restore justice in the house of God. And note, please, that neither Jesus nor his apostles took up the sword to wage wars against infidels. Whether people later put on Christian cloaks and launched crusades in the name of Jesus is a different matter."

"I remember a Cypriot deacon," I added, "who justified his involvement in the guerrilla movement against the British as a matter of justice sanctified by God. 'Christ showed us the way,' he told me, and he used this very example of Jesus chasing the moneylenders out of the Temple as a justification for his own participation in the violent underground movement to chase the British out of Cyprus."

Father Maximos responded that these are the results of human shortcomings and spiritual imperfection. It has nothing to do with Christ's teaching and message. "Christ is our archetype," he elaborated further, "and our challenge is to come as close to our archetype as we can. The anger of Jesus was not the product of any earthly passions, nor was it the outcome of egotism. Jesus was perfect God and perfect man. When Jesus told his disciples that he had to go to Jerusalem, surrender to the Romans, and eventually be executed, Peter was outraged. He rebelled against such a prospect and declared that he was not going to allow that. Then Jesus reprimanded him. He told Peter that he spoke in the voice of Satan. He said that to his foremost disciple! You see, Jesus had all the powers of his soul in a state of perfect equilibrium."

"Jesus reacted in a similar way," Antonis added, "when Satan offered him worldly power. He became angry and chastised him."

"Jesus used anger only to resist temptation. This is the example he wanted to give us, what is being asked of us to do," Father Maximos said. "I always remember the way Elder Paisios handled cases like these even though he was frail and weak from excessive fasting and all-night vigils. There were times, in fact, that he could hardly keep himself upright. Yet, when it was a matter of conscience and of confronting evil he was transformed into a warrior. Old Paisios, frail as he was, had no fear in his struggle against evil."

"Have you ever witnessed him in action under such circumstances, Father Maxime?" I asked.

"Many times. One day I watched how he handled a fellow from Crete who apparently was under the influence of demonic energies. He was tall and powerful and he asked Old Paisios to have a private audience with him. Then he started talking nonsense. At one point he demanded that the elder kneel down and worship him because, he claimed, he was 'God.' Obviously, he was out of his mind. The late Paisios stood up, pushed him away, and told him 'You are not God, you are an ass.' Then the Cretan threw the elder to the ground. Once again Old Paisios stood up and, pointing his finger at that ferocious-looking fellow, warned him 'Tonight I shall take care of you.' "

"Did he really threaten him like that?" I asked, laughing.

"Oh, yes! It was the devil, of course, that he threatened, not the poor fellow himself. What Elder Paisios meant was that during the night he was going to pray for the Cretan fellow in order to free him from the demon that possessed him. That young man didn't know what he was doing or saying. So when he heard Elder Paisios say he would take care of him that night, foam started flowing out of his mouth and he jumped on Old Paisios to tear him apart."

"Well, did you save him?" I asked half seriously.

"He didn't need any help. I was with another young monk that day and I thought we would all die. Things developed so rapidly there was hardly any time to react. Before we had a chance to intervene, the elder, frail as he was, stood up and gave him a slap so hard that he almost fell on the ground. Then the Cretan began cursing not only the elder but also the Holy Virgin. At that moment Old Paisios delivered him such a sharp slap on his mouth that I thought his teeth would fall out."

"Wasn't he afraid that this person could kill him?"

Father Maximos dismissed that possibility with a gesture. "Old Paisios was not afraid of demonic possession. He was not afraid of Satan. He was a master exorcist. The struggle that day was not with that troubled fellow but with the demon who was inside him and kept tormenting him." Elder Paisios, Father Maximos went on to tell us, spent all night praying for that man, whose mental health was eventually restored.

Father Maximos smiled as he remembered something else. "You know, there are many stories in the lives of saints that demonstrate these qualities of anger and defiance in the face of worldly power and injustice. When Julian the Apostate [fourth-century Roman emperor who fought Christianity and tried to restore pagan religion] passed by Caesarea, where Saint Basil lived, he was offered all sorts of expensive gifts befitting a powerful emperor. People were diplomatic, trying to ingratiate themselves with him. The great Basil, who had been Julian's classmate and friend while they were students at the philosophical school in Athens, also sent him a gift. It was a loaf of bread made of barley. When the emperor received it he threw it on the ground in anger and disgust. 'Isn't he ashamed to send me this? I will show him,' he roared. Julian ordered his servants to offer Basil as his own gift a bundle of hay used to feed donkeys. When Basil received it he laughed and said, 'I sent him a loaf of barley bread because that's what I eat and in exchange he offered me a gift of what he eats.'

"Saints are like that, you know. When it is a matter of fundamental principles of faith they are fearless and can muster extraordinary power regardless of who their opponents might be. Sweet and humble as they may be, they often act provocatively against the powers that be. In matters of injustice, in matters related to possible accommodation with sin, and in matters of faith they are uncompromisingly intransigent. They are real fighters."

"That's how the prophets of ancient Israel were," I said. "They thundered against injustice and were not afraid of the ruling powers."

"Men of God are never afraid of worldly powers," Father Maximos added. "I remember reading about the life of the great Antonios [Saint Anthony, founder of Christian monasticism during the fourth century] who was living alone in the Egyptian desert. Yet when he realized that the *Ecclesia* was in danger because of the Arian heresy [movement within the church questioning the divinity of Christ, headed by a priest named Arius], he left the desert and rushed to the city to become a witness to the faith. So you see, struggle and conflict within the *Ecclesia* are not something unusual or new. They have been going on throughout its history. We are obligated to fight when necessary, but always with discretion and discernment."

"But isn't this a tricky argument, Father Maxime?" I protested. "This is what can lead to religious wars."

"Such developments take place when people act out of egotistical desires and self-interest."

"But one can argue that Islamic suicide bombers today act selflessly and out of love for their particular group and religion," I persisted.

"Look! We must fight only within the context of the spirit of God and always with love for all living beings. We must always have the welfare of others as our central motivation. Saints like Elder Paisios offer us a good example. We must never act on the basis of motives that are contaminated by worldly and personal considerations. When the saints fight for justice and for the preservation of fundamental principles of faith they never do so in order to promote their own careers or interests or any particular group. They would ask nothing for themselves, be it glory, praise, or any other human recognition. They do everything for the glory of God and for the love of their fellow human beings, all human beings. That's when anger is necessary and without sin. But again human beings can express this form of anger only after they reach a point when they act naturally, like the saints."

"A person may think he or she is acting selflessly but it may not be so in reality. You can kill for your God or for your country, for example, and imagine that you are acting selflessly."

"That's right," Father Maximos replied. "Spiritual maturity is a precondition."

"Can you please make this notion of anger without sin more concrete?" Eleni complained. "It is somewhat unclear to me."

"You are a mother, right?"

"Right."

"Well, as you know from experience, often a mother, in order to offer her child a certain lesson, needs to show anger. A mother who gets angry at her child, having in mind only the good of her child, is an example of anger without sin."

Eleni nodded.

"Of course, keep in mind that this is really a very subtle principle. It is very difficult to differentiate between a state when one is angry and does not sin and when one is angry and commits a sin. Given where we are in comparison to the saints, we must assume that when we are angry we simply express our egocentric self. Very few among us can be angry without sinning, really."

"Therefore," I added, "to tell ourselves 'now I am angry but I do not sin because my anger is freed from any selfishness,' would be presumptuous and a self-serving rationalization, a sin in itself."

"Quite right. Even saints would often succumb to the temptation of anger. I have in mind the case of Abba Makarios, who got angry one day when he was stung by a fly. He killed the fly. He then became so remorseful that for six months he lived naked near a swamp. He was literally eaten up by flies and other insects. He was so badly swollen that when he returned to the monastery nobody could recognize him. They finally figured out who he was from his voice."

"He punished himself just because he killed a fly?" Antonis asked with astonishment.

"No, not because he killed a fly but because he got angry. We kill flies all the time and Abba Makarios did so himself many times before. He inflicted this punishing penance on himself because he succumbed to the temptation of anger."

Father Maximos realized the incredulity that this story created in us (but not in the nuns, who listened silently with smiles on their faces) and went on to point out that in the life of a saint like Abba Makarios what was of paramount importance was his relationship with God. He was a saint graced by the Holy Spirit. Anger cut him off from grace. It was for this reason that he was so harsh on himself. His anger, like a light switch, interrupted the currents of grace flowing through him. To those of us who are not in conscious communication with divine realities and experiences, Abba Makarios's behavior appears bizarre and incomprehensible."

"In our times we call such behavior a form of mental illness," I said.

"Forgive me for asking a naive question," Eleni interjected, "but how do we know whether we are graced by the Holy Spirit? Are there any criteria that we can use to recognize such an experience?"

Father Maximos remained thoughtful for a while. "Being graced by the Holy Spirit means attaining purification of the heart from egotistical passions. People can examine themselves and find out whether they have a clean heart or not."

"But how?"

"It is very simple. Explore the fruits of the Holy Spirit and see if you have them. Christ tells us that from the fruits you shall get to know the tree. Do you want to know if a tree offers good fruit? Cut one and taste it. The Apostle Paul says 'Brethren, the fruits of the Spirit are the following,' and Paul lists such traits as love, joy, peace, gentleness, forbearance, goodness, honesty, faith, temperance, humility. Take the catalogue he offers us and do a self-analysis. Are these characteristics present in you? If yes, then the Holy Spirit is active within you. If not then it means that the fruits of the Holy Spirit are not yet manifest in your life. It means that the fruits of your heart are different. If within our hearts we find darkness, confusion, agitation, despair, evil, hostility, vengeance, hatred, hedonism, stinginess, narcissism, egotism, and the like, then we should consider it as a given that the Holy Spirit is inactive. That means we are dominated by these passions, which keep the Holy Spirit away or hidden from us. It means that we need *metanoia* and hard work to purify our hearts."

We contemplated for a while the meaning of Father Maximos's words. I am certain that each one of us made an instant self-analysis. Antonis broke the silence. "To get back to the issue of anger, I suppose a general rule for us would be to avoid it, period."

"That would certainly be wise. Practicing humility in a conscious way will help us overcome anger and assist us in purifying our hearts from whatever keeps the Spirit of God dormant rather than active in us. We just need to learn to curb our desires and personal will by being more accommodating to the needs of others rather than our own. Do you understand what I mean?"

"It is hard, Father Maxime, to follow such a principle," I said. "Modern individuals will find such a prescription rather bitter. It goes against the grain of individualism, which is encouraged by contemporary life. Perhaps such a rule can work in a monastery, but it is difficult to put into practice in the so-called real world."

Father Maximos shook his head and insisted that such a rule is possible whether one lives in a monastery as a monk or whether one lives in the world. He admitted, however, that it is more challenging to maintain such an attitude while living in the world.

"I remember an abbot who used to say that in his monastery there were some monks who were not very accommodating to others. They were very difficult. 'Since,' he reasoned, 'they themselves could not behave properly toward the rest of us, we ourselves must behave properly toward them.' That is how they maintained peace in the monastery."

"But again, Father Maxime," said Antonis, a businessman who often complained of the "dog-eat-dog" atmosphere of the marketplace, "given what Kyriacos just said, how can one apply such a rule in the world outside the monastery? The monastic setting is much more supportive of such an attitude."

"Let me ask you this," Father Maximos said and fiddled with his *komboschini*, which he always held in his hand. "Suppose you have a problem with your spouse, your employer, your workers. Suppose you don't see eye to eye with them. Okay, why don't you take the first step and accommodate your position in their direction? Place yourself in the right way toward them. Accept others as they are, without losing your peace of mind. That is the way to cut off the causes of anger. Is it difficult? Absolutely. But for someone with spiritual ambitions, such provocations must be welcome and seen as opportunities for growth."

"What if you cannot cut off the cause of your anger, Father Maxime?" I asked. "Then what?"

"Choke the anger. Don't let it come out."

"But that could be disastrous," I said. "Are you suggesting that we should suppress our anger and store it in our subconscious and keep it there simmering like a time bomb?"

"No, Kyriaco! You know the answer. Remember what I told you the other day? Our elder said that we should be ready to suppress our anger to such a degree that, as he put it, smoke could come out of our nostrils. Now, why would he say something like that? Because anger is like a mighty river that can sweep you along the way. You lose control of yourself and you say things and do things that you will later regret."

"But how do you control your anger without storing it in your subconscious?"

"It is simple. As you suppress your anger you fall on the ground and ask for God's help. You can say 'God have mercy on me. Liberate me from this anger.' Then you will truly find peace within yourself. When you learn how to do that then the grace of God will enter inside you and free you from that passion."

"So the key to avoid storing anger within your subconscious," I said, "is to recognize your weakness and seek God's help. That's how you learn to manage anger."

"That's what the holy elders teach and this is what we know from personal experience. They teach us that when we are angry we should remain silent. Then we must immediately ask for God's mercy and assistance so that we can get rid of our anger."

"What if we lose our temper and strike back, saying or doing something offensive against another person? What then?" I asked.

"Then the medicine against such a weakness is to go to that person and ask for forgiveness."

"It is terribly difficult to do that," Antonis complained and shook his head, perhaps thinking of the serious problems he once had with one of his business partners. "It is a terribly humiliating act to do, particularly if you feel that the other person's behavior toward you was unjustifiable."

"But it is humility that will take the energy out of your anger," Father Maximos stressed. "This is the needed medicine and we must recognize it as such. I should also add that for this medicine to work, your approach to the other person must be genuine and not forced or pretentious."

"How?" Antonis asked.

"Avoid saying, for example, 'If I caused you any grief or if I saddened you, I ask for your forgiveness.' Such a wishy-washy, superficial attitude is not helpful. Be brave and just go over to the other person and say, 'Brother, or Sister, I am sorry for causing you grief. I apologize. I am responsible for this.' Don't approach the other by starting to justify yourself, by finding excuses such as 'Well, I am sorry but I was very upset,' or 'I was sad because of what you said,' and so on."

"At least it could be a first step! It's better than not saying anything," I said.

"Okay, I can accept that, Kyriaco. If you are not ready for total humility, do at least that much. But if we are serious about spiritual work, we need to be tough with ourselves. I do recognize that it is very difficult to go and tell someone 'Please forgive me for causing you grief,' but that's how we progress spiritually. I remember how difficult it was for me as a young and inexperienced monk when I faced this problem for the first time. My elder required of me to ask forgiveness from a brother with whom I had some problems. And the difficulty for us monks is that not only are we expected to ask for forgiveness but also touch the ground and make a prostration in front of the other person."

"I am afraid I am not ready," Antonis said with comic discomfort. "It would be virtually impossible for me to do such a thing." The rest of us burst into laughter.

"Imagine if I were to go to a colleague at the university," I said, "and kneeling in front of him, ask for forgiveness. In no time he will reach for the phone to call health services."

"It is certainly not easy," Father Maximos conceded. "Of course you don't kneel in such a case but, following the spirit of this principle, you humble yourself by genuinely apologizing to the other. That's what is needed if you take the spiritual life to heart."

I remembered the day when a young monk at Saint Anthony's monastery in Arizona kneeled in the middle of the church and, in front of all the pilgrims and monks, asked forgiveness from his brothers as they walked out. His "crime" was oversleeping and coming late for *Orthros*. However, such a demonstration of remorse seemed to me more like a spiritual exercise than a punishment for lack of punctuality. Of course, as a sociologist I also interpreted that scene as the unavoidable necessity of all social groups to create their own "deviants" as a tool for "boundary maintenance." If someone didn't violate the rules nobody would know what the rules are and without rules no social group is possible.

Father Maximos told us another story in his usual casual manner. "During the first year I was a monk on Mount Athos, there was some kind of a misunderstanding between a young hieromonk and his elder. The young hieromonk was very upset because he heard a rumor that his elder was planning to change his work schedule. Being young and inexperienced he started bad-mouthing his elder. The rest of us, naive and younger than he was, would not waste a moment. We went straight to the elder and reported him. The elder's reaction was 'I'll take care of him during vespers. I will make him feel so much shame he won't know where to go and hide his face from the rest of us.' We thought he was really going to reprimand him.

"I remember it was Saturday before vespers. The elder walked down the steps from his cell, which was on the second floor, and called for this hieromonk. 'Come to the sanctuary. I want to talk to you,' he said to him somberly. 'Holy Mother of God,' the rest of us murmured among ourselves. 'Alas to him.' The elder was going to take care of him right inside the sanctuary. All of us were tense, waiting for the developments. We expected to hear raised voices and reprimands as the elder scolded him. I happened to be inside the sanctuary helping with the service as I had just been made a deacon. And what do you think I witnessed? As they entered the sanctuary, the sixty-five-year-old elder fell on his knees in front of the twenty-five-year-old monk, kissed his feet, and asked for forgiveness. 'I am sorry, my brother,' he said to the young monk, 'I must have done something to cause you grief. Please forgive me.' The other of course was shattered and began sobbing while asking forgiveness from the elder. By the grace of God, tranquility was restored in the monastery and a valuable lesson was offered to all of us."

Father Maximos paused in reminiscence. "You know there was more to this story. On Monday I visited Elder Ephraim [another charismatic elder and spiritual guide to Father Maximos] at Katounakia. His hermitage was hours away from our monastery. The moment he saw me he became inquisitive. 'What happened on Saturday night at the monastery?' he asked me. 'What do you mean?' I replied, pretending I had no idea. 'During my prayers,' he explained, 'I saw an angel putting a golden wreath over the head of your elder. Something must have happened.'"

"How could he know, Father Maxime?" Eleni asked puzzled. "Did anybody tell him?"

"No, nobody could have told him. Elder Ephraim was a saint. He saw those scenes in a special way, through the grace of the Holy Spirit. Now, you may wonder what I am driving at. Anger requires head-on confrontation. Don't let it sit inside you. Most important, never justify yourself when you are angry. Self-justification is a weakness and is counterproductive to our spiritual development. Always remember that."

"Woe to us, Father Maxime. What you advise us to do is extremely tough. We all tend to get angry with the slightest of provocation," Antonis muttered and sighed.

"Of course we get angry. We are all human. But we must gradually learn to turn our anger not against others but against our selfish passions."

"Psychologists would warn that such an attitude could make us all into severe neurotics," I said playfully.

"It is possible to achieve that without neurosis, anxiety, or depression," Father Maximos responded. "We must become merciless judges of ourselves whenever we catch ourselves with anger in our hearts. We must humble ourselves by learning how to say 'I am sorry.' Do you know how much better our lives would be if we got accustomed to saying that word?

"I am reminded of an experience of Saint Anthony when he said 'I saw the traps of the devil wrapped around the earth.' Horrified, he sighed and asked in despair 'How can one get through these traps?' God then replied, 'It is humility that defeats Satan.' Notice that he didn't tell Saint Anthony that it is through fasting, or all-night vigils, or even through prayer that the devil can be defeated. No, none of that. Just humility.

"Believe me, it is true. Only humility can destroy the traps of Satan. Why? Because the devil is our pride and egotism. Their practical symptom and outcome is anger. Therefore, that which destroys anger is humility. You see, serious spiritual work presupposes the development of the habit of intentionally humbling ourselves, cutting off our desires, and rejecting our own opinions: 'I think this way . . .' or 'I believe this . . .' or 'I consider this to be good . . .' Go beyond these personal claims. Transcend yourself and empty yourself in the way Christ emptied himself for us. That is how we learn of the Christ mystery. It is this *kenosis*, the rejection of our will and desires, which will lead us back to God.

"There is an icon called the *Akra Tapinosis* [Absolute Humility]," Father Maximos continued. "It depicts Christ in the tomb, dead and naked. That is the ideal model of perfect humility. Are we capable of such a state of being in the world? If yes, then the mystery of the Resurrection will begin to get energized within us. A person in that state experiences peace, joy, freedom. I will never forget those holy elders of Mount Athos who lived in the cenobitic or communal monasteries, how happy and accommodating they were. If you asked for their preference about anything, their standard reply was 'As you wish.' They were accommodating with whatever solution others would find to a problem. They were always joyous and whatever the outcome, their standard reply was *'Nan evlogimeno'* [may it be blessed]."

"Imagine if people treated each other like that in marriage?" I asked lightly. "Saying *'Evlogison'* [your blessings] to each other every time they had a disagreement, giving in to the wishes of the other."

"Then you will have happy marriages," Father Maximos retorted. "When spouses focus on pleasing each other rather than themselves you have peace and love within marriage."

"You mean accommodating yourself to every whim and request of your spouse?" Antonis said with raised eyebrows.

"Such an attitude must be matched with discernment, of course," Father Maximos hastened to add. "It is important to remember that as long as we fail to learn the art of transcending ourselves then we will never be truly happy. We will never be content, no matter what others do for us. You know, I used to think that what is described in the *Gerontikon* on the life of holy elders is useful and valid primarily for monks. But now that I live in the world and I hear all sorts of difficulties and tragedies that people face in their families and daily lives, I am convinced that everybody can benefit spiritually by studying the *Gerontikon* and by learning how the holy elders confronted life. Such a study can help us handle our worldly problems better and it can be a guide toward our own perfection. We can become perfect just as readily as married or unmarried men and women living ordinary, worldly lives as we can living in the monastery."

Before we dispersed that night Father Maximos repeated the main points of our conversation. "Anger is a natural propensity of the soul that can help us resist evil and sin. We must marshal our anger only against sin, never against human beings. This is an axiom. We can be angry against injustice, never against the unjust person. We are asked not to hate even the demons. Saints did not hate demons. They hated, however, demonic acts. Believe it or not saints loved even the demons. Their hearts were on fire with the love of the whole world. Abba Isaac the Syrian wrote that the heart of the saints was in flames for the love of the entire creation, including the demons. It was impossible for saints to accept that there were entities who were cut off from God. When we reach such a state then, as the prophet David says, we can be angry without sinning."

Father Maximos stood up. "It is past midnight and tomorrow is going to be a long day," he said and stretched his arms. Before getting into bed I walked with Antonis around the boat a few times and reflected on the points Father Maximos had raised on how to think about anger, the source of all our personal and collective problems. Since that night I could never again relate to anger the same way. Whenever I would catch myself boiling up, the words of Father Maximos would come to mind and my anger would lose some of its steam.

FIVE

A

DIFFERENT HOSPITAL

e reached Tinos at sunset on rare tranquil seas. The island was reputed not only for hosting a most venerated miraculous icon of the Holy Virgin but also for the notoriously troubled waters that surrounded it. The serenity of the sea was a soothing counterbalance to the upheaval that had just taken place on board. A man in his seventies almost choked to death when a piece of bread got stuck in his throat over lunch.

"Had the ship's doctor arrived a few seconds later the old man would have been a goner," Antonis said with a sigh of relief. "He lost consciousness and his face turned purple. I was terrified and took him for dead. There was no sign of life in him."

Antonis, who rushed to help even though he did not know what to do, confided to me that he was concerned not only for the man's life but also for the possible negative consequences to Father Maximos's reputation had the pilgrim died. "His enemies back in Cyprus would have welcomed it as a great opportunity to hit him hard."

"Perhaps," I mused, "the Holy Virgin wanted to demonstrate her presence with a little miracle." Antonis nodded as if it was a self-evident empirical fact.

The church with its miraculous icon was two miles up the hill from the harbor of Tinos, a distance we covered slowly on foot in a meditative procession while chanting hymns to the Holy Virgin. Father Theophilos (Friend of God), a young deacon, recited by heart verses from the Salutations to the Holy Virgin. At the end of each verse Father Maximos and his companions rhythmically sang *Chere Nymphe Anymphefte* (Rejoice, O Bride Unwedded). Walking near Father Maximos, I had the uncanny feeling that the fathers in their solemn procession carried on a literal dialogue with the invisible presence of the *Theotokos* (Mother of God), patron of the island.

> *Rejoice, heavenly ladder by which God came down;*
> *Rejoice, bridge leading those from earth to heaven . . .*
> *Rejoice, surpassing the knowledge of scholars;*
> *Rejoice, dawn that illumines the minds of believers . . .*
> *Rejoice, arable land yielding an abundance of compassion.*[1]

By the time we reached the hundred or so steps to the church, perched on the top of the hill, we had covered all the stanzas typically chanted during services in honor of the *Theotokos*.

As we climbed up the steps we avoided a young woman on her knees as she painfully, slowly, and tearfully crawled her way up the steps, her prayers interrupted by uncontrollable sobbing. "God knows," Antonis whispered to me, "what tragedy she is going through."

The church smelled heavily of incense and beeswax candles. It was packed to the brim with pilgrims who were squeezed in line, awaiting their turn to pay homage to the miraculous icon. At the same time, a choir of nuns filled the space with their perfectly delivered chants. It was an emotionally charged atmosphere that could trigger, I felt, a string of healing miracles. The famed icon of the *Theotokos* was covered top to bottom with expensive-looking jewelry, from diamond rings to golden crosses, which people left behind as gifts for their recovery from some incurable illness. Innumerable were the tales we heard of people who, after arriving on the island physically disabled, departed completely healed, leaving behind their clutches and wheelchairs. It is these stories that keep pilgrims coming to Tinos by the thousands.

When people neared the icon they would light their candle and then, after a prostration and after crossing themselves a few times, they would kiss the icon at a spot kept free of jewelry. An attendant would then quickly wipe the kissing spot with a piece of white cloth wetted with rosewater perfume, making it ready for the next pilgrim. As we waited in line, Antonis winked at me, nodding at the elderly man who had almost choked to death only a few hours earlier. Being squeezed like everybody else, the man patiently waited his turn to pay his respect to the Holy Virgin. He showed no traces of his ordeal.

We returned to the boat near midnight, right after the evening prayer vigil was over. The crew was preparing to lift the anchor for the overnight journey to Lesvos, known to the Western world as the island of Sappho, the ancient poetess and contemporary icon of the women's liberation movement. But for Orthodox pilgrims Lesvos is the island of extraordinary miracle stories attributed to Saint Raphael[2] and to Archangel Michael, or as he is referred to by the locals, the *Taxiarchis*, literally meaning "The Brigadier General." It was for the purpose of visiting these holy places that we arrived early the next morning in Mytiline, the major harbor of Lesvos.

Unlike Tinos, Lesvos is one of the largest Aegean islands and lies a few miles off the Turkish coast. The shrines of Saint Raphael and the *Taxiarchis* were situated at opposite sides of the island. It was an all-day affair to visit them. I made sure that I would be on the same bus with Father Maximos, who sat in the front next to Fathers Theophilos and Isaac. The two nuns from the monastery of Saint Anna's in Cyprus also sat in the front of the bus.

The person assigned to escort us on our pilgrimage was a Greek-speaking German tourist guide who was married to a man from Mytiline. How that guide could have assumed that the bus carried ordinary tourists was unclear to me. Over the loudspeaker, in her accented Greek, she proceeded to speak about the island and its history, extolling its rich pagan past and details from the life of Sappho. The speech may have been appropriate for European tourists but was hardly what monks, nuns, and pilgrims expected to hear. At the next stop Antonis, who sat next to me in the back of the bus, took the liberty to speak privately and gently with our knowledgeable and talkative guide. Extremely embarrassed over the misunderstanding, she burst into tears while Antonis tried to comfort her.

The atmosphere in the bus warmed up when the tour guide returned and shifted her emphasis to the legends around the local saints and the miracles attributed to them. Pagan Greece was placed on the back burner and the miracle culture of Byzantium took over, something I found deeply amusing. It triggered memories of my cousin Hector, a leading Cypriot architect and poet who had lived in Paris for most of his life. A lover of ancient Greece, Hector had reservations about "the glory of Byzantium." A passionate Hellenist, he never reconciled himself to the displacement of classical Greek culture and its free, creative spirit by the conservative Byzantine theocracy. It was a subject of animated conversations every time we got together. He thought of me as somehow leaning in favor of Byzantium while his uncompromising preference was Homer and the golden age of Periclean Athens.

Father Maximos was pleased with the switch of focus and made his own contribution to the repertoire of legends related to Saint Raphael and the *Taxiarchis*. "There are innumerable miracles that people attributed to Archangel Michael," he interjected as the German guide, with obvious relief, handed him the microphone. "Let me share with you one that I just learned about. A few years ago, a pilot from Lesvos took a group of elementary school children for an aerial tour over the northern Aegean. It was at first a good day. But the weather suddenly changed and the pilot lost his orientation in the midst of heavy rain, thunder, and lightning. The navigational instruments stopped functioning. The pilot became desperate when he realized that only two minutes of fuel remained. Certain they were about to crash into the sea he cried out to the *Taxiarchis*, his patron archangel, for help. At that very moment there was a flash of lightning and through an opening in the clouds he recognized that they were over the airport. He landed the plane safely."

More stories followed about the healing interventions of Archangel Michael in the lives of the local faithful and visiting pilgrims from all over Greece. The tales about the miraculous interventions of the *Taxiarchis* put us in the right reverential mood as we lit our candles and paid homage to his icon. Given the purpose of our visit to the island, it certainly made more sense to speak of the miracles of Saint Raphael and Archangel Michael than the erotic poems of Sappho or sensual lyrics of Odysseus Elytis, the contemporary Greek Nobel laureate from Lesvos.

From Lesvos we headed north toward Mount Athos. We sailed around the Holy Mountain while Father Maximos continued to casually relate stories from his stay there. The captain anchored *Calypso* five hundred meters off the coast from the Vatopedi monastery, situated on the northeastern coast of the peninsula. Then the abbot of the monastery, accompanied by a group of monks, came on board carrying with them holy relics and conducted a liturgy. We then unloaded the gallons of sweet wine brought over by Father Maximos as a gift to his "alma mater." After a brief visit to the monastery, where he was given a hero's welcome by his former fellow monks and friends, we returned to the boat. We then began the long journey south to Aegina, the island next to Salamis, famed for the final victory of the Greeks over the invading Persians during the fourth century B.C.E.

Our visit to Aegina, of course, was not to light candles and pay homage to Themistocles for skillfully setting up a naval trap for the Persians. That victory saved Western civilization, allowing it to serve as the cradle not only of democracy but also of Christianity. The aim of our trip, rather, was to honor Saint Nektarios, the patron saint of Aegina. At the grave of this contemporary saint, Father Maximos kneeled, took the silver *engkolpion* (chain with an icon that bishops wear) from his chest and, after placing it as a symbolic gift over the marble plate covering the saint's grave, unburdened himself, sobbing.

I was following too far behind during that episode to witness the scene but I was told about it by other pilgrims who were next to Father Maximos.

It was an emotional catharsis for Father Maximos from the extraordinary strains he had gone through as a result of the hostility shown against him by some of his colleagues in the church and their relentless efforts to destroy his reputation and force him out of Cyprus. Father Maximos identified with and drew inspiration and strength from the saint of Aegina.

At the start of the twentieth century Saint Nektarios was a consecrated bishop. Like Father Maximos, he was a much loved, charismatic clergyman to whom people flocked for solace and healing. He too faced envy and hostility from members of the Greek clerical hierarchy who accused him of being a philanderer and of fornicating with scores of nuns who gave birth to his many illegitimate children. Because of the slander against him he had no diocese. Although innocent, Elder Nektarios never defended himself. Instead, he literally "turned the other cheek" and died in infamy. The humble bishop from Aegina was posthumously declared innocent by a clerical tribunal. With miracles continuing to happen around his home and grave, the very church that tried to defrock him declared him a saint now, one of the most venerated contemporary saints of Greek Orthodoxy. No wonder Father Maximos wept over the grave of Saint Nektarios.

News traveled quickly about what transpired at Aegina. In the minds of some of us lurked nagging questions about the nature of a church that would allow such low behavior from its very custodians. Alas, any historian of the Church or any sociologist of religion could not be surprised by the recurrent phenomena of misuse of ecclesiastical authority and power.

Nevertheless, Father Maximos would repeatedly urge his followers not to indulge in negativity and not to be scandalized by the actions and behavior of individual priests or bishops, but to focus instead on the spiritual mission of the *Ecclesia*. For him the *Ecclesia* does not stand or fall on the basis of the actions of individuals who make it up. He would often say that as a spiritual institution the *Ecclesia* is a reality in and of itself, over and above any particular religious functionary. That is why, he argued, it is imperative to have a clear understanding of what its real mission is.

The episode in Aegina offered the opportunity to discuss this issue in some detail as we headed to our next and last destination, the island of Kos, home of Hippocrates, the ancient father of modern medicine. After lunch, a small group of us sat around Father Maximos in a shaded area outside his cabin while the boat, trailed by hundreds of seagulls, steamed along. In a few hours we would drop anchor at Kos, where pilgrims would have a free day to shop and visit its archaeological sights, foremost of which are the ruins of Hippocrates' medical school. Appropriately, the focus of the discussion centered on the potential healing role of the *Ecclesia* in the modern, secular world.

"If we don't have a clear understanding of what the *Ecclesia* really stands for, the consequences could be catastrophic," Father Maximos said in response to a question by Marina, a medical doctor and a friend of Stephanos and Erato. "We could get scandalized very easily by the actions of individuals and become distracted or get to the point whereby we would even be ready to reject the *Ecclesia* altogether."

"These are strong words, Father Maxime," I said.

"But Kyriaco," he retorted, "a misguided approach to the *Ecclesia* could lead us to a counterfeit relationship with God. And by extension it could also lead us to a false relationship with ourselves and with our environment."

"I am not sure I see the connection, Father," Marina said, expressing the feelings of the rest of us. Father Maximos stroked his beard as he reflected for a few seconds.

"Let me put it in a different way so that you are able to understand what I mean. There are two dominant perspectives on how to view the *Ecclesia* and its teachings. The first considers it simply as a religion aiming at making people pious and well-behaved. The second perspective considers the teachings of the *Ecclesia* as some sort of a religious philosophy with the founders of the *Ecclesia* as religious philosophers and contemplatives. As such they are supposed to deal with philosophical systems, with ideas and values, very noble and worthwhile values. Fair enough. One can say that this is good. But if we wish to seriously examine how the holy elders, the authentic interpreters of the *Ecclesia*, like Saint Nektarios, viewed it and continue to view it, we will recognize a different reality, we will see a surprising picture. We will notice that the holy elders considered the *Ecclesia* as having little to do with religion as commonly understood."

I looked around and saw a great number of puzzled faces. Father Maximos explained, "Many holy elders understood religion to mean the way people try through various ceremonies and rituals to appease an all-powerful and fearsome God who created the universe and themselves. This attitude has been the trademark of the average person's understanding of what it means to be religious."

"And you say, Father Maxime," Antonis intervened with a quizzical look, "that the holy elders rejected this understanding and approach to God?"

"Most definitely. But they also rejected rational philosophy as the key tool of the *Ecclesia*. That is, they rejected philosophy as the way to search for and get to know God."

"Why?" Marina asked.

"Philosophy is based on intellectual contemplation, on hypothesizing, on building theorems."

"What's wrong with that?" Antonis asked.

"There is nothing wrong with that. Philosophy is good as far as it goes. But it does not cease to be a human creation, a product of the human mind and imagination."

"I don't get it, Father Maxime," complained Marina, a newcomer into Father Maximos's spiritual orbit. "If the real teaching of the *Ecclesia* is based neither on religion nor on philosophy then what is it?"

Father Maximos smiled. He turned toward the horizon, where the famed island of Hippocrates was beginning to appear. "The *Ecclesia* must be properly seen as being part of medicine. In reality it is a spiritual hospital. Do you understand what I am saying?" It was clear hardly anyone really understood, and he elaborated: "A hundred and fifty years ago, when the University of Athens was created, those in charge, following Western European models, placed theology under the school of philosophy and law. That was a terrible mistake."

"Theology and religion are traditionally considered part of the humanities," I explained. "At least that is how they are considered in American universities."

"Wrong, terribly wrong," Father Maximos said raising his voice. "The holy elders would have placed subjects like theology, and the subject matter of the *Ecclesia*, within the medical school, not philosophy or law. Do you understand?"

"Perhaps we need a more concrete explanation," I suggested. I was beginning to sense what Father Maximos was driving at.

"I will explain. The *Ecclesia* is preoccupied essentially with the ultimate fate of human beings. It teaches that human beings are God's creation and came out of their Creator's hands absolutely healthy. All their powers functioned perfectly. This state was characterized by the total love of human beings toward God, toward one another, and toward Creation. The holy elders teach that human beings in that state were in constant contemplation and memory of God."

"You are referring to the state before the Fall," I said.

"Of course. According to the holy scriptures humanity has been fallen from that state of grace since time immemorial. From that point on, human beings have been characterized by confusion, destructive passions, and sinfulness. This is an abnormal state of existence."

"So, the 'normal' person is in a paradoxical way 'abnormal,'" I said.

"That's exactly what the holy elders would say. 'Normality' is a state of corruption."

"But it is not recognized as such."

"Of course not. Only the holy elders can recognize this type of pathology lurking at the depths of every human being. Humanity has been marching on this road of passions, confusion, and sin since the Fall. God has been sending his emissaries and prophets, however, to help humanity and prepare the way for the appearance of Christ himself.

"We Christians believe," Father Maximos continued, "that with Christ's Incarnation we are offered the opportunity to see a different human being, a God-man. So, according to the teachings of the *Ecclesia* there are three categories of human beings. First, there is the original Adam, which means human beings as they came out of their Creator's hands. Then there is the fallen Adam, meaning human beings after the Fall, as they live in this world. And third there is the birth of the New Adam, meaning Christ as the ultimate archetype of what we may become." Father Maximos stopped to see if we understood what he was talking about and then proceeded.

"It would have been a tragic error to assume that Christ came into the world in order to give us a set of good teachings or a book called the New

Testament. Had it been so he could have given it to us in many other ways. But he did come into the world himself so that we may be able to participate in his own perfect presence and see in the flesh, in a concrete way, our own archetype. As Saint Athanasios said, 'God became man so that man may become God.'

"The *Ecclesia*," Father Maximos added, "was created for purely therapeutic purposes, for healing the split between us and God."

"How is that?" Marina asked.

"The *Ecclesia* takes fallen, sick, and confused human beings, who suffer from all sorts of destructive passions and sins, and with its very tangible therapeutic methods helps them attain real health."

"You mean spiritual health."

"Yes, of course. That's the ultimate form of healing. The body sooner or later will die, decompose. Spiritual health is eternal and, therefore, more real."

87

Father Maximos then went on to point out that the *Ecclesia* may often help a person get healed from physical and psychological illnesses but that is of secondary importance. "After all, even if, let us say, a person is healed, through prayer, that person sooner or later will die like everybody else. But spiritual healing is beyond the body and touches eternity."

"But to call the *Ecclesia* a hospital means that it employs medical therapies," Marina said.

"Absolutely. And the medicine for the restoration of health is to assist human beings to get into the habit of following and implementing the commandments of God in their lives."

"Skeptics will say, Father Maxime," I said, "that such arguments are nothing more than presumptions and theological speculations. They would ask, 'What evidence can you offer that what the *Ecclesia* teaches has any basis in truth?' It is an extremely difficult task to convince someone that the *Ecclesia* is closer to medicine, which is based on science, rather than religion, which is based on faith."

"The truths of the *Ecclesia*, like the truths of science, are based on observation and on experiments that can be repeated time and again before its axioms are proven and established," Father Maximos replied forcefully. "The *Ecclesia* has concrete proofs of its therapeutic efficacy."

"I wonder about that," Marina said with skepticism.

"Wait and things will become clearer," Father Maximos said lightly. "When I suggest that the *Ecclesia* has proofs of its therapeutic efficacy I do not speak in metaphysical terms. The *Ecclesia* does not accept that the real therapy of the human soul is a metaphysical event."

Father Maximos paused. Upon realizing that his statements were hardly comprehensible to his increasingly expanding audience, he clarified them further. "I am reminded of the words of a venerated elder of Mount Athos who would jokingly say, 'Suppose you go to a doctor when you are sick. He checks you out, makes an accurate diagnosis about your problem, and then gives you the appropriate medicine. He then tells you, 'Take this medicine but you should know that you will get well after you die.' The *Ecclesia* would act like that doctor had it instructed us to follow its therapeutic methods without any hope of getting well until after we are gone from this world.

"Now, my dear doctor, do you understand what I am saying?" Father Maximos asked and turned toward Marina with an inquisitive look on his face. "The therapy that the *Ecclesia* offers to human beings is not metaphysical. As with good medicine, therapy for the *Ecclesia* must take place now, in this present physical life, not after death. We must not forget that this healing has distinct and identifiable attributes in the same way that a therapy for bodily illness has distinct and identifiable characteristics. Do you remember Paul's epistle to the Galatians? Like the good doctor of the soul that he was, he identifies what the symptoms of sin and spiritual illness are: hostility, jealousy, anger, idolatry, murder, drunkenness, debauchery, adultery, and so on.

"He then points out that the therapy from such illnesses is not something abstract and vague but something concrete and clearly recognizable. He goes on to enumerate the tangible fruits of spiritual healing: love, joy, peace, forbearance, goodness, gentleness, faith, and the like [Galatians 5:22]. In other words, the Apostle Paul shows us that the *Ecclesia*'s therapeutic interventions have real and tangible results. That means we can identify and test for ourselves whether we have been spiritually healed from the illnesses that haunted us. Such therapy has practical consequences in our lives."

"Based strictly on these reasons you claim that the *Ecclesia* belongs to medicine and not to religion or philosophy," I said.

"It is not what I claim. This is what the holy elders understand as the deeper meaning of the *Ecclesia*. They clearly show us how persons who have undergone this therapeutic treatment demonstrate definite and concrete results."

Father Maximos welcomed more pilgrims as they gathered around. "Let me make this clear," he continued. "When we raise the question 'What is a human being?' we must also ask 'What is God?' Since God is our archetype and we are created in his image, understanding ourselves presupposes understanding our archetype. It's like trying to determine how authentic the portrait of a person is on canvas. We must see the person in real life and then compare the two. We need to contrast the painting with the person in the flesh. If we have never seen the person then we cannot judge one way or another."

Father Maximos laughed. "A story about the pope I heard lately just came to my mind. A painter went to the Vatican to offer the pontiff a gift, a portrait of the pope that he himself had painted. The pope had the habit of kindly accepting presents from the faithful. He would then sign them and offer them back to the donors as gifts from him. In addition to his signature he would search for an appropriate extract from the Gospels and add it above his name. When he looked at the portrait he realized that the painting had no resemblance to him whatsoever. But, being a kind man, he said nothing while he searched to find an appropriate extract from the Gospels to inscribe on the painting before he offered it back to the painter. He flipped the pages of the New Testament and found a fitting extract. It was that part when the disciples, in a state of utter fear, saw Jesus walking on the water. So, the pope wrote what Jesus said to put them at ease, 'Fear not. It is me!'"

Father Maximos continued in a serious tone. "So the archetype is real and concrete and human beings are images of the archetype. The Gospels tell us clearly what God is. John the Apostle says, 'Brethren, God is love.' Since God is love then we as human beings, created in his image, are also love. And God gave us the medical prescriptions for how to heal our split from him, how to repair the damage that made us unrecognizable in terms of our divine archetype."

"What prescriptions are you referring to, Father Maxime?" I asked. "I assume you mean the methodology and the spiritual practices to abide by the Ten Commandments and the teachings of the Sermon on the Mount."

"Yes, exactly," Father Maximos said. "Those who have implemented those prescriptions are the saints. Once they learned to authentically love God and their neighbor they healed themselves. It is the saints who manifest in practical terms the reality of the healing that takes place within the *Ecclesia* as a spiritual hospital. Let us say they embody the ideal of the truly healthy individual and provide the empirical evidence of the *Ecclesia* as a healing institution."

"This is the first time I've heard such a notion, that the *Ecclesia* is a hospital," Marina remarked with surprise, shaking her head in disbelief.

"It is indeed a hospital. As in the case of an ordinary hospital, in the *Ecclesia* we can meet doctors, nurses, recovering patients, sick people, and very sick people. Sometimes we can even find corpses."

"Do corpses have a chance?" Antonis asked lightheartedly.

"Naturally they do. Doesn't the *Ecclesia* call Christ the *Zoodotes* [Giver of Life]? In whatever category we may belong within this spiritual hospital, we always have the hope and the possibility to achieve our own resurrection and the restoration of our spiritual health.

"It is extremely important," Father Maximos continued, "that we never abandon this role and outlook on the *Ecclesia* as a spiritual hospital. If we give up on it then the *Ecclesia* becomes nothing other than a worldly institution."

Father Maximos's mother, who had joined us for the pilgrimage, came out of her cabin and joined our group. Smiling widely, she brought a bag of pistachios she had bought on Aegina, a pistachio-producing island, and passed it around. Munching on the pistachios, Father Maximos went on to answer and discuss more questions from his impromptu audience. Marina asked why certain "circles within the *Ecclesia*" urge the faithful to simply believe, have blind faith, and avoid the temptation of investigating God. "A true science," she said, "cannot accept these kinds of limitations and censorship. Yet today you are suggesting a radically different way of looking at the *Ecclesia*."

Father Maximos shook his head and sighed. "Nowhere in the New Testament or even in the Old Testament is there anything that supports such nonsense, which some people preach in the name of the *Ecclesia*. There is nothing of the sort in any of the writings of the holy elders. The saying 'believe but do not search' is nothing more than superstition. To ask of someone to have blind faith in anything is really idiotic, an affront to human intelligence. On the contrary the *Ecclesia*, properly understood, encourages the search for God. I am reminded of the *troparion* [chant] during the Sunday of Saint Thomas which celebrates the fact that 'Christ is joyous when he is investigated.' "

"Why so?" asked a young black-clad woman, who added that while growing up, "blind faith" in Jesus was what she had been taught.

"Because," Father Maximos replied, eyes shining, "Christ is given the opportunity to reveal to the searching soul the glory of his existence."

Our conversation was interrupted when we heard over the loudspeaker the voice of Yianoula, the travel agent who had organized the journey. She announced that we would shortly be arriving at the harbor of Kos. She then offered a brief overview of the history of the island focusing on the story of Hippocrates and his medical school.

As we approached the island most of the passengers from the lower and upper decks leaned on the railings and began taking photographs. The rest of us remained in our seats around Father Maximos. Marina, who had come on board after strong encouragement from Erato and Stephanos, was keen for further discussion around the topic of the *Ecclesia* as a spiritual hospital. The moment the loudspeaker was turned off she resumed her questioning.

"If I am not mistaken, Father Maxime, there are parts of the Bible that deal with medicinal matters. I remember, for example, that in the case of Samson, an angel told his mother before he was born that she should avoid certain foods and refrain from wine so that the baby might be born healthy. There are similar dietary prescriptions here and there in the Old as well as in the New Testament. Three thousand years later modern medicine discovered that the embryo is really aware and affected by the mother's physical and mental condition. We know today that the fasting that the *Ecclesia* prescribes is also good for health, such as in lowering cholesterol levels and boosting the immune system.[3] Would these prescriptions also be part of your claim that the *Ecclesia* should be considered as a type of hospital?"

91

"No," Father Maximos replied emphatically. "We need to clear certain misconceptions. If certain statements in the Bible related to health or geology or history or whatever else came to be scientifically supported, fair enough. But the Holy Bible is not a medical text that offers us guidelines about the health of the physical body. It is not a biology primer, or a book on geology or history for that matter. The Holy Bible is purely a spiritual text that speaks about God's energy in the world. If those parts of the Bible that deal with physical health, or with geology, or history are proven to be scientifically false it should not have an iota of an effect on its therapeutic, spiritual significance."

"Well—" Marina began saying in a skeptical tone.

"My dear, as I have argued time and again, the essence of the Bible, its very meaning, is to heal us human beings from our psychic illnesses, from that which separates us from God. Now, if three thousand years ago human wisdom knew about certain recipes for good bodily health, well and good. But even if the opposite turned out to be true, again, well and good."

"This is an important point to keep in mind," I suggested. "A lot of scholars today focus exclusively on the scientific accuracy of the Bible and conclude that since it is replete with historical and scientific inaccuracies and contradictions it must be nothing more that folklore. On the other extreme are the fundamentalists who interpret everything in the Bible, such as the age of the planet, as literally true."

"That is how both the rationalists and the fundamentalists fail to understand the spiritual meaning of sacred texts and the purpose for which they were written," Father Maximos responded.

"In my practice, Father Maxime," Marina said after a while, "I meet people who may be actively religious and spiritual but who have serious psychological problems. However, they don't dare seek professional help from psychotherapists or psychiatrists lest they are committed to an asylum. What can the *Ecclesia* do to help such people?"

Father Maximos reflected for a few seconds. "The *Ecclesia* as a spiritual hospital has its own physicians who can help such people. These are the spiritual elders."

"You mean the ordained priests and bishops?"

"No. Spiritual elders are not necessarily those who are simply anointed by the mystical ritual of anointment but those who have the experience of the energies of the Holy Spirit. They are individuals whose existence has been filled by divine grace. These are the real physicians who can heal people because they are gifted with the ability to discern whether a person actually needs psychiatric care or spiritual guidance and training. This is important. If a human being needs medical treatment because of some biological malfunction then that person should be treated by a psychiatrist, not by a spiritual guide. The *Ecclesia* does not handle psychiatric problems. If someone suffers from a schizophrenic breakdown due to some problems in the brain the spiritual pedagogy of the *Ecclesia* will not be helpful or relevant. On the other hand, if a person suffers from spiritual maladies, from destructive passions, then that individual may be helped by a spiritual physician. In such case a psychiatrist is not the appropriate person to seek help from. We need, therefore, to develop the appropriate discernment so that we know whether a problem belongs to traditional medicine or to the spiritual pedagogy of the *Ecclesia*."

There was a pause as Father Maximos pondered further on the subject. He continued: "I advise confessors that they need to become knowledgeable about mental maladies and develop the kind of discernment that would allow them to distinguish between a real psychiatric problem and a spiritual illness. Sometimes on the surface they may manifest similar symptoms."

"I assume demonic possession may also mimic mental illness," I said, remembering an earlier conversation with Father Maximos when he described dealing with people he diagnosed as suffering from demonic possession.[4]

"Oh yes! That is why it is crucial that spiritual guides and confessors must learn how to differentiate between a mental illness and demonic possession. Unfortunately, there is much confusion there. A person is sick in the brain and people think he is under the control of demons. All he really needs is medication and a little counseling and his problem will be taken care of. No matter how much exorcism you do for such a person you are not going to help him. It is his biological, material brain which is damaged, not his soul. Or someone is suffering from possession and they assume he is mentally ill. They load him with drugs that do nothing to free him from his problem. In fact such treatments will make his condition much worse." Then Father Maximos added that it is possible for someone to have psychological problems but be spiritually healthy. Similarly someone can be psychologically well and yet spiritually ill. This understanding, I learned, is based on the distinction in the teaching of the holy elders between the levels of the *psyche* and of *pnevma* or spirit, a category not found in psychological texts.

Father Maximos's comments reminded me of a colleague who had some psychological problems that he traced back to his childhood, problems that he considered as impediments to his academic career. However, because of these very psychological difficulties he plunged into a relentless struggle to understand himself and master his problem. In the process he gradually discovered God and was transformed from a thorough agnostic to a deeply spiritual person. Some of his personality difficulties may not have gone away completely but he felt, and he looked, like a person who was spiritually healed. Without the psychological problems he would have been just a successful professor, knowledgeable and honored within his field but without any interest in God or spiritual development. The elders would have diagnosed my friend as someone who had problems on the level of the psyche but who was healed on the level of the *pnevma*, or spirit.

"I wonder, Father Maxime," Antonis asked with a joking tone in his voice, "what is worse, being schizophrenic and feeling that you are possessed by the devil or actually being possessed by the devil and appearing as if you are schizophrenic?"

"Believe me, it is preferable to be mentally ill than to suffer from demonic possession. At least in the first case a person is completely innocent and with some drug therapy and psychological counseling he may get well. In the case of possession the person has opened the gates to the diabolical energies for spiritual reasons and it is much more difficult to free him from such a state."

"But what causes mental illness?" Antonis asked.

"From our point of view it doesn't matter what the cause is. That's a medical issue. It may be just physical deterioration. It may be problems of aging, biological inheritance, whatever. It does not matter whether a person is spiritually advanced or not. After all, even saints get sick, just like the rest of us, right? They suffer from cancers, from their hearts, their livers. Should one be scandalized if a saint loses his memory or suffers from Alzheimer's? There is no reason to assume that being a saint means being immune to mental diseases."

"That is clear. But is it possible to help people who suffer from serious psychological problems that are not biologically based?" Marina asked.

"In theory, of course it is possible. After all the *Ecclesia* encloses the mystery of God's presence. Nothing is impossible for God. Individuals who have problems may, through their prayers and faith, find the appropriate spiritual guide that could help them."

Father Maximos then went on to point out that it is important for a person to search well in order to find a spiritual guide who is a real doctor of the soul. Just as there are differences among physicians in terms of knowledge and expertise, it is the same with spiritual guides. There are good and excellent spiritual guides and there are also those that are mediocre. A person must find someone he or she can trust after some real exploration.

"There are also people who may claim they are doctors but in reality are quacks," Father Maximos said and laughed. "When I was in *Nea Skete* [a set of hermitages on Mount Athos, each made up of a small group of monks] we had someone who claimed he was a medical doctor. In reality he served as an assistant nurse during the Second World War. But he tried to convince us that he was as good a doctor as two other monks in our company who were trained physicians and who had practiced medicine before they became monks. I asked him one day to tell us the names of those he healed. He started mentioning some names: 'The late Father Constantine, the late Father Kosmas, the late Father Makarios . . .' There was not a single living person on his list!"

"Father Maxime," Marina asked when the laughter died down, "how can we know when one needs psychological treatment and counseling and when spiritual guidance? Can a spiritual elder know when to give spiritual advice and when to send a person to a professional psychologist or psychiatrist?"

"When a spiritual guide masters his science then there is no problem making such an assessment. Problems emerge when a spiritual physician, a spiritual guide, intervenes in areas that are beyond his capabilities and expertise. Likewise problems emerge when psychologists and psychiatrists enter spiritual regions that are beyond their capacities or understanding. When such confusion takes place they can hurt a person either spiritually or psychologically. I personally find cooperation with psychologists and psychiatrists very useful in helping people. There are certain problems that are more psychological or psychiatric than spiritual. Therefore, I send such cases to a psychologist or a psychiatrist. But I must say that the *Ecclesia* is closer to psychiatry than psychology."

I remembered the shock a very materialistic and bombastic Greek psychiatrist experienced when, during an exchange with an Athonite abbot, he was told that the real psychiatrists are the holy elders. It was an affront to his overdeveloped professional ego.

"In one of the prayers of the holy liturgy," Father Maximos continued, "we address ourselves to Christ and call him the physician of our souls and bodies. That means the authenticity and the real seal of our healing will be offered to us by Christ himself via the energies of the Holy Spirit. The medicine and the pedagogy are very clear. It is a road much traveled and carefully mapped by the elders of the *Ecclesia* in the same way that medical texts are written by experienced doctors as guides for practicing physicians. So if someone consults an authentic spiritual elder he or she will receive the appropriate guidance on what needs to be done. The problem arises when people do not ask, or they ask the wrong way. For example, instead of consulting a real physician, patients may open a medical text and draw conclusions about their particular ailment and how to restore health. This can create serious complications and problems."

"Father Maxime," Marina asked as the boat entered the harbor with the usual excitement and noises of docking, "quite often in our medical practice we doctors are constantly witnesses to healing phenomena that go beyond medical knowledge. For example, a patient is terminally ill and we throw our hands up and say that only God can save that person. Sometimes a miracle takes place and the people get healed from incurable cancers and the like. We also hear that contemporary holy elders like Porphyrios and Paisios were able to heal people from terminal illnesses. Yet they themselves died from cancer. Should we assume that they have taken up such a burden consciously just like Christ did on the cross? Is their action some kind of a model for us to imitate as a means to reach perfection?"

"Let me explain," Father Maximos said. "Miracles are in reality extraordinary interventions by God who on special occasions suspends the laws of nature. But the extraordinary is not the law. So, we can say that fifty people were healed miraculously from cancer this month. At the same time, however, fifty thousand others died from this disease. There was no suspension of the physical laws in their case. The purpose of the *Ecclesia* is not to simply heal a person physically. Because if a person is healed, say from incurable cancer, he will die anyway within the next ten or twenty or thirty years. The *Ecclesia* heals the person not temporally but eternally, without the biological death interfering and interrupting this process."

"In the case of Stephanos," I said, "God did make an exception and he was healed from certain death. Why?"

"We can never know the 'why.' Only God knows that. But even if the person, in spite of the efforts of the *Ecclesia*, dies it does not mean that the therapeutic efficacy of the *Ecclesia* is canceled out. On the contrary. A person can transform the existential fact of inevitable human mortality into eternal life. Such a radical shift in our attitude toward death can have a liberating effect against it. The saints were not seeking to be delivered from death but to transform biological death into eternal life."

Our conversation with Father Maximos ended when our guide instructed us on disembarkation over the loudspeaker. When Father Maximos stepped onto the harbor he was welcomed by a delegation of clergymen who drove him to the local bishopric where he was to meet with the local bishop. The rest of us were free to roam around the streets of Kos and visit the ruins of Hippocrates' medical school. The religious part of our trip was over and the five hundred pilgrims were now transformed into tourists visiting archaeological sites and spending their remaining dollars in the local souvenir shops. Before boarding the ship for our journey back to Limassol, I joined Antonis and his group of family and friends for a fish *meze* at a local restaurant by the harbor.

SIX

ALTERATIONS

OF THE

SOUL

fter I returned from the pilgrimage and set-
tled in our apartment in Limassol, I had to
now find a way to have frequent contact
with Father Maximos. These thoughts were in my mind
when the telephone rang. "Join me at the Farm," Lavros
urged me over the phone. "I just learned that Father Maximos will be there at four. I'm sure there will be opportunities for serious talk."

"Good," I replied without a second thought. I intuitively
knew that the coincidence of Lavros's telephone call and the
opportunity to be with Father Maximos that afternoon was
not accidental. I looked at my watch. It was already three.

Lavros had earlier confided to me his rather unconventional way of meeting with Father Maximos. On occasion, a practical way of meeting the busy bishop was to learn in advance where he would be for the day and then set up an "ambush." That was an effective way, he told me, to have regular access to him. As a close advisor to the bishop, Lavros had inside information about Father Maximos's moves. This most unorthodox manner of trapping him for conversation was based on Cypriot realities and the circumstances that emerged with his change of status.

In the past, while he was still an abbot at the Panagia monastery I had daily, casual access to him during my visits there. All I needed to do was simply to knock at his door. But with his election as bishop, he was forced to abandon his monastic sanctuary in the mountains and relocate himself at the center of a noisy city. His daily responsibilities and activities were now stretched over a wide geographic area. They required travel to various parts of his diocese for a myriad of reasons, ranging from consecrating new churches and presiding over liturgical services to meeting with local groups, mediating conflicts, and offering confessions to an exponentially expanding number of the faithful. Consequently, it was not as easy for me to access him. Unlike the "good old days" when I served as his temporary chauffeur at the Panagia monastery, I now had few occasions to play that role. Because of his new official status, Father Maximos had a regular driver, Father Theophilos, the young deacon who was also assisting him with various rituals associated with his new position.

Bumping into Father Maximos in the corridors of the Panagia monastery and having a leisurely chat on matters related to my spiritual interests was a thing of the past. For this reason I had to be innovative, a bit bold, and ever ready to take advantage of opportunities to spend time with him as they arose. The "ambush," Lavros's methodological innovation, was a way of continuing my exploration into Athonite spirituality. It had already worked many times.

Father Maximos must have had his suspicions about our unconventional approach to contacting him but he never showed any signs of discomfort or objection to our methods. On the contrary, given his reactions, I felt as if my new modus operandi was agreeable to him. After all, he could not give me formal appointments and information about his whereabouts

99

in advance. Local cultural habits did not permit long-term scheduling, as is the practice in modern academic and corporate settings. Unlike the Panagia monastery, the bishopric was not a place where I could reside and have casual encounters with him. Consequently, I was on call at all times to take advantage of opportunities as they arose.

I shut my computer and placed a notebook and a mini-recorder into my handbag. I then walked down the steps from the fourth floor of the apartment building to the street level and waited for Lavros, who arrived promptly in his dark-green Range Rover. Thanks to the Cypriot tradition of the afternoon siesta during the summer months, we exited Limassol swiftly, reaching the Farm at a quarter to four, ahead of the bishop.

The Farm was a large piece of land equal in size to several large American university campuses. It was filled with citrus, cypress, and palm trees as well as a vegetable garden. There was a small artificial lake at its center, an unusual sight for a dry island like Cyprus. The Farm also had its own sandy beach, mercifully inaccessible to tourists.

The first time I visited the Farm with Lavros, its interim manager, I had been startled at the abundance of birds that found refuge in its tranquil, green environs. The lake buzzed with ducks, pelicans, and a variety of migratory birds coming from Africa on their way to Europe during the summer months and returning to Africa during the winter.

Adjacent to the Farm there was also a sanctuary for stray cats. A zoophile Englishman had set it up decades ago to rescue abandoned kittens from starvation and from the asphalt of the city. After the British benefactor passed away, the cats, Lavros informed me, came under the protection of three elderly nuns living in a stone house next to the sanctuary. For this reason people began calling the nuns' retreat "the monastery of the cats." An official road sign pointed in the direction of "Saint Nicolas, monastery of the cats."

In order to get to the Farm we had to pass by the cats. It was quite a sight as we drove by on the dirt road leading to our destination. Hundreds of cats lazily enjoyed their siesta under trees and on three branches, stretching themselves and relishing the start of the afternoon sea breezes.

The Farm, the cats' monastic sanctuary, and the residence of the three nuns were all located inside the boundaries of the British military bases, an out-of-bounds area for hunters and developers. Due to security concerns, the authorities prohibited any commercial construction. The unintended and benign consequence of that remnant of British colonialism was that the area was preserved in its pristine state, a real *biotopos* (place of life) at the borders of a city that had been calamitously seduced by the fatal attraction to cement and concrete.

Most important, the Farm belonged to the local bishopric. Father Maximos, as the new bishop, inherited the role as its custodian. It was he who appointed Lavros, a seasoned agriculturist, to temporarily administer the place. A former American-trained professor of agricultural economics, beekeeper, and occasional entrepreneur, Lavros gave his full attention after his retirement to ecological issues. In the process he developed a reputation as a leading advocate for the environment, particularly as a dynamic defender of migratory birds threatened by unscrupulous poachers. Of average height and somewhat on the heavy side, with a short white beard, Lavros possessed an abundance of good humor. It was a quality that had made him an ideal companion during an earlier pilgrimage to Mount Athos.

When we reached the Farm there was hardly anyone there except a few migrant workers from Sri Lanka. In Mexican hats, they were picking oranges, tangerines, and lemons from the orchard. After packing them in special containers they loaded them on a truck headed for the local market. Lavros chatted with the Sri Lankans for a few minutes and we picked a few oranges from the trees. We then sat outside his modest makeshift office at the center of the property, waiting for Father Maximos to arrive.

As we peeled and ate the oranges, Lavros revealed to me what Father Maximos had in mind for the future of the Farm and the reason for his upcoming visit. The bishop, he informed me, wished to develop it into a nature preserve for educational purposes. Part of the property was to be reserved and developed into an environmental park for public use. In addition, Father Maximos wished to create a summer camp for youth. Teenagers were to spend summers there swimming, working, and learning about the ecosystem. Such lofty goals, however, required money, plenty of it. The reason for Father Maximos's visit to the farm, I learned, was to escort a prospective donor.

It was about four thirty when Father Maximos finally arrived with his companions. He was pleased to see us but showed no particular surprise other than to grin with an implicit understanding of our intentions.

Losing no time, Lavros took the initiative, playing the role of host to Father Maximos's guests. They included the wealthy benefactor, his wife, as well as Erato, and, to my surprise, Marina, the doctor I met on the boat. Apparently, the time she spent on the pilgrimage with Father Maximos aroused her interest in further encounters and conversations. I was pleased.

For the next fifty minutes Lavros gave us a tour of the grounds, sometimes on foot, sometimes by car. In his enthusiastic way he expanded on the uniqueness and importance of the Farm. During the tour Erato whispered to me that the middle-aged couple walking next to Father Maximos were Mr. and Mrs. Leventis, well-known philanthropists who contributed lavishly to charities, not a very common practice among the local rich. Both husband and wife looked humble and unassuming, in spite of their reputed wealth.

Humility and detachment from worldly possessions were qualities of supreme importance for an Athonite elder. What attracted this wealthy couple to Father Maximos was that he himself exemplified these qualities, an assurance that the money would be put to good use. There were too many scandals in the Church that could raise concerns for potential contributors to ecclesiastical institutions. Father Maximos's reputation was such that people like the Leventises trusted him. In fact Stephanos had told me sometime earlier that while he was still abbot of the Panagia monastery, Father Maximos refused two hundred thousand dollars because the donor lacked the right attitude and motives. If the intentions of a prospective benefactor are less than pure, I was told, this fact may contaminate and undermine a project irrespective of the amount of cash offered and the loftiness of the project's goals.

Father Maximos's guests had passed the test of purity of intention on several occasions. They had already committed four million Cyprus pounds (about eight million dollars, at the time) for the restoration of an old, archaeologically significant but abandoned monastery at Mesa Potamos right at the center of the Troodos Mountains. Its ruins were located in the middle of a lush, pine-filled valley with robust springs flowing around it, a dream location for a retreat reserved for prayer and contemplation. Father Maximos had plans to develop it into another spiritual center for the region.

All signs showed that the wealthy couple was ready to donate additional funds for the development of the Farm. After an hour's tour during which Father Maximos explained his plans, the prospective benefactors, looking satisfied, got into their car and drove away. The rest of us remained at the Farm a while longer. We strolled up and down the beach chatting and breathing the carbon monoxide–free air coming from the west. In the distance to the east, we could see the rising skyline with the new hotels and the string of apartment buildings that had turned a once-emerald town into a sea of gray.

Finding the time to walk on the beach and relish the sights and smells of the coast was a rare opportunity for Father Maximos. He lamented that as a child growing up in Limassol, swimming was second nature to him, but the moment he put on the monk's robes at the age of eighteen he had to renounce that source of worldly delight. Since then he had never set foot in the Mediterranean. It was not customary for monks to take off their clothes and abandon themselves to watery pleasures. Given my love for the sea, it was a monastic habit that I found difficult to accommodate in my mind.

After our walk, we followed Father Maximos to the "monastery of the cats" where the nuns treated us to freshly squeezed lemonade, coffee, and special homemade sweets. They seemed pleased and animated by the unexpected appearance of their new bishop at their doorstep.

Sitting at the veranda of the nuns' monastic retreat offered a unique view of the Farm and the sea beyond it. The monastery was at a slightly higher elevation than the Farm, allowing us to see the horizon as the sun was about to sink into the Mediterranean. As always, Father Maximos was willing to share his knowledge of Orthodox spirituality to anyone who showed interest. That was a major part of his mission in life to serve others, his *diakonia*. life's task

Marina was eager to explore further some of the issues that we began discussing the previous week on the boat back to Limassol and lost no time in jump-starting the discussion. It was fine with me.

103

"Human beings are never steady, emotionally or spiritually," Father Maximos responded when Marina raised a point about emotional stability. "They undergo alternations in their moods and predispositions. You must know from personal experience that this is happening to us constantly."

"This is unavoidable insofar as we are human beings," Marina agreed.

"Good. From the point of view of the patristic tradition, however, this state of ongoing alterations of the soul emerged only after the Fall." Father Maximos paused to sip his tea. "The holy elders teach that prior to the Fall human beings were in a singular, steady state of uninterrupted contemplation of God. When we lost that primordial unity we became subjected to continuous instability in our moods and spiritual states. Sometimes we are euphoric and joyous. Other times we are sad and depressed. Sometimes we are overwhelmed by feelings of debility, awe, toughness, anger and many, many other types of sentiments and emotions."

104

"That's self-evident," I said. "I suppose that the type of sentiments that we experience depend to a great extent on our state of spiritual growth, our mental state, and of course, the general circumstances of our lives."

"Naturally. Even holy elders, who have more or less transcended this world, are subjected to psychic and spiritual alterations. They are not always in a state of divine euphoria or joy.

"Based on their own experiences and their own methods of dealing with the wide range of emotions and sentiments that all human beings are subject to," Father Maximos continued, "the holy elders identified what they called the 'law of alterations.'"

"To call it a law," Lavros interrupted, "implies a scientific approach to the issue. But is it?"

"Of course it is," Father Maximos responded more loudly. "The holy elders were spiritual scientists. They made discoveries about the spiritual laws that govern human existence in much the same way that natural scientists make discoveries about the laws that govern the material universe."

"That's a bold statement," Lavros interjected. "But I think I understand what you are driving at."

Father Maximos's words brought to my mind a point raised by the Cypriot lay mystic I had studied with during the 1980s. He insisted that whereas scientists make their observations on how the external world works from lab experiments, mystics throughout history have turned themselves into their own laboratories. Their methods are just as "scientific" in the sense that they are based on observations and experiments and their conclusions are then corroborated by other mystics who have replicated these inner experiments. It is a theme that is echoed today in the work of leading transpersonal theorists.

"It is always important to remember," Father Maximos continued, "that the law of alterations is a *metaptotic* phenomenon, meaning that it occurred after the Fall, a development that exposed us to various sources of influence that cause different types of changes or alterations in us."

"What types of changes are you referring to, Father Maxime?" Erato asked, as the three elderly nuns brought some extra chairs and joined us.

"The elders concluded that the soul's alterations come from four major sources," Father Maximos replied and brought forward the four fingers of his right hand. "One category of alterations may come directly from God. They may be the result of the activation of the energies of the Holy Spirit that resides within us. These, of course, are the type of alterations that we all strive for. They form our ultimate goal in life."

"To say that there are alterations coming from God implies that there must be alterations coming from the opposite source. You cannot have the good without its opposite," I suggested. I knew what Father Maximos's answer would be.

"A logical deduction to be sure," he nodded. "The elders teach, and we know it from experience, that there are indeed demonic alterations. We will talk about them later. A third type of alteration springs neither from God nor from the demons but from within ourselves. And a fourth source of alterations may be the environment within which we live.

"It is a basic axiom of Orthodox spirituality that we are psychosomatic beings. We are not just body. We are not just psyche. Nor can we say that we are a combination of psyche and body, which are united but separated in their own individual domains. We cannot say this is where the body ends and this is where the psyche begins. We are one entity. Our soul is knitted together with the body in the same way that flour and water are

four
major
sources of
the soul's
alterations
1. from God
2. from
   demons
3. from
   within
   ourselves
4. the
   environment
   within
   which we
   live

diabolic assaults
demonic conditions

mixed together to make up dough." Father Maximos brought his two palms together in a gesture that implied making bread. "Can you determine where the water is and where the flour is? Once you bring them together you have a new reality. Therefore, since we are a psychosomatic entity, we are subjected to influences springing from spiritual levels, both benign and destructive, as well as from environmental conditions within which the body operates. We are also subjected to conditions of our own making.

"But first let's look at alterations that spring directly from God and how they get activated. Let us imagine that we are in a neutral psychological state. Let us assume that we live our lives being neither spiritual nor anti-spiritual. Then at a certain point in time we seriously subject ourselves to the pedagogy of the *Ecclesia*. We engage in systematic and ceaseless prayer, we fast, we go to confession and take communion, we participate in all-night vigils, and so on. At some point our heart may crack open and begin to feel God's living presence. As we undergo such an experience we become overwhelmed by a sense of love for all human beings, a sense of awe, *metanoia*, humility, a feeling of tolerance toward everybody. We feel our hearts getting ignited with a burning love for God. I should add that such states are usually accompanied by the shedding of tears. Believe me, these things do happen to people when they engage in systematic spiritual practice."

"At what point, Father Maxime, should we expect to have such an experience? I mean under what conditions does it take place?" Erato asked with animated interest. Stephanos had confided in me that she'd had some spiritual experiences of her own in times of deep prayer.

"You cannot predict such developments. This is up to the discretion of the Holy Spirit. Such alterations can happen through a diversity of conditions. A divinely inspired experience could happen while we walk, or while we pray, or even while we are asleep."

"Asleep?" Marina responded.

"Yes. Believe it or not, persons who are engaged in a spiritual struggle to reach God can often experience visitations from grace while asleep. Such persons can then experience great joy and comfort. Their hearts are vigilant. They may be asleep, they may be resting, but their hearts are awake."

"Does God visit only people who are subjected to the pedagogy of the *Ecclesia*?" I asked. "I have in mind the episode on the road to Damascus. Paul was not a member of the *Ecclesia*. He was a persecutor of Christians. Then he had that mystical experience and was transformed into Saint Paul."

"God can directly visit people's hearts through a myriad of ways. All human beings have such a potential within them."

"So, a person who has no relationship with the *Ecclesia* and walks down the street may suddenly be visited by God and undergo such an alteration," I said, trying to pin Father Maximos down to a universalistic conception of the religious experience, a position that dogmatic believers find impossible to accept.

"Absolutely. All human beings have God within, and therefore, the prospect and possibility of salvation is open to all. But, again, we can never know when grace will visit a human being or whom God will touch with his grace. Keep in mind also that only the Spirit of God can penetrate into the furthest reaches of our existence. Nobody else."

"What about unclean spirits?" Lavros asked.

"Fortunately, they are barred from those regions," Father Maximos replied. "Only the Holy Spirit has the authority and power. So the Holy Spirit can penetrate into the heart of any human being and cause these good alterations."

"Based on what you are saying, Father Maxime, it seems to me that our innermost being is like the depths of the oceans," Lavros said. "No matter how much turbulence there is at the surface, the depths are always peaceful and quiet."

"A very good metaphor."

"I presume such experiences and alterations can also manifest on the bodies of those who have them," Lavros added.

"Given the fact that human beings are psychosomatic entities, everything about them becomes sanctified as they undergo a divine alteration. It shows on their bodies. When you come in contact with holy men and women you will notice that everything about them emanates holiness: their glance, their faces, their behavior, even their very clothes. It is the energy of the Holy Spirit that was once dormant and then became manifest, affecting the total person, soul and body."

"Is that why the remains of saints are venerated in the *Ecclesia*?" Marina asked.

107

"Exactly. We honor and pay homage to their remains because their bodies have literally turned into temples of the Holy Spirit. So even their bodies become sanctified."

"A friend of mine who is a connoisseur of philosophy objects vehemently to what he calls the 'worship of bones' in the Orthodox tradition. He considers such practices as nothing more than macabre forms of superstition and idolatry, a leftover of medievalism that undermines people's intelligence and capacity to reason," I said provocatively.

"Your friend is simply a rationalist who, lacking direct experience, cannot understand that the remains of saints emanate holy energy," Father Maximos replied and made a dismissive gesture with his right hand.

I went on to confess that before my first visit to Mount Athos I shared my friend's opinion about bones. Yet, the theory behind them started to make sense only after Father Maximos mentioned that just as locations and objects can be charged with positive (or negative) energy, so too can the remains of saints be charged. Their divine, holy energies or "elementals" are embedded in their very bones. Father Maximos always carried with him a tiny piece of bone from the remains of Saint Arsenios the Cappadocian, given to him by his elder, Paisios. He always used it as a shield of spiritual protection, particularly whenever he conducted an exorcism.

"It is important to be aware that when humans struggle for spiritual perfection, God periodically offers them a certain degree of comfort in order to sustain them on the path," Father Maximos stated. "It is like giving water to a marathon runner during the race so that he can quench his thirst and continue for the finish line. That is how God offers struggling individuals periodic relief. He does so through alterations brought on by brief visitations from grace. Clever spiritual scientists try to store and preserve that grace within themselves."

"Like trying to preserve water during periods of drought," Lavros mused.

"It's actually something like that," Father Maximos said. "It's like what we try to do here in Cyprus. Whenever it rains we try to preserve water in various dams because we know that next year there may not be any rain."

"Fortunately, we had good rainfall this year!" Lavros announced with a satisfied look.

The remains of saints emanate holy energy because their bodies are sanctified

"But next year or the next six years we may get no rain," Father Maximos responded. "That's why we are urged to save even a single drop. That's what smart people do when they experience these divine alterations, when their hearts open up and are filled with prayer. Really, we should try to have our hearts watered by grace and nurtured during these periods of good alterations in the same way that a thirsty man drinks incessantly and tries to fill up with water."

"Greediness in the pursuit of grace is no vice," I joked.

"Absolutely so," Father Maximos said. "When it comes to the grace of God we have a license to be greedy and avaricious. It's the only form of greediness that is music to the ears of God. Believe me, such good greediness has no limit or point of satiation. That's when moderation is truly not a virtue but a vice. A spiritually intelligent person will never say 'I tasted grace and had enough.' We are invited to indulge in this good greediness. As our hearts open up we must proceed to ask more from God: more grace, more love, more compassion. Can you imagine a limit to compassion? Impossible. The period of grace's visitation is the period of the good rainfall. Whatever seeds there may be inside our hearts will begin to sprout, blossom, and bear fruit. Those of us who know this grace of God, specifically those who tasted the freely given grace—"

"Freely given grace?" Marina interrupted. "Is there a different kind of grace other than freely given?"

"Of course. The freely given grace is the grace that God, as the Great Fisherman, offers periodically to people as a bite to attract them to him." I noticed Erato smiling as Father Maximos spoke, apparently understanding what Father Maximos was talking about. She had been a faithful disciple and apprentice to Father Maximos to such a degree that many considered her as some sort of an eldress. That was how Stephanos thought of his wife and that was how Emily felt toward our friend.

"I don't think *I* understand," Marina murmured, emphasizing the "I" after noticing Erato's reaction. Marina was a newcomer to Father Maximos's ways of spiritual thinking.

"I'll explain," he replied. "Under certain circumstances God will give generously of his grace, free of charge. Consequently, human beings are enchanted with the grandeur of grace and their heart is moved with greater ease toward *metanoia*, tears, love, joy, veneration. For such persons who are so touched by grace, the moment they begin to pray they immediately find themselves in a paradisiacal state of mind. Destructive passions begin to recede and the persons experience emotional and mental as well as bodily peace. They experience an overwhelming sense of well-being. Grace reigns within their entire personhood. This is the freely given grace that God often gives to human beings.

"Of course," Father Maximos added with a wily smile, "ultimately grace is not really free. You must eventually work hard to earn it and keep it."

"Now, that's paradoxical." Marina protested good-naturedly. "You just said that God's grace is freely given to people."

"Yes and no. Look, once you have tasted grace, freely given by God, then you will have to work hard at it in order to bring it back and make it a permanent resident in your heart. You will no longer rest until you do so. You are hooked, so to speak. And that's what is not given freely. You must work at it. Elder Paisios used to say that God is like a clever manager of an ice-cream parlor. In order to attract customers he offers free ice cream for a day or two to get people hooked. But the next day, and the day after, they must come with their money. Likewise, God will offer his grace freely on occasion in order to make you an addict of grace. But after the initial taste, in order to get back that same grace and to possess it on a permanent basis you must struggle and sweat for it."

"You have tasted paradise and then you lost it. Only then do you become fully conscious of what you are missing," I volunteered. "Is that the meaning of the motto 'Give blood in order to get Spirit' that some elders talk about?"

"Precisely."

"This is true in every field of endeavor."

"It is the same with spiritual endeavors. You cannot attain spiritual goals without serious and focused hard work. You cannot get things freely all the time. You simply have to gain grace through your free will and spiritual efforts."

"It is impossible for us, Father Maxime," Marina said, "to imagine what it feels like to be filled by the grace of the Holy Spirit. We are so ignorant that we really don't know what you are talking about, what we are missing. How does it feel, really?"

Father Maximos smiled. "Those of us who have tasted grace, whether freely given by God or earned through hard spiritual struggles know that when grace works inside us everything around is joyous, filled with light. Even if we step into hell itself it is automatically transformed into paradise for us. I recall an incident with an old Athonite monk who was descending the mountain with a tall walking stick. He was full of luminosity. He looked so brilliant, it was as if he were an Old Testament prophet coming down Mount Sinai. I asked him with curiosity, 'What's happening, Father?' 'Oh my dear brother,' he replied, 'the bird is singing, the bird is singing.' He meant that his heart was filled with grace. He was undergoing a period of spiritual alterations and everything about him and around him became numinous, divine."

"Why does God offer his freely given grace to some but not to all human beings?" Marina asked.

"But he does offer it to anyone who is ready. God wants his grace to be experienced by all human beings. He stands outside the door of our hearts and knocks and implores us to open it up, even for a short while, to create even a minor crack in our armor so that we can taste the sweetness of his presence. Our own freedom is the key to our success or failure in letting God in."

"And failure to allow God in may often imply allowing the opposite energy to take over," Erato stated. With her intervention she shifted the discussion from alterations resulting from God's grace to alterations resulting from diabolical assaults. It was a topic that she had raised in earlier conversations with Father Maximos.

"Sadly, it is so," Father Maximos replied somberly. "Remember, this is the second source of alterations. A human being may, from a variety of reasons, begin to feel within his heart turmoil, confusion, despair, hopelessness. He may experience hell, darkness, terrible demonic conditions. Such inner states are also manifested externally. You can see such alterations in a person's looks, in his glance, in his words, in his actions, in everything about him."

"Do these possessions happen accidentally, like how we catch a virus or a cold?" Marina asked.

"No, no! Definitely not. Alas if it was so. Demons are not free to do as they please without being accountable to anyone."

"Demons are not free?" she said, surprised.

"They are free," Father Maximos acknowledged with a nod, "but their freedom cannot neutralize our own freedom. They are forced to respect it. However, demons do something else. They try to besiege us. For those who struggle for their spiritual perfection and try not to allow demons to enter through their heart's door, they surround them and wage war through various means. Demonic arrows come from the outside to the inside. But they remain outside the hearts of those who are spiritually engaged. This is important to keep in mind.

"Unfortunately, there are people who do offer Satan the right to take over their hearts, either because they are careless with their lives, or they lack vigilance, or they are impious, or because of insolence toward God. Then these demonic energies may find a way to invade their hearts, turning them into a gristmill. Such people will then truly taste the bitterness of hell."

"People may be in hell but they don't know it," I suggested. "Often, what is hell for one may be paradise for another."

"True. People who are cut off from God do not necessarily realize that they are in hell. They live in darkness but they are so blind that they are not even aware that they reside in darkness."

"Why can't we say, Father Maxime," Marina asked, "that such people are simply suffering from mental illnesses rather than being demonically possessed?"

"No. In our understanding of these matters mental illness is an entirely different phenomenon. Strictly speaking, mental illness is a problem of the physical brain and the nervous system. Demonic possession is a spiritual malady of the most serious type. It is not a problem of brain malfunction. It is an assault on a person's soul. In such cases what is needed is spiritual intervention, not conventional psychotherapy or medical treatment."

"Are people who struggle spiritually always protected from Satan's arrows?"

"As long as they are vigilant, Satan will remain outside. He will keep throwing his 'fiery and cunning arrows,' as the prayer goes, but the arrows won't touch them. However, if people lose their watchfulness then anything is possible. Lack of alertness is a powerful satanic arrow against the spiritual life. It is similar to when you go for an operation and the anesthesiologist gives you a shot that you barely feel, but in no time you are completely knocked out. In that condition you are totally at the mercy of the doctors. With a minor sting your entire existence is paralyzed."

"What causes Satan's arrows to sting us, Father Maxime?" Lavros asked, stroking his short white beard.

"It could be from a variety of causes. As I just said, it may be produced by carelessness and negligence of the spiritual life. No matter what the cause, the result is the same: our consciousness gets paralyzed and is at the mercy of the enemy of our salvation.

"I have noticed," Father Maximos continued, "that many people afflicted by the malady of carelessness are often characterized by a state of lifelessness and a lack of interest in anything. And this state, which we all occasionally experience, becomes a permanent and chronic condition for these people. Such people in reality are the unburied dead. They have no life in them. I have known such people who desire nothing and are interested in nothing, nothing pleases them and anything they do appears onerous and tasteless. It is similar to how you feel when you are sick and no matter how tasty the food may be in front of you, you don't want to touch it. Let me tell you, it is tragic to meet young people who live such lives of veritable hell. You can't motivate them to get interested in anything, anything at all. They are lifeless."

Father Maximos tapped his foot on the ground and leaned back on his chair. "So demonic alterations take place in situations when people lack experience and are careless. That's why I advise whoever comes for confession to get into the habit of prayer as a form of protection against demonic assaults. It is a shield against the arrows of the demons. For us being in church with the holy icons, where God's energy is concentrated, is another way of being protected against such assaults."

"I assume," Erato reasoned, "that, likewise, if you carelessly enter into areas where there is negative energy then the opposite may happen."

113

"Yes. Some people out of curiosity may experiment with magic or visit locations of devil worship. As a consequence they expose themselves to diabolical energies and symbols. These symbols have power. It is like visiting a radioactively infected area. That's dangerous for their spiritual and mental well-being. I should warn that visiting places where sinful acts are being committed, where people curse and act with irreverence, is also risky. In such places there is an intense concentration of demonic energy that can penetrate the inner world of a naive person, someone who is not experienced and who is not spiritually protected."

"How can you know that a place has such energy, Father Maxime?" Marina asked with interest.

"People of God have discernment. When the soul tastes the fruits of grace then she develops the appropriate sense organ to know what grace is, what diabolical energy is, what delusion is, and what the difference between them is. A person with spiritual discernment knows whether a particular locale has grace or demonic energy in it, believe me."

Father Maximos paused. "There is a phrase that we monks often use. We say 'I don't feel rested in this place,' or 'that person doesn't comfort me' or something to that effect. Likewise, we would say 'this place comforts me,' or this person, this atmosphere, this energy, makes me feel at ease. We know when something is not in harmony with our heart. It reacts. It is similar to situations when we are offered food that we don't like. We can force ourselves to eat it but our stomach reacts.

"I remember a pilgrim who visited Mount Athos asking a hermit 'Father how do I know that I will be saved?' And the hermit replied 'Go to church and see how you feel. If you feel suffocated and wish to run out the door it means that your spirit and the Spirit of God that resides there are not compatible. On the other hand if you feel good being in the house of God then that would be a sign that your soul is in harmony with the Holy Spirit.

"You see, that is what happens to the spiritually experienced souls when they come in contact with places and objects that have demonic energy in them. When the soul is spiritually healthy and knows what grace is, then there is an automatic reaction within: 'I cannot be in this space. It is impossible for me to be in this room or in this house. I will burst. My soul cannot find comfort in a place where the spirit of God is absent.' "

I tried to hold back a smile as Father Maximos said those words. I wondered whether his soul could find comfort in any part of the modern, secular, consumer-oriented, materialist world. Yet, that's where the elders of Mount Athos sent him, in spite of his own preferences.

"How our soul gets accustomed to the objects that surround us is a huge topic. That's why the space where we live should be sanctified." There was a long pause and reflection after Father Maximos went silent. It seemed to me that what may feel like a spiritually comforting space would depend to a great extent on one's cultural conditioning. For example, the fact that Father Maximos was singularly and exclusively steeped in the culture of Eastern Orthodoxy would cause him difficulties within a Hindu ashram or a Tibetan lamasery. Likewise I presumed spiritual people from those traditions or people who lived in multicultural, secular cities would feel less comfortable following the spiritual regimen of an Athonite monastery. Those were issues that I did not wish to raise that day. I had no idea how to negotiate such cross-cultural considerations with what Father Maximos was saying. When I raised those issues with my friend Mike Lewis he suggested in a note that "Father Maximos's generalizations help us understand the broad parameters on how to think about these matters. But the spiritual value of an individual or a place can only be really known by God. Each tradition is unique and things that may appear to be contradictory to human rationality may in fact derive from God's will."

"Father Maxime, what about alterations that originate neither from God nor from the demons?" Erato asked. "What are they? So far you haven't talked about those."

"Perhaps the best way to start is with an example," Father Maximos replied and paused for a second. "Suppose we are prejudiced against a particular person, or against a particular group of individuals. Such prejudice is neither from God nor necessarily from demons. Let's say I cannot be in the presence of people who have beards or wear cassocks! Every time I see such a person I begin to experience alterations within me. I feel uncomfortable in their presence. I may feel angry. Many times in Greece I experienced all kinds of abuse from people who could not stand seeing a monk. I remember I was in a hospital once waiting for an examination and this nurse started cursing and calling me all sorts of names, 'dirty monk,' and the like. Perhaps some monk may have done something to her. Who knows? She just didn't like monks for some reason."

"We carry plenty of nonsense in our heads, thanks to ignorance and prejudice," I said.

"The cause of such alterations may not be due to ignorance or prejudice. We may not like to eat certain foods or we may find it hard to live in the countryside. We may prefer the city. These are strictly human preferences that can cause alterations in our psychological and spiritual state. For instance, in our everyday lives we may get tired of our work, such as being in an office all day long. We may wish to go out and enjoy ourselves, find some relief. Or we may decide to go to the mountains and be alone in a forest for awhile. We may wish to hear some music, or go see a friend who gives us comfort, someone who is pleasant and makes us feel good when we see him. Even great saints often have such needs and experience these types of alterations."

"How is that possible?" Lavros said lightly. "I assumed that saints reached a state beyond the human, beyond human needs."

"Not so. Let me tell you a story. Many years ago when I was at Katounakia [a rugged area in the southeast of the Athonite peninsula] I would often spend time with that great contemporary holy elder Father Ephraim, Papa Ephraim, as he was popularly called. I am not sure whether our century will give birth to another great elder like him, a man of continuous prayer who radiated the abundance of God's grace.

"When a group of us visited him at his hermitage one day he complained that he was tired of Katounakia and expressed a wish to go live at Monoxylites for awhile. That's an area near the borders of Mount Athos. It is a valley between two mountains filled with pine-tree forests, vineyards, and olive groves. It is a very beautiful area with abundant running waters, an earthly paradise. He said, 'I want to go there and rest. Here at Katounakia there is nothing except rocks and prayer, prayer and rocks, day in and day out. I am really tired. I need a change.'

"I was shocked when I heard him say that. I wondered how it was possible for a great saint like him to have a desire to change his environment, to go to Monoxylites? I could see young monks like ourselves having needs of this sort. But how is it possible that this great saint in whose life God is always present has such needs? It was then that I realized that even saints are human beings subject to the law of alterations.

"I heard later that Joseph the Hesychast [d. 1959], the great elder of Papa Ephraim, expressed similar needs during his life. Elder Ephraim himself told us once that his elder underwent a period of deep sorrow and was subjected to many temptations. One day he asked his then disciple Ephraim, 'Papa Ephraim, go and bring Pseudo Vasili here to amuse us.' Pseudo Vasili was a layman who lived and worked near the *skete* of Saint Anna. He was a simple man who was reputed for his outrageous lies. In his presence it was impossible not to roar with laughter. As in my case, Papa Ephraim was scandalized. 'How is it possible,' he reasoned, 'that the elder has a need for a jester like Pseudo Vasili to amuse him? Why can't he do something else, like more prayer?' As you can see, even great saints occasionally have such needs by virtue of their being human."

"I am pleased to hear you say that, Father Maxime. It makes the spiritual struggle more accessible to us common mortals. Otherwise I was ready to give up," Lavros said with his usual humor.

"Saints may be God realized but they don't cease to be human beings. This is important to keep in mind. We notice such alterations in our lives all the time. I see it, and you can see it. When I confess adults all day long I feel very different in comparison to the times when I confess little children. Confessing little kids is a form of relaxation for me, even entertainment. Children act as sponges for me, absorbing all my fatigue. When I visit elementary schools and spend some time with them I feel I am in paradise and the children are like angels. Of course, I am not sure whether their teachers share my feelings . . .

"Let's say," Father Maximos continued after a pause, "I go somewhere to enjoy nature or to listen to music. This will generate changes in me. Or, let's say I meet a friend who gives me great joy. Or I accidentally encounter someone else and I feel my blood freezing, as we say. I feel inside me discomfort and wish to run away. These are alterations that spring from within me. Of course, ideally, a person should become free of such prejudices. We

117

must have love and show love to all human beings. This is the ideal, the perfect way of relating to others. All human beings should be sources of comfort for us. But unfortunately until we get there we will experience these alterations that spring from our own imperfection. We will need to work on this for our spiritual development."

Father Maximos remained silent for some time. It seemed he had nothing more to say, so I reminded him that there was a fourth source of alterations that he had mentioned but had not yet elaborated on. These are the alterations that spring from the environment.

"Look at the night. What does it mean to you?" Father Maximos nodded at the sky, which was getting dark. Before I had a chance to respond, he went on. "It causes special alterations of its own. At night we normally feel different than during the day. We feel different during midnight than during noontime. We feel different in the morning and different in the afternoon, different also during twilight. I have known people who feel depressed with the setting of the sun and others who are inspired and write poetry. In the morning the same persons who feel sadness with the setting of the sun may feel joyous.

"Even the *Ecclesia* has adapted its services to this cycle of light and darkness. In the morning we chant '*Doxa si to dixanti to fos*' [Glory to Thee who has shown us the Light], an upbeat, wake-up chant. In the evening we chant the more subtle melody '*Fos Ilaron Ayias Doxes*' [Radiant Light of the Holy Glory]. The *Ecclesia* says different things during vespers, reminding us of other things than it does during the morning services of the *Orthros*. We are normally in a different mood when we open our door to welcome the new day. We can notice such alterations particularly when we wake up before sunrise, as we do at the monastery. There we experience the various changes in the atmosphere with the sun gradually appearing in the east. We live through these magnificent alterations of the environment, which, unfortunately, people who live in cities are unable to experience. They are deprived of that sense of awe and wonder in witnessing the emergence of yet another day.

"When I was living on Mount Athos at a time when we had no electric lights our day ended at five in the afternoon, at sunset. All we had at that time were candles and kerosene lamps. The night was truly night. We did not have electric lights that would let us turn nights into days. Without lights we were able to enjoy the night in all its majestic glory, its darkness, its silence. We just went to our room to do our spiritual exercises and then sleep. So, a human being is emotionally affected by environmental factors."

"But this is self-evident," I said. "It's common sense. This is what we sociologists teach, particularly as we deal with the social and cultural environment within which people live."

"Of course it's common sense," Father Maximos replied and with humor went on. "What do you think, holy elders taught nonsense? It is common sense when I feel different in my city and different when I am in a foreign land. I feel different when it rains, different when it snows, different when the sun is up, different during the summer, different during the winter.

"The holy elders were meticulous students of their environment. They would even point out that the direction of the winds can affect us. They said that southerly winds have a different impact on people than when northerly winds are blowing. I remember whenever that humid southerly wind was blowing on Mount Athos many of us would suffer from headaches and lack of energy. On the other hand when cold northerly winds blew we were full of energy. Everything looked clear and we felt good."

"What about food? I assume the elders talked about that also," I asked.

"Oh, yes. They observed that we feel differently when we eat fatty foods and differently when we fast. Even food can cause alterations. For example, I would never eat before offering confession. Somehow for good spiritual counseling I need to have an empty stomach. Otherwise the Holy Spirit doesn't help me. The elders also claim that the place we live in can be a cause of alterations in us. I would feel different if I lived in a palace and different if I lived in a slum. I would feel different if I sat on a throne and different if I sat on a pile of garbage. I would feel different yet if I sat on a comfortable couch and different if I sat on a stool."

"Speaking about the environment," Erato said, "is it more appropriate to stand when praying, particularly when engaging in the Jesus Prayer, or is it equally effective to sit in a comfortable position?"

"Look, you will feel different when you kneel and pray than when you pray standing. And you will feel different when you pray while lying in bed." Father Maximos suddenly laughed.

"Your question, Erato, brought to my mind my friend Chris, an American classmate of mine. We were students at the University of Thessaloniki. We went to Mount Athos one day to visit Papa Charalambos for confession. He was a great Russian elder from the Caucasus and a friend of Papa Ephraim. When we went there he asked us if we do any prostrations during our prayers. 'Yes,' we replied. 'How many?' We said twenty-five to fifty. 'Only fifty! You must do at least five hundred every night.' While he was a young novice himself under the tutelage of Elder Joseph, the Hesychast was doing seven thousand prostrations per day, he informed us. When he got old he was doing only three thousand.

"So we went back to Thessaloniki with the instruction to perform five hundred prostrations every night, a difficult task for us students. It took about an hour to do them and we had to study. One night I saw my roommate lying in bed. He kept raising his hand up and down, up and down. 'Chris,' I said. 'What on earth are you doing?' He replied, 'I do the prostrations ordered by Papa Charalambos.' He said, 'Look, I can't do this thing. I just imagine that I do prostrations by raising my hand up and down. I do them noetically.'

"Well," Father Maximos continued after we stopped laughing, "it's better than doing nothing. So, you see, the setting of our prayer generates different types of alterations in us."

"I assume," I said, "that the more spiritually advanced one is, the less the environment plays a role in causing alterations in our heart."

"Yes, of course. That's how it should be. The environment plays a very decisive role in our spiritual life while we are not perfected. When we reach perfection we transcend the influences of the environment. The environment in such a case plays only a minor role at best. But for us who are not there yet, the environment can be of great help in our spiritual struggle and advance."

"Or depending on the type of environment, it can have the opposite effect."

"Naturally. Notice how the churches are decorated with icons, candles, and other religious artifacts. The temple of God must be characterized by such an atmosphere that could facilitate one's spirituality. That is why the elders incorporated icons into the worship of the *Ecclesia*."

"Some people raise questions about all the expense that goes into painting the inside walls of the churches with saints," I said. "While I was at the Panagia monastery, a visitor asked me what the justification was for spending so much money to bring Russian iconographers. Russians were up on scaffolding, painting the inside walls of the church of Saint Gregory Palamas. He objected to what he considered to be an unnecessary expenditure of the monastery's wealth."

Father Maximos shook his head. "It is *ecclesiastical* marketing," he said. "But seriously, the *Ecclesia* is keenly aware of how a person functions in the world. The *Ecclesia*'s intention is that the moment people enter a church they should leave behind all the worldly images that they carry in their heads. They should feel that they are entering into a space that is holy. Therefore we, as the custodians of the *Ecclesia*, must be careful how we decorate the churches. We cannot have excessive lights illuminating the place as if it were a five-star hotel. We must not allow loudspeakers and megaphones that remind us of nightclubs or discotheques. The atmosphere of the temple must be such that the moment people step in they are inspired to generate in their minds good *logismoi*, good thought-forms, which will assist them in their ascendance toward God. For imperfect beings like us there is the need to see the image of Christ or the image of the Holy Virgin so that our soul may experience joy. So, as you must know from experience, the contemplation of icons generates benign *logismoi*."

I recalled an incident during which Father Maximos explained to a critic that icons in the Orthodox spiritual tradition are nothing other than objects that help us to concentrate our minds on the reality or content behind the icons. It was a notion that excited my artist friend Mike Lewis, who exclaimed that this is the basis of all art. It would be a form of idolatry for Father Maximos to worship the icons themselves. He claimed that this was the misconception that led the Western churches to abolish icons from worship. Icons, he insisted, are simply venerated as aids that help us

121

I cons come in contact with the reality that the icons represent. When we view them in this light, icons create a spiritually charged atmosphere that is conducive to prayer and contemplation.

I also remembered a discussion I had with two colleagues and friends back in Maine about these issues. After an evening talk on Eastern Orthodoxy at the Orono Methodist Church, the organizers and I walked to the local pub to continue our discussion related to issues of faith and worship. They lamented the fact that few young people from the university community attend church these days. In order to attract students they initiated a program in which a rock band played in church every Friday night. The band would set up its stage next to the altar and play rock with religious lyrics. Few students, however, attended those concerts. They asked my opinion on how to attract more students to the church. Why, I asked, would students come to church to hear religious rock and not attend the real thing at a rock concert? But the lyrics are Christian, my friends pointed out. Sacred music, I argued, comes from a different source. Those who compose such music are spiritually inspired. I suggested that a first step to make the church more attractive to students was to create an atmosphere whereby when a person entered the church he or she experienced the sacredness of the space. Rock cannot do that. The church has to offer a clear distinction between the ordinary "profane" world and the realm of the sacred so that a person who enters the church will leave the "profane" world behind. That is the power of Mount Athos, I went on to say, and that is why now that it is being discovered it's inundated by young pilgrims.

I mentioned that experience in Maine and Father Maximos nodded. "When we enter the church," he said "our whole person partakes in spiritual experience through smell, sight, hearing, and taste, through communion with others. The elders included candles, incense burning, and chanting as ways to get into a spiritual frame of mind. Why do you chant in church, you may ask? Couldn't we, let us say, spend an hour in silence? Incidentally, silence is a more perfected mode of worship."

"How so? Is chanting an imperfect way of worshiping?" I asked surprised.

"Yes it is. It is not meant for those who are perfect. Those who are God realized pray noetically, through the heart. They don't need to pray through sounds, chants, and music. But we need all these things ourselves. Even great prophets needed chanting, sometimes in order to get into that state of spiritual receptivity and experience."

"What are some examples of that, Father Maxime?" I asked with curiosity. I was reminded of the Native American drumming and other similar activities used when shamans try to enter into what modern anthropologists call "shamanic states of consciousness."[1]

"In the Old Testament there was this prophet who wished to make contact with God in order to offer a prophecy to his people. He tried to pray but it was impossible to do so, even though he was a prophet. He said to his people, 'I can't pray, therefore I cannot get information from God.' Then he instructed them to bring cymbals and trumpets in order to chant an ode to the Lord. And the people came and started chanting and played their trumpets and cymbals. Then suddenly the spirit of the prophet was awakened and he offered a prophecy. You see, he needed the chanting and the sacred music to get into the necessary state of mind. If a prophet needs these methods before he can attune himself to God, imagine how much more we ourselves need such methods of spiritual practice."

"Who creates such music, Father Maxime?" Marina asked.

"In the Eastern Orthodox spiritual tradition it was the holy elders themselves who composed the music appropriate for spiritual work. They constructed the temples and the churches of God using a special architecture. We don't just construct a church in accordance with the whims of an architect. Also, the painting of the icons in the church is governed by clear rules and they are very specific. You cannot paint saints the same way that a painter would paint people on a canvas. The holy elders through grace were able to set down the type of music and the type of iconography that are conductive to the good alterations, helping the heart to also move toward spiritual directions. The liturgical vestments that we use in church are not ordinary garments. They are endowed with religious meaning and significance. The *typikon* of the *Ecclesia* must be followed at different hours and for different occasions in minute detail and focus. Everything in the *Ecclesia* has a meaning behind it. Nothing is put together haphazardly. We believe that all of these rituals have been created with the help of divine wisdom so that they become aids for us to transcend the earthly and temporal domain and move us on to the heavenly and everlasting realms. They can alter our hearts in a positive direction."

"How can we who live in the world create an environment that is conducive to spiritual development?" Marina asked. "It is difficult to create such environments."

"Elder Paisios used to advise both monks and pilgrims: 'Make the space where you live conducive to your spiritual development, regardless of whether you are in a monastery or in the middle of a city.' Have a corner in your house where you gather spiritually charged objects like icons and have a lit candle or a lamp in front of them. You will notice that the entire space in your house will be transformed. You will experience a sense of comfort in your immediate environment. And, believe it or not, you will notice that spiritual objects like icons will have an impact on the people who live in that house."

124

"It will be a pole for the attraction of the energies of the Holy Spirit," Erato added in a soft voice. She spoke from direct personal experience. Erato had filled her and Stephano's apartment with several icons, candles, and pictures of holy elders. I always felt good in their home but I attributed that to the good energy that she and Stephanos radiated.

"You know, after much research and reading about the lives of the holy elders, I realized how much they were helped by the environment they lived in," Father Maximos said. "They carried good memories from their parents. The families they grew up in, particularly their mothers, were holy."

"But what about your case Father Maxime? You did not come from such a holy family." I was referring to the fact that Father Maximos's father was a communist. An atheist, he strictly forbade young Father Maximos to go near a church.

"First and foremost, Kyriaco, I am not a saint," Father Maximos clarified. "Second, I did have my grandmother who was an exemplary model for the spiritual life. Without my parents' approval she would secretly take me by the hand to church. But since you raised the issue I can tell you how the environment of the Holy Mountain had such a profound impact on me. Upon waking from a dream involving Mount Athos, I feel refreshed and full of energy. It's the way I feel when I conduct the liturgy."

"I assume when you dream of Limassol and your life in Cyprus you feel otherwise," Lavros interjected. Father Maximos laughed.

Stephanos had told me earlier that Father Maximos gets very little sleep since he sometimes sees people for confessions past midnight. Then he has to wake up before five for *Orthros*. During his ordeal with the other bishops he spent most of the time that he would have otherwise spent getting some sleep in a state of continuous prayer. He did so, I was told, sitting on a chair until sunrise.

"Why do you feel so good when you dream of Mount Athos, considering that you are not there anymore?" Marina asked. "Wouldn't the contrast create unhappiness in your soul?"

"Not at all. What I've experienced there is securely stored in my memory. It's part of me and can never be erased. It's what I truly own. I have as an integral part of my inner world the good images of those holy men that I was so blessed to have known, people like Old Paisios and Papa Ephraim. Who can snatch out of my mind the memories of these spiritual giants, and so many others?" There was emotion in Father Maximos's voice. "All those images of the *agrypnias* [all-night prayer vigils], the liturgies . . . Who can erase them from my memory? Nobody can. It's like painting a white cloth. No matter how much cleaning powder you use you can never remove the color. When I first saw Papa Ephraim conducting the liturgy, I felt as if Moses had returned to earth. I can never forget that liturgy—"

"Speaking about good images and good memories, I am really concerned about the images children get exposed to through the mass media," Marina interrupted. "I see the results in my practice."

"It is disastrous," Father Maximos agreed. "Children should be exposed to good images so that they can store them in their memory. If day in and day out they see nothing else except diabolical images on television, people hitting and shooting one another, then they are bound to be affected. When a child sees demons, fights, and T-shirts with monsters on them, how are these images going to help that child be peaceful? Sometimes I go into the rooms of children when I am invited to conduct a sanctification service at various homes. I get horrified at what I see. Posters of monsters, wild rock stars, ferocious-looking black panthers. Had you locked me up in such a space I would have gone paranoid. Yet they have

[handwritten margin notes:] at Mt. Athos

I have warm childhood memories that can never be erased.

125

Children today are not exposed to good images that they can store in their memory their children live in such environments." I marveled at how Father Maximos's innocent eyes looked with such freshness and insight at taken-for-granted images of modern culture.

It was eight in the evening when Father Maximos abruptly pulled his watch from his pocket. "It's time to go," he said urgently. "I have business to attend to at the bishopric."

We understood that the "business" was the long line of people who waited for him for confession. We thanked the nuns for their hospitality and they urged us to return there soon for further discussions. When we dropped Father Maximos off at the bishopric he asked me in passing whether I wished to drive him to the Panagia monastery the following evening. Those were, of course, the opportunities I was looking for. Lavros's ingenious method of the "ambush" had worked again.

SEVEN

SPIRITUAL STAGES

opened the door of my old Honda the mo-

ment I saw Father Maximos coming out the

front door of the bishopric. "For God's sake,

Kyriaco," he reprimanded me with a laugh and, brushing

me aside with his right arm, he bent down and sat on the

front seat. "Just because I am bishop doesn't mean that I

need you to open doors for me."

"It's fine with me. My car, after all, isn't exactly fit for

VIP treatment," I joked as I started the car for the journey

to the Panagia monastery.

I was pleased to be Father Maximos's unofficial chauf-

feur once again, even for the brief period of only two days.

He understood these were my rare opportunities to discuss Orthodox spirituality with him and did not object when I pushed the button of my minirecorder on the dashboard. He buckled himself up as we exited the bishopric's parking lot.

It was eight thirty in the evening when we left Limassol and began to climb up the southern slopes of the Troodos Mountains for the two-hour journey. After we casually chatted about various mundane issues for some time, I asked Father Maximos to shed some light on a question that had been puzzling me. On a number of occasions I had met a few Athonite elders whose views on political and social issues struck me as anything but enlightened. From my vantage point, I told Father Maximos, I would categorize their views as, if not downright reactionary, at least embarrassingly off the mark. Nationalistic would be more precise. How could a man who speaks and writes with such profound wisdom on subjects related to spirituality hold what I considered to be grotesque views on contemporary social and political issues. "How come," I asked, "there are such glaring blind spots in the development of people whom large numbers of devotees consider paragons of spiritual attainment?"

I felt free to speak openly to Father Maximos because I knew that he himself was liberated in his heart from all traces of nationalistic fervor, a criticism, in fact, that many levied at him as a way of undermining his chances for the archbishopric throne. The unfortunate history of the Eastern Orthodox world had been driven by the merging of religion and ethnicity, a tragic contamination of religion, the outcome of the long centuries of Ottoman occupation when religion and national identity became indistinguishable in the minds of the common people. That was when the Ottoman occupiers recognized the religious leaders as the political representatives of the subjugated Christians.

"Listen, Kyriaco," Father Maximos responded wearily. "This is of course a problem that troubles me personally. However, you must keep in mind that to be considered a holy elder does not imply that you are perfect. Spiritual elders are not infallible. Nobody is. There could be areas in their lives that may remain underdeveloped."

"That is what most people do not understand, and they lose their faith when they hear an elder speak in ways that people may consider unacceptable. The opposite can also be true. Gullible people may take the nonsense that such a person may utter as profound wisdom."

"That's why people must develop critical discernment when they embark on a spiritual path," Father Maximos said. "You must also keep in mind, however, that such a shortcoming on the part of an elder does not imply that he is prevented from attaining salvation."

"What do you mean?"

"The measure of his holiness is the depth of his *metanoia* and humility, not his knowledge about world events or the advocacy of the right political ideology. He may be ignorant and misguided on many issues, but it is his humility that matters in the eyes of God. Do you see what I mean? God does allow for holy elders to have blind spots such as in the case of an elder who may have remained stranded in his nationalism."

"But they can do much damage nevertheless," I insisted and kept driving in silence for a few seconds. "In any event," I added, "I am personally put off by such an elder. I must confess that I have a difficult time separating his reactionary, backward social and political views, which can generate hostility between groups, from his acclaimed spiritual development. In fact I would consider such an elder a dangerous person rather than a spiritual guide."

I was waiting to hear Father Maximos's reaction but it was his turn to remain quiet. I turned for an instant and noticed that his head was bent way down. For a moment I thought he was deep in contemplation based on what I said. Perhaps he was steeped in the Jesus Prayer to dissipate whatever negative energy I may have generated with my critical comments. But I then realized that, in fact, Father Maximos had dozed off. I did not disturb him and instead let him get his much-needed nap, the engine roaring monotonously under us as we climbed the Troodos Mountains. Tomorrow, I mused to myself, is another day, another demanding day, to be sure, for Father Maximos. I could raise my questions when he was more rested.

Between four thirty and seven in the morning, while the *Orthros* was going on, Father Maximos was in the confessional attending to as many monks as possible, one at a time. His weekly visits to the Panagia monastery were primarily for the purpose of counseling the monks and for maintaining his ties with the monastery where he had served as the abbot for several years. Visiting the Panagia monastery was like going home for him.

After the morning service we had a brief communal breakfast and at eight we headed off for the monastery of Saint Anna, a two-hour mountain drive. I looked forward to further discussing some of the issues we had covered the previous day. But after an hour's discussion, Father Maximos had another much-needed nap. It was his way, he told me earlier, of replenishing his meager sleep.

We arrived at Saint Anna by ten in the morning. Erato had already informed me that the new abbess was none other than Rosa. Several years ago Rosa was a young architect whose father waged a relentless war against Father Maximos, accusing him of "seducing" his daughter into monasticism. When the old abbess of the Saint Anna's monastery passed away, the rest of the sisters elected Rosa, who as a nun changed her name to Sister Ioanna. At the tender age of twenty-seven Sister Ioanna was probably one of the youngest and most educated abbesses in the entire Eastern Orthodox world. Erato, who was close to the young abbess, told me that Sister Ioanna had already developed a reputation as a formidable eldress, reputed for being graced by gifts of the Spirit. Stephanos confided that he also resorted to her often for spiritual guidance.

We found Abbess Ioanna with a couple of nuns in her office, going over architectural maps. A government official was also present to help the abbess determine the exact number of plots owned by the monastery. The eldress was putting her architectural skills to work as she planned to build a church next to the monastery in honor of John the Baptist, whose name was given to her during her tonsure. They were delighted to see Father Maximos. After chatting briefly about the monastery's holdings, Father Maximos went right to work, offering confession to one nun after another.

After lunch and a brief siesta for some much-needed rest, Father Maximos spoke to a *synaxis*, a gathering of the nuns, on a topic that I felt was in some way triggered by the issues we touched upon during our sojourn. Father Maximos told me on several occasions that as a rule he did not prepare for his speeches. Instead he would mostly rely on inner illumination and guidance. "Every time I went prepared for a talk," he told me once, "it was a disaster."

Being the only man around besides Father Maximos, I was invited to attend the lecture. I was not bold enough, however, to ask permission to tape the talk. Instead, I kept notes in my head. I assumed I could ask Father Maximos any questions later, during our two-hour journey to Nicosia, where he was to give yet another lecture, this time to a basketball club.

The subject of his talk to the nuns was on discernment, specifically, on the importance on the part of a spiritual advisor in recognizing the way that the energies of divine grace manifest themselves within a given individual. The spiritual elder or eldress, Father Maximos instructed the nuns, must learn the way God works in people's hearts to avoid wrong counseling that can potentially harm a person.

Father Maximos was brief and spoke in general terms, leaving me with many unanswered questions in my mind. I did raise those questions, however, during our trip to Nicosia. I was pleased to see that he was fully rested. At first I was hesitant, not wanting to tire him before his upcoming evening talk, but the signals he gave me were such that I quickly overcame my initial reluctance. It was an easy ride down the mountain as we passed by one picturesque village after another, heading toward the capital city.

"You see Kyriaco," Father Maximos replied to my question related to one's spiritual maturity, "when you are charged with the spiritual guidance of people you must figure out what stage they are at. Otherwise you might give them the wrong advice." Father Maximos explained that by "wrong advice" he meant advice that would not help a person advance spiritually. It was like giving the wrong medicine to a patient.

"What do you mean by stages, Father Maxime?"

"There are three spiritual stages that the elders identify. Each of these stages has distinct characteristics that we must become aware of."

"How did they come up with the number three?"

"It was, of course, the product of their personal experience. Their wisdom, as you know, was not based on just reading books." As ironic grin showed through his beard.

"So what's the first stage?" I insisted, trying to keep Father Maximos focused on the subject we had just started discussing.

"The holy elders call it the stage of the 'Slaves of God.' People at this spiritual stage can be deeply religious and devout. They may have a strong relationship to God and a genuine wish to serve him. They may do their best to obey his commands and harmonize their lives in accordance with what they consider to be the will of God. However, it is fear that motivates them and propels them along the avenue that will lead them toward God."

"This is the attitude of most religious people as far as I can tell."

"Not exactly. Yes, a large number of people do seem to be in that stage of relating to God, like slaves to a master. Such people would say to themselves: 'Look. If I don't obey God's commandments I will go to hell. I will be sentenced to eternal damnation."

"Is that a helpful way of looking at God?"

"It's helpful if you are at that stage of spiritual maturity. This fear of God functions like a barrier against sinning and as an inducement in obeying God's commandments. Furthermore, a person with such an attitude who is at that stage of development can indeed progress toward God. It's a spiritual condition that is real for many people."

"It doesn't seem a very mature way of relating to God."

"So what? They are no more and no less immature than infants and young children. But you're right. It's an infantile stage. It's the first stage of spiritual growth, which although imperfect, is real, just like the stage of being a child is very real but imperfect. When a human being is a child it doesn't mean that he or she is less of a human being—just a human being who is imperfect in terms of maturity. Do you see what I mean?"

"Yes. You cannot become an adult until you first go through the stages of infancy, childhood, adolescence, and so on."

"Exactly. During this condition of spiritual maturity people see God as a master, an implacable and fearsome despot who is ever ready to condemn them eternally to hell if they violate his commands."

"But is this a helpful way of seeing God?" I asked rather absentmindedly as I focused on the road.

"Here you go again!" Father Maximos said teasingly. "I just said it is helpful only when dealing with people at that stage of spiritual maturity."

"Okay. Give me some examples."

"Such an attitude toward God helps people who are coarse, brutish, and of a violent disposition. That's when they are biologically adults but spiritually children. Nevertheless, such personality types can be helped spiritually by injecting the fear of God or the fear of eternal punishment in them. Since they cannot be persuaded otherwise to be decent to others, then a healthy dose of fear of hell and damnation may be the only way to keep them out of trouble, from harming others and themselves, both physically and spiritually. God, in his absolute love for humanity, wants everybody to be saved regardless of their level of maturity. Such methods that use fear are, therefore, appropriate only for pedagogical reasons, taking into account the stage of maturity of a particular person. Do you see what I am driving at?"

I nodded. Father Maximos began laughing as he thought of an incident that was related to what we were discussing. It was about the case of a woman who came for confession and asked him to pray for her daughter to get married.

"As she entered the confessional I asked her about the kind of work she was doing. She mumbled something without giving me a straight answer. Now, ordinarily when people come for confession I never ask them for their work or profession. But for reasons unknown to me I was persistent. I asked her three or four times to tell me the kind of work she was doing. She finally revealed her true profession. She said she was managing a 'house.' 'You know, I have to make a living,' she said. Then I realized what 'house' she was managing. She was the madam of a prostitution parlor!" Father Maximos said with a grimace. "I told her she must immediately quit and find another job and that I was not going to pray for her daughter until she promised to give up her 'profession.' She said, 'But I have many debts. I'll go to jail if I give up my job.' I promised that I would give her two hundred pounds myself toward her debts. She looked at me and said, 'But I make that in an hour.'" Father Maximos waited for me to finish laughing. "I warned her that hell was awaiting if she continued in that line of work. She fell on the floor and started crying and screaming. After that outburst she agreed to give up her profession. She did so because she was afraid of the consequences. This is an example of how fear of hell can help someone advance spiritually. In fact, on occasion we can apply this understanding of God to ourselves regardless of our stage."

"How?"

"At some point in our lives, for example, we may be tempted to do something that goes contrary to the will of God. We may face a temptation that is so powerful that it can literally suffocate us. At such critical moments, which may appear suddenly in our lives, we may threaten ourselves with the thought that eternal estrangement from God is awaiting us if we succumb."

"Scaring ourselves . . . That's a novel idea," I said.

"This attitude may serve us like a brake that we can step on sharply, bringing our vehicle to an abrupt stop before a precipice. It can be helpful on certain occasions but it could be disastrous on other occasions."

"Such as?"

"I have heard of parents trying to plant in the hearts of their children the fear of God as a way of forcing them to behave properly. You often hear of parents warning their children that God will punish them if they curse, or if they don't behave the way they want them to behave."

"But this sense of fear may have immediate practical results," I said. "The child may say 'Okay I will not do this or that because God will punish me.' Then there may be peace in the house."

"But when that child grows up, he will realize that such a fear was unfounded and unhealthy. It was not a mature way of relating to God. In fact it could lead to a complete rejection of God. For children who are sensitive, such a tactic can really be devastating. I mean threatening a child with demons, and pots of boiling oil and all this nonsense. I always tell parents to speak to their children about God in a mature, serious way and not in a 'childish way.'

"Some parents trying to seduce their children to get communion tell them that they will get a 'golden little birdie.' Imagine that! Sometimes they even force their children to get communion. They drag their kicking and screaming kids in front of the holy altar."

"I've witnessed such scenes many times," I said. "The poor kids are scared looking at you in your cassocks and beards."

"Better that they keep them at home watching cartoons. I tell parents how important it is that their children establish a serious relationship with God. I have heard from spiritual people who come to me for confession that as children they had certain experiences that were clearly experiences of grace but which they had later forgotten. When they matured and looked back they recognized that those experiences were real spiritual experiences, authentic stuff, not hallucinations or fantasies. Injecting the fear of God as popularly understood may be terrible for such children, who may be young in age but spiritually advanced. So discernment is crucial as to when to employ such methods."

"Yet the scriptures speak positively of 'the fear of God.' "

"But that's different. The scriptures properly understood don't speak of a psychological fear of the Almighty. God is not a punishing and fearsome tyrant. They speak of a spiritual fear of God."

"I'm not sure I see the difference."

"Look. When I say psychological fear I mean fear that is the product of some guilt, like breaking the law and fearing the police and the courts. During the Eucharist when the priest announces 'With the fear and love of God come forward,' it is an entirely different kind of fear he is alluding to. It has no relationship to the fear that springs from negative emotions. Spiritual fear is simply the sense that God is holy and I am a sinner. And this sense of the holiness of God, the purity, the immaculate and unpolluted nature of God in contrast to my own sense of unworthiness and impurity generates a sense of awe, humility, and personal weakness. At the same time this recognition fills me with courage and hope because this fear is won over by God's love."

135

"What you say reminds me of the state of John the Baptist when he first met Jesus at the Jordan River."

"Right. That's a good example. We are told that when Christ went to John the Forerunner for his baptism, John's hands trembled with fear while his heart was filled with joy. This is often what happens when as a priest you conduct the mysteries of the *Ecclesia*. You tremble, as it were, because you are dealing with God, but at the same time you don't want to separate yourself from the mysteries. You are filled with joy."

"Your interpretation of the fear of God, Father Maxime, is really at odds with a lot of Christians' understanding of that fear."

"My understanding of God is based on the experiences of the holy elders. They are the experts who can speak about the nature of God. Everything else is an ideological distortion." Father Maximos suddenly chuckled. "Do you know why Saint Barbara is considered by the military as the patron saint of the artillery?"

"No."

"Well, I didn't know either until I was invited to preside over ceremonies at some military barracks where they were celebrating the name day of Saint Barbara. Then I found out why poor Saint Barbara is the patron saint of the artillery. When her father killed her after discovering she was a Christian, lightning struck him on the head, turning him into charcoal. So from that episode the generals, in their 'wisdom,' decided that she was the protectress of the artillery. Artillery, after all, also throws lightning against its enemies. Now figure that out!"

We were close to the main highway that was to take us to Nicosia and I was eager to cover the topic we were discussing before we reached our destination. I realized that what he was referring to had implications for contemporary psychology and the understanding of the self. I reminded Father Maximos that he had so far mentioned only the first stage of spiritual maturity, the stage of the slaves.

"The holy elders, who were great psychologists," Father Maximos replied as if he read my thoughts, "call the second stage of spiritual maturity the stage of the 'Employees of God.' Most of us are at that stage of spiritual development. Such people have gone, at least on the surface, beyond the fear of hell and do what they do because they wish to inherit paradise, they want to enter into the kingdom of heaven. In exchange for good works a person expects to be rewarded by God in this life and in the life to come."

"What you say reminds me of a sociological theory that states that human beings are primarily motivated by exchange. We do things to others because we expect something in exchange from them. I give you a gift with the implicit understanding that you will give me a gift back. It is called 'exchange theory.' Some would say it's a capitalist theory of the self."

"Well, your sociological theory is valid for people who are at the second stage of spiritual maturity. They are the Employees of God and want to get paid with his grace on the basis of their good works. It's as if someone is saying: 'Look, I work eight hours a day and I expect from you, my employer, fifty pounds in exchange for my labor. I am entitled to this money as a hard-working individual. A person establishes, in other words, an exchange relationship with God. I give to God good works and I expect grace, good fortune, paradise, whatever."

"There isn't much to admire in such an attitude."

"Maybe so. But it's important to keep in mind that at a certain spiritual stage such an attitude may be helpful. You tell yourself, 'Why should I fast and deprive myself of food?' Then you answer to yourself: 'God will reward me as a result of this small sacrifice. He will bless me and my family when I wake up early on Sunday morning and go to church. As a result of my sacrifices, he will prepare a place for me in his kingdom.'"

"I am sure a lot of people think like that when they give to charities."

"But of course. People know that when they give, God will return what they give many times over. We know that from experience. I have noticed that there are people who are very stingy and miserly but at the same time devout. So out of their stinginess they may become charitable."

"Doing good works out of stinginess sounds like an oxymoron. Like good businessmen, most of us think in terms of costs and profits," I said in jest.

"I remember several years ago when I visited a hermitage with Elder Paisios and they offered us something to drink and eat. It was some sort of a sweet. I kindly declined, trying to appear more 'ascetic.' Then Old Paisios said to me, 'Eat blessed one, eat! When they offer you something to eat, do so and in that way you are doubly the winner.' 'Why?' I asked him. 'First,' he said, 'you exercise the virtue of obedience. Therefore, God will reward you just because of that. Second, you get some nourishment for your body.'" Father Maximos laughed. "So," he emphasized, "people can be avaricious and charitable at the same time."

"They are good spiritual investors."

"That's a pretty good way of putting it. You tell yourself, 'I have money. I will give some so that the rest of my property may be blessed. On top of that I will get them back in some way. So I go to sleep with a peaceful conscience that I have done my duty to God. I am covered.'"

"But isn't this a mercenary understanding of God?"

"No. When you are at that stage you are still close to the spiritual child's understanding of God. But it's something. It's a step higher than that of the slave in the same way that adolescence is a step higher in maturity than childhood. It exercises the soul in its journey toward God. It is definitely better than that terrible rigidity of the heart, that refusal to do anything to help fellow human beings in need. The 'I don't give, I don't care,

I'm not interested' type of mentality. This is the attitude of the completely self-absorbed, narcissistic personality. In comparison to that, the stage of the Employee of God is a spiritual advance."

"So how do you approach this category of human beings, I mean the Employees of God?" I asked.

"As I said, for the crude, violent type of individual, toughness may be needed. Hit him on the head, so to speak, to crush the toughness of his heart, because it must be crushed. Or you crush yourself with fear. And you do that by reminding the other and yourself of the hell that awaits you if you do this or that. You remind yourself of the earth that will eventually receive you and so on."

"But these are terror tactics that could backfire," I protested.

"You need to use extreme discernment based on whom you are dealing with. You don't follow this therapeutic method for everybody or apply it to yourself at all times. You may need to instill the fear of hell in a person who is plotting and thinking of committing a terrible act.

"In reference to the stage of the Employees of God," Father Maximos continued, "you may engage yourself in a dialogue, pushing yourself, for example, to be more generous by saying 'What are you thinking about, blessed one? You are thinking of money? Just think of the kingdom of God. Think of what God will reward you with. You are exchanging perishable and meaningless things with eternal rewards. Replace the perishable with the imperishable, the temporal with the eternal, the zero with the infinite.' Saint Chrysostom said, 'If you are smart and learn how to be generous and charitable you have become a great merchant. It is a treasure that needs no protection and that gets more and more plentiful as you spread it out.' Saint Chrysostom asked, 'Do you want me to show you this treasure?' He then goes on to talk about charity that when given out to the needy grows and sanctifies your life."

"Regardless of its positive outcome, in the long run this remains a businesslike attitude."

"Okay. But, again, it is on a higher lever of spiritual development than the stage of the Slaves of God. Such a pedagogical approach is useful when you are dealing with people who are still not perfected spiritually or not mature enough and they need some kind of a motivation to move forward. You tell a person, 'Come closer to God and you will see how much more God will offer you. God will sanctify you and your family for the rest of the week or month or year.' "

"But isn't it problematic, Father Maxime, when too many promises about divine rewards are made and eventually things don't go well with a person? Then how can he or she maintain faith?"

"Yes, you are right about that. It is the myriad of temptations that will unavoidably come along the way to shake up the very foundation of the Employees of God. That is how the self gets purified. That is how the person will sooner or later realize that just because you give to charities, you go to church, you pray, and you do good works, it doesn't mean everything will be fine and dandy with you. No. You will feel pain, you might go bankrupt with your business, you may go hungry, terrible things may happen to your family, everything can be ruined for you. Are you ready? You must go through all these without ever complaining to God 'Why me? Why was my business ruined even though I gave so much to charities?' God allows these things to happen to people for their *catharsis*, their purification.

"The third spiritual condition," Father Maximos went on, "is that of the 'Children of God' or the 'Lovers of God.' This is the only stage that is real, the only stage that we must project as reflecting the true teachings of the *Ecclesia* on the nature of God. That is when individuals have come to understand and feel that God is their loving Father, speaking metaphorically of course. They act and do what they do not because they are afraid that God might send them to hell or because they want to gain a ticket to paradise but because they love God.

"I remember a good example that Old Paisios once gave us. Imagine, he said, if during the second coming of Christ mistaken calculations were made and at some point, as more and more people entered paradise, there was no more room for some of those still remaining outside. Then God comes and tells them, 'Folks, I'm sorry but unfortunately paradise has filled up. Find somewhere else to accommodate yourselves.' Then, Old Paisios said, the persons who lack nobility of character will begin to wail and start protesting. 'Why didn't you tell us before? Isn't there a chance that we can go back so that we can do all the things that we wanted to do? We sacrificed the pleasures of the world for the sake of heaven and yet we lost paradise as

139

[handwritten margin note:] The third spiritual condition is that of the Children of god or the Lovers of god. Individuals do what they do because the love god

well.' On the other hand the Children of God will respond, 'It's all right that paradise is full. Don't feel bad, dear God. It is good that paradise is full and you are happy. We will find a way to take care of ourselves.'"

"God wants us to think of him as a parent."

"This is the healthy way of relating to God. He wants us to relate to him as his children. As we say in church during the liturgy: '*Kai Kataxioson emas Despota meta parresias akatakritos tolman epikalesthai se ton epouranion Theon Patera and legein,*' which means 'Make us worthy, O Holy One, to dare call you Father, the God of Heaven.' Then we recite the Lord's Prayer: Our Father . . .

"Christ himself taught us how to pray and how to call God our Father. He did not teach us to call him either 'Master,' 'Heavenly Ruler,' 'Absolute One,' or anything else. Just 'Our Father.' This is very important. God has revealed his true nature to us. He said, 'Do you want to know what to call me? What my name is? What I feel for you? I am your Father. Therefore, you are my children.'"

"So, is this understanding of God what you consider the most mature?"

"It is by far the most mature and the most healthy. Whatever we do we must do it within the context of this loving relationship. Then we will feel a certain sense of nobility. How should I put it? It is like a child who feels totally comfortable and at home within a loving household. We do not feel like strangers in our Father's home, but members of the family. The *Ecclesia*, the world, the entire universe is our home, the house of our Father. We are neither slaves nor employees in this universe. We are the children of this omnipotent, omniscient, and totally loving God."

"At the same time, however, we are asked to see our lives with God as a relationship of freedom."

"Of course! I often feel so disheartened to see spiritual people, priests, monks, and laymen, who turn their relationship with God into some kind of a torture chamber. Old Paisios used to say to such people, 'My dear! God is oxygen and you turned him into carbon monoxide.'

"In other words," Father Maximos went on after we stopped laughing, "they turned their relationship with God into anguish, anxiety, and neurosis. When I meet people in such states, psychologically constrained and miserable-looking, I marvel at the distortions they manage to create in their relationship with God. How is it possible, I would ask such religious people, that you as children of God and inheritors of the saints have managed to reach such states of psychological misery? How can you present yourself as an image of God to those who come to you for spiritual advice?"

"That's the surest way to put somebody off God." I went on to unleash my lifelong frustration with the priests and theologians I had known since childhood who put me off so completely that I couldn't have a meaningful relationship with the church. The theologians I had known in high school, I told Father Maximos, were stern, humorless, intolerant of differing views, virulently nationalistic, and extremely authoritarian. They emanated everything but the love of God that Father Maximos claimed should be the predominant characteristic of the Children of God.

"You know," Father Maximos said, "I often thought that the survival of the *Ecclesia* through the ages is a standing miracle in itself. It exists in spite of the fact that those of us who represent it, priests, bishops, theologians, are so inadequate and unworthy of the task. Why should people want to come near the church when those who represent it project an image of a God who is stern, punishing, and dictatorial? A lot of people come and tell me, 'But why, Father, should I come to church when you, the representatives of the church, are so full of anger and intolerance? Why should I want to be like you?' And they are right."

"Many people of the church," I went on to say, "prefer a God who is like a slave master: stern and punishing. Obviously it is a reflection of the personality of those who hold to that image. I'm afraid a lot of people who represented the church throughout history are individuals who seemed to be in the first stage of spiritual development."

"Unfortunately it is so. I always tell the official representatives of the *Ecclesia*, the priests, the monks, the theologians, the Sunday school teachers, that they must be extremely careful to teach the true doctrine of the *Ecclesia* about the nature of God—that God is our Father and not a fearsome despot or a wealthy employer. This is a serious problem with the people who represent the church. People come to them to hear about God and they are taught instead about Satan and hell and the like. They present God as a punitive tyrant. They may, for example, tell a student 'Go to church and God will help you pass your exams.' What if that student does not pass his exams? Isn't he then going to turn against God? Or they may visit a sick person and tell her 'Pray and God will make you well.' And when the patient does not get well or she dies, God is to blame. These are tragic mistakes."

"What do you tell a dying person, Father Maxime?"

"Put your trust in God because God loves you, period. Love God whether you get well or whether you don't get well. We must never waver in our love toward God no matter what. We should not believe in God because he will make us well."

"That's the Employee's understanding of God," I pointed out. Father Maximos nodded. "But you did say that one should employ a different strategy in discussing God's way based on a person's stage of spiritual development."

"Of course! We must do everything we can to help the person not get stuck at an immature spiritual stage. I am particularly concerned with the case of young people. I tell catechists that under no circumstances must we deprive people of having this experiential understanding of God as total love. So during our spiritual struggles even though we may occasionally invoke the lower understanding of God, that of the Slaves and of the Employees, we must never forget that the most authentic way of understanding God, and the one that is expressed through the *Ecclesia*, is that we are all Children of the loving God and that at the end everything will be good. So the notion of God as a tyrant or God as the big boss disseminating rewards and punishments is ultimately false."

"But again, you said that the other two stages are useful for our spiritual advance."

"Absolutely. If the first stage is infantile, the second expresses the average person and the third is the understanding of God through the experiences of the saints, the perfect way of relating to God. But God is not unjust. All stages are helpful in our ascent toward God. What is important is to advance spiritually. When the time comes, God will reward those who have obeyed his commandments."

"What I find intriguing and puzzling is the notion that even if people are at the third stage of spiritual growth they can also employ the two lower levels."

"You see, Kyriaco, the perfected human being does not cancel out the previous stages but wisely uses them at appropriate times."

"Why is there a need for the lower stages?"

"Because even a perfected human being can have spiritual lapses and temporary regressions. So depending on the nature of that regression we can employ the appropriate medicine. Even Saint Silouan, who was a perfected human being, would cry and wail on occasion that this was his last night and that his 'miserable soul' was going straight to Hades, away from God."

"It is hard to fathom something like that," I said shaking my head.

"But it helped Silouan to remember his mortality and hell during the time of his temporary spiritual lapse. There are times when you marshal the fear of hell for your own spiritual good and there are other times when you choose the image of God as an employer that rewards your hard work. You must find within yourself what suits you at appropriate times, what helps you advance spiritually. Does the fear of God help you? Then use that image during that specific situation. Does the image of God as the great Employer help? Then have that as your working image.

"However," Father Maximos continued, "those of us who serve as spiritual guides and are often called to speak about the nature of God must never present a God who is either a despot or an employer. Why? For the simple reason that this is not his real nature. The true image of God is that of the loving Father.

"Now, we as human beings are on an evolutionary path toward God and we often have the sense of a God who can send us to hell or who can reward us for our good works. But we must always keep in mind that useful as these conceptions of God may be on occasion they are also imperfect and immature ways of understanding and relating to God. If you wish to know how to relate to God, study the lives of saints and see how they viewed God. Do you know what saints used to say about God? *'Tetromenos eimi tes Agapes Sou ego.'* In other words, 'I am wounded by your Love.'"

"God is the Great Beloved," I said.

"This is what many Christians don't understand. The saints were literally in love with God. Everything they wrote, everything they said, all the spiritual exercises they engaged in, all the hymns and chants they composed were nothing more than the overflowing of their hearts, which were erotically attached to God. There is no greater love than the love of God.

Nothing in this world, nothing can transcend or surpass the love of God. When someone truly falls in love with God then he transcends even his own physical nature."

"In what way?"

"Take a look at human erotic relationships. What happens to the person who is passionately in love? That person may not be able to eat, or drink, or think about anything else except the beloved. Such a person may be absent-minded, may look like a fool, not be able to rest, read, or sleep. The mind is glued on the beloved and wants to be with him or her all the time."

"That's what makes for great literature."

"Well, that is the state of the person who has fallen in love with God. Such a person cannot find rest anywhere else except in God."

"They are intoxicated with divine Eros," I added and mentioned the name of Saint Maximos the Confessor, who coined the term *Eros Maniakos* [Maniacal Eros] to describe the condition of the person who has come under the spell of God's divine love.

"That's why under the power of that erotic paroxysm toward God some of these saints would do, from the point of view of human logic, really crazy things."

"Are you referring to Saint John Stylites?" I said and smiled.

"Yes. How can you explain logically the behavior of such a saint, who piled up one stone after another and sat on top of them for forty years, never moving from there either in the midst of snowstorms or during the scorching heat of the summer?"

"Another good example of what you are saying is the case of Saint Neophytos of Cyprus." As I mentioned his name I recalled the incredulity I felt when as a boy I first heard about his strange life.

"For a rational person such behavior is totally crazy. Here is a man who came under the spell of God's love and shut himself into a cave for sixty years, praying continuously without seeing any other human beings during that time. Yet, miracles were taking place all around his cave."

"Alas, Father Maxime," I sighed, "we turned his cave into a tourist attraction."

"But the grace and the healing energy still reside there," Father Maximos reminded me. "Such saints often pretended to be crazy. Their experience of the love of God was so overwhelming that nothing else could distract their attention, nothing else could steal that love.

"It is said in the *Gerontikon*," Father Maximos continued, "that while in church Abba Therapon was approached by a beggar asking for alms. He gave the beggar everything he had. He walked outside and another beggar approached him. At last Abba Therapon was left only with the cloak he was wearing. Farther down another beggar asked for his cloak. He took it off and gave it away, remaining completely naked. Similarly, another elder went around giving everything he had to the poor. A beggar asked him to give him something too. Having nothing else left to give him he handed over his only possession, a copy of the Gospel. His disciple complained that he had gone too far. The saint then replied, 'I gave that which taught me to give everything away.'"

[handwritten margin note: Abba Therapon gave everything away]

Our conversation was interrupted when I had to stop the car at an intersection just as we were about to get to the main highway. We were at the outskirts of Nicosia, near the village of Lakatamia and a herd of sheep crossing the road had stopped traffic. The shepherd followed behind, hardly paying attention to us as he was absorbed in a conversation on his cell phone. We remained silent, taking in the pastoral sights and colors, knowing full well that they were remnants of a Cyprus we knew as children but which was rapidly disappearing as the island prepared to become part of the European Union. When the last sheep crossed the road I shifted into first gear and we crossed over onto the main highway. The sun had disappeared behind a forest of eucalyptus trees.

"In the Gospels there are images of God that can be identified with all three stages that you mentioned," I noted. "It can be very confusing."

"Jesus offered different images of God on the basis of what audience he had in front of him and on the basis of what spiritual stage they were at. In the Gospels there are several images of hell, of eternal darkness, of eternal fire, and so on. But we must interpret these things properly and within the context of the perfection of God's love, which accommodates itself to our own weaknesses and to our own spiritual situation."

"So these images that we find in the Gospels, the ones the fundamentalists use to the extreme, are there only for pedagogical reasons."

"Naturally. In a sense God makes an accommodation to our own weaknesses and spiritual illnesses in order to help us on our path. Even the Commandments of God, 'Don't steal, Don't kill, Don't commit adultery,' are not necessary in reality."

"What do you mean?"

"We were created in the image of God. We did not need commandments. We are good by nature. But we lost that state of oneness and goodness. So God offered us his injunctions as guideposts to help us out on our return journey. Once we reach our destination we will have no need for them."

"Oh, I see what you mean," I said nodding. "Based on what you've said one can get the wrong image of God by a careless reading of the Gospels. There are so many interpretations. The fundamentalists love to trumpet the image of God as a punishing despot who ejects sinners into the fires of eternal damnation."

"That's a problem. That's why I would never encourage people to read the Gospel without spiritual preparation and assistance. If someone reads the Bible without prior spiritual pedagogy he can easily reach the conclusion that it's a pile of nonsense. Take for example the image that God will sit on a throne separating the sheep from the goats . . . On the other hand, if you are prepared spiritually then you will realize that the Gospel is a vast wealth of divine wisdom."

"But who can recognize this wealth? I don't think that many of the fundamentalist Christians obsessed with the Apocalypse and eternal damnation can recognize this wisdom."

"Holy Scripture was written with the help of the energy of the Holy Spirit. Therefore, if you are to truly comprehend scripture, you must have within you the Holy Spirit as a living reality and presence. Did you know that in the early *Ecclesia* the catechumens, those who were being prepared to become members, were never exposed to the Gospel of John?" I sent a quick puzzled look over at Father Maximos. "They needed prior pedagogy to understand the high theology of John. Before their baptism they were allowed to hear only the Gospels of Matthew, Mark, and Luke. Never of John. Only after they were baptized and only at Easter were they allowed for the first time to hear John's Gospel: 'In the beginning was the Word, and the Word was with God, and the Word was God.' They had to acquire those spiritual preconditions so that they could penetrate into the mystery of the Gospel."

"Are you saying now that a person who does not have these spiritual preconditions or instruction by spiritual guides should not read the Gospel?"

"No. I'm not saying that. All I am saying is that there is a risk of misunderstanding the meaning of the Gospels when people don't have the spiritual preconditions to penetrate into its wisdom. They may develop a childish understanding of God."

"And they can get stuck there for a lifetime." I mused on the occasional preacher who would come to our university and create pandemonium at the steps of the student union building screaming about Jesus, sin, repentance, the end of the world, and hell and damnation to indifferent students.

"Unfortunately, distortions are unavoidable if we do not base our faith on an experiential understanding of God."

Thinking like a sociologist, I pondered the idea that regardless of our stage of development some distortions were unavoidable, period. After all, as human beings we are products of culture and historical circumstances. Even our most profound religious experiences have to be filtered through the channels of culture and society and therefore, to some degree, distorted. But I did not have time to externalize this thought and discuss it with Father Maximos. The bishopric car was there waiting for us at an appointed side street, a couple of hundred meters from the basketball club.

Father Theophilos, the deacon, was in the driver's seat. He was to escort Father Maximos to the formal function, the commemoration of the tragic life and martyrdom of Archbishop Kyprianos, the archbishop of Cyprus during the Greek war of independence against Ottoman rule in 1821. I simply sat in the audience listening.

EIGHT

CONVERTS

y stay in Cyprus was coming to a close and after visiting Father Maximos several more times at his bishopric I prepared myself for the long trip back to Maine and to Emily. We planned to return to Cyprus together in January of 2003 for a nine-month sabbatical stay, she to continue her work on peace and ecology and I to have further conversations with Father Maximos.

In mid-July, at the "ungodly" hour of four in the morning, I left the island for London. My plans were to stay in England for several days before heading back to the States. I had already made arrangements to interview Kallistos

Ware, bishop of the Greek Orthodox Church and leading scholar of Eastern Orthodoxy at Oxford University. An Anglican convert, Bishop Kallistos did more than anyone I knew to create bridges and understanding between Eastern Christianity and the West, making the spiritual wisdom of Eastern Christianity accessible to readers and spiritual seekers throughout the world.[1]

Given his unique and double role as university scholar and bishop, I had many questions I wished to discuss with him as I tried to deepen my understanding of the Eastern Orthodox spiritual tradition. Bishop Kallistos was an academic of Western background and so I felt a certain intellectual affinity with him that I could not have with Athonite monks, including Father Maximos, who had no experience of modern Western culture.

It was seven in the morning when we landed at Heathrow airport after a four-and-a-half-hour nonstop flight. As soon as I cleared customs I took the underground to the last stop on the Piccadilly line where Emily's brother, Akis, a longtime resident of England, awaited me at a Cypriot-owned shoe repair shop.

Heavy clouds covered the sky during the two-hour drive to Lincoln, the town where my brother-in-law had just bought a home. He planned to retire there with his English-German wife, his daughter and son-in-law, and their young twin daughters. After spending more than thirty years as a London businessman, unable to fulfill his dream of retiring to his beloved Famagusta due to the continued Turkish occupation of the city, Akis made the decision with his family to move to a less crowded part of England. "It's better for the girls to be in the countryside," he told me on the way to Lincoln, referring to his lively six-year-old twin granddaughters.

Every time I visit England I feel a sense of familiarity and a certain connection with the place. It is as if I have lived there before, an understandable feeling considering the centuries-old link between Cyprus and England. It began with Richard the Lionhearted, who conquered Cyprus on his way back from the Crusades. This connection was further romanticized by Shakespeare, who chose the Famagusta castle as the setting for his Othello. This special relationship between Cyprus and England was finally cemented by eighty years of British colonial rule, which lasted until the island's independence in 1960.

149

I was raised in Cyprus while it was still a British colony. Consequently, besides the Byzantine chants that I heard in church I also absorbed in my consciousness the colonial symbols that were around me. Seeing the red mailboxes in the streets of London with the British Crown on them and the red telephone booths stirred in me certain uncanny emotions and a nostalgia for my long-gone teenage years. The nationalists back in Cyprus, bent on eradicating every trace of the colonial inheritance, removed the red mailboxes and painted the telephone booths with an emetic yellow color.

There is no Cypriot who does not have a relative in England and who, like myself, does not feel an affinity with the British. Most of the Cypriot politicians and presidents since independence have been British-trained lawyers. Because of the many years of British rule, thousands of Cypriots emigrated to the United Kingdom, forming one of the largest and most thriving communities of Cypriots outside of Cyprus. It is believed, in fact, that a major factor in the prosperity of the island has been the steady flow of money that Cypriots living in England regularly send to Cyprus either in the form of investments or as cash to support poorer relatives. It is estimated that over 250,000 Cypriots live in England today, a huge number considering that the total indigenous population of Cyprus, both Greek and Turkish, does not exceed 700,000. It is ironic, if not amusing, that several of the diehard underground guerrillas who fought to overthrow British rule during the fifties migrated to England as soon as the island was given its independence. At the same time large numbers of British retirees chose Cyprus as their final residence. A celebrated author like Lawrence Durrell immortalized his stay on the island during the troubled fifties with his classic novel *Bitter Lemons*.

No wonder I felt at home in England, enjoying my two days with Akis and his family. We visited the magnificent Lincoln Cathedral and went to some local pubs, where we caught up on family news and talked about prospects for the reunification of Cyprus and return of refugees to their homes. Very early in the morning on the third day, my good-humored and ever-optimistic brother-in-law dropped me off at the train station in the nearby town of Newark, where I took the train for Oxford. My appointment with Bishop Kallistos was at one.

After checking in at the Galaxy Hotel, a homey English inn, I walked the distance to our appointment on Canterbury Road. Conscious of British punctuality, I rang the bell of the Saint Theosevia Centre for Christian Spirituality at exactly one o'clock. Bishop Kallistos opened the door and welcomed me warmly. It was the second time I had met with him, the first being four years earlier. Tall and gentle looking, the sixty-six-year-old bishop wore the black robes of an Orthodox monk, his face hidden behind a white, robust beard. As with my earlier visit I felt as if I were meeting a resurrected stately prince of Byzantium, right in the heart of Oxford.

"How do they relate to you in this town, seeing you dressed in your black cassock?" I asked as we walked to an Italian restaurant nearby.

"They are accustomed to seeing me around by now," Bishop Kallistos replied in jest. "Most people, of course, don't understand what I represent but they are used to my strange appearance. When I was ordained a priest, my elder on the island of Patmos, Father Amphilochios, told me that I should always wear the black cassock and let my beard grow. He said that in this way I would constantly be acting as a witness of Orthodoxy in the West."

After lunch we walked to the Orthodox chapel, next to the Saint Theosevia Centre. It was a simple round structure. "It will be quiet here for our conversation," Bishop Kallistos said as he escorted me in. Then he shut the door behind him and, after reverentially making the sign of the cross in front of the altar, as all Orthodox priests and faithful do upon entering a church, he proceeded to the iconostasis and kissed the icon of Christ and then that of the Holy Virgin. After this ritual we sat near the wall on chairs that were arranged in a semicircle facing the sanctuary.

"We are soon going to build a new church based on Byzantine architecture," Bishop Kallistos said, seeing me gaze upon the room. I had expected to see an old church similar to the traditional, Gothic-style cathedrals one finds on every corner at Oxford. Instead I found myself in a simple, octagonal structure with a tall ceiling. Clearly, I thought, it must have been used for something else, perhaps as a storage warehouse, before the bishop turned it into the Orthodox Church of Oxford. In fact, he explained to me, it was originally built as an Orthodox Church in 1973 but to a very simple plan, for resources were limited. Its unique simplicity was actually very agreeable to me. The church housed all the sacred symbols of

Eastern Orthodoxy: icons with hanging lamps, an iconostasis, candles, and a psaltery for the chanters.

"Well, where do we start?" I asked as I unfolded the paper with the ten questions that I had sent him several months earlier in anticipation of our meeting. Bishop Kallistos placed his hand into his cassock and pulled out his own copy.

"Let's start with number five," he said as I pressed the buttons of my two mini-recorders.

I read the question aloud: " 'Who is going to be saved and what does that mean?' An old monk from Mount Athos who spent all his life there once asked me whether I believed there were saints outside of Orthodoxy. I answered him with my own question. I said 'Father, are we to limit God within the boundaries of Mount Athos?' So, what is your answer to that question? Is it possible to reach *Theosis* outside of Orthodox Christianity? If the answer is 'no' then what can be said of the billions of humans who are not Orthodox?"

"As you can see," I continued, "this is a question concerning Christianity in general. So, I am trying to explore the issue of whether, according to Orthodox belief, *Theosis* is built into the very structure of human nature itself. If so, then it must be possible for all humans to become God-realized regardless of the culture or religious tradition they happen to be born into." The same question, of course, had been posed to me during my workshop in Sedona. I wished to find out how Bishop Kallistos as an esteemed official of the Orthodox Church would respond to such a challenge.

He thought for a few seconds and then responded, slowly and authoritatively, in his distinct Oxford accent. "I would start in my own thinking from two texts in the New Testament. The first is from the opening chapter of Saint John, from the prologue of his Gospel. It says with reference to the Logos, who is Christ, that he is 'the true light that enlightens everyone who comes into the world.' That for me is a fundamental principle: the light of Christ shines in the heart of every human being."

"If so," I interjected, "that light will manifest itself within the consciousness of the individual who is ready in a way that will be relevant to his or her own state of consciousness and level of understanding."

"Yes, yes! And they may not always understand that this *is* Christ."

"Exactly. The Logos of John's Gospel."

"Often there is an anonymous presence of Christ—"

"I like that phrase, 'an anonymous presence of Christ.' "

"Yes. Christ is there. But people do not recognize him. They do not know his name. And this would lead me on to another important text in the New Testament, in Acts, Chapter 17, at Saint Paul's visit to Athens and his speech at the Areopagus. When he speaks to the Athenians he does not begin by saying 'You are in darkness. You are in error. You are going to be damned.' But he starts by commending them for having an altar to the Unknown God. Then he says, 'The One whom you are worshiping in ignorance, he it is that I will declare to you.' In other words he starts from what they already believe in and he affirms it. But then he takes them further. He talks about the presence of God in everyone. 'In him we live and move and have our being,' he says. 'He is not far from us. We are his kinsfolk.'

"Now, these are ideas from Greek philosophy that Paul deliberately uses," Bishop Kallistos continued with a marked excitement in his voice while pointing his finger forward. "But having started from the affirmation that there is a revelation of God in every human heart, Paul then goes on to take a further step. Passing far beyond Greek philosophical notions, he speaks of Jesus Christ and his Resurrection from the dead. Having begun with beliefs shared in common by Christians and non-Christians, he ends up by preaching a message that is distinctively Christian. Such is his missionary strategy. He doesn't start by telling the Athenians that they are all wrong, but he says: 'You are on the right path, yet you need to go further.' I like that."

"That is certainly not the principle many Christian missionaries followed during the last few centuries when they encountered native peoples," I said, alluding to the often disastrous consequences of such contacts when missionaries denounced native religions as diabolical and often tried to convert the "heathens" forcefully.

"Paul's way was different," Bishop Kallistos said, nodding. "He adopted a positive approach. In common then with Saint John and Saint Paul in my thinking about non-Christians, I would start in a positive way. We are all made in the image of God, and that means in the image of Christ. Therefore, there are seeds of the Truth in everyone. But not everyone recognizes

153

the full meaning of this Truth. So I would say Christ is the Truth, and that all Truth is of Christ. But Christ may often be present even when he is not named."

"He is not recognized."

"Yes. He is not recognized. So that is my starting point. But at the same time I also remember how in the book of Acts, Chapter 4, Saint Peter speaks of Salvation 'only in the name of Jesus.' I firmly believe that the Incarnation is unique and that Jesus Christ is the one and only Savior of the world. But Christ may be present in a hidden way, and many people in this life don't actually recognize him."

"You are raising a very important point. If we take the reality of Christ the Logos as the reality beyond culture, beyond time and space, then we cannot limit the Christ Logos to a particular culture at a particular space and time. Therefore, by definition, no one can find salvation outside of the *Christos Logos*. It's like saying the obvious: no one can attain Christ consciousness outside of Christ, or attain God realization outside of God. They are one and the same thing."

"Right."

"But the *Christos Logos* can manifest in a personal way within the context and meaning system of one's culture and individual level of understanding."

"Yes," Bishop Kallistos said softly. "And I believe, then, that those who live in this life by the best that they know will have the chance to meet Christ after death. And when they meet him, then there will come a moment of recognition. They will say, 'Yes, now we understand that you, Christ, do indeed fulfill all that we believed in, only during our life on earth we did not know you for what you truly are.' "

"How would you speak, let us say, to a Hindu or a Buddhist, or a Jew or a Muslim in that context?" I asked. Being a layperson and a nontheologian I felt I had the luxury of going beyond any denominational boundaries.

"Obviously there is a mystery here. It is not for us to say who is saved and who is not saved. God is the one who decides that. And we do not have the right to say of any particular person, that he or she is *not* saved. We do not know. As to *how* people are saved, we know for certain that they can be saved only through Christ, the unique, only-begotten Son of God. But

Christ can act in different ways: sometimes explicit, sometimes hidden. My own belief is that, bowing before this mystery, nonetheless we may say: 'If a Muslim, a Hindu, a Buddhist, a Jew has lived according to the highest and best in their tradition, then in some way they already believe in Christ, because all Truth is from Christ."

"I have many friends who are not Christian," I said. "By what you are suggesting, they do manifest the Christ love that the Gospels speak of. But they are not Christians by any stretch of the imagination."

"Yes. And if you ask them 'Are you Christian?' they will reply, 'Of course not.'"

"You are saying then that such people are *Christian*, as it were, in their inner being, and not Christian in any culturally recognizable way. Rather they manifest Christ as the Logos which is God's love. So persons who express that love are 'Christian' deep down. It is the degree to which humans can express love that determines to what degree they come close to the Christ."

"This is what I believe," Bishop Kallistos stated. "It is my deep conviction that after death everyone is going to meet Christ. And the way they react to him at that meeting will depend on the way they lived their life here on earth. I am not saying that after death we can suddenly make a set of completely new decisions and become completely different people from what we were in this life. But we have to remember that in this life many things are veiled. There is much unfinished business. Death comes as the moment of truth. After death those who did not know Christ at all in this life or who knew something about him but did not know him fully and directly, will have the opportunity to meet him face to face."

"Of course, if what you believe is a spiritual law then it means that it will impact also those who claim to be Christians in this life."

"It will include the Christians, of course!" Bishop Kallistos exclaimed.

"It will include Christians who had no relationship to the *Christos Logos*, who did not know Christ."

"Absolutely. But the opposite could also happen," Bishop Kallistos noted. "Many Christians who in this life thought that they believed in Christ may find, when they meet Christ after death, that he says to them: I do not know you! You are not my servants. You used my name but you were

155

not close to me. So, we cannot say that you will automatically be saved just because you happen to be a member of the Church, and we cannot say that you will automatically be condemned simply because in this life you did not belong to the Church."

Quoting from Saint Augustine, Bishop Kallistos added: " 'There are many wolves inside and many sheep outside.' I understand this question about who is to be saved in terms of the story of the sheep and the goats told by Christ in Matthew, Chapter 25. The sheep, those whom Christ welcomes into his kingdom, did not realize that they had in fact accepted him in his life. When he tells them, 'Come, blessed ones, enter into the joy prepared for you,' they are surprised. They had served Christ through serving their fellow humans, but they themselves weren't aware that all the time they were actually serving and meeting Christ. But then came the moment of truth when they met him, and he said: 'I am the One you were serving all the time.'

"But let us not forget that the goats also were surprised," Bishop Kallistos added in a light tone. "They are the people who think that they are good Christians but when they meet Christ he will tell them: 'You didn't serve me in this life.' So in this way I believe that salvation is only from Christ. But to repeat, there are many people who in this life believe in Christ without knowing that they do so, and there are many people who truly belong to the Church without belonging to it outwardly."

"So there is an inner *Ecclesia* that people may belong to without knowing it. They are unconscious members, so to speak. Hmm . . . How would someone who, let's say, grew up in the Jewish tradition, or in any other religion for that matter, respond to what you just said? How would you talk to the Dalai Lama, for example?"

"Yes, yes! Naturally I would not speak to him the way I have just spoken to you. We speak now as fellow members of the Orthodox Church. But, in speaking to non-Christians, we Christians must take care not to be, as it were, imperialists. It might appear as if we were saying, 'You think you are Buddhists but we know better than you do. You are really Christians.' And that would sound very arrogant. They could legitimately answer, 'Well, we ourselves know better what we believe than you do.' So we must be careful not to speak in such a way as to deny their own integrity.

"How, then, would I begin if I were talking with a Jew or a Hindu or a Buddhist? Like Saint Paul, I would not start with points of disagreement, but would try to discover common ground on the level of the spiritual life."

"I am glad you clarified this," I said with relief. "It's important."

"I would want to understand how they prayed. With what feelings do they stand before God? What is their sense of the sacred, of the numinous, of the transcendent? That is where I would want to begin. Statements about dogma, if they are taken in isolation, and are not understood in the context of prayer, become somehow distorted. Therefore, I would start by trying to appreciate their way of experiencing the divine presence. But I am not saying that Truth is relative. I am not saying that all religions are the same."

"How can one say that?" I agreed. "There are religions like that of the Aztecs with rituals that involved human sacrifices. The high priest himself, with a stone knife, would take out the heart of the sacrificial victim."

"Yes, yes! As a bishop of the Church I believe very firmly that the full Truth is to be found in the Christian Church—to be more precise, in the Orthodox Church. I believe that God became incarnate only once, that Jesus Christ is unique. He is not on the same level as the different incarnations of which the Hindus speak, for example. Jesus Christ is indeed the one and only savior of the world. Yet at the same time there are seeds of the Truth in all the great religions. And we should start from there, not from the differences but from the seeds of Truth which are already present."

I remained silent for a few seconds as I looked at the icons that decorated the church. I was fully cognizant of the fact that Dr. Ware, as he is known at Oxford University, is also an ordained bishop of the Orthodox Church. "I am reminded," I said, "of the world conference on religion that took place in Chicago in 1993, a hundred years after the first one that took place in the same city. There were leading representatives from all the religions and they came up with a very comprehensive, life-affirming statement for a twenty-first-century global ethic. They set up that manifesto on areas of agreement between the different religions. It is a very impressive protocol for ethical behavior. Unfortunately the Orthodox were not represented. Those few—I believe, two—Orthodox representatives who were present walked out of the hall because they felt offended at sitting around

157

a table with representatives from tribal religions. Now, I think this is unfortunate because instead of presenting the position of the Orthodox Church they just ran away from that dialogue, leaving an impression that they were arrogant and racist, a very un-Christian posture indeed. So where do you base your faith? I mean, your assertion that the incarnation of the Logos took place only once in Jesus of Nazareth? What is the foundation of that belief? Let's say that I am not an Orthodox, or even a Christian. What kind of an argument can you offer me that can possibly convince me that you are right?"

"That is certainly not an easy question to answer." Bishop Kallistos paused thoughtfully. "If you ask me first why I personally believe, then I simply reply: I believe because of what I read in the New Testament. The Gospels speak to me with an entire authority that I do not find elsewhere. But there is more to be said than that. Belief is not a solitary thing. Belief is activated within the community. And so I believe through belonging, through membership in the Church, through receiving the sacraments, through Holy Communion. And I believe not so much because of abstract arguments, although sometimes they have their uses, but I believe because of my own experience gained through reading the scriptures and through living and praying within the Orthodox Church."

There was a long pause, then Bishop Kallistos continued. "How would I seek to share that faith with others? Not primarily through arguments. In a way arguments only are helpful when a person is already well on the path of accepting Christianity and then sometimes the arguments, the explanations, will help to remove objections. But I would start with what is said in the first chapter of John's Gospel: 'Come and see.' I would invite people to come to the church to be present at the divine liturgy. My starting point would be that Christ is present in the heart of everyone, that there is a *natural* knowledge of the Truth, part of our human nature, because we are made in God's image. Therefore, when we speak about Christ to others we are not simply speaking to those who have no knowledge of the Truth within themselves. In a sense there is already a spark of the Truth within them, and we are doing no more than to kindle that spark into a flame. When we speak to others we are addressing the hidden, implicit faith that is already in their hearts. So, while I am speaking to them outwardly I would at the same time trust Christ to speak to them inwardly."

"How then do you see your role as a bishop living among the non-Orthodox?"

"Simply as that of a witness. We cannot force people to believe, and we should not try. Belief has to be free, based on liberty of choice. I remember what is said in the Letter to Diognetus, a Christian text of the late first or early second century. 'God persuades. He does not compel, for violence is foreign to him.'"

Bishop Kallistos extended his right hand forward and said in an animated tone, "That is a golden saying. I wish that Christians through the centuries, not excepting the Orthodox Christians, had listened to it."

There was a long pause as I looked over my questions. "Okay," I said after a while, "I think to some degree we have touched upon question number eight." I read that question: "How would you respond to the Bible scholars who question the historical accuracy of the New Testament? Are the saints of all ages in contact with the cosmic Christ, irrespective of the details of the historical facts that took place two thousand years ago? How can we answer that question if we project ourselves a billion years in the future?

"In regard to this question let me raise a possibly heretical *logismos* that came to my mind just now," I rushed to add. "This world will come to an end at some point, a few billion years from now. The *Christos Logos*, however, will not disappear, for according to the teachings of the holy elders he always was, he is, and he will always be. One could then propose to someone from another religious tradition something like this: 'Look, I cannot know on empirical, or scientific, rational grounds what happened two thousand years ago. Nevertheless, I don't have to base my faith completely on the details of the events that took place during that period, events that could be questioned by someone coming from another religion. Bible scholars are caught up in these contradictions as if the whole Christian faith depends on the historical accuracy of the Bible. But if we take a different route, that the New Testament is an overall revelation of divine wisdom and Truth, then it becomes independent of any possible historical contradictions because every saint of the *Ecclesia* manifests and therefore empirically validates the reality of the *Christos Logos* as a state of God realization. And we have seen in the lives of saints individuals who have reached that stage of christification. They think and act in the world in a Christlike way, which leads me to assume that the evolutionary potential of every human being is to be one with the *Christos Logos* and manifest that Christ which is a reality lying dormant within every human being. Therefore, what I am wondering is whether I need to totally ground my faith on the absolute historical accuracy of the events that took place two thousand years ago. Sooner or later this planet is going to disappear, along with all its accumulated and recorded historical memories. Therefore, taking these empirical facts into account, my faith has to be based on something much deeper and timeless, which is the Logos, the light that lightens every human being who comes upon the earth. I am reminded here of what Saint Silouan said, that in the event of a massive global catastrophe like an earthquake where everything will be destroyed, the Gospels can be rewritten when external conditions permit it, for the Gospels, he said, are already written in the hearts of every saint.[2] This is pretty mystical stuff. What do you think about this?"

"Partly I agree with you, though I might not put it exactly in that way," Bishop Kallistos responded and I noticed a certain trepidation in his voice.

"Of course," I pointed out lightly, "my remarks are simply personal reflections."

The Bishop said, "We have to balance and hold in harmony two things: first, the universal revelation of the Logos to every human heart; second, the specific historical revelation through the Logos incarnate, through the life, death, and resurrection of Jesus Christ two thousand years ago. Let's now take up the question of the historical accuracy of the Bible and the place of biblical criticism. God has given us a reasoning brain. And we should use this gift to the full. Therefore, the critical study of the New Testament, using all the resources of scholarship, is something that we Orthodox should approve. We do not serve Christ who is the Truth by simply shutting our ears and eyes and refusing to listen or to look. So there is certainly a place for the critical study of the Bible. We Orthodox may not always agree with the conclusions of the liberal theologians, but we do affirm the principle of free inquiry. Second, we Orthodox in our approach to the Bible are not adopting exactly the viewpoint of Protestant fundamentalists. Like them, we believe that the Bible is true. But we do not isolate each sentence, each word on its own. We look at the total message of the Bible. This has always been the Orthodox principle of scriptural interpretation: that we take the Bible as a whole and we understand one part of the Bible in the light of another. So we don't isolate texts in the way some fundamentalists do. But I would go further than that. We also need to say that there are many ways of expressing truth and that literal truth of a worldly factual type is not the only kind of truth."

"Can you give me an example?"

"For example, when we read the first chapter of Genesis, the point to hold fast to is that this world around us is the creation of God and that it is very good, altogether good and beautiful, *kala lian*. That is what the opening chapter of Genesis is affirming. But we do not have to assume that the seven days of creation each mean twenty-four hours measured in our clock time, and we are not bound to argue that the order in which things emerged in this world is exactly as described in Genesis 1. Genesis 1 is not geology or prehistory. It is religious truth, expressed in narrative form and through pictorial language. There are, then, many different kinds of truth and fundamentalists go astray in assuming that everything has to be taken literally.

"I said just now that we Orthodox interpret scripture as a total unity, understanding each part in the light of the rest. We understand the Old Testament, for example, in the light of the New Testament. We are interested in the Old Testament above all because throughout the Old Testament God is speaking to us everywhere of Christ. The Incarnation is the center of everything. But we should go beyond that and say that the true understanding of scripture comes not just through historical inquiry about biblical origins but through seeing how scripture has been lived and understood in the Church. This is the difficulty of the historical-critical approach, that it isolates the reasoning brain and is carried out in the scholar's study, whereas the true understanding of scripture comes through the total person, and we have many other ways of understanding as well as the reasoning brain. It comes not just through sitting alone in a library, reading books. It comes also, and much more fundamentally, through worship, through sharing the life of the community, through praying together—praying with our understanding but also with our heart, which is something far deeper than just the emotions or the reasoning brain. And so the true understanding of scripture comes through participating in the worshiping life of the Church. The true interpreters of scripture are not so much the learned scholars, though we should listen to them. The true interpreters of scripture are the saints."

"This is exactly what Father Maximos has been saying."

"We will have a much more all-embracing understanding of what scripture is saying if we take into account the lives of the saints. It is the way scripture is lived by the holy men and women through different generations that is our decisive test."

"Right. However, much of contemporary Christianity," I said, "ignores the reality of the saints. Therefore contemporary Christians in the West have no access to that unique source for the validation of spiritual teachings as found in the New Testament. As a result they become literalists. The letter becomes all-important at the expense of the spirit embedded in the writings. This has had a twofold tendency: either people become too rigid and intolerant or too liberal to the point that Christ himself is not the Logos of God but an ethical philosopher. Hence the emphasis among this latter category to turn the *Ecclesia* into a forum of worthy causes for social betterment."

"I agree. There is a tendency to isolate the letter of scripture," Bishop Kallistos said. "But to truly understand scripture we have to understand it liturgically and experientially: through the celebration of the divine liturgy, through participation in the sacraments, through the preaching of the Church, through the lives of its spiritual fathers and mothers. All of these form part of the total richness of the Church. This is the context we have for understanding scripture. We allow full scope to the witness of the saints. Let us remember what was said by a great Serbian bishop Nikolaj Velimirovic, who is already regarded as a saint by the Serbian Church. He said: 'The opinions of the scholars may be marvelously clever and yet they may be completely wrong. Whereas,' he added, 'the words of the saints are often very simple but they are always right.'

"Well, we should not reject scholarship," Bishop Kallistos hastened to add, raising his voice for emphasis. "But as I pointed out, we should recognize that, alongside the use of the reasoning brain, the *dianoia*, the truth is apprehended more profoundly through prayer, through a life of holiness, a life of living compassion. The true understanding of the Bible comes through God's revelation on this level to the heart, to the *nous*, to the spiritual vision, not just to the discursive reason. This is the way whereby we are to find the true meaning of spiritual life."

"I couldn't agree with you more. I would also add that the sheer experience of life itself, paying attention to the world as it unfolds around us with its myriads of spiritual signals that come our way, can help us move step by step in the direction of God. In fact I was thinking along this line today as I was riding on the train and gazing at the English countryside. Science itself doesn't have to be a contradiction to faith as it has come to be viewed but an affirmation of faith in the sense that the aim of science is to acquire knowledge of the empirical world of ordinary consciousness. Anyone who has eyes to see will realize that this observable universe has God's signature all over it, regardless of our religious or cultural background."

"Quite right."

"And therefore," I went on, "through discipline and focus the mind gets trained to search for objective knowledge and truth. And if the ultimate objective Truth is God then science may be a step in the direction of developing that kind of discernment that can lead us to the Truth. Unfortunately, that is not how science has been perceived and how it has functioned in the world. But in the wider scheme of things perhaps it's part of the way Providence works to bring humanity back to God."

"Yes!"

"So I don't see science as contradictory to the aims of religion, properly understood. Though I do read some of those critical Bible scholars, I refuse to give them the final word and the power to define for me the nature of ultimate reality. And I would rather hear what Elder Paisios has to say about God, or some other great elder of the *Ecclesia*."

"Good. We must listen to what scholars and biblical critics have to say. But we must keep in mind that the Church also has its own vision, its own way of understanding. And so what the scholars say has to be submitted to the test of the concrete experience of the Church shown in the lives of its saints. The same applies to science. All truth is from God. Therefore, the

163

honest search for Truth is something we should not be afraid of. We should cultivate it. But scientific inquiry by itself cannot give us the whole Truth."

"We agree on so many points!" I said. It was comforting for me to meet a member of the higher clergy of the Orthodox Church who was also a Western intellectual.

"When science is isolated and is set up as an end in itself it can give a very distorted picture," Bishop Kallistos went on to say. "We believe that in the end it is only through Christ that we can understand the Truth. Science has a highly positive role to play, so long as it acts as a handmaid. But when science considers itself all powerful, when it becomes what we may call not science but scientism, then it can be misleading."

"Yes. In this sense, I think science can become an instrument in stimulating our egotism. It can keep us away from God."

Bishop Kallistos nodded. "Science relies strictly on the evidence of sense perception. But we also have other ways of apprehending Truth, through revelation, through prayer, through the word of God in the heart. So sense perception is not the only source of Truth. And another thing is that we believe the world around us is a fallen world. It is not as God intended it to be. And science, with its reliance upon sense perception, can tell us only about this fallen world. But it is only through revelation that we can learn of the divine plan, which is greater than what we see through our senses."

Conscious of time, I suggested that we move on to the other questions. "Can Orthodoxy speak to the non-Orthodox today? Is Orthodoxy ready for the global village?" I also added the third question: "Can Orthodoxy find common ground with Hindus and Buddhists, without dismissing these spiritual traditions as dangerous heresies?" I looked at my list of questions. "We have touched on number two. Is there anything else to say about it? We were talking about that while having lunch, that the Greek Orthodox Church is not yet ready to accept the global village. I have noticed similar tendencies toward ethnocentrism in the Russian expression of Orthodoxy also."

"Alas, the element of nationalism, of ethnic narrowness, is a fact that we can see very widely in the contemporary Orthodox Church. And it has of course deep historical roots. It is *not only* a problem of today," Bishop Kallistos stressed.

"The patriarch of Constantinople, Bartholomew, and other patriarchs denounced nationalism as a heresy."

"Yes, indeed! 'Phyletism,' setting nationalism above Orthodox catholicity, was defined as a heresy by the Church of Constantinople in 1872. We must keep in mind, however, that there is nothing wrong in itself with nationhood and our loyalty to our own particular people. In fact it is good. Patriotism is a noble feeling. But this feeling of national identity that humans have when they lead a balanced, full life, has to undergo *metanoia*, repentance, a change of mind. It has to be baptized. And very often this repentance, this change of mind, hasn't taken place and we have an untransformed nationalism. So while nationhood is precious and can be a means of grace, we must remember that Christ stands higher than all ethnic differences. 'There is no longer Jew or Greek . . . for you are all one in Christ Jesus,' Saint Paul instructs us [Galatians 3:28]. And we have to emphasize that what matters about the Church is its universality, its catholicity. Nationalism can be a servant but it must not be allowed to become master of our heart. And, as we said, there is a negative narrowness in the kind of intense national feelings that one encounters, yes, in Greece, and in Russia and also among British people, of course. None of us is without sin.

"Actually," Bishop Kallistos continued and rested his back, "I have noticed while visiting Romania that though Romanians are proud of their nation they don't have the hostile, aggressive attitude toward the West and the fear of non-Orthodox churches that I encounter in other Orthodox countries. In Romania I don't hear, or only very occasionally hear, people talking about 'Judeo-Masonic conspiracies' against the Orthodox world. So, in my experience at least, Romanians seem to be more balanced than many other Orthodox in their views about the rest of the world.

"But of course we mustn't generalize," Bishop Kallistos rushed to add. "In Greece, in Russia, there are also people with a wonderful vision of the universality of Orthodoxy, who value and love their native land, their national tradition, Greek or Russian, but who at the same time are universalists; and this is surely what the Western world needs. Not an Orthodoxy that is ethnic but a *Catholic* Orthodoxy. Not an Orthodoxy that is always condemning, but an Orthodoxy that is generous, humble, *kenotic* [self-emptying]. Not compromising, but not attacking the others.

"Speaking for myself," he continued, "as someone who has been the only Orthodox member of the theology faculty here in Oxford, who has taught in a British university for the last thirty-five years, I can testify that people are thirsty and eager to hear about Orthodoxy. But, if we Orthodox simply condemn the West in a sweeping way, they will stop listening to us. They are not interested," Bishop Kallistos stated with passion in his voice. "But if we speak in affirmative language about our vision of the Truth—"

"This is what people are searching for," I exclaimed. "They are searching for an authentic experiential pathway to God. When they hear this kind of negative rhetoric they are put off and turn elsewhere."

"Precisely. And this is tragic. Because this could be the *kairos*, the moment of opportunity for Orthodoxy. But we Orthodox are not ready. We are not Orthodox enough," Bishop Kallistos concluded in a sad tone.

"That's my feeling. I had seen time and again this narrowness of mind and heart among a large number of the higher Orthodox clergy I encountered."

"I can only speak for myself," Bishop Kallistos said. "For me Orthodoxy is the one true Church of Christ, in the sense that it has a fullness of Truth not to be found elsewhere. Yet at the same time I believe that the other Christian communities have parts of the Truth, and they often live out their partial Truth far better than we Orthodox live out our fullness.

"I became Orthodox forty-three years ago," Bishop Kallistos went on. "I have never regretted that. I have always believed I made the right choice and I bless God for calling me, unworthy though I am, to belong to the Orthodox Church. I see that as the best thing that has ever happened to me in my whole life. But it is sometimes quite hard to be Orthodox. What has again and again saddened me is the divisiveness within our Orthodox Church. There is so much rivalry, so much suspicion. People think in terms of Constantinople against Moscow, Moscow against Constantinople, or the ecumenical patriarch against the archbishop of Athens, and so on. And too often we Orthodox allow national particularism, chauvinism, to dominate us. And we don't bear witness to the all-embracing wonder of the Orthodox faith. That pains me profoundly, although it doesn't make me regret that I became Orthodox. At the same time I am sure that I too have many fears and suspicions, that I too am frequently guilty of the very things that I am ascribing to others. Yet truly we do need to rise above our national differences, especially here in the West, so that we may bear witness in Western Europe and in North America to the unity and universality of Orthodoxy in a way that we aren't doing at the moment."

what/who causes for this alienation?

"I think we must integrate the Enlightenment tradition of the West with the inner enlightenment of the holy elders, the patristic tradition," I interjected.

"Yes, yes!"

"Once we bring these two together," I continued, "I believe we will have a more holistic understanding of reality and our purpose in this infinite universe."

"What North America has, which is good, is respect for the freedom of each individual. The Enlightenment tradition of the West has taught us the value of liberty of conscience, the right of people to choose, and the rejection, therefore, of moral violence," Bishop Kallistos added.

"Right!"

"And we Orthodox need to learn this from the West, to respect people's freedom of conscience."

"I wouldn't like to live in a world without the Western Enlightenment. It is a Providential gift. We might still be living in the Dark Ages otherwise."

"Yes!"

"Now, if I had the choice of living, let us say, in the Athens of Socrates and Pericles, in the fifth century before Christ, or in ninth-century Constantinople I would probably have chosen ninth-century Constantinople. In Byzantium I could visit monasteries where, if I searched hard enough, I could find holy elders radiating the love of Christ, something I couldn't do in downtown Periclean Athens even at the zenith of its luster. Having said that, I wouldn't want to live in a world where democracy, openness to new ideas, respect for and acceptance of other traditions were absent. That's why on balance I cast my vote in favor of today's open American society, notwithstanding its monumental problems, rather than for ninth-century Orthodox Constantinople. American society today, and the West in general, embody more than anywhere else the values of the Enlightenment tradition even if on the surface it appears as antireligious."

167

"Yes. After all, Christ is the lord of history," Bishop Kallistos added. "And we are not to say, then, that we reject totally a whole movement, an entire development in human culture, such as the Enlightenment. That does not mean, however, that we necessarily accept it on its own terms."

"Exactly."

"In every great culture and in every intellectual movement there are surely lessons for us to learn. The Greek fathers in the early centuries were conscious of the differences between Christianity and Platonism. But they were willing to use Platonism as an instrument for the expression of the Truth without accepting all its presuppositions. And for us today the world of the Enlightenment is the equivalent of what the world of the Greek philosophers was to the Early Church."

"I like this analogy."

"We must look, then, for signs of the Truth, traces and footprints of the Truth, throughout our modern culture," Bishop Kallistos added.

"Some great philosophers did see that, Hegel for example," I suggested. "They perceived these truths perhaps only partially, and hence the flaws in their systems. But I think a corrective to the external Enlightenment of the West would be its integration and accommodation with the inner Enlightenment of the holy elders."[3]

"We Orthodox, particularly those of us who are Western converts," Bishop Kallistos said, "are often in danger of becoming church mice. We just live inside the church and nibble at the crumbs in the church, but we don't look outside at the presence of Christ in the world as well.

"We Orthodox who live in the West are heirs to the entire cultural and intellectual tradition of the West, much of which indeed is profoundly Christian. We are heirs to Dante, to Shakespeare, to Milton, to Wordsworth," Bishop Kallistos continued passionately. "Of course we have our own Orthodox interpretation of their work. But if we are to play our role as Orthodox in the Western world we must be willing to listen and to learn from the spiritual masters of the Western tradition—yes, even from the world of the Enlightenment. Because this for us, and I speak as a Western convert, this for us is our own cultural heritage. We must not simply reject it and say 'I shall only read Orthodox authors.' Sometimes Orthodox say to me 'Oh, I'm not going to waste my time reading Dante; he wasn't Orthodox,' which is a pity: for, if they did read Dante, they might learn a lot. Well, perhaps some people should just read Orthodox books. But others of us must surely engage in a dialogue with Western culture. Otherwise we are betraying our roles as Orthodox placed here in the West as mediators and witnesses. God did not put me in ninth-century Byzantium. He placed me in twenty-first-century Oxford. There must be a reason for that. Moreover, what is asked of us Orthodox is to listen as well as speak. All too often we carry on an Orthodox monologue. But we need to hear the voice of the other. Somebody said to a friend of mine (my friend is Christian, the person speaking to her was not): 'The trouble with you Christians is you want to give us the answer before you bother to find out what our questions are!'"

I joined Bishop Kallistos in a hearty laugh. Then he continued, "Now, I think we could apply that to Orthodoxy in the modern Western world. Before we give them all the Orthodox answers, which in any case we ourselves know so incompletely, we need to listen to what their questions are. We need to consider where these questions are coming from, what is the meaning of the whole experience of the Renaissance, the Reformation, the Counter-Reformation, the Enlightenment? As a Westerner I should start from where they are."

169

"And be able to share your own understanding, by understanding where they come from," I added.

"That's right."

"Again, speaking for myself," I said, "I cannot give up the Enlightenment tradition. I am myself a product of it and I consider it a spark of the divine in history."

"The Spirit," Bishop Kallistos declared, "is working in all kinds of ways—even in a movement like secular feminism. It's very easy for us Orthodox to be ironical about that, and certainly sometimes within the feminist movement there are some things that are just silly. But we would be very, very much in error to dismiss the movement as a whole. It is a serious movement, there is a real searching there, and the Spirit speaks in the most unexpected places. And so there is something in the feminist movement, even in its more anti-Christian forms, to which we ought to be listening and from which we can learn."

"I couldn't agree with you more. Emily, my wife, will love you for this!"

He is adamant about listening to the voices of others to learn.

I exclaimed. "She finds some of the patriarchal, authoritarian tendencies within Orthodoxy most disturbing.

"Now, in reference to what we said earlier," I continued, "a lot of people may overtly appear antireligious but deep down they may manifest the love and compassion of the Christ Logos, who is inside them after all."

"Indeed!"

"I must confess that I feel a certain discomfort with the tendency of some elders to make this clear-cut division between that which is beyond this world and the world, the 'This-is-worldly-and-therefore-not-spiritual' attitude. I would hope that the Spirit is also working in the world in ways that are not recognized. It has to be that way if we believe in Spirit. I do think that democracy and the open society are a Providential gift and Orthodoxy must come to terms with this fact and not operate with models of authority that belong to a nondemocratic, authoritarian era. There is a cultural gap there."

"I have reservations about modern democracy, but in principle I agree. At the same time, let us never forget that the world we live in is a fallen world. I have already mentioned that. This is not the world as God intended it to be. However, we Orthodox do not think that this world is totally fallen. We do not speak of a total corruption of human nature, as has sometimes been done in the West, in particular by the extreme Calvinists. We accept there is a reality of sin in the world but there is also the presence of God the Holy Spirit. And the Spirit blows where he wills. We cannot restrict the Spirit simply to the walls of the Church. The Spirit is present throughout the created order, everywhere present and filling all things, as we say in the prayer, 'Heavenly King.' And so in this fallen world there is also good. The presence of the Spirit comes in many anonymous forms, and it may even inform the writings of those who see themselves as atheists. We are not to view things simply in terms of black and white."

"Yes," I murmured. I felt an affinity with Bishop Kallistos on these issues.

"We have to allow for the fact that spiritual fathers are directing their advice to particular persons," Bishop Kallistos continued. "Often they see that these persons are not very strong in their faith and must therefore remain rooted in what is firmly Orthodox. It is not for everybody to explore the frontier lands. In such a case, the elder may say, 'Don't read non-Orthodox books. Just concentrate on your own Orthodoxy.' But, we should not turn this into an absolute rule. We need to exercise *diakrisis*, discernment. We cannot make a stark and unqualified contrast, as if everything is light within Christianity, and everything is darkness in the world beyond. Much depends what we mean by 'the world.' Different people have different vocations, and not everyone is called to engage in dialogue with the world of the Enlightenment. But let us not exclude that possibility because there are indeed some who are called to do so. And Christ can be present in the most unexpected places."

"I have just read a couple of books by the Russian philosopher Tatiana Goritschewa," I interjected. "She made some interesting points, that what helped her overcome nihilism and the stifling Soviet mentality was studying the existentialists."

"Yes!"

"Even atheist existentialists like Sartre, who emphasized the freedom of the individual, helped her in the direction of discovering Orthodox spirituality within the world of Soviet oppression. This supports what you just said about the Spirit manifesting in ways that we least expect."

"That is certainly a very good example."

"I would go as far as to say," I continued, "that Marxism could be included in this light."

"Yes."

"It helped us to become conscious of the distortions in our lives that come from gross inequalities."

"Marxism, perhaps," Bishop Kallistos conceded, "but not Leninist-Stalinism."

"Well, that goes without saying."

Bishop Kallistos interrupted me by saying that in a few minutes someone else would be coming to see him. We had already spent almost three hours talking.

"I would like to quickly comment, if I may, on some of your other questions," Bishop Kallistos said. "Let's look at question seven. 'The Pope asked forgiveness for the sins of his Church toward the Orthodox. What is your reaction to this development? Has the Orthodox Church itself committed any errors that should at some point be corrected? If yes, what do you think are some of them?'

"First," Bishop Kallistos answered, "I respect the present pope for his transparent sincerity. As to whether the Orthodox Church itself committed any errors that at some point should be corrected, the answer is a resounding yes! Let us not think that we Orthodox have never done wrong to other people. Let us recognize that we too are fallen and sinful human beings. As members of the Church, we Orthodox have to repent of much that we have done and to ask for pardon. We shouldn't expect this to be simply unilateral. For example, yes, the Crusaders did sack Constantinople in 1204. But it was Byzantines who invited them in. The tragedy happened because there were quarrels and divisions, rivalry and selfish ambition among different claimants to the Byzantine throne. Let us not think that the Crusaders were simply aggressors. That, of course, does not justify the days of pillage and sacrilege that took place at the sack of Constantinople. Yet let us recognize that there were mistakes on our side. For example, long before the disaster of 1204 in 1182 there was a shocking massacre of Western residents in the city of Thessaloniki.

"On other occasions also it has been we Orthodox that have been the persecutors. I think, for example, of the whole story of the Eastern Catholics, or Uniates [Christians living in the Orthodox world who give their allegiance to the pope]. Now it is true that the Greek Catholic churches in Ukraine and elsewhere were established partly through political involvement, and even through the use of force. There were a lot of mistakes committed by those who set up the Greek Catholic churches. Yet there was also much sincere desire for unity and Truth. But what did *we* do? I mean we Orthodox when we were in power? Under the Russian empire of the nineteenth century the Greek Catholics were definitely persecuted, and political pressure was directed at them to become Orthodox. Again in 1945 and in the years following, when Stalin suppressed the Greek Catholics in Ukraine, we Orthodox said nothing. Well, perhaps the Moscow patriarchate couldn't say anything because it was itself under very heavy pressure from the Soviet state. But a great wrong was done to these fellow Christians, the Greek Catholics, in that by means of violence on the part of an atheist government their churches were closed or given to the Orthodox. And we Orthodox just accepted this."

"If for no other reason," I said, "this injustice must be acknowledged at least for the sake of historical truth. Such a public admission could be an antidote to the rise of Orthodox fundamentalism and chauvinism." I found it interesting that the bishop, a Briton who was called Timothy before ordination, used the word *we* to refer to what Byzantines did centuries back.

"Now that Communism has fallen," Bishop Kallistos said, "shouldn't we Orthodox ask pardon from the Eastern Catholics for the immense suffering that was inflicted on them after the Second World War and for the way we Orthodox profited from this? When Communism fell, should we not have taken the initiative in restoring their churches to them? Could there not have been, from the side of both Orthodox and Eastern Catholics, an act of mutual pardon and forgiveness? A great opportunity was lost."

"Such a development would have had a healing effect between Eastern and Western Christianity," I lamented. "After all, collective *metanoia* would be consistent with the teachings of the *Ecclesia* itself. Unfortunately, I don't see much of such an attitude prevailing among Orthodox Christians. The tendency is to view the world from purely Orthodox historical perspectives, from the perspective of a total victim. With such a mindset a dialogue is impossible, not only with other Christians but with people from other religious and cultural traditions."

After a pause I read another question from my list. "Do you think the so-called 'New Age' is a movement to rediscover religion or a movement away from religion? What could Orthodoxy say to New Agers?"

"That is huge and complicated." Bishop Kallistos took a deep breath. "The New Age means so many different things. A great deal that goes by the name 'New Age' is very contrary to Orthodoxy. There is a kind of neopaganism in much of the New Age that we should be deeply suspicious of. But I am unhappy when people make a global denial of the New Age. I say this because in what is called the New Age there *is* a genuine searching for a spiritual meaning in life. Many people are attracted to New Age groups precisely because they are dissatisfied with modern materialism. The institutional churches, including the Orthodox Church, have failed these peo-

173

ple. We have presented Christianity in a way that doesn't interest them. We have made Christianity seem to be nothing more than moralistic teaching; often we say little more than what a sociologist might say. But people don't want to hear from us what they could hear elsewhere, often much better expressed. They don't want to come to church simply to listen to our views about social issues and politics. Often we Christians have failed to bear witness to the transcendent reality of the living God and to the divine kingdom hidden within the heart. At how many Orthodox churches in America, I wonder, do you hear a Sunday sermon about the Jesus Prayer or the sacrament of confession? All too often you hear the kind of things that could be said better by a liberal humanist. So, I think the New Age has behind it a real seeking for spiritual truth that institutional Christianity has failed to satisfy. The movement may have gotten into very dubious side alleys, but there is also a sincere quest that we should not simply dismiss."

"You mentioned the sacraments—"

"Let me see whether these people have arrived," Bishop Kallistos said suddenly. He stood up and walked out of the chapel. After a few minutes of chatting with a couple that had just entered the church, he returned. I suspected that they had an appointment with him for spiritual advice or confession. The bishop was not only an Oxford professor of religion but also a practicing priest offering confession and administering the sacraments, a very unusual combination of roles, indeed!

"About the sacraments," he began and proceeded to read my question aloud, " 'Must we see them as the method of the *Ecclesia* for the attainment of union with God or as the absolute prerequisite for the salvation of all peoples, Orthodox and non-Orthodox alike?' I would make here just one comment. There is a Roman Catholic saying that we Orthodox can also endorse: *Deus non alligatur sacramentis sed nos alligamur*, which can be translated 'God is not bound to the sacraments, but we are.' "

"Meaning?"

"Meaning that God can save whomever he will. He can save people who have never been baptized. We cannot set any limits to the divine freedom. But we, from our human side, have to say, 'I need the sacraments. I cannot do without baptism. I cannot do without Holy Communion.' "

"It can be a help for Christians in their spiritual struggles."

"Well, I would put it a great deal more strongly than that. I would say it is essential and necessary for *me* personally to have the sacraments. But what God does with others is not up to me to decide. So God's action is not restricted to the sacraments, but on my side I cannot afford to neglect them. I would also add, while we are speaking about the sacraments, that I like the Orthodox term for a sacramental action, the word *mysterion*, mystery. Of course a *mysterion* does not mean here an unsolved problem, an enigma. The word *mysterion* suggests that there is so much about the sacraments that we don't understand. They initiate us into a realm which we know as yet very little."

Thinking of the time, I turned to another question. "Is there anything else to add to number nine?"

"Yes," said Bishop Kallistos and he read the question. " 'What is the unique contribution of Orthodox spirituality for the modern seeker not found in other religions?' Let me answer in a personal way, from my own experience."

"I meant to ask you at the end, if you don't mind," I interrupted, "to tell me something of your autobiography."

"Yes. You can read a little about that, on how I became Orthodox, in my recent book, *The Inner Kingdom*."[4]

"I read it some time ago. But I also would like to hear it from you directly."

"Fine. What first attracted me to Orthodoxy was the experience of Orthodox worship. Originally I got to know Orthodoxy not through reading Orthodox books, nor at the beginning through meeting Orthodox people. My first contact was from going to an Orthodox church and being present at the worship."

"Was it in Patmos?" I asked since I remembered how the elder at the monastery there, Father Amphilochios, played a key role in the bishop's spiritual development.

"No. In London."

"In London!"

"Yes. It was the experience of Orthodoxy as a way of liturgical prayer that originally drew me in. Attending an Orthodox service in person for the first time gave me nothing less than a vision of the heavenly kingdom."

"A reenactment of the story of the Prince of Kiev," I mused. It is said that Orthodoxy was adopted by the Russian people in the tenth century, after a delegation from Prince Vladimir of Kiev visited Hagia Sophia (Holy Wisdom), the great church of Constantinople. They reported back to the prince that they were not sure whether they were in heaven or on earth, so enchanted were they with the beauty of the liturgy. It was allegedly because of their report that the prince decided to adopt Orthodoxy as the religion of his kingdom.

"Yes, indeed, indeed! But, of course, in my case it was in a much more humble way. What I felt in Orthodox worship was above all the unity of heaven and earth. I felt the communion of saints, not just as a theoretical belief but as a living reality.

"I felt in the Orthodox service," the bishop continued in a stronger voice, "that we are being taken up into an action far greater than ourselves, that we, the few visible people in the Church, are taking part in an event that is not just cosmic in its dimensions but supracosmic, because it involves the heavenly realm. And this I see as the most precious thing in Orthodoxy—the experience of the communion of saints, mediated to us first and foremost through prayer, during the divine liturgy and the other services. That was how I first came in.

"Then there was a second thing that attracted me deeply when I began to know Orthodoxy better through reading more about it. This was the sense of living tradition. I found in Orthodoxy a continuity with the Apostolic Church, with the Church of the martyrs, of the early fathers, of the ecumenical councils. I felt that the Orthodox Church had a direct and unbroken continuity with this ancient tradition, which indeed was not just ancient but contemporary. Tradition is not just our past, but our present and our future. And so a second thing which drew me in was that within Orthodoxy I found a living tradition, a living and unbroken continuity through early Christianity with Christ himself.

"Then there are two other things that attracted me and that remain particularly important for me: martyrdom and inner prayer. I was very moved back in the 1950s when I read about the suffering of Russian Christians under Communism. This was at the time when Stalin was still in power and the memories of what had happened in the twenties and thir-

176

ties were very vivid. I was deeply moved to learn how women and men of our own time have continued to lay down their lives for Christ. I saw that martyrdom was not something of the past alone but a living reality in the present. I saw Orthodoxy as a Church of martyrs. Later I read about the Turkish period in Greek Christianity and about the *neomartyres*, the new martyrs, and here again I saw that, at a time when Christianity in the West was privileged and powerful, Orthodox Christianity in the Ottoman period was weak in outward resources, was trampled down and oppressed. The new Greek martyrs came from all classes: some were monks and hierarchs, but most were laypeople, cooks, shopkeepers, and barbers. At the same time I noted how in Orthodoxy this cross-bearing goes with an emphasis upon transfiguration and resurrection.

"Along with all this," Bishop Kallistos went on, "along with the liturgy, living tradition, the witness of the martyrs, I was deeply attracted by the Orthodox understanding of inner prayer. I learnt about the Jesus Prayer[5] and then I read the *Philokalia.*[6] I discovered the teaching about the divine light in Saint Symeon the New Theologian and Saint Gregory Palamas. So these were four elements of my conversion. Well, we had better stop now."

I mentioned that I had a few more questions, but Bishop Kallistos smiled and said that since we had run out of time we should perhaps leave them for some other occasion. He then jokingly said that he hoped my tape recorder worked this time, alluding to the fact that in our previous encounter I had some technical problems with the recording.

"I think I am prepared to allow my own name to appear with almost everything I've said. But I will have to think about that!"

"Great," I said, and after we exchanged pleasantries for a reunion in the near future I walked to my hotel, stopping along the way to take in the cultural richness around me. At the same time I tried to digest the rich texture of Bishop Kallistos's responses to my questions. I knew that at some point I would have to return to Oxford for further conversations, particularly on the role of Orthodox spirituality within Western culture.

NINE

CUNNINGNESS

 spent the following year processing the material that I had gathered during my summer visits with Father Maximos and my encounter with Bishop Kallistos. In this effort Emily and my colleague and friend Michael Lewis played, as before, a pivotal role. Our frequent walks through the university woods provided the context for discussing, among many other things, the spiritual lessons I was exposed to. With their help and encouragement my interest and energy to pursue further explorations was nourished and sustained while my understanding of the teachings was sharpened. Yet, I felt that I still needed more contacts with Father

Maximos and further experiences and lessons for a fuller understanding of the Eastern Orthodox spiritual tradition, the *Hagia Paradosis* (Holy Tradition), as it has been known through the centuries in the Greek-speaking Christian East.

I looked forward, therefore, to visiting with Father Maximos once more during my upcoming sabbatical leave, most of which I would spend in Cyprus. In the meantime the tragic events of September 11 were a signal for me to bring my work to fruition as questions of life and death, spirituality, and the meaning of life acquired an urgency among the many people struggling to cope with the aftermath of those horrendous acts.

It was in early January of 2003, right after the celebrations of Epiphany, when I returned to Cyprus. Emily was to join me a few days later after spending some time with her brother in England. We were to stay until summer in Limassol, where I could have easier access to Father Maximos and to the sea. In addition, many of our friends and Emily's relatives lived there. It was in Limassol where the majority of refugees from Famagusta settled after the Turkish invasion in 1974. With a harbor like that of Famagusta, Limassol had a natural attraction for the refugees who resided there, temporarily, as they believed, waiting in vain year after year for a resolution of the Cyprus conflict and the opportunity to return to their own city.

I landed at the Larnaka airport during a critical period for Cyprus and for the world at large. The drums of war were beating again as the Bush administration prepared to invade Iraq, a singularly unpopular prospect for the Cypriots, and most of the world for that matter. The island was only a few hundred miles away from Iraq and hosted two large British bases, a leftover of the colonial past. The bases would be used as a staging ground for an attack on Iraq. The Cypriots felt vulnerable not only in terms of safety but also in terms of financial repercussions. The local economy relied heavily on tourism at a time when Cyprus was preparing to join the European Union. "Tourists," the minister of commerce once said, "are like birds on a tree. The moment they hear noise they fly away."

An index of the magnitude and complexity of the political problem of this small and vulnerable island republic is that it has on its soil six different armies controlled by six different states and military establishments:

the Greek Cypriot National Guard, controlled by the Republic of Cyprus; the Turkish occupation forces and the Turkish Cypriot militia controlled by Turkey; the British army at the two bases controlled by England; a Greek military contingent controlled by Greece; and the United Nations force, made up of soldiers from several nations, dispatched to the island in 1964 with the mandate to keep the fragile peace. Equally depressing is the fact that in a small island half the size of New Jersey there are seven different international airports: two run by the Republic of Cyprus, two by Turkey, two by the British, and one by the United Nations.[1] It is no wonder that the refugees have been waiting thirty years for their return home.

Before moving to Limassol my plans were to stay at Meneou, a village next to Larnaka airport where my sister owned a small summer apartment. At her generous suggestion, I would settle there for a few days to overcome jet lag while waiting for Emily's arrival. Meneou, with its deserted two-mile-long sandy beach, was an ideal place for a person like myself, who enjoys walking, to adjust to the new time zone.

Upon arriving in Meneou, I called my friends Stephanos and Erato. I was pleased to hear that Stephanos was back to his "old self" after recovering from his heart operation. I looked forward to being within walking distance of their home during the following months.

"By the way," Stephanos said to me over the phone, "do you know that today Father Maximos is celebrating his name day? He will be at the bishopric throughout the day welcoming well-wishers."

Forgetting the jet lag, I got into our aging Honda and headed for Limassol. If time and circumstances allowed it, I would catch up on news with Father Maximos. We hadn't met since summer.

Name days carry particular meaning for the Greek Orthodox. It is believed that a person who is named after a saint during his or her baptism will have a special affinity with that saint, who will act like a spiritual guide to that person. This is particularly so for monks and nuns who, at their initiation, are given a new name, that is, a new saint and a new name day.

The custom for both laypeople and monks is to celebrate the saint with special services. According to the Orthodox calendar, every day is the name day of a particular saint or saints who are honored during church services. Their names are recited while major saints are celebrated with special chants composed by recognized and gifted hymnologists. Persons, therefore, who bear the name of a saint keep an open house for well-wishers to honor both the saint and those who bear his or her name. Father Maximos would keep an open house at his bishopric until late in the evening and would welcome individually each well-wisher. If past experience was any guide, I knew that it was going to be an excruciating task for him since he would be required to remain standing in one spot for hours. Like thousands of his parishioners, I too, following tradition, had to wait in line to offer my good wishes.

I reached Limassol within the hour and parked my car close to the bishopric by the sea promenade with the tall palm trees. I then walked for twenty minutes through the narrow streets of the old city until I reached Father Maximos's residence. As I expected, it was crowded with visitors. I had to stand in line for over half an hour before I managed to greet the bishop. What a change since 1991, I mused, when I first met him on Mount Athos as a simple young monk quietly engaging in his spiritual practices with hardly anyone noticing. "Now," he lamented to me once, "I can't even walk down the promenade without people following me and without the newspapers reporting it the next day."

"Let's meet at the monastery on Sunday afternoon," he said, looking at the long queue behind me. "We'll have time to talk there. As you can see, it's impossible to do so today."

"Wonderful," I replied and helped myself to the *kerasma*, the wrapped sweet pastry offered for such occasions. "I'll be there." Every Sunday Father Maximos visited the Panagia monastery, and every Monday morning he traveled from the Panagia monastery, where he would stay overnight, to the monastery of Saint Anna to provide his confessional services to the nuns. Like their brothers at the Panagia monastery, they structured their monastery's activities around his weekly visits. As this detail of Father Maximos's weekly routine crossed my mind, I elbowed my way back to the reception room and asked him whether I could drive him to Saint Anna's on Monday morning so that we could spend a few extra hours together. He signaled to me with an affirmative nod and proceeded to greet the next person in line.

"Mission accomplished," I announced to Lavros triumphantly when I met him outside in the yard. "The 'ambush' approach worked once again." When he learned the details, my retired friend decided to join us at the monastery.

Sunday was cool and cloudy when I set off late in the morning from Meneou heading from the eastern part of the island toward the Panagia monastery up on the Troodos Mountains. I turned the radio on and the weatherman predicted rainfall all over the island for the next two days. That was always good news for Cyprus, which suffered from chronic drought conditions. It was an unusual, pleasant sight for me to see the island exceptionally green. I usually visited Cyprus during the summer months when the predominant color, with the exception of the mountains, was straw yellow reminiscent of Arizona and the deserts of the Southwest. But on that January morning I felt as if I were driving through the Irish countryside. The fields of growing, green wheat under a gray sky made the Cypriot plains an unusually deep, emerald green.

As I drove by the airport next to the Salt Lake, which in years past provided most of the island's salt, I noticed thousands of flamingos. The elegant-looking birds, a tourist attraction, spend the winters by the Salt Lake's shallow waters, feeding on tiny shrimp, before they begin their spring journey back to the northern, cooler climates of continental Europe. Cyprus, my friend Lavros once told me, serves as a resting station for over 120 million birds every year when they make their way from Africa to Europe and from Europe back to Africa. As a leading environmentalist on the island he fought valiantly to protect the feathered creatures from unscrupulous poachers.

At the western bank of the Salt Lake, amidst an oasis of palm and eucalyptus trees, stands the Hala Sultan Tekke, one of Islam's sacred sites, whose minaret extends above the treetops. During the seventh century, as Islam was sweeping across the Middle East, one of Mohammed's aunts, who happened to be visiting the island, fell off her mule and died instantly. When the island was under the control of the Ottoman Turks a mosque was built on the spot where the fateful accident took place. Today it is a tourist attraction and a place of pilgrimage for devout Muslims.

Only four miles to the east of the Hala Sultan Tekke, at the very center of Larnaka, lay the final burial ground of Lazarus. According to the legend, after he was resurrected by Christ, Lazarus found refuge in Cyprus. The ancient church that stands over the grave of Lazarus was built by a devout Russian nobleman and, very much like the Tekke, it serves both as a tourist destination and as a place of pilgrimage for devout Christians.

Heading west toward the Troodos Mountains in an almost straight line from the Tekke and the church of Saint Lazarus I passed under the shadow of Stavrovouni, the Mount of the Cross. During the fourth century, Saint Helena, mother of Emperor Constantine, built a monastery there upon her return voyage from the Holy Land. As a gift she left behind a piece of the Holy Cross, which to this day forms the center of veneration both for pilgrims and for the thirty or so monks who live there. Stavrovouni was the monastery that nurtured Father Maximos's love for the monastic life during his youth.

As I turned the radio on to hear news of the gathering storm in the Middle East, I suddenly realized that Mohammed's aunt lay buried between these two important Christian sites. I sighed as I pondered the long and tragic history of the island, fatefully situated at the fault lines between Christianity and Islam.

It was two in the afternoon when I arrived at the Panagia monastery. Silence and a sense of serenity prevailed. On Sundays hundreds of visitors would arrive and spend the day there, particularly during the hot summer months. But the influx of pilgrims in the heart of the winter was substantially reduced. Most of those who had braved the weather had already left and the monks had retreated to their cells for their scheduled afternoon rest. Only Father Joseph, the young monk in charge of the *archondariki*, the guest room, was up and about. Father Maximos, he informed me, had arrived an hour earlier and was resting. Father Joseph assigned me to a cell next to Father Maximos. It happened to be the same cell that was assigned to me when I carried out my earlier field research in 1997.

While handing me the key, Father Joseph mentioned in passing that there was soon going to be a *synaxis*, a gathering of all the monks. Father Maximos was to deliver an informal talk to them. I hoped that for the first time I would be able to attend a lecture given by Father Maximos to the

183

monks under his supervision. I had heard him speak to lay audiences many times before but never to monks. Perhaps, I thought, this is why Father Maximos asked me to join him at the monastery.

I placed my tape recorder in my handbag along with a notebook and waited. Father Joseph had promised that he would check with Father Maximos about my possibly joining the *synaxis*. Within the hour he knocked at my cell and I got ready to follow him.

"Sorry," he said apologetically. "There are several laypeople at the monastery and Father Maximos feels that in order to avoid any hurt feelings and misunderstandings on the part of the others no layperson can attend this particular lecture. It is strictly for the monks."

Hiding my disappointment, I said I understood and resigned myself to spend the time in my room reading. "Oh, by the way," Father Joseph said in passing while stepping outside, "Father Maximos asked me to let you know that he is going to have a special gathering for lay visitors right after his talk with us. He will meet you at the *archondariki*."

"Great!" I said. Bearing that in mind modified my feeling of being left out when I overheard periodic outbursts of laughter coming from the large room next door where the *synaxis* was taking place. I never found out what father Maximos told his monks that generated so much hilarity.

"They are all at the *archondariki*," Father Joseph informed me a little after eight when most of the other monks had already retired to their cells for the night. "The elder will begin the discussion in a few minutes. Your friends Lavros and Antonis have just arrived and have been asking about you. They are with Father Maximos."

I thanked Father Joseph again for the information and headed straight to the *archondariki*. I had made prior arrangements not only with Lavros but also with Antonis to be at the Panagia monastery on Sunday and even stay overnight in the hope that we would have some good discussions with Father Maximos. Apparently our plan was going to work. Father Maximos intended to offer us a lesson on certain aspects of Orthodox spirituality, an inexhaustible subject, as I had come to realize. I had no idea what the topic was going to be. The modus operandi of Father Maximos was primarily to surrender his mind to inner inspiration and to the discretion of the Holy Spirit after a prayer. He felt that that was the approach which worked the best for him. An academic theologian, he once told me, had criticized him for being too casual about his presentations, which the theologian found lacking in order and rigor.

"He was, of course, right," Father Maximos said and grinned. "I tried once to follow his advice and prepare ahead of time. I had everything written down. It was a disaster! Ever since that time I just surrender to the Holy Spirit for guidance. That way I have no anxiety as I enter a room to give a talk."

For the evening gathering, the Holy Spirit led Father Maximos to a seminar-like discussion centering on a part of the work of Saint John Climacus (also known as Saint John of Sinai), considered to be one of the most important spiritual texts of Eastern Orthodoxy.[2] It was written by Saint John during the seventh century, when he was abbot of Saint Catherine's monastery. This fourth-century institution was built at the foothills of Mount Sinai, in the heart of the desert.

I later learned that, along with the Holy Spirit, my friend Lavros had also played an important role in choosing the subject of our discussion. He had struggled with the ancient text after having visited the monastery a few months earlier. Lavros told me that his late wife, Maroulla, had felt throughout her life a special affinity with Saint Catherine. In fact she even died the day that the church commemorates the saint. For this reason Lavros vowed to visit the monastery often in honor of his late wife.

"Perhaps tonight we could explore the way the holy elders view the problem of *ponyria*, or cunningness, as an obstacle to our divine ascent toward God," Father Maximos began, after welcoming me with a gesture into the group of seven pilgrims that included my friends Lavros and Antonis. "More specifically, I would like us to examine the way Saint John Climacus addresses this issue.

"In his twenty-fourth homily," he continued as he put on his glasses and opened the ancient Greek text, "Saint John elaborates on the nature of equanimity and simplicity. Within that homily he also addresses the problem of cunningness. He points out that before we look at that issue we must always remember that God created human beings in his own image and that in their very essence they are simple and uncomplicated."

"Naturally," Lavros interjected with a grin, "this does not imply that human beings are naïve or unintelligent in their very essence."

185

"What is meant by simplicity," Father Maximos replied, "is that the individual's powers, whether they be physical, intellectual, or emotional, form a unified whole." He removed his glasses. "As we have said before, the aim of life is the transcendence of our lower passions and the reunification and reintegration of all our powers into this unified whole. The Fall shattered this original unified state that was given to us by God, causing our primordial existential illness. Our after-the-Fall state is characterized by confusion, the pursuit of contradictory and mutually exclusive goals. Our desires are harmful and go contrary to God's laws. We relentlessly fight in an effort to impose our own will upon our fellow human beings, causing havoc for ourselves and for them. We want one thing and we do another. We love certain things but we act in ways that undermine that which we love. In short there is chaos within our very being."

"I assume," Lavros said, "that the cunning individual is he who moves within this complexity of confusion that appears to be the very symptom of the Fall."

"This is what Saint John tells us. However, in addition to the confusion and complexity inherent in the fallen state itself, the cunning person contributes even further to this complexity and confusion. It's as if we have a piece of cloth that is a unified whole and then we pull up each thread one at a time and transform that piece of cloth into a bundle of disjointed threads. That's the complex individual, a bundle of disjointed threads. His psyche is in constant turmoil and confusion. Keep also in mind the fact that we are encouraged to be cunning by the environment within which we live. I remember the case of a boy who gave money to a beggar and his mother reprimanded him, charging that the beggar was a devious impostor. The outcome of her intervention was to turn her own child into a cunning and calculating person by implanting in his mind cunning *logismoi*."

"To be a cunning person is considered a virtue," I interjected. "World literature and popular culture is filled with images of the cunning individual as an admirable hero. We admire the exploits of Odysseus, 'the man with the many skills,' and we try to imitate his cleverness and enterprising spirit."

"We are told to protect ourselves from the cunningness of others by becoming cunning ourselves," Antonis added. He routinely complained that the business world within which he found himself was undermining his spiritual life.

"The saints were not naive people, you know," Father Maximos said. "They were intelligent and clever human beings, but their cleverness was free of egotism. This is the difference. In fact they were the cleverest people on earth because they were never deceived by the allurement of this world. They did not pursue chimerical objectives like ordinary human beings, who suffer from cunningness, do.

Father Maximos paused briefly when Father Arsenios, the current abbot of the Panagia monastery, joined us. "Saint John incorporates his homily on cunningness within the homily of equanimity and simplicity in order to show that a person who has a propensity to be angry and to create turmoil around him cannot be simple."

"In what way?" I asked.

"Anger is a child of egotism and egotism is the source of all evil." Father Maximos went on to read another homily from Saint John's ancient text. "A cunning person makes false conjectures and projections and fantasizes that he understands the thoughts of others on the basis of what they say. He claims to understand the secrets of their hearts from their external actions. So the cunning person is he who makes false assumptions and projections. He imagines things will happen that can never happen."

Father Maximos paused and placed Saint John's work on the table next to him. "Someone came to my office the other day and said that he heard rumors that our bishopric would sell a plot of land so that I could use the money to become archbishop. Look how people think!" Father Maximos spread out his arms as the rest of us laughed. "Instead of seeing that the bishopric needs the money to pay the many debts that we inherited, instead of showing understanding and sympathy that we are forced to resort to that sale, he presumed unseemly motives on our part. He ignored the financial burden of charities that the bishopric is daily engaged in and he fantasized that somehow I will use that money to gain favors and be elected as the new archbishop.

"All I know," Father Maximos said with a sigh, "is that I am not spending money in order to become archbishop. These are the false projections that Saint John speaks of in reference to the cunning individual who dis-

187

torts reality and spreads falsehoods. This is the nature of cunningness, an integral part of the fallen state of human nature. When people notice that John the Baptist refrains from both food and water while living in the desert, they assume that he is possessed by demons. Down goes the Precursor!" Father Maximos chuckled. "Then Christ appears and moves about among the people, eating and drinking, and some point their fingers at him, saying that a man who eats and drinks wine like that cannot be a man of God."

"Perhaps that's why Jesus called the human race 'the cunning generation,'" Lavros said.

"Quite true. By 'generation' of course he meant the after-the-Fall state of humanity," Father Maximos explained.

"One can say that cunningness is the state that leads to war, not only among individuals but also among nations," I added. "War often breaks out because of a lack of clear understanding of other people's intentions."

"Again, this is part of our nature due to the Fall. That's why great effort and struggle is needed to overcome our predicament, to overcome our cunningness, our tendency to misread other people's intentions and words."

"I have always felt," I said, "that an essential part of our spiritual development is the capacity to perceive reality clearly, without prejudice. That's why I believe that the inner purpose of science, a science broadly understood, is actually a spiritual enterprise. It is part of the training of the soul to overcome confusion and ignorance."

Father Maximos made no comment to my speculation. He just smiled and went on. "Let me give you another example. The other day I met with some pious people and as is the custom they greeted me by kissing my hand. At a certain point while someone kissed my hand I unthinkingly murmured something that we customarily say on Mount Athos under such circumstances. I said to her 'May God forgive you.' I didn't realize at that moment that such a phrase has a different meaning outside Mount Athos. She spent her entire day crying in the belief that I somehow thought of her as a common woman who needed God's forgiveness. Poor woman, I just uttered a simple blessing!

"Another time," Father Maximos continued and shook his head, "I was offering communion at the monastery and as is the custom I mentioned the name for each person who came for communion. We say, 'The servant of God so and so receives the Body and Blood of Christ for life everlasting.' In the case of this particular individual, I just forgot to mention his name. He was terribly upset and he later complained that as far as I was concerned he was just a nameless nobody. He was tormented because I forgot to mention his name and assumed that I thought he did not deserve to have his name mentioned. These types of insecurities are symptoms of cunningness, symptoms of the Fall."

"Imagine being married to such a person," Lavros blurted out.

"It would be hell. This is what I hear in confessions day in and day out. Married couples misread each other's intentions all the time. Several years ago a man committed suicide because he believed his wife was cheating on him. He left behind a note that life was meaningless for him and jumped from his twelfth-floor apartment. The tragedy was that his poor wife was totally innocent."

Father Maximos sighed and then proceeded to read another passage from the homilies of Saint John. "They [the cunning persons] try on the basis of external signs to presume to know the secrets of people's hearts." He then proceeded to comment on what he had just read. "I hear people say 'Such a person dislikes me.' And I ask 'How do you know?' 'From the expression of her face,' is a typical answer.

"You know," Father Maximos continued, "when the devil realizes that you are predisposed to think this way he will create the right circumstances that will bring about that which you believe."

"After all, he is the epitome of cunningness," Antonis mused.

"There is an axiom in sociology," I mentioned, "which stipulates that when things are defined as real they become real in their consequences. Therefore, even an originally false definition of reality tends to become a self-fulfilling prophecy. Of course sociologists do not attribute this human weakness to the devil."

"Well, it is nice to know that the way the devil works and the way sociologists see things converge," Father Maximos quipped. "Let me give you another example from personal experience. While I was at Mount Athos, there was this brother who believed that I somehow disliked him. Of course it was totally untrue. He never externalized his feelings and showed

189

no signs that he felt that way. But things unfolded in such a way that everything confirmed his entrenched belief. One day, I was casually chatting with some other brothers in the central yard of the monastery. For some time during our chat I had wished to withdraw to my cell but I was still waiting for an opportune moment to leave the group. However, the conversation had proceeded in such a way that it was difficult for me to disentangle myself. At some point this brother joined us and there was a brief interruption in our conversation. I sensed it was the right moment that I was looking for. I mentioned hurriedly that I had work to do and left. Alas, this brother assumed that my action was further proof of my dislike for him. Things got worse when during the next day I had to walk to another monastery for some errands. He asked me whether he could come along and give me a hand. Not wishing to unnecessarily burden him I thanked him and mentioned that I really did not need any help. On the way I met another brother. He asked me where I was heading. It so happened that he also was going to the same destination for some errands of his own and so we walked together. This innocuous development was a further confirmation for the other brother that I indeed disliked him. Naturally, the problem was within his own mind. External events confirmed time and again his false beliefs about our relationship and my attitude toward him. The devil brought things together with such admirable precision that it added one problem on top of the other. Things were getting from bad to worse.

"At last, he could not bear it any longer. He was so overwhelmed by *logismoi* of rejection that he gathered his courage and one day spilled it all out and told me exactly how he felt. Of course, I was taken by surprise. I had absolutely no clue that such thoughts went through his mind. So we cleared up the misunderstanding and I apologized profusely for my oversight and insensitivity.

"Now, do you see what Saint John meant when he said that the cunning individual draws conclusions and judges people about their intentions by focusing on their external behaviors and actions? This is what he meant by cunningness. I always tell people that when the devil recognizes such a predisposition in us he will match everything: the words, the gestures, the external actions, so that he will prove to us each time that things are the way we assume they are."

"Cunningness is a form of *plani*," Lavros murmured.

"Yes. It is totally a state of *plani*, or delusion," Father Maximos said. "Cunningness, Saint John says, is a demonic science, or better, the ugliness of demons. Although they are bereft of truth they hide this fact and deceive many.

"Elder Paisios used to tell us time and again that we must learn to entertain only good *logismoi* in our minds. It is a form of protection against the manipulations of demons. It is really emotionally draining to relate with cunning and complicated persons and be able to have a mutual understanding with them. They distort everything in their mind."

"What is the solution to this problem?" I asked. "I mean how do we resolve this difficulty of communicating with cunning persons? It's a major problem that we all face constantly in our personal, social, and political life."

"Pray. That's the only thing you can do. Let God handle such a problem," Father Maximos replied and moved on. "Further down in his homilies, Saint John repeats that cunningness entails thoughts of *plani*, of delusion. You believe rigidly in your own opinion, without any trace of humility. It is the syndrome of 'I say so. Therefore it is true.' The elders teach that the persons who suffer from *plani* believe in their own *logismoi*. Nothing can lead them to change their opinion, no matter what you tell them. You cannot have a dialogue with such people.

"The cunning heart, says Saint John, is like the depths of the sea. Impossible, in his time, to get there. Furthermore, within the heart of the cunning individual there are terrible and complicated alterations that no one can disentangle, not even the person himself. Elder Paisios used to say that some persons are so cunning that they could offer lessons to the devil himself. It is terrible to contemplate where the mind can take a person if he is not vigilant.

" 'It is an abyss of duplicity,' " Father Maximos read further. "I have known people who admire their own capacity to deceive. They are so accustomed to telling lies that they forget what is true and what is false. In fact they have to exert themselves to remember what the truth is. Such persons come to believe their own lies."

"This is a great hazard in the careers of politicians," I said and I saw

191

many heads nod. I was certain that they all had in mind the current campaign for the Cyprus presidency. I had in mind the brewing war in the Middle East.

Father Maximos read another homily. " 'Cunningness is a malady that came to be considered as normal.' People suffering from this malady are not necessarily aware that they have such a problem. They are unlike the persons who pray to God and say, 'God have mercy on me. I am egotistical, I am stubborn, I have this malady, this illness.' No, persons who are not aware of their problem consider it natural. People in that state of mind cannot get healed from their problem. Healing will begin when a person realizes that he has a problem in the first place.

" 'Cunningness is an enemy of humility,' " Father Maximos added in reference to another extract from the work of Saint John. The humble individual is ready and willing to listen to others and hear their advice. Even great saints who became witnesses to revealed truth that descended directly from God sought the advice of others because they did not rely exclusively on their own perceptions."

"Who do you have in mind, Father Maxime?" Antonis asked.

"Saint Paul is always a good example. He experienced Christ on the road to Damascus and the entire Gospel was later revealed to him during his years in the desert. So Paul learned the Gospel without anyone teaching him other than Christ himself, whom he never met in person. In spite of that fact, Paul, who was the vehicle of God's choice, mentions in one of his epistles that he traveled to Jerusalem to find Peter in order to discuss his experiences with him just in case he was mistaken. Just imagine," Father Maximos marveled. "Paul had a direct contact with God and yet he placed a question mark about his spiritual experiences and actions lest he be deluding himself."

"Why did Paul need advice, Father Maxime?" one of the other pilgrims asked.

"Because he was humble, that's why. The humble person always seeks a dialogue and is not rigidly trapped in his own opinions and ways of thinking. He leaves space for a conversation with others. He is always ready to listen. The humble person does not believe blindly in his own *logismoi*. He always places a question mark at the end of his thought and seeks the advice of others."

"This is a problem that we witness both in our public as well as in our personal lives," Lavros suggested. "I mean this absolute certainty in one's opinions."

"I see this attitude during confessions all the time. Most of the problems in marital relations are caused by people's incapacity to engage in a dialogue. Many people are rigidly stuck in their beliefs and opinions because they lack humility. The proud, cunning individual cannot retreat from his own views and ways of seeing things and lacks a capacity to be lenient to the possible mistakes of others. Being tough and unrepentant, such a person cannot live with another human being. It is impossible."

"How is that so, Father Maxime?" a young man asked whose wedding was to take place in Limassol the following Sunday.

"Because love is a child of humility in the same way that anger and evil are children of egotism. To be able to love the other person implies humility and readiness to retreat from your position and make concessions in the event of possible disputes and conflict. The proud, rigid, and cunning person cannot do that. Therefore, living with others becomes very difficult." Father Maximos went on to read from Saint John's text: " 'Cunningness is hypocritical *metanoia* [radical change of heart and mind accompanied with humility].' "

Father Maximos looked up from the text. "The cunning individual may pretend to repent, he may say 'sorry' to another person, but deep down he is unrepentant. Inside his heart and mind there is no trace of *metanoia* and he continues to rigidly hold on to his position. You cannot build a bond of love under such conditions. Many people who come for confession, instead of being critics to themselves, try to convince me that the other person bears all the responsibility for their troubled relationships and try to find rationalizations for their own actions."

"Then it's a pointless form of confession," I noted.

"Of course! Hypocritical *metanoia* is to ask for forgiveness from another person without feeling or meaning it. You do so for practical reasons, such as when it is not in your interest to be in conflict with the other person.

" 'Cunningness means distance from mourning,' " Father Maximos went on as he read another homily of Saint John's. "When you do not truly repent," he explained, "and you always find excuses for your actions then there is no chance that you will mourn and shed tears for your sins. The person who sheds tears for his sins is a person who takes full responsibility for his actions. Cunningness is the enemy of true confession, says Saint John. It distorts everything within the individual, who finds no reason for confession, displacing the need for such action onto others. The cunning individual always justifies himself. Saint John goes on to say that cunningness is the cause of carnal sins. He claims that cunningness is a child of pride and pride is mother to debauchery."

"How are the two related?" I asked.

"You must remember that Saint John wrote his homilies for his fellow monks. So, cunningness and pride are related because the proud individual is abandoned by God, so to speak, and is demolished. On the other hand, the humble individual is protected and covered by the grace of God. Even if the humble person succumbs to personal weaknesses, he will not be crushed. When he falls he stands up and with humility asks for God's forgiveness and God will cover him with his grace. The proud person falls apart when he falls. He becomes a thousand pieces. He cannot accept the comfort of *metanoia* given by divine grace. Why? Because pride is incompatible with grace. The two don't mix. Somewhere in the text Saint John says that God opposes the proud. Imagine how terrible this must be, to have God not only withholding his blessing for your actions but having him as your opponent! God becomes your enemy, so to speak. At this point your only alternative is to be demolished. That is why cunningness is the cause of carnal infractions. The cunning individual gets crushed, always of course within the context of God's philanthropy.

"You see," Father Maximos continued, "the cunning heart cannot be healed until it is broken. It requires demolition. It is not amenable to any medicine. It is not like an illness which can be taken care of by, let's say, some antibiotics. No. It needs to be crushed, to be split into a thousand pieces and then reassembled from the beginning."

"How does the heart get crushed, Father Maxime?" one of the pilgrims asked. "It rings like a paradoxical statement."

"As I said time and again the heart is crushed through the many tribulations, sorrows, failures, humiliations, and so on that a human being goes through. The heart can then get broken in a way that may potentially lead to one's salvation. That can happen when the individual, at that point of the demolition of his proud heart, undergoes deep *metanoia* and uses those painful experiences to his spiritual advantage. Under such circumstances, the demolition of the heart becomes a cause for one's salvation. If not, the individual runs the risk of ultimate destruction in terms of body and soul.

"Cunningness itself is an obstacle to those who have fallen," Father Maximos went on after pausing for a few seconds. "Those who have fallen, who are under the spell of cunningness, do not believe that they have fallen. Therefore, they do not have the motivation to raise themselves up. Before you can take action to overcome your problem you must first accept that you have a problem. Saint John goes on to say that the cunning individual reacts to others' curses and attacks with a smile and a false aura of serenity. His aim is to show that he is not affected by whatever the other person is doing. But inside his heart he is boiling and is already plotting his revenge. Saint John further writes that cunningness is 'meaningless, mindless, and unnatural toughness combined with a false sense of devoutness.' And he ends his homilies on cunningness by saying that it is 'a life similar to that of the demons.' "

"That's a very harsh conclusion," Lavros said.

"Well, Christ said it in the Lord's Prayer: *'alla resai emas apo tou ponyrou'* . . . 'and lead us not into temptation' [*ponyros* in Greek means the cunning person]. He meant the devil, the archetype and archangel of cunningness. Therefore, the person who has embraced cunningness as a way of life is akin to the demons. Everything inside him is diabolically altered."

"After all, the word *diavolos* [demon] in Greek literally means he who distorts the truth," Lavros pointed out.

"Exactly. He is the one who distorts God's work as in the example of Genesis. The devil distorted God's words by marshaling his own cunningness."

"Father Maxime, how can we overcome cunningness" asked Mikis, a

195

thirty-year-old lawyer who was flirting with the thought of joining the monastery. "As a lawyer, I am expected to be cunning."

"No wonder I don't know of any lawyer who became a saint," Father Maximos said and the rest of us burst into laughter. "Well, the holy elders, as good spiritual physicians, set down the principles that could help us overcome cunningness. First and foremost, we must bear in mind that it is the Holy Spirit that will help us overcome cunningness and work out our salvation. Of course this is possible only with our full and unfettered cooperation. We cannot be saved unless we fervently and freely wish to be saved. This is an axiom.

"For the cure of this particular ailment of cunningness," Father Maximos went on, "it helps immensely to come in contact with a spiritual physician who is freed from this primordial distortion of our nature. Then through frequent contacts with him we confess openly and honestly and begin to take upon ourselves full responsibility for our predicament without self-justification and rationalizations. A person will have to learn not to look for scapegoats when faced with difficulties but to accept the full burden of responsibility."

"This is extremely difficult for us both individually and collectively," I said. "For example, we blame foreign powers all the time for problems we ourselves have created."

"But what if you are not really responsible for a certain situation? What if you are really innocent?" Mikis asked.

"It's important to maintain such an attitude anyway as a form of spiritual exercise," Father Maximos advised. "This is the way of the saints. Saint Nektarios was persecuted by the ecclesiastical hierarchy of his time and lived until the end of his life in a state of dishonor after being falsely accused of having sexual relations with nuns. Yet he refused to defend himself and clear his name." Father Maximos paused for a few seconds. "I will never forget what Elder Paisios told a visiting priest one day. 'Father,' he said, 'the times when I experienced most intensely the visitations of grace were during periods when I was treated unjustly.'

"Of course," Father Maximos, reading our thoughts, added, "you should employ such a self-critical method of spiritual practice up to the point where you are able to withstand it. That's when you will truly begin to work on yourself. You move away from the point of self-justification that tries to absolve you from a sense of guilt and instead fearlessly begin to take full responsibility for your life."

Father Maximos suddenly laughed. "I was offering communion to an old man during Eucharist when disaster broke loose. He lost his step and spilled it on the ground. I was horrified, but it was done and I could do nothing about it. So I went to Papa Charalambos, one of the elders, for confession. I told him what happened. 'Oh,' he said, 'you are responsible.' 'But how, why?' I protested. 'It was the other fellow who spilled it.' 'But for you to be there at that point in time means that you are responsible in some way. It is not accidental. You must have done something for the creation of the circumstances that caused the accident.' 'Well, what must I do now?' I asked him. 'Five thousand prostrations for you and five thousand for the other fellow,' he replied. 'Since we cannot find him, you will have to do them on his behalf.' I had to do ten thousand prostrations! Now why did Papa Charalambos, who was a simple old man but a great elder, say that? Because he wanted to give me a lesson that whatever happens to us is not accidental. *Metanoia* means never looking for personal excuses. The moment you are into excuses and self-justifications you are not into *metanoia*. The two are like fire and water. They don't mix.

"So a key point that the holy elders stress in order to overcome cunningness is to never put blame on others for whatever grief or pain you go through. Always remind yourself that you are not totally innocent of the seemingly bad things that happen to you. A judge in court may find you innocent and absolve you of any responsibility for whatever happened. But spiritual laws do not work out that way. On principle we must assume that we contributed to whatever happened to us. It is spiritually safer to maintain such an attitude. The moment I assume responsibility, I have entered the process of *metanoia* and humility. At that moment there emerges a radical alteration in the way I relate to my fellow human beings. When I approach another person with whom I have differences I do not go to him with the intention of judging or correcting him. I approach the other instead with the goal of judging and correcting myself. I go there in order not to vindicate myself but in order to find out in what way I hurt the other person. That's the only way to have a real interaction, a real dialogue. The moment you ignore your own responsibility and go to the other person in order to correct his or her mistakes you have already created the circumstances for the emergence of a quarrel and a vicious circle of mutual incriminations. We must move away from an absolute belief that our own *logismoi* are correct.

"That's how one can begin to overcome cunningness," Father Maximos continued. "Then with prayer, mourning, *metanoia*, and the spiritual methodology offered by the *Ecclesia*, our heart and mind will gradually get cleansed and we will begin the return journey to our primordial simplicity and integrity, the way God created us. This is the meaning of Jesus' words when he said that if we wish to inherit the kingdom of heaven we must become like children. In time this practice will give birth within our soul to a sense of spiritual mourning which will gradually develop into what the holy elders call 'joyous mourning.'"

"Joyous mourning?" I asked. Father Maximos assumed that we knew the meaning of his paradoxical statements.

"After this self-criticism or self-loathing there emerges a feeling within us that we have caused grief within the very heart of God and that we have distanced ourselves from him. We then realize that we carry the seeds of evil and cunningness within the depths of our being and become conscious of this fundamental distortion of our nature that God originally created to perfection. We gradually begin to mourn and shed tears for our predicament. This existential form of mourning is accompanied by tears. The elders say that it is these tears that are needed for the cleansing of the human soul. It is like taking a spiritual bath. When a person, through his spiritual struggle, begins to mourn and shed tears from the realization of the apostasy of his soul from God, then his soul becomes increasingly softer and mellower. As a first step, he repudiates this evil distortion. This is followed by visitations from grace that begin to work more systematically within him in a way that reconstructs his existence. Then a human being reaches the point from which he started, the point of his original simplicity. All his powers are now reintegrated around one single movement, a movement that points directly toward God. Any trace of cunningness is erased from his soul and the person reaches a state of blessedness.

"Self-criticism, self-abnegation, confession, and spiritual mourning are transformed for the spiritual person into ceaseless and intense prayer and an agonizing invocation of God's mercy. Do you remember Saint Seraphim of Sarov who for three years shed bitter tears on a rock in that forbidding Russian land, imploring God's mercy for his sinful nature? That's the way of the saints."

"Why this state of agony, Father Maxime?" Mikis asked softly.

"All the saints have gone though this dramatic and agonizing search for God's mercy because they become conscious of the distance that separates them from God. They understand the meaning and the horror of this estrangement. They have noticed where God is and they have seen where they are themselves. Their prayer is like fire that cleanses them and brings them face to face with God. For such a person everything then works perfectly. As Saint Paul said, *ta panta kathara tois katharies*, everything is clean for those that are clean. Nothing is done that displeases the holy spirit of God.

"That is how one gets freed from cunningness," Father Maximos said, concluding his long, spirited monologue, and leaned back on his chair to rest his back. "For us all these processes take place within the parameters of the *Ecclesia* and under the supervision of an experienced spiritual physician."

It was nine thirty in the evening when we dispersed, very late for the monastic time schedule. The *symantron*, with its penetrating metallic sound, would begin to ring at three, waking everybody up. But Lavros and Antonis joined me in my room for an additional hour of further exchanges related to the issues Father Maximos raised during his impromptu lesson.

199

TEN

PRAYER POWER

 sat on the balcony of our apartment in Limassol, enjoying the warmth of the morning sun, taking notes and looking upon the blue expanse of the Mediterranean. The sea was calm, sparkling with intense luminosity, and the temperature neared seventy degrees Fahrenheit, a far cry from the February weather of Maine.

A month had passed since Emily joined me on the island to pursue her work related to peace and environmental issues; it was already the last day of February and the almond trees were in full bloom. My work with Father Maximos was moving along at a steady pace amidst far-reaching political changes on the island. The European Union had accepted Cyprus for full membership by May 1, 2004, a turning point in the troubled history of the island and a cause of massive outbursts of local exuberance.

Due to these developments there were urgent and intense efforts by the United Nations and the Europeans to resolve the Cyprus problem so that by May of 2004 the whole of the island could join the Union. Kofi Annan, the secretary general of the United Nations, in a public statement told both sides, the Greek Cypriots and the Turkish Cypriots, "You have an appointment with destiny. Solve this problem now." Then in no uncertain terms he warned, "Otherwise, the UN will close its books on Cyprus." It was a subtle but ominous threat. The UN had played a key role in keeping the peace after Turkey invaded the island in 1974. The invasion caused the de facto partition of Cyprus and a festering international problem for close to thirty years.

At that time the criticism coming from the UN secretary was directed mostly against Rauf Denktash, the Turkish Cypriot leader who since 1964, enjoying the full backing of the Turkish military, had controlled the fate of Turkish Cypriots. "Only Fidel Castro could match such a record time in power!" I wrote down. But unlike Glafkos Clerides, the then president of the Republic of Cyprus, who tentatively accepted the proposed UN plan for the reunification of the island, Mr. Denktash rejected it, triggering huge demonstrations among Turkish Cypriots in the north. Apparently, the majority of Turkish Cypriots wanted reunification so that they too could become European citizens.

During the evening news we were stunned to watch close to 100,000 Turkish Cypriots carrying not the red flag of Turkey but the blue flag of Europe, demanding the acceptance of the "Annan Plan" for reunification. It was a promising sight, a possible light at the end of a very dark and long tunnel in unhappy Greek–Turkish relations.

My reflection on these political developments, the major topic of local news, was suddenly interrupted when Antonis called me over the phone. He had persuaded Father Maximos, he announced triumphantly, to take a break from his busy schedule and visit his home for afternoon tea and conversation. Only Antonis and Frosoula, Stephanos and Erato, Father

Joachim (a priest friend of Antonis and close associate of Father Maximos), and Lavros would be there. Emily and I were invited.

We gratefully accepted the invitation. Antonis's seaside home, surrounded by eucalyptus trees on the eastern outskirts of Limassol, was an idyllic venue for a tea party and spiritual dialogues. The couple had held such gatherings periodically in the past but the nature of those encounters had been mostly philosophical. Their house had often served as the equivalent of the French salons of the eighteenth century. But after Antonis discovered Mount Athos, philosophy lost its luster and the topic of conversation, in addition to local politics, shifted to Eastern Orthodox spirituality.

It was a rare occurrence for Father Maximos to take time off from his busy schedule. Antonis, who first introduced me to Mount Athos and to Father Maximos, knew of my interest in finding opportunities to have dialogues with the elder. I had a feeling he organized the tea party in part with this in mind. "We must make sure," I told him half-jokingly over the phone, "not to spend the time talking about the Cyprus problem, the European Union, and the demonstrations in the North."

"Don't worry," Antonis reassured me, laughing. "We'll talk only of things that are not of this world! By the way, can you pick up Father Maximos and drive him here?"

By three thirty I was at the bishopric. "I'm glad you came," Father Maximos exclaimed, raising both of his arms as I entered his office. "We have a problem here. We need a translator."

He introduced me to an Austrian journalist, a woman in her thirties, who had just arrived. She explained to me in excellent English that she was sent to the island by Austrian national radio to produce an hourlong program on the issue of the Annan Plan for the reunification of Cyprus. Her focus was on the role of the Church of Cyprus during the current stage of negotiations for resolving the problem.

Father Maximos was the first bishop she had met and it had been by accident. After arriving from Larnaka airport and checking into her hotel, she took a casual stroll to familiarize herself with the town. She noticed activity in the Katholike church and entered. That's where Father Maximos was carrying out confessions. She explained to me that there were reports in some European papers that the Cyprus church opposed the UN plan and was lukewarm about the island joining the European Union. The Austrians wanted to know what was behind those rumors. Father Maximos agreed to be interviewed on the spot.

The foreign journalist, dressed in blue jeans, apologized for not wearing proper attire. "Had I known that I would meet you today," she said, "I would have been more appropriately dressed." Father Maximos smiled and reassured her that he was not the least bothered. Then she proceeded with her questions.

"Is the Church of Cyprus against the Annan Plan for unification?"

"Not that I know of," Father Maximos replied, and asked her how such rumors spread all over Europe. Obviously, some members of the higher clergy did make such statements. But the church itself at that time had not officially taken any position.

"What can the Cyprus church offer Europe once the island joins the Union?"

Father Maximos answered that it could offer the experience of the Christ and show how Europeans can get to know God. When the Austrian journalist asked him to elaborate, Father Maximos pointed out that the Orthodox Church preserved in an intact form those mystical pathways leading to the direct experience of God. This is an aspect of Christianity that has been driven underground in the West because of its overemphasis on rationality and as a result of its primarily intellectual and cerebral approach to the divine.

As I was translating Father Maximos's words, I noticed the Austrian journalist nodding in agreement. She told me later that she was familiar with these ideas because she had a master's degree in theology. That was the reason she was sent on this assignment.

"Are you in favor of Cyprus joining the European Union?" she then asked.

"Yes, absolutely," Father Maximos replied. I breathed a sigh of relief. I knew that there were some ultraconservative Athonite monks who were not favorably predisposed toward Europe.

"Why? Why are you in favor of Cyprus joining Europe?"

"Because Cyprus is too small and vulnerable an island to exist by itself in this troubled part of the world. And because Cyprus is part of European culture."

"Have you met with the Mufti in the north?" she asked, referring to the Muslim religious leader of the Turkish Cypriots.

"How can I meet him?" Father Maximos said. "Mr. Denktash does not allow it."

I briefly explained to her that there was a 120-mile-long "dead zone" separating the Turkish-occupied territory from the rest of the Republic of Cyprus, which kept the Greek Cypriots and Turkish Cypriots apart. I mentioned that there were seventeen thousand landmines separating the Greeks from the Turks with no movement of people permitted between the north and the south of the island, except at the Ledra Palace checkpoint in Nicosia. It was kept open primarily for diplomats and UN personnel. This rigid separation had been enforced by the Turkish military for almost thirty years.

"Okay Kyriaco, let's go," Father Maximos said. The journalist thanked him profusely for giving her an hour's interview without a prior appointment.

I hadn't had time to explain to the young woman the "ambush" methodology that worked for me. She had unconsciously practiced that approach, given the informal ways things are done in Cyprus. At that point, however, Lavros dropped in quite unexpectedly. After being introduced, he volunteered to become her informant on the situation in Cyprus and to speak with her further on the role of the Church. The two of them made plans to meet the following day. In the meantime, we all got into Lavros's green Panjero and set off to pick up Emily before heading out for Antonis's tea symposium. I hoped that the political discussion would end the moment the interview was over.

"By the way, how did I do?" Father Maximos asked with a wily smile as soon as we got into the car.

"I didn't realize until today how good a diplomat you are," I joked, as Lavros turned the ignition on. I assumed it was Father Maximos's first interview by a foreign journalist.

It was past five when we reached the home of Antonis and Frosoula, with its large veranda overlooking the sea. Stephanos and Erato were already there, along with Father Joachim and his wife. A former bank director, Father Joachim was ordained as a priest the very year he retired from his job, at the age of sixty. He decided to become a priest, he told me, after undergoing a religious experience over Christ's tomb in Jerusalem. Under the most unusual of circumstances he was somehow led to spend the night there with Father Maximos on a special all-night vigil and the two of them prayed all night long over Christ's tomb. The experience was so overwhelming that it turned his life around. Father Maximos ordained him and assigned him, in addition to serving as a priest in a local church, the task of managing the finances of the bishopric. Father Joachim, humble and unassuming in his black cassock and white beard, was a close friend of Antonis as well as of Stephanos and Erato. I liked him the moment I met him, and so did Emily. Father Joachim was the quintessential good-hearted parish priest. "I was a usurer all my life," he said to me humorously, "so I became a priest to pay for my sins."

After serving ourselves tea and pastries, we sat around the living room with its large glass windows, which offered us a spectacular view of the sea. On the walls hung some old, original paintings with religious themes and in a discreet corner there was a special cluster of hand-painted Byzantine icons that Antonis had accumulated over the years from his many yearly journeys to Mount Athos. Two lit lamps hung in front of the icons, creating a feeling of holiness in that corner of the room. Father Maximos always taught that the presence of holy icons creates good energies in a place, and Antonis was a committed convert to the Athonite spiritual tradition and practice.

It was getting cool and Antonis started a fire in the fireplace, which quickly took the chill out of the room and created an atmosphere conducive to conversation. Eager to start, I asked Father Maximos to clarify for us the importance of prayer as a method of spiritual practice. "People today," I mentioned, "living within the modern world have a difficult time getting into the habit of prayer. This is particularly so for people like academics, writers, journalists, artists, and so on. For them the notion that God is listening when someone prays is considered wishful thinking or mere naiveté. In fact they would feel embarrassed if they were ever caught praying. So modern individuals living in the center of Manhattan find it much more comfortable to practice 'meditation' rather than prayer. It is more compatible with the individualistic ethos of our times. Somehow meditation appears culturally legitimate whereas prayer is associated with the fundamentalists and people of less sophistication."

Father Maximos listened quietly and took a sip from his teacup. He took a deep breath in his characteristic way and responded to my comments. "Prayer is not like meditation. It may have similarities with meditation but it is altogether different. Prayer is a formidable science that must be studied and practiced so that it can lead us to a union with God who is a Person. From the little I know of what meditation is, it seems to me that it does not have as its primary aim union with the personal God.

"Prayer hides great surprises," Father Maximos continued. "It reveals the nature of God and opens for us unimaginable spiritual landscapes within our very being." The faces of Father Joachim and Erato lit up in agreement. They seemed to know from personal experience what Father Maximos was talking about.

"This is territory that is completely alien to most people today, or perhaps of any previous period," I pointed out. "My feeling is that prayer is often done in a mechanical way and therefore is not very conducive to the discovery of the kinds of inner landscapes that you have referred to."

"That is the reason why one needs to be coached by those who have traveled the mystic pathways of prayer," Father Maximos replied. After a long pause he continued in a serious tone. "Believe me, prayer is potentially the greatest power that human beings hide within themselves."

" 'Why should I pray?' This is a question people often ask," I said. "I was talking with a friend of mine the other day who insisted that prayer is an insult to God. He felt that somehow those who pray assume that God needs to be begged in order to give us things we need."

"This is a gross distortion of the purpose of prayer." Father Maximos waved his right hand. "To tell you the truth, as far as I am concerned, it is disrespectful to ask favors of God to help us fulfill our worldly desires—"

"So you agree with the criticism of Kyriacos's friend," Antonis interjected.

"No, not really. I can see his point in terms of exclusively focusing our prayers to attain worldly goals, such as to succeed in our jobs or stay in good health and so on. In reality it's like asking our mother 'Please mama, keep me well.' It's an insult to the Almighty. Thank God he doesn't feel offended," Father Maximos said, laughing with the rest of us.

"Nevertheless," Father Maximos continued, "within the *Ecclesia* there are prayers for the attainment of all sorts of practical ends. During services we pray for peace, for good harvest, for the protection of those at sea and so on. We even have special services for a good rainfall."

"I read the other day," Stephanos said, "that Saint Arsenios the Cappadocian instructed Elder Paisios on how to use different parts of the Psalms for very mundane ends such as what prayer to recite when you lose the keys to your house."

"Yes, I remember that part," Father Maximos said. "It is legitimate to ask God for good weather, rain, good crops, peace, and so on. This is fine, assuming they do not become priorities in terms of what we ask of God."

207

"So what must we first ask of God, Father Maxime?" Antonis wondered.

"Jesus instructed us that when we pray we must not ask for superfluous things like the idolaters do or those who do not know God. He tells us exactly what we must ask of God, namely his kingdom. Everything else will then be offered to us. What we need first and foremost is to experience God's love."

"I suppose this is the essence of the Jesus Prayer," I said, "the 'Lord Jesus Christ Have mercy on me.'"

The Jesus Prayer, Father Maximos told me earlier, is the most powerful way of contacting God. It fills the mind with grace as the person keeps this prayer in his or her heart and mind. Ideally one should reserve a certain amount of time every day and engage in this form of prayer. Furthermore, as one engages in routine activities such as washing dishes, taking a walk, or waiting at a bus stop one can recite the prayer. Then the person will reach a point when the Prayer will be an ongoing activity within his or her consciousness even while asleep or even while one engages in intellectually challenging activities like solving mathematical equations. Prayer becomes a form of breathing, an ongoing activity within the person that sanctifies his or her entire being.

"The Prayer," Father Maximos responded, "literally means 'Jesus Christ grant me your mercy, which is what I need in order to meet you, in order that you may live inside me and that I live as you wish me to live, so that you may find rest within my own being and existence.' This is the mercy of God. It is the love of God."

"So true prayer is the means by which to ask God to help us love him," Antonis said.

"That's exactly the meaning of real prayer as understood by the saints. God's love is a given. It is we who need to learn how to love God. We don't ask God to love us. His love is total and unconditional. It is we who need to heal ourselves so that we may be able to experience God's love. It is we who have a problem in this relationship. Therefore, the mercy that we seek is so that God may heal our existence in such a way that we may allow God to find rest within our own hearts. It is as if we ask of God to create a space within us so that he may be allowed to bring about our own union with his love. This is what we must first and foremost ask of God. When that happens then God offers us whatever else we might really need."

"I suppose when your primary need for union with God has been satisfied then all other needs fade away. This perhaps explains why saints are so indifferent to worldly goals, honors, and possessions," I speculated.

"Precisely so. Our true existential need is union with God. The craving for worldly goals and objectives is a false substitute for that inner need. When that is satisfied then our heart and mind work in their natural primordial condition, in a continuous memory and contemplation of God. A person in reality enters within the furthest regions of his own being."

"We can say then that prayer is the method that helps us penetrate into the center of our existence," concluded Lavros, who had been uncharacteristically silent.

"In fact, Christ instructs us that when we pray we should retreat into our 'treasury,' that is, into the depths of our being, free of external distractions, so that we may let ourselves cry out to God the pain we experience in his absence. Our passions and the consequences of our transgressions that torment us, which form the sum total of the problems we face, can become a powerful force for prayer.

"I am convinced," Father Maximos continued, "that the antidote against all the problems people face as a result of their isolation living in modern cities, or anywhere for that matter, is prayer. The systematic practice of prayer will lead them to that space within themselves where God resides, where they will discover their true personhood and uniqueness. They will find their wholeness not in external events and in ephemeral phenomena but within the context of their relationship with God. I do believe that the best resistance and inoculation of the person against atomization and loneliness is prayer."

"That is certainly a factor that neither the sociologists nor the existentialist philosophers considered as a means to overcoming modern alienation," I said. "The subject of alienation has been at the heart of modern sociology."

"Through prayer," Father Maximos said, "a person may recover his existence. This is what monks and hermits try to do in monasteries and hermitages."

"Again, ordinary people living in the modern world would find such a position untenable," I pointed out. "They believe that monks and nuns waste their life living in such places. It is the standard critique directed against monasticism."

"But when you live in an authentic monastery you recognize that it is in reality a place where not only are you not lost but rather it is a place where you may truly find yourself. That is where you can discover the strength of your personhood."

"Meaning?"

"Meaning that you can develop the capacity to commune with God and as a result of that you learn to commune with your fellow human beings. Once you do that you can never again experience loneliness or anxiety or the feeling of being lost."

"This is, after all, the meaning behind the commandment to love God first and then love your neighbor," Stephanos said.

"Of course. If you learn to love God through prayer then it is natural to love your neighbor. In fact it is inevitable since the two go together. Furthermore, through prayer we discover who we really are. And when that happens all the fears and insecurities that we hide in our hearts vanish forever. Prayer gives us a certainty which allows us to have a different outlook on life. We develop the certainty that God is always present in our life."

"That's why hermits and monks never feel alone or lonely," Lavros added. Like Antonis, Lavros had visited Mount Athos several times.

"This is their secret," said Father Maximos. "Wherever we are, we are conscious of God's presence. So it is important to keep in mind that prayer is like a harbor that is always nearby. It is unavoidable that there will be many storms and rough seas in our life which can lead some of us to despair, even to suicide. Prayer is the harbor where we can enter at all times and at all occasions. Only there can we find real peace and serenity. Nothing can shatter that peace because God is there, in the very depths of our being. No worldly upheaval, therefore, can undermine that tranquility, none at all. If people really knew the power of prayer they would put in the effort to gradually learn how to pray. I really believe this."

"If the best antidote to contemporary loneliness and alienation is prayer," I reasoned, "then Western philosophers and intellectuals have ignored one of the most potent medicines for coping with the difficulties of life."

"Obviously. But to attain results requires persistence and stamina. When you first enter into that space of your heart you will confront great resistance. It is like stepping into a room where no human being has entered for years. It is full of dust and mold. You initially feel despair and you may say to yourself 'My God, how am I going to live in this place full of cockroaches?' This is how you feel when you first enter into your heart. That is why a person today is reluctant to penetrate into his own heart and take a good look. He is terrified of the emptiness and the negativity he discovers there."

As Father Maximos made that remark he looked at Stephanos, who nodded with understanding. We all knew what that silent exchange meant. Stephanos had once described to me how, one day, during a state of deep prayer, he foolishly asked God to reveal to him how he actually looked spiritually. That invocation triggered in Stephanos a negative mystical experience that led him into great despair. It plunged him into a nightmare. Erato explained to us that he almost went mad and could not keep from weeping continuously for six months. A sociable man with a wide circle of friends, Stephanos could not even appear in public because he could not control his ceaseless crying and weeping. He told me that he felt like the foulest garbage dump. He rushed to Father Maximos, who, after hearing what had happened, reprimanded him for making such a request of God. "Not even the most experienced hermits of Mount Athos would dare ask God such a thing," he told Stephanos. It took months of close and constant monitoring and guidance from Father Maximos before Stephanos came back to his senses. It was a spiritual emergency of the utmost severity, which may have weakened Stephanos's health, paving the way to his heart problems later.

"If there are such prospects," Frosoula asked, "then why should people open themselves up to such dangers?"

"Once you know what is going on and are under the supervision of a spiritual guide, you can overcome these initial difficulties. It's important that we never become desperate in such situations. Once we genuinely pray to God or to the Holy Virgin for help then healing will begin to take place in our hearts. It's like calling on our neighbors and friends to come and help us clean the room. Likewise, with prayer we call on God to come and cleanse our heart, our very existence. That is when our agony and despair are transformed into intensified prayer. As the elders instruct, tears often follow such states. But please, don't ask of God to reveal to you how you look spiritually, as Stephanos did!" Father Maximos warned with a grin.

"Why the tears?" Frosoula asked.

"It is an integral part of real prayer," Father Maximos replied. "If you wish to dynamically enter the path for the discovery of God and to experience his presence within you, then you need to learn the secret of praying with tears."

"This is not easy to comprehend," I said. "How is that done?"

"Just let go of your resistances and allow yourself to break down and cry."

"As in the case of Stephanos?" I asked.

"No. That was a different matter altogether. He made a dangerous invocation."

"And if you cannot shed tears during prayer?" Antonis asked.

"It means that the doors of your heart are still firmly shut. That means you need to work harder at prayer. The first sign that the door is broken and that you have entered into this particular spiritual space is the phenomenon of tears. As I said, during intense prayer, tears begin to flow."

"I assume the ease with which a person can experience these tears will depend to a great degree on a person's idiosyncratic nature. Some people cry more easily than others," Frosoula pointed out.

"Quite so. Many people today don't know how to cry. They are emotionally handicapped. In fact I am horrified to hear during confessions the incapacity of people to express themselves to each other. Husbands don't know how to relate to their wives, parents don't know how to caress and kiss their children. Relationships within the family are stale and unalive. Such people are stunted in their development and consequently they cannot express themselves either in their relationship with each other or in their relationship with God."

"We can conclude then that our personality may be an obstacle to our capacity to pray," I said.

"Perhaps so." Father Maximos paused. "A human being is not just spirit. We need to express our love with our entire being. In the early years of Christianity, during the Eucharist and soon after it, when the priest would say 'Let us love one another so that with one heart we may confess,' people used to embrace and kiss each other. Today we don't know how to express our love toward God because we don't know how to express love to one another.

"When I first met those holy men on Mount Athos, like elders Paisios, Porphyrios, and Ephraim, I was extremely impressed by their capacity to express themselves. For example, if you read the letters that Elder Joseph the Hesychast sent to his spiritual children you will see an amazing sensitivity and beauty in the way he offered them counseling. He was a master of communication."

"And you believe," I said, "that these gifts are products of their capacity for deep prayer."

"I've said it before. Being in a constant state of prayer these elders learned first and foremost to commune with themselves. This entrance into their very being taught them how to communicate with themselves."

"This is strange talk," Lavros interjected. "What does it mean?"

"It means to look yourself straight in the eye, the way you are with all your faults, shortcomings, and difficulties. But you do not remain there. You do not remain enclosed within yourself as many people do with contemporary methods of self-exploration."

"Such ways may often degenerate into the trap of self-absorption and narcissism," I pointed out. "I have known people who are obsessed with 'spirituality' and yet their entire spiritual work is nothing more than an exercise in ego absorption and narcissism."

"Exactly. That is why the next step in this self-exploration must be to turn your gaze toward God. Otherwise you may be stuck within your own ego."

"It seems as if in order to establish a real dialogue with God you must transcend yourself," Stephanos said.

"That goes without saying. You implore God to put in order your shattered existence. When you do that, a dialogue opens up between you and God. Something marvelous takes place. Without realizing it, the moment God visits your heart you will simultaneously unite with the entire world in a fullness of love.

"When you fall in love with God and his love floods your entire being then you witness your heart opening up and accommodating all of humanity. A human being in such a state is united in love with the entire creation, with birds, plants, rocks, mountains, rivers, with everything. What he feels is what the holy elders describe as the first experience of grace, the *logoi ton onton.*"

Father Maximos reflected for a few seconds. "The *logoi ton onton*, as the elders say, are the purposes and the reasons hidden behind the existence of every single thing. A human being learns, not intellectually but experientially, that everything has a purpose to its existence."

"Creation is not irrational," I said, "It has a purpose. This theme preoccupied most of the great philosophers."

"For Orthodoxy this purpose is none other than the *Gnosis,* or the knowledge of God. The purpose for the existence of anything is the knowledge of the Creator and the deification of the created. Through the knowledge of creation you are guided to the knowledge of God, which eventually

213

leads to your own *Theosis* [union with God]. Persons who realize this truth are masters of creation and that creation itself was made for them as a means of knowing the Creator."

"Some people today react negatively to what they would consider to be dangerous anthropocentrism that leads toward the destruction of the environment," said Lavros, a passionate environmentalist.

"No, no. This is a clear misunderstanding," Father Maximos said impatiently. "When the holy elders say that everything was created for human beings, it does not mean that they are given a license to mindlessly subjugate and abuse the natural environment. The environment must be seen as a sacred gift, an arena that could help human beings toward the knowledge of God and their deification, their *Theosis*. When that happens a human being begins to function in accordance to his true nature. He communes with himself, with God, with other human beings, and with the whole world."

"How does that state manifest itself in a person's life, Father Maxime?" Frosoula asked.

"The moment love enters your heart, all fear evaporates. That's the key sign that grace has visited your heart. That is why the saints were so fearless. They loved everybody and everything. They reached that state through continuous prayer. A saint is at home with the entire creation. In fact the most awe-inspiring realization is to witness creation being tamed in the presence of saints. Many saints lived peacefully among wild animals without ever being harmed by them. Saint Gerasimos in Palestine had a lion as a pet. Saint Seraphim of Sarov enjoyed the company of a wild Russian bear and Elder Paisios befriended snakes. Phenomena of this sort were and still are common on Mount Athos and in the lives of the desert fathers of early Christianity. As Abba Isaac the Syrian says, nature has within itself the sense of Adam prior to the Fall. Just like Adam, who lived peacefully among wild animals without being harmed by them, human beings who are restored to their primordial, paradisiacal state relate to nature in an identical way."

"Of course, for modern-thinking individuals such arguments appear incredulous," I said in jest.

"When human beings attain that state of spiritual development then creation is no longer a threatening force. It is for this reason that saints on various occasions transcend the laws of nature without being harmed. Nature by itself protects the person who has discovered in his very being his primordial beauty given to him by God at his very creation. That's what you notice when you study the biography of saints."

Our hosts intervened and suggested that we take a break by sitting around the dinner table, which was set up with all sorts of delicacies. The tea party had evolved into dinner. "This is part of the way of the 'ambush,' " said Lavros, winking at me as he moved toward the table.

While we stood around the dinner table, Father Joachim, who up to that point had silently listened to the ongoing exchanges with Father Maximos, offered a short prayer. Father Maximos then blessed the food by making the sign of the cross with his right hand and we proceeded to eat a light dinner. Unavoidably, the conversation turned into an exchange of opinions about the political developments related to Cyprus and the brewing war in the region. That was the type of "temptation" that not even Father Maximos, who had once abandoned the world for the Holy Mountain, could resist.

215

ELEVEN

FAITH

OF

SAINTS

he "Kofi Annan Plan," the effort launched by the United Nations for the reunification of Cyprus, was the central topic of conversation around the table. Our hosts, as well as Emily, were born and raised in Famagusta, the only occupied city in the world surrounded by barbed wire. There was palpable excitement in the air with the prospects for a political solution and the possibility of return to family homes left abandoned thirty years ago. Given the intense interest that all of us shared regarding a peaceful future for the island, I assumed there would be no further discussion that evening on spiritual matters.

As soon as we finished eating, Father Maximos blessed the leftovers with a short prayer and then we moved back to the living room. Lavros, ever mindful of the reasons of my stay in Cyprus, took the initiative to shift the discussion back to the topic that dinner had interrupted. "Father Maxime, systematic prayer for us laypeople is not easy. How should one pray?"

Father Maximos smiled, apparently sensing Lavros's intention in asking the question. He looked at me as if he suspected collusion between us and then, upon reflecting for a second, he said: "First and foremost we must be very serious when we address ourselves to God."

"I thought this was a given."

"What I mean is that we must avoid addressing ourselves to God in a superficial, casual way. For this reason Elder Sofrony goes as far as to say that the language we use in prayer must be different from the ordinary language of everyday usage. That is why he insisted that the language of the liturgy should not be translated into the contemporary spoken vernacular."

"A lot of people today would strongly object to that suggestion," I pointed out. "They demand that church services be conducted in the spoken ordinary language so that they can understand what is being said. Why did Elder Sofrony hold to such a position?"

"Elder Sofrony claimed that when we conduct the liturgy using everyday language, we lower the level of our communication with God."

"How is that so?" I asked.

"He believed that ordinary language carries meanings and images from our daily reality that usually lack the element of holiness and purity. On the other hand when we address ourselves to God in a language that has, as it were, an exclusive usage within the boundaries of the *Ecclesia*, the very words and sounds of that language evoke sacred feelings and images that facilitate communication with God. A special language that offers precise and exclusive meanings can automatically be experienced as the language of the *Ecclesia*. It carries greater spiritual force."

"Okay. I see what you mean. It makes sense even on purely psychological grounds."

"Well, it's just a theory proposed by the late elder born out of his spiritual experience."

217

I explained that in contemporary sociology and psychology the notion that language structures our way of apprehending the world is well established. From my own personal experience, translated versions of the New Testament in modern Greek are less appealing than the original New Testament Greek. Similarly, the King James Version of the Bible is of greater appeal, as far as I am concerned, than the Standard Revised Version. Given Elder Sofrony's theory, I wonder whether the total abolition of the Latin mass by the Catholic Church was a wise decision. This becomes even more interesting when one considers the fascination of many New Agers with Eastern religions. Disenchanted with the rationalization of their own religious tradition, they turn toward Buddhism or Hinduism, reciting mantras and chanting Sanskrit prayers they do not understand. But they still find such rituals aesthetically and spiritually more palatable than the Sunday church service.

218

"Of course," Father Maximos said, "it is important to keep in mind that for a more effective way of praying we must know and understand what we say. Saint John Chrysostom made it clear that if we do not pay attention when we pray then we should not expect God to pay attention to our prayer."

God will not pay attention to us if we do not pay attention when we pray

"I have heard several people claim," Lavros said, "that they don't pray because they cannot focus. Since they cannot focus they consider prayer a fruitless and meaningless exercise." *I can connect!*

"This is not a wise position to take. The words of Saint John Chrysostom are not directed to those who have such a specific problem. You see, what is important is to struggle with sincerity during our prayer, to do our best given our abilities and limitations. Gradually we will learn how to focus our thoughts and pray with intensity."

"So we should not despair if we keep falling asleep during prayer or if our mind is wandering during prayer," I said.

It isn't easy to stay focused. It is heartening to know that others experience this same struggle

"Naturally not. All of us suffer from such shortcomings. We may read whole pages from the Psalms and after a while we realize that our mind was not there and we have no clue what we read. Only angels and those who have reached their angelic condition do not suffer from such problems of focusing the mind on prayer. When we are in elementary school we must first learn the alphabet, and then move on from there. We do not punish little kids when they face difficulties as they clumsily try to read a book. It takes time, practice, and growth to master such skills. We could not expect a child to act as if he is a university graduate. It's the same with prayer. When we are beginners we are bound to face difficulties and make mistakes. We will pray in an imperfect way. Having that in mind, we must not lose our courage and interest in getting into the habit of prayer."

"After all," I mentioned, "persistence and hard work are necessary to master any skill. But what did John Chrysostom really mean when he said those words?"

"He referred to persons who were indifferent," Father Maximos answered. "Such people may go through the motions of prayer without any personal investment in what they are doing. They don't struggle and they don't care. God will not listen to such prayers—"

"I have known a number of clergymen who are like that," Lavros interjected. "They conduct church services in a mechanical way, and it shows."

Father Maximos nodded. "The person who is willfully indifferent, yet goes through the motions of prayer will not be graced by the presence of God in his heart. On the other hand, the grace of God will eventually visit the person who carries on a spiritual struggle sincerely even though he may continuously lose his concentration while praying. Providence works in such a way that grace gradually strengthens the mind of the praying person to stay focused. It is a never-ending effort to remain focused on the prayer. What is important is not how well we succeed but how sincere we are in our endeavor."

This is comforting!

"This is encouraging. I always have problems focusing," Antonis said, probably echoing the feelings of most of us in the room.

"Sincere efforts are never in vain. The proof of that is the fact that when we stop praying, no matter how imperfectly, we feel spiritually depleted."

We remained pensive for a few moments as I assumed that the evening conversation had come to an end. I was certain that Father Maximos would be very tired by now since he had been up since well before sunrise. But he had more to tell us about prayer. The conversation had apparently invigorated him.

"It is very important in our spiritual struggle, and in life in general, to get training so that we pay attention to the words we utter. I mean this literally." Father Maximos turned toward me to make certain that I heard what he said. "We need to observe our words as we utter them. If it were possible to see the words coming out of our mouths, one at a time, it would have been a great lesson in itself. It would help us recognize the power embedded in words. Imagine how important these words are when we use them to address ourselves to God."

It was clear that we needed further clarification and he went on to illustrate his point with a story.

"During my stay at Mount Athos a friend of mine, a young monk like myself, was plagued by doubts. He would go to church before the start of a service and begin wondering, 'What are we doing here? We live alone and every single day we repeat the same words and hear the same prayers, over and over.' He felt dispirited. It was the time of the *apodypnon*, the short prayer service that we conduct after dinner. The presiding priest began with the words that are recited at the beginning of most services: *Evlogytos oh Theos ymon pantote, nyn kai ai kai es tous aeonas ton aeonon Amen* (Blessed be our God, now and forever and unto the ages of ages, Amen). During that *apodypnon*, at that very moment when my friend heard these words, God offered him a spiritual experience. Through the help of the Holy Spirit he understood what it means for a human being to eulogize God 'to the ages of ages.' He told me 'It was as if all the horizons of the entire creation, of time, of space, of everything, opened up in front of me.'"

"It's always difficult, if not impossible, to imagine someone else's mystical experience," I said, shaking my head in frustration.

"Well, yes. In this particular case the way he tried to explain it to me was similar to the situation when we utter a loud cry in a canyon and we hear the echo go on and on into the depths of the canyon. That is what happened to him when the priest uttered those sacred words. He literally felt the blessing endlessly moving unto the ages of ages. He realized experientially what a serious matter it is when you open your mouth to address God. It is the greatest of tasks and the greatest privilege that a person may exercise.

"So words have power," Father Maximos emphasized again. "Most important, the specific words that human beings choose to address God have an eternal dynamism and an extraordinary spiritual energy accumulated within them."

"Is this also the case when words are being aimed in the opposite direction?" I asked.

"Oh yes! Blasphemies against God are ejected into the eons. Every word we utter and every thought we project is a tangible reality affecting our world."

"Including foul language?" Antonis asked.

"Absolutely. It is terrible to get into the habit of using bad language. And it is a terrible sin to blaspheme God. According to the Gospel the demons themselves dare not commit such an act. When demons hear the name of God they shudder. Unfortunately, we humans lack that sensitivity.

"When we get ready to pray we must have in mind that God is literally present and that we must speak to Him in utter earnestness of heart and with precision. We must remember that God is listening and is registering our every word, our every thought, and our every feeling. I am always awed by the seriousness with which the saints addressed God during their prayers. They were totally focused and very precise, something that we must learn to do as a matter of course."

Father Maximos then suggested that we all do a simple exercise for an hour each day by becoming aware of the words we utter during that hour. "Say to yourself that between nine and ten in the morning I will observe every word I speak as if I am seeing each word written down as it exits my mouth."

"This type of exercise," Father Maximos explained, "will train us to be attentive to the words we utter and help us to have focus and precision. Ideally, our prayer must sound like an intense cry that goes up to God, a point that is mentioned in the Psalms. King David calls prayer a 'cry.' That means that the person who prays must appear like someone who cries with all of his might."

"I thought prayer is quiet," Lavros said half-humorously.

"It is the need for inner intensity during prayer that David refers to," Father Maximos replied. "Imagine someone pushing another person from

221

I wonder if I can ever do that.

the twenty-fifth floor of a building. That person will cry out a heart-wrenching, terrified call for help. It is his ultimate, desperate cry. That is the power that ideally one should muster while praying."

"But how realistic or possible is it, Father Maxime, to be in such a frame of mind when praying?" Antonis asked.

"Theoretically it is possible. But practically it is not. We are human beings and the circumstances of our lives do not normally allow us to engage in this intense form of prayer. When, however, we are confronted with life's tribulations and sorrows then we are like water that is being compressed and in such a state it spills upwards. When the soul is pressed in this manner then it is possible to cry out to God for help in the way that David speaks of in the Psalms.

"When a person is crushed by sorrow then his prayer may become more intense," Father Maximos continued. "Saint Silouan, the twentieth-century Russian elder from Mount Athos, knew a layman, a worker who prayed with great intensity. 'Where did you learn to pray like that?' he asked him. The laborer replied that he did so during the war when it was a tossup whether he was going to live or die."

To further illustrate the point, Father Maximos related the extraodinary experience of an Athonite elder he knew personally: "One day after vespers were over the elder went to his cell to continue praying on his own. While doing that, he marveled at the thought that everybody—all two thousand or so monks on the entire Athonite peninsula—was praying during that very moment. Then, he wondered what the Holy Mountain looked like under such intensive prayer.

"At that very moment he experienced himself being catapulted by the Holy Spirit high up in the air. It was as if he were looking down from an airplane. From that high point, he saw the Athonite peninsula spurting out flames like an active volcano, as if the entire mountain was on fire. Some of the flames went straight up to heaven. Others seemed weak, like the flame of a small candle, while yet others were flickering and barely visible. Yet, there was one, this elder claimed, that was like a fiery river that went straight up. He then overheard a voice coming from heaven saying 'What you have witnessed is the Holy Mountain and these are the prayers of the monks that go up to God.' Then the elder asked, 'And whose prayer is this great river of fire?' God replied that it was the prayer of a certain abbot at a certain monastery, whose name cannot be revealed since this abbot is still alive.

"You see," Father Maximos went on and rested back on his armchair, "God is not some kind of impersonal intelligence. God is personal and communicates with us, speaks to us, and can catapult us to other parts of his kingdom as in the case of that abbot."

"If that were not the case, it would be pointless to pray," I reasoned aloud, having in mind the fashionable notion among many modern and well-intentioned theologians of not referring to God in personal terms but of using the more neutral term "the Ground of all Being."[1] "It's hard to pray to the Ground of all Being."

"It is absolutely impossible to pray to an impersonal intelligence," Father Maximos declared. "To do so would imply that God suffers from either inattentiveness or nonexistence. God is personal, not some kind of an abstract idea."

"For many ordinary people like myself," I said, "this is a difficult reality to digest. Most of us feel that when we pray nobody really listens."

"This is part of the tragedy of contemporary men and women. Our models of what it really means to pray should always be the saints and the prophets, be it King David or Elder Paisios. I remember one day when I happened to be at Elder Paisios's hermitage preparing to have a lunch of bread and a few olives. We stood up to pray and he began the Lord's Prayer. Unfortunately, I cannot convey to you how I felt when that old hermit began saying 'Our Father who art in heaven . . .' Now, you see, I had heard and recited the Lord's Prayer several times a day, thousands of times each year. Yet, when Elder Paisios began saying those sacred words you knew that he was communicating directly with God, that he was standing in front of God in the same manner that Moses stood in front of the burning bush on Mount Sinai. There was no barrier between him and God."

Responding to Frosoula's question on the role of study in a person's spiritual struggle, Father Maximos stressed that the elders considered prayer and study as twin and necessary preconditions for the road to holiness. "In addition to the practical aspects of engaging in spiritual exercises, such as managing anger, being kind to others, praying, working toward developing a charitable predisposition, and so on, we must also devote time to study. Studying is a way of preoccupying our mind with God. Drops of water hitting marble rhythmically over a long period of time will crack it in two. It is the same with our hearts. Preoccupation with spiritual work along with the study of the lives of saints can keep our minds focused on God and the *Agathon*, or the Good. Over a period of time our hearts will open up."

"The other day, Father Maxime," Stephanos said "you mentioned in passing that there are two types of faith but you did not elaborate. Since we have been discussing prayer I wonder whether you could explain further what you meant by the two types of faith."

Father Maximos pondered Stephanos's question for a few seconds. "Yes," he said. "Faith has basically two stages. The first stage is what the average person usually believes in, namely that there is a God. I believe in one God, in Christ, and in the Holy Spirit. I believe in the essential teachings of the Gospel and the *Ecclesia*. In the language of the holy elders this form of faith is called *introductory faith* or the faith of children."

"Did they mean that one should not have such faith?" I asked.

"No, of course not. It is a necessary stage in our spiritual development but it is an infantile stage. It is a starting point, a base from which you begin your journey back to God. And that is good. This form of faith, however, does not have much power."

"One should not get stranded on that stage," Stephanos stated.

"Exactly. Simple faith is not the aim of the *Ecclesia*."

"Yet most people think of faith in God in this very manner," I added. "They become pious and feel 'born again,' and so on."

"The teachings of the *Ecclesia* go beyond belief. If you believe without having any proof then you are in reality naive. You must prove the existence of God first to yourself through your own direct experience before you can tell others about God. You can claim that you believe in God. Fine. But where is the evidence of God's existence? Saint Paul tells us that a person can reach a spiritual point where faith will be abolished. At that point both faith and hope will be canceled out and what will remain will be love."

"So faith in God is not an end in itself but only a stage that will lead us to a loving union with God," I added.

"Yes. It doesn't mean, of course, that the person is no longer a believer in God but that God for such a person is no longer a matter of faith but of direct experience. The elders teach that through this introductory faith a person is ushered into the second stage of faith, which they call *Pistis tes Theorias*. It implies the kind of faith that is based on the direct vision of God [*Theoria*] rather than a philosophical contemplation about the reality of God. You no longer believe in something unknown and remote but something that is known to you firsthand. It is concrete and tangible."

[handwritten margin note: second stage direct vision of god or the Theoria]

"I suppose it is like having faith in someone close and dear to you," I suggested. "You have faith that your close friend will not cheat or steal from you. You have this faith because you know your friend on a heartfelt level. You are absolutely certain of his integrity."

"That's a good analogy. It is not sufficient to have others describe realities that are beyond your capacity of knowing and verifying. It is not sufficient for someone else to describe to you the sweetness of being one with Christ. You must yourself taste that sweetness." Father Maximos thought for a few seconds. "I must emphasize that it is only when you have the direct experience of God that you will have the stamina to continue on the difficult spiritual path. This is so because sin is experiential, and it is often mixed up with the allurement of the senses and with pleasure. You cannot fight the attraction of worldly pleasures with only a theory of God. But you can fight the attraction of sin with the overwhelming sweetness of the presence of God. As an elder put it, 'We fight the erotic with the Erotic.' That means you can overcome worldly temptations with the infinitely more pleasurable direct experience and love of God."

"According to the great saints and mystics of all the centuries the direct vision of God's love is the most powerful experience anyone could have, overshadowing every other," said Father Joachim, who up to that point had remained silent. It was direct experience that turned him from a successful banker to a black-clad, bearded, ordained priest.

"I assume that the introductory faith is characteristic of the 'Slaves' and 'Employees' of God that we talked about before, whereas the stage of the direct experience of God is more characteristic of the 'Lovers of God,' " I said.

"Yes, exactly."

225

"The natural question that an ordinary person could ask," I continued, "is the following: How does one advance from the introductory faith to the second faith of the direct vision of God, of the *Theoria*?"

"Just follow God's commandments and be patient. They are forms of spiritual exercises. It is the equivalent to having a teacher give you tests to find out how much you have learned from the assigned material. For example, God asks of us that we must not return evil with evil. But then a time comes when circumstances push us in the direction of revenge or of seeking justice or of experiencing jealousy. But because of Christ's commandment we try to resist the temptation of seeking revenge or allowing ourselves to feel jealousy. This ongoing struggle to remain faithful to the commandments 'unto death,' so to speak, is a necessary precondition toward true faith. This kind of faith, according to Abba Isaac, is the outgrowth of temptations. Through temptations, sorrows, trials, and tribulations, God comes and rewards, as it were, the struggle of the faithful person and gives him as a trophy the experience of the splendor of his own presence. This experience is so overwhelming that the next time around the person struggles with an even greater force to regain it."

"You become addicted to God, as it were," I said.

"Yes! You fight with greater energy as grace shows its presence even more intensely. It is impossible for a person who reaches that state to have any trace of doubt about the reality of God. That is real faith."

Father Maximos went on to repeat that systematic prayer is of utmost importance in the effort to move to the second stage of true faith. "Prayer offers us the strength that will eventually lead us to the experience of God. In the same way that a person needs to eat in order to be healthy and have strength to face the tasks of everyday living, so too does a person need prayer to develop resistance and immunity to temptations and evil acts. It is like the system of antibodies we have within our physical body that keeps it in good health. When a virus enters the body the antibodies are activated, offering resistance."

"Is this foolproof?" I asked. "Can't one succumb to temptation no matter how advanced one is in prayer?"

"Of course it's not foolproof," Father Maximos replied. "Even great saints and prophets have succumbed to temptations in disastrous ways. They fell from grace precipitously. That is why the holy elders keep their vigilance until their last breath."

Father Maximos suddenly pulled his watch from his pocket as if he remembered something he had to do. Then he excused himself, saying that he had to rush back to the bishopric. It was nine in the evening and there were people waiting for him at the confessional.

"I have one question, Father Maxime," said Emily, who had remained uncharacteristically silent throughout the evening's discussion, as Lavros drove us home, Father Maximos in front and Emily and I in the back. "You've talked so much tonight about prayer and its power, particularly the constant repetition of the Jesus Prayer. What can you say to those who are not Orthodox but wish to practice the prayer within their own denomination?"

The Jesus prayer or

227

The Prayer of the heart

"Anybody can engage in the 'Jesus Prayer,' the 'Prayer of the Heart' as we sometimes call it. What is important, however, is to pray with humility and not reduce the prayer to some kind of a mental technique. Such an approach can backfire and lead to unpleasant developments."

Father Maximos did not elaborate on what these "unpleasant developments" could be but went on to point out that the systematic practice of the Prayer can solve three fundamental existential problems that all people face. He turned back, looked at Emily, and held up three fingers of his right hand. "First, it liberates us from loneliness. We cannot feel lonely when we are connected with the Christ. Second, we are freed from any form of anxiety, about our health, our property, our work, our children, and so on. Third, we are liberated from fear. By surrendering to Christ we overcome the fear of death, for in reality there is no death. So as we know from experience, the Prayer of the Heart helps us overcome our fundamental existential problems."

I mentioned that for people who are not Orthodox I often suggest the innovation of Saint Gregory Palamas, who for hours used to pray 'Lord enlighten my darkness,' 'Lord enlighten my darkness,' 'Lord enlighten my darkness,' on and on. Apparently it had the same effect as the original formulation of the Jesus Prayer. I suggested that this second version may be easier for people from other religious traditions. Father Maximos did not comment. Then I pointed out that this form of prayer may be helpful to people who live alone in big cities.

"Oh yes," Father Maximos said in an animated tone. "The modern city is the equivalent of the desert that the early fathers sought for their spiritual practices. You can be a hermit in a big city without anyone noticing."

"So the anonymity that one can attain in the modern city is the equivalent of the deserts of Egypt," Lavros marveled.

"Right. Even something that is considered a problem, I mean the loneliness that many people experience in the city, can be transformed into a life-giving desert for prayer. As Elder Paisios used to say, what is important is to turn yourself into a 'desert' free of destructive and egotistical passions."

"I have a request, Father Maxime," Emily said with determination in her voice. "How can I get to know Eastern Orthodox spirituality better and how can I personally get to know God experientially? Please don't send me to any holy books," she said lightly as Lavros parked his Panjero in front of the bishopric's gate.

"Go to the women's monastery in Patmos for ten days," he said as he stepped out of the car.

"What? Why?" Emily was taken by surprise.

"You will find out when you get there. But you must follow the instructions of the eldress," he replied cryptically and walked up the steps, waving goodnight.

TWELVE

DEATH

A N D

NEAR-DEATH

learned from Stephanos and Erato that early

in January, several days prior to my arrival in

Cyprus, Father Maximos had had a public

discussion with a well-known local psychiatrist on the na-

ture of death and the "near-death experience." This "NDE,"

phenomenon was first identified and made widely known

by Dr. Raymond Moody, the celebrated American psychia-

trist and philosopher.[1] According to my friends, the hall

where the discussion took place was packed with people

eager to learn about death and the afterlife. I regretted

having missed the event by only a few days but my wise

friends and informants advised me that I could bring up

the issue with Father Maximos at an opportune moment. They were certain that he would address once again at least the major points of that discussion.

I was particularly interested in the near-death experience for two reasons. First, I considered it an extraordinary development in our understanding of the death process. In fact I believed that the phenomenon itself might unravel revolutionary possibilities for an understanding of the nature of death itself and possibly the life beyond. Before Professor Moody's breakthrough research, it was unthinkable that people certified as deceased by doctors employing state-of-the-art scientific instruments could come back to life and report stupendous and fully conscious experiences that they had while in their "death" state. Furthermore, I was fascinated by the similarities between reported mystical experiences[2] and the near-death state. Such experiences tended to radically transform people's outlook on life and, among other things, liberate them completely from the fear of death.

I was also interested in the phenomenon because of my wish to learn of Father Maximos's views on this controversial subject. His outlook, I reasoned, would reflect those of the elders of Mount Athos, the specialists, as it were, of the "death phenomenon." My curiosity peaked when I learned from Raymond Moody himself during a conference in Canada that Christian fundamentalists in his native Alabama had demonized his work as "anti-Christian," making life sometimes difficult for the doctor.

The opportunity to follow my friends' advice came up when I accompanied Father Maximos on a trip to a village located at the eastern slopes of the Troodos Mountains, an hour and a half drive west of Limassol. As bishop he had established a policy of visiting a different church each Sunday where he would preside over the liturgy. That was his way of remaining in touch with all the communities in his diocese. It was the custom, after the formal service was over, to have lunch at someone's home. The host considered it an honor to offer a meal to the bishop and his companions, in this case Father Nikodemos and myself.

That particular Sunday in mid-March, lunch was offered at the home of the local doctor, who was also the mayor of the community. It was a bright, warm day. The sky was crystal clear after a weeklong continuous rain that brought joy to the Cypriots, who were accustomed to chronic droughts. The dams were filled, promising a summer of adequate running water. Our hosts set up the table in the middle of the courtyard under a canopy of vines, typical of mountain villages. The house was surrounded by cherry and apple trees in full bloom. It was springtime in Cyprus and the island was at its best.

I could not imagine a more pleasing setup and looked forward to a good meal and a lively discussion. *"Because of the basil the pot is watered,"* I whispered to Father Maximos as we entered the doctor's newly built stone house. He chuckled at the well-known Cypriot proverb, meaning that thanks to him, who was the "basil," I—the "pot"—had also been invited.

As soon as we finished eating the generous portions of fish, salads, and fruits there followed an almost predictable question-answer period related to spiritual concerns. People had grown accustomed to relating to Father Maximos in that fashion, a process that he encouraged himself. He considered such discussions as part of his duties as bishop, an integral aspect of his "job description." Through these Socratic dialogues he would disseminate to the faithful the wisdom tradition of Orthodox spirituality.

Coincidentally, one of the guests at the table had recently had a near-death experience herself during an open-heart surgery. Margarita, a middle-aged cousin of our host, claimed that she literally "died" but returned to life as a transformed human being. She was eager to bring the subject up and get Father Maximos's feedback. The prophetic advice of Stephanos and Erato, that an opportune time was bound to come up when the near-death issue would be discussed, was right on the mark.

Margarita was present at the public discussion of the subject, but out of shyness she did not volunteer to reveal her extraordinary experience in front of a big audience. But, in the small and informal gathering of eight people at her cousin's home, she opened up and shared with us her life-changing ordeal.

Margarita, a high school teacher of English literature, described in minute detail her near-death experience. Her story matched closely the stages of the near-death experience that Raymond Moody describes in his work, and that are repeatedly confirmed by other researchers of this extraordinary phenomenon. She found herself out of her body, watching the doctors work on a body that was in a comatose state and that the doctors eventually pronounced dead. She knew exactly what was happening in other parts of the hospital and could watch the agony of her relatives and other friends. She then traveled through a tunnel at the end of which there was an indescribable light waiting for her. There was a Christ entity inside that light which emanated the most profound personal love that she had ever experienced. It was as if she had met her loving parents after a prolonged absence. So much did she feel the intensity of that love that she wished to stay there, in her "real home," as she put it. The Christlike entity, however, counseled her to return to her body and to life on earth because her time had not yet come to cross the threshold into the realm of the spirit world. Margarita was told that she had unfinished business in this life that she needed to take care of first.

"Before I had that experience I was full of doubts about life after death," Margarita revealed. "In fact I was more of a nihilist than a believer. Until that time I had not read any books written by saints that would have given me an intellectual understanding about the light that they all refer to and that I witnessed during my near-death experience."

Margarita went on to claim that the absolute beauty and love she experienced as she encountered the light at the end of the tunnel radically transformed her outlook on life and profoundly changed her beliefs about death.

Margarita's story brought to my mind the case of Dannion Brinkley, one of Raymond Moody's subjects and collaborators, who had not one but three near-death episodes, one after being struck by lightning and the other two during heart surgery. When I first met him during the 1993 conference that established the Office of Alternative Therapies at the National Institutes of Health in Washington, D.C., he described almost verbatim what Margarita experienced. He completely lost his fear of death after he realized that there was life beyond the grave. Furthermore, the experience itself was absolutely magnificent. Mr. Brinkley in fact claimed that he was "kicking and screaming," as he had no desire to return to his body since he felt that during his near-death state he was "home."

I described his experience to the people around the table and Margarita was pleased that her own experience was corroborated by others in different parts of the world. Father Maximos listened with interest, often nodding.

"I am really very pleased to hear that science has begun to explore such phenomena," he said after pointing out that what Margarita had described and what he had heard during the public discussion of the near-death experience were hardly at odds with the Christian spiritual tradition as it is found in the teachings of the holy elders.

When I brought up the negative reaction to the work of Raymond Moody and other pioneering thanatologists Father Maximos shook his head and said, "On the contrary it seems to me that in many ways all these phenomena support the teachings of the *Ecclesia*. Or I should say there is a convergence on many points between what science discloses and what the theology of the *Ecclesia* professes about the nature of death."

I was fascinated that Father Maximos was so positive about the near-death experience. I knew that other Orthodox elders, like the American convert from Protestantism Father Seraphim Rose, took a much more negative view.[2] I was curious to hear the details of Father Maximos's position.

"Perhaps, Father Maxime, you can summarize for us what the basic teachings of the *Ecclesia* are on death so that we can compare them with what scientists like Raymond Moody tell us about the near-death experience and with what Margarita has gone through," suggested Yiannis, our physician host.

Father Maximos glanced casually around at the keen faces waiting to hear what he had to say about this primordial concern. "As we try to understand this issue, we must keep in mind the fundamental position of the *Ecclesia* that God created everything *ek tou me ontos* [ex nihilo], as we say. God also created human beings in his own image and placed them within a paradisiacal world where there was neither death nor suffering of any kind. Humans were in continuous contemplation of God and had the potential to live in that state eternally. We must also keep in mind another important belief of the *Ecclesia*, that a human being is a psychosomatic unity. The *Ecclesia* does not accept the permanent separation of soul and body but sees both as an indivisible unity. This is the natural state as ordained by God. This is what the *Ecclesia* teaches.

"It is with the Fall," Father Maximos continued, "that death first came into the picture, leading to the split between soul and body. People often ask me whether this is some sort of punishment for Adam and Eve's transgressions. My answer is a categorical no. God is not punishing anyone for violating his commandments."

"But how else should we understand it, Father Maxime?" Yiannis asked.

"You can view it simply as the natural consequence of the disruption of the relationship between human beings and God. Nothing more, nothing less. Based on the experiences of the saints and on what is written in the Holy Scriptures, the *Ecclesia* speaks of three types of death. First, there is the biological death of the body that we all know about and we all dread so deeply," Father Maximos said humorously. "Then, there is a psychic death when a human being is cut off from God, from life itself. Remember what Jesus said? 'I am the way and the life—'"

"We find a similar reference in the Apocalypse," interjected Father Nikodemos, who sat next to Father Maximos. "That's when Jesus tells an unworthy bishop that he is alive only in name but in reality he is dead."

"Good. That bishop had no relationship with God, the source of life. He was biologically alive but psychically dead. The *Ecclesia* teaches that psychic death is abolished the moment the individual, through spiritual practice and effort, reestablishes contact with the Christ that is Life everlasting. In addition, according to the teachings of the *Ecclesia* even biological death will eventually be abolished with the Second Coming of Christ. Then there will be the resurrection of the dead and the reunification of the body of each individual with the soul."

"Excuse me for interrupting," said Helen, our hostess, "but would you like to have coffee?" Turkish coffee was traditionally served at the end of any meal in Cyprus when guests were present. Although Father Maximos rarely had coffee, he asked for a *sketos*, meaning black without sugar. Others followed suit and while the coffees were individually prepared we talked about other matters: the coming war in the Middle East, the political developments related to the Cyprus problem, and the condition of the archbishop, whose health was deteriorating, rendering him incapable of fulfilling his archiepiscopal duties.

"What's the third type of death, Father Maxime?" Margarita asked after the short interruption and after our hosts completed the coffee ritual.

"The *Ecclesia* speaks of eternal death," Father Maximos answered somberly.

"I must confess I have some reservations about this notion, Father Maxime," I said. Somehow the resurrection of bodies and eternal death did not sit well with my way of thinking.

"This notion is not really meant to imply a state of death as we understand it," Father Maximos hastened to explain. "A human being is never lost. The way the holy elders understood real death was simply being cut off from direct communion with God's love."

Not wishing to detract from our main theme I did not follow up with another question on the matter of eternal death.

"The near-death experience," Father Maximos repeated, "is not inconsistent with the teachings of the holy elders."

"In what way?" Margarita asked.

"As you yourself described, people who undergo such experiences demonstrate unusual powers and abilities. People in such a state have experiences such as traveling in different places, and hearing and seeing what the doctors have been doing during the time that the patients were supposed to be dead. Then after they come back from their near-death experience, they talk about it. They shock their doctors with what they report. The doctors realize that what their patients said they saw happening somewhere else during the duration of the near-death state actually did happen just as they described it, as if they were fully present. Isn't this what the scientists who have studied this phenomenon say, Kyriaco?"

"Yes, yes," I replied. "The patients were aware and conscious in some other way while their bodies remained in a comatose state and were considered clinically dead by the attending physicians."

"That was true with my experience," Margarita said earnestly. Yiannis, the physician, confirmed what his cousin had related.

"Well, such experiences should not be surprising," Father Maximos said. "Throughout the ages there have been stories like these in the lives of saints. For those of us who have lived on Mount Athos, such phenomena, and some even more extraordinary than that, are routine."

"How are they being explained?" our host asked.

"You see, my dear Yianni, such phenomena are real because the soul in reality is endowed with extraordinary powers. That's how God made us, in his own image. Deep within our human nature we are gifted with extraordinary abilities that have been buried there due to the distortions created by the Fall. But in critical moments such as the near-death experience, these powers may come to the surface. Such gifts of the spirit do often emerge after systematic and prolonged spiritual *askesis*.

"To give you an example, we learn from the study of the lives of saints," Father Maximos continued, "that when they were in a state of *Theosis*, their physical functions were often suspended. That is why a saint like Paisios the Great [not the elder of Father Maximos] was reported not to have eaten for seventy-two years. According to his biographer he kept himself alive only with Holy Communion."

"Medically speaking this is impossible," Yiannis retorted, who in spite of his devout predisposition could not suppress his skepticism.

"But in a *theosized* state the laws of nature are sometimes transcended," Father Maximos explained. "Osios Savvas, from the Vadopedi monastery, who was considered a 'fool in Christ,' was immobilized for three months without food and water. He was neither hungry nor thirsty because during those three months he was in a state of ecstasy under the direct energy of *Theosis*."

"In such a state a person can literally walk on water," Father Nikodemos pointed out.

"Of course," Father Maximos added as if it were a self-evident truth. "I would even add that sometimes people under ordinary physical conditions could tap into inner powers that would be considered extraordinary. It happens to people all the time."

Father Maximos's words reminded me of what a pilgrim once told me. He claimed to have been present when an extraordinary phenomenon unfolded before him on Mount Athos. Having witnessed that phenomenon, he underwent a radical change in his life. Encouraged by my hosts and by Father Maximos I shared the details of that case.

"I met this pilgrim a year ago thanks to a mutual friend. Over a beer at a local pub frequented by peace and environmental activists he narrated to me in great sincerity what he had witnessed. He was a regular visitor of Mount Athos for the past seventeen years and he was quite familiar with the Holy Mountain and its ways. While attending vespers at a remote monastery during one of his visits, he noticed that a monk who was holding a candle while praying in front of the icon of the Holy Virgin began to gradually levitate until he was a meter high. Terrified, he turned toward his companion and asked him whether he was seeing the same thing. His companion was equally stupefied. 'Later on during dinner,' this person told me, 'we both kept looking at this monk who was quietly eating at the edge of the table. We just could not eat and we kept staring at him, speechless. Then without raising his head to look at us and while he was focused on his food he muttered: "Fellows, eat and forget what you just saw tonight."' As I listened to his story I remembered that Marco Polo too, after his twenty-year voyages to the East, reported to his fellow Venetians that he had witnessed such a phenomenon. He had seen a Tibetan monk rising up during a state of meditative ecstasy. But he stopped talking about his experience after the monks in charge of the Inquisition began showing an interest in his tale."

Father Maximos went on to repeat that such phenomena are not surprising or uncommon on Mount Athos. They are the products of relentless and focused spiritual work.

"Can such phenomena be witnessed outside the boundaries of the *Ecclesia?*" asked Yiannis.

"But of course. These are powers deeply buried within human beings by virtue of their humanity and of their creation in the image of God. They appear as supernatural phenomena but in reality they are perfectly natural. Such abilities simply transcend the sphere of the three-dimensional world that we are in contact with through our five senses but they are still part of this world. They don't belong to the world beyond, they are part of the created cosmos."

"What about near-death experiences, like the one Margarita just described?" Yiannis asked. "Isn't that an experience of the world beyond?"

"Well, not necessarily," Father Maximos replied, with some hesitation.

"No?" The doctor's eyes widened.

"Let me explain. While I was on Mount Athos I must have met at least ten people who shared such experiences during confessions. I became curious and tried to search within the context of the experiences of the holy elders for an explanation. In order to really understand these matters we must differentiate the created cosmos from the uncreated world of the energies of God and of the spirit world. We must bear in mind that although these are 'near-death experiences' they are not experiences of death itself. At best, they tell us something about the process of death but not about the real thing. Nobody has died and came back to tell us about it. I am delighted and reassured, however, to hear that the majority of people who undergo such an experience report that while it lasted they were filled with joy."

"Not only that, Father Maxime," I interjected. "People who have such experiences report radical shifts in their worldview. For example, they lose their fear of death. Many of them change their lifestyle, become more loving and caring and turn into avid learners. They discover, they claim, that the reason we are here is to love and to learn. They discover that knowledge and love last forever and that they are the only things that we take along as we depart from this life."

238

"All of that is very good, of course," Father Maximos said. "However, what I mean to say is that these experiences are part of this world of creation even if they take place in a different dimension than the one we are ordinarily conscious of. They do not occur in the spirit world, in the world of angels and demons, which is beyond this world. To my knowledge nobody has visited those regions and returned to report on them. From the point of view of the *Ecclesia*, whatever we do know about that world is based on what the saints have been telling us by means of the Holy Spirit.

"Scientists tell us," Father Maximos went on, "that during the near-death experience there are five stages. What about the sixth stage? From there on the trip has no return. For as long as you are in the fifth stage there is no problem. You go up on the ceiling, see what is going on below as the doctors try to resuscitate you, and so on. It is at the point beyond the ceiling, beyond the possibility of return, that the mystery begins."

"Oh, I see what you mean," Yiannis said. "Scientists that explore the near-death experience tell us about processes related to the space that they have authority over, namely the world of creation. Therefore, science can help us understand the near-death experience but not death itself and spiritual dimensions beyond creation."

"You got it! Science does not have the methodology to explore the worlds beyond the created universe. This is the province of the saints, those who have become true vehicles of holy wisdom, the *theosized* human beings. Now, as we said before, we know for a fact that human beings have hidden within themselves extraordinary abilities that, as I am told, science is only now gradually beginning to document and discover."

"What abilities, Father Maxime?" Yiannis asked.

"Some human beings have the capacity to see with closed eyes and from a distance. I have witnessed it many times, as in the case of the late Elder Prophyrios. On Mount Athos such phenomena are taken for granted. I have met many elders and ordinary monks who have such abilities. In fact they seem to have such experiences the moment they step into a monastery and begin their monastic life. This is nothing to get excited about for us monks. It is a routine matter in the lives of monks and ascetics."

"Parapsychologists call it 'clairvoyance,'" I said.

"We call it seeing *en Pneumati Agio* [through the Holy Spirit]. There are many other types of phenomena that people experience. I hear about them in the confessional all the time. Such experiences, however, are within the natural boundaries of our existence. And the light that is being seen during the near-death experience and what holy elders themselves see and report is usually not the Uncreated Light of God but the created light of human beings."

"What's the difference?" Yiannis asked.

"The Uncreated Light is the light that is God himself. The great saints have had such contact in a state of *Theosis*. The created light springs from human nature itself."

"I don't understand," Margarita responded.

"Look. Since God is Light and resides in Light so too do human beings, who are created in God's image have light inside them. The foundation of their existence is light. It is the created light that the holy elders also speak of and identify as one stage on the progress of human beings toward God. It can emerge during the practice of the *Noera Prosefchi* [Noetic Prayer, or the Jesus Prayer]. So what I wish to say here is that the light that people who have near-death experiences see may be the light that emanates from within themselves rather than the Uncreated Light, which is beyond the created world."

"The Uncreated Light is the ultimate stage of spiritual attainment," I volunteered to clarify. "It is the final union of the soul with God."

"But it is beautiful," Margarita said, alluding to her own experience.

"Of course it is beautiful!" Father Maximos exclaimed. "We are made in the image of God and what we see is the beauty of our own existence." Father Maximos claimed. "This is no trifling matter. However, there is a possible trap here. People who come in contact with the magnificence of their own existence and experience the radiant light within themselves may become so enamored with it that they may feel they have reached God and experienced God's Light. In fact, all they experienced was the beauty of the light that is inherent in their very essence, the light that emanates from within themselves."

240

"These subtle differences are difficult for us mere mortals to comprehend," I said jokingly.

"As I mentioned earlier, the light that people see after the experience of the tunnel during their near-death experience is not necessarily the Uncreated Light of God that the saints have talked about. It should not be confused with divine grace that usually comes after an arduous spiritual struggle, after the purification of the self, after *Catharsis*. It is instead the created light inherent in the deepest recesses of our existence that can surface during extreme conditions, like the near-death experience."

"Or during deep prayer and spiritual practice," I added.

"Precisely. The holy elders know this light very well as they themselves have experienced it. They can therefore differentiate between this light, which precedes the experience of the Uncreated Light of God, and the light that emerges after the self is purified from egotistical desires."

"So what people usually experience in the near-death experience is really a first stage of experience on the ascent toward God," I said.

"In a sense this is what seems to be the case. Human beings do not need a near-death experience to come in contact with that light. When they pray systematically they will first reach that stage of experiencing the light that is found within every human being. The holy elders have an entire theology around the nature of light and the various stages of experiencing light during prayer. Before you reach the Uncreated Light you must go through that stage of experiencing the light embedded in your own nature."

"Is that a problem?" I asked.

"Of course it is not a problem. But we must remember it is only a stage for the reasons we mentioned."

I remembered vividly a relevant passage from the work of Elder Sophrony that supported what Father Maximos had said. I summarized it for them: "The theologian who is an intellectualist constructs his system as an architect builds a palace. Empirical and metaphysical concepts are the materials he uses, and he is more concerned with the magnificence and logical symmetry of his ideal edifice than that it should conform to the actual order of things. . . . Many theologians of the philosophical type, remaining essentially rationalists, rise to suprarational . . . spheres of thought, but these spheres are not yet the divine world. . . . People in this category . . . come to realize that the laws of human thought are of limited validity, and that it is impossible to encircle the whole universe within the steel hoops of logical syllogisms. This enables them to arrive at a supramental contemplation, but what they then contemplate is still merely beauty created in God's image. Since those who enter for the first time into this sphere of the 'silence of the mind' experience a certain mystic awe, they mistake their contemplation for mystical communion with the divine."[3]

"This is good," Father Maximos said, nodding.

"So what happens to a person who has such an experience?" I asked.

"If he stays there he may enter into *plani*, or delusion, and may end up, as the chant of the *Ecclesia* goes, worshiping the objects of Creation rather than the Creator. It seems to me that this could happen either to people with near-death experiences or people who pray systematically and begin to experience their own light, or people who have exosomatic experiences of various types, or to theologians enamored with the beauty they discover with their intellect. In fact it is said that the real reason behind Lucifer's fall as an archangel was this mistake. He became enchanted with the beauty of his own existence, his own light."

"However, such experiences," I proposed, "open up people's realization that there are worlds out there beyond the world of our five senses. So far I have personally seen only good coming out of such experiences."

"I don't doubt it. Experiences like Margarita's can lead to very positive spiritual consequences. All I am saying is that for serious seekers caution is needed to overcome the temptation of feeling self-important. Humility and guidance are essential so that they may be able to differentiate the created light present within themselves and the Uncreated Light of God, which is the ultimate spiritual prize."

"I have a question Father Maxime," Yiannis said. "Since the time I was young I've had a problem with the notion of 'the resurrection of the dead' that we recite every Sunday in church. What is the meaning of it, really?"

"Again, always according to the official teachings of the *Ecclesia*," Father Maximos replied with a broad smile, "a human being is a psychosomatic unity, made of soul and body. The death of the body is an abnormal phenomenon, an affront to and degeneration of God's perfect work. For this reason God does not allow death to become victorious at the end. Through an eventual resurrection, God restores the unity of body and soul that was put asunder as a result of death."

"Body and soul will be resurrected at the end?" Yiannis asked.

"No. The soul never dies. It is only the dead body that will be resurrected in a new, imperishable and incorruptible form, just like Christ's body after the Resurrection. Human beings will then be in a position to experience the joy of the Uncreated Glory of God not only as souls but also as a psychosomatic unity."

I had told Father Maximos in an earlier conversation that for a modern individual the notion of the resurrection of bodies appears ludicrous at worst and only symbolic of a deeper truth at best. I also mentioned that for modern individuals, a symbolic interpretation of these teachings may be more palatable, such as the notion that the "resurrection of the dead" is the reunion of human beings with God and the attainment of *Theosis*. With such an understanding, the "dead" are all human beings who are not in conscious communion with the divine. Father Maximos claimed that this is only one side of the story. As a functionary of the *Ecclesia* he was also committed to the notion of the resurrection of bodies and to the fact that we as human beings are a psychosomatic reality and will remain so within eternity but within a different context.

"How would the billions of people who died come back to earth and acquire flesh and bones as they were before?" Yiannis asked and shook his head in disbelief. "And if things are like that how are we going to deal with the problem of overpopulation? How will this world be organized? How are they going to make their living and so on?"

"A very logical question," Father Maximos replied amidst chuckles from everybody. In a more serious tone he went on. "We believe in the resurrection of all human beings, regardless of religion, ethnicity, or whatever. All human beings from the first humans to the present will undergo this transformation. But, at the same time, according to the Christian doctrine we anticipate not only the resurrection of the dead but also a new heaven and a new earth. That means it is not on this perishable earth that we will all live but on a new creation. This creation will be renewed so that it may become ready for the new bodies of human beings who will no longer be dressed with this perishable flesh that grows old and dies. All human beings will be at an age that will be imperishable just like, as I said, the body of Christ after the Resurrection. There won't be young and old and middle-aged people and infants."

"Will they need to eat?" Yiannis asked playfully.

"There will be no need for food that is perishable. Instead human beings will get their energy through the sheer love and contemplation of God. So there won't be any need for money or buildings," Father Maximos added with a smile. "Also, as the saints teach, there will be no danger for one's safety and sense of well-being. The 'garments of skin' will no longer be necessary. We won't have all this deterioration and perishability which we experience in our present form. All the elements of nature will be transformed and humanity will live within a radically different dimension of reality."

"I see. This is the 'different context' you mentioned," Yiannis said. "So the resurrection of the dead will take place within a new Creation altogether?"

"This is what the *Ecclesia* teaches. It will take place within a restored Creation, the way God intended it to be. How else could present conditions accommodate the magnitude of the Second Coming of Christ and the resurrection of all bodies?"

"One more question, Father Maxime," said Yiannis. "When the soul

243

separates from the body, where will it be until the final resurrection? What does it do? Does it evolve or does it remain in a state of, let's say, deep sleep?"

"Another logical question! Unfortunately, it cannot be answered through logic. The notion of space belongs to this world. So where the soul will be until the common resurrection can only be answered this way: it will be in the world of the spirits where the angels reside. It is a world beyond time and space. We are speaking here of a radically different world, a radically different dimension beyond our capacity to know, through logic that is. Nobody can describe with words that world that lies beyond space and time. At the same time, during that period of waiting there is, let us say, an evolutionary process of the soul toward God. It is a dynamic process as the soul marches up toward the greatness of God."

"So the soul continues to grow," I said. "It does not enter into some sort of a static condition awaiting the Second Coming."

"Right. That's what the holy elders say. Had it been otherwise, had the soul been in a state of inertia, of stasis, then at some point it would experience fatigue and boredom in its vision of God, regardless of how good and beautiful God is. Anything that we focus on continuously without change would unavoidably lead to fatigue and lack of interest. But a human being proceeds in an evolutionary upward march toward a God that is infinite. The life of a human being within this infinite 'space' of God is a continuous and uninterrupted motion that leads, so to speak, from one surprise to another surprise of God's magnificence. That is why saints, like angels, ceaselessly glorify God—because they are continuously witnessing the greatness of God's love as it unfolds within their own hearts. So again, this is an evolutionary movement within the infinity of God's grandeur. It is not a static condition that breeds boredom. At the same time, however, it is at stasis."

"What's the meaning of this paradox?" I asked.

"It is both evolution and stasis at the same time, Kyriaco," Father Maximos replied. "While you stand in front of God you move toward God and vice versa."

"But what does it mean?" I asked again. I was reminded of the *koan* riddles of Zen teachers.

"We cannot say that the soul is stationed in one particular spot, in some kind of a stationary harbor, because, as I said, this would imply saturation and boredom. At the same time the soul is not in an ongoing state of unquenched seekership."

"So the soul is simultaneously feeling fulfilled and complete but at the same time evolving eternally within the infinity of God's glory," I concluded.

"Yes, you might say it that way. I know it is paradoxical, but remember we are speaking about matters that are beyond language's capacity to pin them down. These are matters that are beyond reason and logic."

"I see what you mean."

"I have a related question, Father Maxime," Margarita said. "When the soul separates from the body does it experience an expansion of its knowledge about the world? I mean, does it know more about reality after this separation than while being confined within the body? Furthermore, can it have any impact on the material plane? Can it, for example, pray for loved ones still in this life who may benefit from this prayer in the same way that we pray for the benefit of the departed during memorial services?"

"That's a lot of questions," Father Maximos protested with humor. "As I just stated, our path toward God is dynamic, not static. Our journey proceeds from knowledge to knowledge and from glory to glory and from one enchanting surprise to another."

"One can make an argument that this is how life is in this world," I suggested. "This dynamic is embedded in human existence itself. It is the source of all creativity, leading humanity from one discovery to another in a never-ending spiral."

"Yes, but with the proviso that the knowledge I refer to is not intellectual, meaning that today I know about things that I didn't know yesterday. Rather, according to the saints, this after-death knowledge is a neverending experiential *gnosis*, or knowledge of God. It is a different form of knowledge from the one we are familiar with."

"On the other hand," I added, "this is also what we experience in this dimension of reality. We can never reach a saturation point of knowledge about this world, just as we can never reach saturation point in our knowledge of God. Our sciences expand within a limitless outward universe. You can never say that you can know everything there is to be known about the physical world, or the social world for that matter."

"If it is true of this world just imagine how much more true it is within the pursuit of the knowledge of God," Father Maximos added. "That's why Apostle Paul gave us those words that our path toward God is from glory to glory and from one enchantment to another in a never-ending process. Therefore, a human being after death continues to maintain his or her powers of consciousness and can continue to commune with the spirit of God. By that I don't mean that the soul will pray to God for this or that object or favor. By prayer I mean the method that unites human beings with God. With this type of prayer the departed can cover and commune with the entire human race in the same way that we commune and pray for the souls of the departed. That's why we have memorials. It is our way of communicating, through the Holy Spirit, with those who have already left for the great journey."

"It has been said, and we hear it in our funeral rites," Yiannis said after a short break in conversation, "that at the point of death the separation of the soul from the body is violent, forceful. Does that mean that it is a painful experience? And if yes, is the pain psychological or somatic?"

"The words 'forceful separation' in the funeral chant that you are referring to," Father Maximos replied, "do not imply pain. Again, let me remind you that according to the theology of the holy elders, body and soul were not meant to be separated. Such words symbolize this belief. After that 'forceful' separation a human being enters within a purely spiritual space and embarks on the march up toward God. It seems to me that whether an individual will experience pain or not at the point of the separation of the soul from the body depends on the spiritual condition of the person. Had he struggled in life for spiritual perfection and had he become victorious over death, while still living in this life, then the experience of death would not be painful but beatific, as we have witnessed in the lives of so many saints."

"Is this why at the entrance of the Stavrovouni monastery there is that paradoxical epigram, 'If you die before you die you shall not die when you die?'" I asked.

"Exactly. This is a motto well known among monks and ascetics. On the other hand, for persons who are hermetically tied to their earthly passions of, say, hedonism or worldly possessions or fame and success, death will be painful because such persons experience separation from the sources of their passions and desires. That can cause terror and fear in their hearts. Having said that," Father Maximos added, "we must also keep in mind that because death is something outside of the essence of human nature as given by God, regardless of how spiritually advanced one might be, it does not cease to be an undesirable fact of human existence and a source of tragedy and grief."

It was three in the afternoon when Father Maximos stood up, bringing an end to our discussion on death, near-death, resurrection of bodies, and the afterlife. "These are topics," he said, "that are inexhaustible. We can never cover them in one sitting."

When I returned at sunset to our apartment in Limassol my mind was still spinning around death, the afterlife, near-death, and the resurrection of bodies. I sat in front of my computer to type out some more notes before they disappeared from my memory:

One thing has become abundantly clear to me: the common notion in mainline Christianity about eternal hell and damnation, an issue that Father Maximos avoided raising, leaves me singularly cold and indifferent. It has been one of those elements in the fundamentalist Christian understanding of life after death that has sent many Christians seeking answers in other religions, particularly Hinduism and Buddhism, where one finds no such grim and unappealing eschatology. I said as much to Father Maximos on several occasions. He always listened with silent understanding to my concerns. His standard reply was that God will judge every person at the "end of times" with total love and compassion. It was a statement that was good enough for me under the circumstances.

The mantra of the connoisseurs of hell, however, is that God has given us freedom to choose (*aftexousion*) that includes the freedom to opt either for hell or for paradise. This is what differentiates us from other animals, we are told. In my understanding, however, this position is in sharp contrast with the totally loving "Heavenly Father." Being a father myself, I too want my children to develop their personalities and show initiative. I too would therefore like to allow them maximum freedom for that very purpose so that they become full adults. But if I see my child ready to fall over a precipice won't I, as a loving father, forget about the *aftexousion* and instead grab my child in the nick of time, preventing his or her death? If this is true of me as a mere imperfect human being with my limitations, how much more true it must be for the absolutely loving and compassionate God "the Father." Will he allow a single soul to plunge into the precipice of an eternal hell, an "eternal death?" This type of problematic reasoning that is often advocated from the pulpit seems misguided to me. It is an interpretation that is based on incomplete spiritual maturity, what Father Maximos called the "religion of slaves."

Fortunately, the teachings of some of my favorite saints seem to me to contradict the formal, external vision that is a favorite of hell-and-damnation theologians. How could I be happy in paradise, said Saint Silouan, if I know that a single fellow human being is condemned to eternal damnation? Then in his authoritative saintly way he goes on to declare:

> My soul knows the mercy of God towards sinful humanity. Standing face to face with God I am writing the truth: that every one of us sinful human beings will be saved. Not even a single soul will be lost, if it undergoes *metanoia*. It is so because the Lord is so infinitely Good in His very nature that it is impossible to describe with whatever words.[4]

Saint Gregory of Nyssa, brother of Saint Basil the Great, speaks of the *apokatastasis ton panton*, the restoration of everything in its pre-Fallen state, implying that in some mysterious way all will be saved at the end insofar as all sinners will sooner or later mature spiritually and undergo their *metanoia* that will open the gates for them to experience the eternal love of the Creator. Even the likes of Hitler will have such an opportunity, but with the proviso, always, that they must undergo a genuine *metanoia*. In my mind it is self-evident and is understood that without *metanoia* no one is saved. At the same time and based on my limited logic, I can't see where the fairness of God lies if he gives me only one brief chance in one insignificant lifetime. It must mean that the choice to undergo *metanoia* must extend even beyond the grave. Life after death must imply an eternal evolutionary process of purification, the catharsis of the soul within the context of the *aftexousion*. The infinite love and compassion of God presupposes such an understanding of the afterlife. At least that's how I see it. How it happens that a Hitler will have the opportunity to undergo *metanoia* is a mystery that I leave up to God. It was comforting for me,

however, to read in the letters of one of the leading twentieth-century elders of Mount Athos to his spiritual children the repeated ending "Don't
despair! We will go to Paradise together. And if I don't place you inside,
then I do not want to sit in there either."[5]

I happened to be reading Huston Smith's latest book, *Why Religion
Matters*, which I had brought to Cyprus with me. Given my admiration for
him both as a person and as the foremost authority on the world's religions,
I was pleased to notice that toward the end of his book he dealt with the
issue of eternal damnation. Most important, I was pleased to learn that he
reached the same conclusion as my own on this topic—there is nothing
more gratifying than to learn that people you respect and admire share your
own views on issues that you feel passionate about.

It was in 1964, Huston Smith wrote, when on a leave of absence from
his university, that he conducted research in India. One day he was con
versing with several gurus, reputed as authorities in their craft, who took
him to the foothills of the Himalayas.

> Suddenly, there appeared in the doorway of the bungalow I was in a figure
> so striking that for a moment I thought I might be seeing an apparition.
> Tall, dressed in a white gown, and with a full beard, it was a man I came to
> know as Father Lazarus, a missionary of the Eastern Orthodox Church
> who had spent the last twenty years in India. Ten minutes after I was intro-
> duced to him I had forgotten my gurus completely—he was much more in-
> teresting than they were—and for a solid week we tramped the Himalayan
> foothills talking nonstop.

Huston Smith went on to tell Father Lazarus that he was very attracted to
Hinduism because of its doctrine of universal salvation. "Everyone makes
it in the end. Its alternative, eternal damnation, struck me as a monstrous
doctrine that I could not accept." "Me too!" I wrote in the margin of the
book.

> Brother Lazarus responded by telling me his views on that matter. They
> took off from the passage in Second Corinthians where Saint Paul tells of
> knowing someone who twelve years earlier had been caught up into the

[handwritten margin note: Why Religion Matters by Huston Smith]

249

third heaven, whether in the body or out of the body he did not know . . . in that heaven the man 'heard things that were not to be told, that no mortal is permitted to repeat.' . . . Paul was speaking of himself, Father Lazarus was convinced, and the secret he was told in the third heaven was that ultimately everyone is saved. That is the fact of the matter, Father Lazarus believed, but it must not be told because the uncomprehending would take it as a license for irresponsibility. If they are going to be saved eventually, why bother? That exegesis solved my problem and has stayed in place ever since.[6]

As in my own experience, he found such a resolution confirmed and reconfirmed in the life and work of sages and seers from around the world. On this reassuring note I turned off the computer and prepared for sleep. I left the notion of the resurrection of bodies for another time. Before sleeping I opened at random a page from Saint Silouan's work and read the first passage that appeared in front of my eyes:

> In the same way that someone alive knows when he is cold and when he is hot, so it is with a person who has known through experience the Spirit of God. He knows when his soul is filled with Grace and when visited by cunning spirits.

In another passage I read: "The Spirit of God teaches the soul to love everything that is alive, so much so that the soul does not wish to cut even a green leaf from a tree, not even to step over a wild flower."[7]

THIRTEEN

REMEMBRANCE

O F

GOD

uring March of 2003 the dogs of war were once again unleashed into the sandstorms of the Middle East. People were dying in droves only a few hundred miles from Cyprus. The noise of the military aircraft at the nearby British bases taking off and landing after their bombing missions day after day brought the war in a nerve-racking way perilously close to home. Like Emily, I was depressed to witness the unraveling tragedy while feeling powerless, like the rest of the world, to do anything beyond protest to prevent what we felt was a disastrous and avoidable war.

I was depressed not only for the innocent Iraqis who

were being killed but by the death of hundreds of young American soldiers. Many of them, I was certain, could not even locate Iraq on the map, nor spell the name of the country to which they were being airlifted. I knew that some of the national guardsmen sent into harm's way were former students of mine, some of whom, coming from disadvantaged families, joined the military to get a university education. Members of this class of Americans were to wet the sands of Mesopotamia with their blood.

For the first time I found myself on the defensive and was compelled, time and again, to explain to friends and acquaintances that the decision of a few people in the Bush administration to wage war did not necessarily reflect the wishes of the majority of the American people. In the meantime Emily and I accompanied Stephanos and Erato to several all-night prayer vigils initiated and presided over by Father Maximos for peace and divine intervention. It is during moments of utter powerlessness and despair that most of us remember God.

One of the minor casualties of the outbreak of hostilities in the region was the cancellation of a plan that I had made with Lavros to spend a few days at the famous fourth-century monastery of Saint Catherine at the foothills of Mount Sinai where Moses received the Ten Commandments. In the midst of the hatreds and the political passions that percolated with the start of the war, we felt it was unwise to travel to Cairo and then take the long bus ride into the Sinai Desert. Instead it made more sense for Lavros and me to join Antonis on one of his regular trips to Mount Athos.

When I asked Father Maximos for his advice as to whether I should take up Antonis's invitation for another pilgrimage to Mount Athos, he was surprised that I would even ask. "Of course you should go," he commanded in a raised voice. "Such opportunities must not be missed. A visit to the Holy Mountain is always beneficial." Thanks to over a thousand years of uninterrupted prayer by Athonite monks, the entire peninsula is heavily charged with divine grace and energy. Depending on their level of receptivity, pilgrims may absorb some of this energy for their own spiritual benefit and for that of others. "You must visit us here at least once a year," a hospitable abbot once urged me in his friendly way while I was on a visit to the Holy Mountain.

After hearing Father Maximos's reaction, I called up Antonis to confirm my decision to join him for the weeklong pilgrimage. It was to be my second visit to the Holy Mountain with Antonis, my "Athonite godfather," as I jokingly referred to him. He was the person responsible for my initial introduction to Mount Athos in 1991 when I met Father Maximos and discovered the spiritual tradition hidden in those ancient monasteries. We were to reenact the journey of more than a decade ago that had proved to be such a turning point in my spiritual life and writing career.

"Mark it on your calendar," Antonis instructed over the phone. "We are leaving Friday the eighteenth of April, and returning on Holy Thursday the twenty-fourth. I already made all the arrangements. They are expecting us at Vatopedi [the second-largest monastery and the place where I first met Father Maximos]. Besides Lavros, we will be joined by two other friends of mine," Antonis added.

Lavros's participation in the pilgrimage was an added motivation for me to join them. He was well connected with a number of monks and abbots and had invaluable insights into the culture and ways of the Holy Mountain. Most important, he was a perfect companion for such ventures, never losing his humor, in spite of his grief at losing his wife of over forty years.

We left the island as the first phase of the war in Iraq was winding down and amidst local euphoria at Cyprus's formal invitation to join the European Union by May 1, 2004. When we arrived at the Larnaka airport the atmosphere was festive as dignitaries waited for the arrival of the Greek prime minister, who presided over the European Union during that period. The European flag was everywhere, overshadowing even the flag of the Republic of Cyprus. It was a major achievement for the Cypriots, who, with help from Greece, had worked relentlessly for decades to persuade the other European countries to include Cyprus in the upcoming major expansion of the Union in 2004. For the first time Cypriots felt less vulnerable toward Turkey, which also aspired to enter the European Union.

Our plane touched the tarmac of the Thessaloniki airport at four in the afternoon. Thanks to Antonis's initiative, a taxi was waiting for us for the three-hour drive to Ouranoupolis, the fishing town at the borderline separating the Chalkidiki peninsula from the thirty-mile-long Athonite promontory. As in previous pilgrimages, we had to stay in Ouranoupolis that night in order to board the ferry *Axion Esti* (named after a miraculous Athonite icon) the following morning for the two-and-a-half-hour ride to Daphni, the western entry point of Mount Athos. The Athonite community, a semi-autonomous republic that operated within the legal bounds of the Greek state, was compelled to protect itself by regulating the daily number of visitors allowed to enter its territory. For this reason we had to secure our *diamoniteria* (visas) at Ouranoupolis before we were given permission to board the ferry. Antonis took care of all the formalities from Cyprus so that by the time we reached Ouranoupolis we could enjoy the night by the harbor. Given the crowds waiting in line, had Antonis not made the arrangements ahead of time we may have been denied a visa and our journey would have ended right at the harbor of Ouranoupolis over Greek wine and octopus.

It was a period of high demand and the twenty monasteries could only accommodate a certain number of pilgrims at a time. No other forms of accommodation existed on the Holy Mountain. Therefore, all visitors had to be given hospitality at the monasteries, an increasingly demanding task in an age of easy access and transportation. Yet the monks continued to offer their hospitality generously to the pilgrims. In spite of its remoteness, Mount Athos has been discovered by a growing number of spiritual seekers, but also by travel adventurers as well as impostors looking for a free vacation. I remember what a concerned Scotsman once said to me during a previous visit while we walked from one monastery to another. "Mount Athos is the greatest secret of Europe. May it remain so forever. For that reason," he added with humor, "I'll never mention its existence to anybody."

There were six in our group. Besides Antonis, Lavros, and myself there were Nikos, a businessman and colleague of Antonis; Andreas, a retired diplomat and cousin of Antonis; and Paul, a physician from Athens. The last two were pleasantly shocked to meet each other at the Thessaloniki airport where we boarded the two taxis for Ouranoupolis. Unbeknownst to Antonis, who was the common denominator to us all, Paul was the personal physician of Andreas.

Unlike the jovial Scotsman I had met earlier, Antonis felt obligated to initiate all his friends and acquaintances into the reality of Mount Athos. Three from our group—Nikos, Andreas, and Paul—had never been to

Mount Athos before. For this reason, the moment we stepped into the taxi for Ouranoupolis Antonis took it upon himself to introduce his friends to some of the basic facts and lore of the Holy Mountain. Everything was new to them. In spite of the inclement weather, they cherished the three-hour drive listening to Antonis's stories, particularly those regarding the ongoing miracles that take place on the Holy Mountain.

When we boarded the *Axion Esti* the following day, the air felt unusually cold. Some passengers, unprepared for such weather conditions, began to shiver. A light drizzle compounded the discomfort, making the journey an even more rugged experience than usual, particularly for Nikos, who boarded the ferry in springtime gear. The whole of Europe was under an unusual spell of rough and cold weather for so late in the spring. It reached all the way to Greece and even Cyprus, reputed to be the warmest island of the Mediterranean.

Despite the weather, we chose to stand around on the unprotected top deck so that we could have a full view of the rare sights as we passed them. Thanks to extraordinarily deep waters around the peninsula, the ferry was able to hug the coastline, offering pilgrims the opportunity for a close-up view of the cliff-hanging monasteries and hermitages, the relics of the arcane and miracle-filled world of Mount Athos.

A seasoned student of the history of the Holy Mountain, Antonis enjoyed his role as guide to his neophyte friends. "This is the Russian monastery of Saint Panteleimon," he announced as we passed by it. "That's the monastery where Saint Silouan began his monastic career." He then explained who Saint Silouan was and went on to say that it was also the monastery of the Russian elder Sophrony Sakharov, disciple of Saint Silouan and founder of the well-known monastery of Saint John the Baptist in Essex, England.

"There was a time when this Russian monastery had close to fifteen hundred monks and looked like a real town. Over the entire Mount Athos there were at the start of the twentieth century somewhere between three and four thousand Russian monks. But after the 1917 Bolshevik takeover in Russia, their source of financial support was cut off and their numbers began to decline. At Saint Panteleimon's there are only about fifty monks today.

"By the way," Antonis added, "Elder Sophrony's monastery in Essex is the only monastery of its kind that I know of where both monks and nuns live, work, eat, and pray together. As you can imagine, it is quite a sharp contrast from Mount Athos." He went on to talk of the one-thousand-year-old history of the Holy Mountain, a refuge for monks and hermits since the ninth century, reserved for them by the then emperor of Byzantium.

Antonis's lesson was based on facts that Lavros and I knew well, but for the uninitiated like Nikos, Andreas, and Paul it was new information. For Andreas, however, the retired ambassador, the Holy Mountain had a special meaning. With some prompting from Antonis he overcame his original reluctance and narrated what had happened to him a few years earlier when he almost died from a cancerous tumor that appeared on the back of his head.

"I can only attribute my survival to a miracle," Andreas said, as we leaned on the railings, holding our umbrellas. "My good doctor here," he added and pointed at Paul, "urged me to have an examination because of the appearance of a lump at this spot." He turned his head and placed his finger just above where his neck met his skull. "When the specialists examined it they ordered immediate surgery. I was petrified with fear. The operation was dangerous. Even if I survived, I was warned, there were serious risks. There was a very high probability that I would remain paralyzed for life, or that I might become mute. Worst of all there was a danger that I might end up in a vegetative state. Yet I had no choice but to take those chances and have the operation. The tumor was going to kill me anyway."

Andreas then went on to reveal to us what happened the night before he entered the hospital. He saw a dream, he claimed, that was not actually a dream but a very lucid and real vision. A woman dressed as a nun, accompanied by his dead uncle, drew him toward her and reassured him that the operation was going to be a total success and that he had nothing to fear. He immediately realized that the nun was none other than the Holy Virgin. He was certain of that, even though up to that point in his life he was only marginally religious. In fact, he thought of himself as a skeptic.

"I was taken to the operating table the next morning as if I were to have breakfast," Andreas said emphatically. "I had absolutely no fear. That same afternoon, believe it or not, I walked out of the hospital. Many years have passed since then and my problem has never returned." That experience, he went on to add as his eyes became moist, changed him from a skeptic to a believer. Therefore, when his cousin Antonis called, he did not hesitate to join him for the pilgrimage. Andreas, now the manager of a company in Athens, suspended everything he was doing and took the opportunity to visit Mount Athos, where the Holy Virgin is at the very center of the monks' life of continuous prayer.

"The entire Mount Athos is a place of devotion to the Holy Virgin," Antonis said. "In every monastery there are icons of the *Theotokos* that are considered miraculous."

"It's interesting that no woman is ever allowed to step on it," Andreas said as we began approaching Daphni.

"Well, it is a problem, particularly now that Greece has become part of the European Union," said Lavros, moving to the edge of the ferry's left corridor where there was some cover. "Several women's organizations consider it a violation of their human rights. I believe, however, there is a great deal of misunderstanding here."

There were lively exchanges after Lavros's remarks that went on for some time. It did not surprise me. Each time I visit or talk about Mount Athos the issue of the *Avaton*, the prohibition that excludes women from setting foot on Mount Athos, comes up repeatedly. I have heard abbots and ordinary monks trying to explain to skeptical visitors that the *Avaton* has nothing to do with a negative predisposition toward women, insisting that its exclusive function is for *askesis*, to assure total and undistracted focus for the work the monks are engaged in. It is for this reason that the emperor of Constantinople made it a rule during the ninth century, a rule that had remained in force ever since. What cemented the imperial edict was the belief that the *Avaton* is in fact the wish of the *Theotokos* herself.

According to legend she chose the Holy Mountain as her private garden where she alone among all women would have the exclusive right to move about. According to Athonite lore, the Holy Virgin, accompanied by Saint Luke, went on a journey to visit Lazarus in Cyprus and got lost along the way because of high winds and thick fog. Their boat turned up instead on the eastern shore of Mount Athos. The moment she stepped on land there was an earthquake and all the pagan statues were demolished. So profound was her enchantment with the beauty of the place that she declared "This is my garden," and asked her son Jesus to offer it to her as a gift. Since then the Holy Virgin has been making her rounds, visiting monasteries and hermitages and appearing in the visions and ecstasies of the great elders and saints of Mount Athos, causing healing and other miracles to happen. As a result of these apparitions and miracles, the belief that she alone can move about on the Holy Mountain has been further cemented.

These manifestations of the Holy Virgin compose the core and backbone of Athonite tradition, reinforcing the taboo related to the presence of other women. Ironically, nowhere else in the world has womanhood in the image of the Holy Virgin been more honored and prayed to than on Mount Athos. Lore and fact got so intertwined over the centuries that it is virtually impossible to separate the two. Regardless of the factuality or mythic nature of the original story, unusual healing and other phenomena do take place that are attributed to the intervention of the Holy Virgin. This is at least the consensus of those who have an intimate understanding of and familiarity with the culture of the Holy Mountain.[1]

However, functionaries of the European Union, who have provided large sums of money that are channeled through the Greek state for the restoration of the monasteries, do not understand this form of thinking. In the name of equality and human rights they have placed enormous pressure on the monastic community to abandon the tradition. This pressure has created a double bind for the monks and hermits. Abandoning the tradition that has been such an integral part of the Athonite worldview and its ascetic ways for over a thousand years may threaten the very existence of Mount Athos itself. Maintaining the tradition, on the other hand, has created difficulties with European feminists and secular activists who have no sympathy for such traditions. Through no choice of its own, Mount Athos found itself in the European Union and therefore subject to laws and edicts coming not from ninth-century Constantinople but from twenty-first-century Brussels. "No wonder," I told my companions, "the Athonite monks have ambivalent feelings toward the West and what it represents."

Nevertheless, Greece as custodian of the Holy Mountain managed to maintain a tense truce on the subject of the *Avaton* by persuading her

European partners that Mount Athos should be considered an exception to European law, allowing for the preservation of and respect for its unique ways. A special provision was included within the charter of Greece's accession to the European Union that allowed the continuation of the *Avaton* of Mount Athos. In spite of these legal provisions the political pressures to open up the Holy Mountain to women visitors continued.

I shared my thoughts with my companions when the boat was close to Daphni. "The fathers of Mount Athos would rather die than change the *Avaton*," Antonis claimed, as the boat docked at Daphni. "For them it is a sacred tradition coming directly from the Mother of God and you don't tamper with that."

"Therefore, only she can change that rule," I concluded. "I can imagine several holy elders experiencing visions of the Holy Virgin announcing to them that the time has come to abandon the *Avaton*. That's the only legitimate way that I can think of that will permit change of that rule without threatening the basic foundations of the monastic community."

"And we never know when that could possibly happen," Lavros added as we began walking toward the minibus that, thanks to Antonis, waited to take us to Vatopedi, the monastery of our destination.

At the edge of Mount Athos several large and thriving women's monasteries have been set up in recent years with the same spiritual program that is practiced in all the other monasteries of Mount Athos. Furthermore, it is in one of these women's monasteries, Souroti, where Elder Paisios, who served as its elder during the latter part of his life, is buried. At another women's monastery at Ormylia, Elder Emilianos, another holy elder from Mount Athos, had served as the elder. It is as if, to accommodate women, a parallel Mount Athos is gradually being created.

Normally, traveling from one monastery to another is done on foot, a part of the total experience of being on Mount Athos. But it would have taken us six hours to get to Vatopedi and Antonis suffered from chronic back problems. To accommodate pilgrims like Antonis and to meet the needs of the monasteries, which faced an increasing influx of pilgrims, the Mount Athos administrators permitted the introduction of a few minibuses and trucks. The roads, however, remained deliberately unpaved. In bad weather they turned treacherous.

259

As we ascended the mountain, the minibus danced around danger-ously in the muddy conditions. I held my breath, feeling that it was a toss-up whether it would stay on the narrow road or slide along with the mud down the mountainside. Things were not made easier when our irrita-ble chauffeur mentioned that his minibus was not a four-wheel-drive. He almost hit the roof in anger when Antonis protested that it was inexcusable to drive a bus on such roads without four-wheel-drive. The chauffeur snapped that four-wheel-drive cars cost a fortune and that the average life of a car on Mount Athos was three years. We remained quiet, not wanting to further irritate our overstressed driver. We focused instead on the beauty of the land, forgetting the mud and placing our trust in the Lady who presided over her garden.

There was a collective sigh of relief when we finally arrived at the monastery. We generously paid the driver, who had by then calmed down markedly. Then we walked straight to the *archondariki*. Father Gennadios and Father Nyphon, monks that we had befriended from previous visits, treated us to liqueur made at the monastery and a piece of Turkish delight. It was part of their tradition of hospitality. Our friends were particularly happy to see Lavros, who after many visits to Mount Athos had forged a special relationship with the young Cypriot monks of Vatopedi. They treated him like a father figure, gathering around him for advice and infor-mation about the turmoil in the Church of Cyprus and the possible up-coming elections for a new archbishop. After Lavros reassured them that Father Maximos's chances for becoming the new archbishop were good, the *Archondaris*, Father Gennadios, the monk in charge of being host to the pilgrims, escorted us to our assigned rooms in a recently remodeled section of the monastery. I stayed with Lavros and Paul, the medical doc-tor. Next door Antonis roomed with Andreas, the ex-ambassador, and Nikos, the entrepreneur. We quickly settled in and then joined the monks for vespers followed by a light dinner for pilgrims only. Monks ate only once a day during the Great Lent.

Soon after the *apodeipnon*, the short prayer service that followed the communal dinner, we were notified that the abbot wished to talk to all the newcomers. Over a hundred pilgrims, as many as the total number of monks residing at the monastery, gathered at the large *archondariki*. The smiling, blond-bearded abbot welcomed each of us to the historic monastery, a place frequently visited, we learned, by Prince Charles, who donated money for the construction of a small chapel nearby.

The abbot sat in the middle of the room and after expressing his happiness to see so many of us present he began a short welcoming talk. The grace residing on Mount Athos, he said, has brought back pilgrims like ourselves time and again. "Whoever drinks the water of Mount Athos will always return." Then in a more serious tone, he continued, "The problem of contemporary human beings is their amnesia. They are overfocused on the present and are totally absorbed by their careers, their families, their communities. Consequently they have become forgetful of God. This is an opportunity for you to be here among us for a few days so that your exclusive preoccupation will be the remembrance of God."

More easily said than done. As soon as we left the *archondariki*, several in our group rushed to their cell phones and stood on the balconies of our third-floor rooms trying to get the right signal, a phenomenon unknown in 1991 when I first visited Mount Athos. Paul, the doctor, was concerned to hear news about his patients. I overheard him prescribing some drugs. Antonis called his wife, who was going to meet him in Thessaloniki for an Easter in Greece. Nikos called his hotel manager on some urgent business. The outside world managed to intrude even on this remote monastery in a relatively inaccessible peninsula in northern Greece where pilgrims come with the purported aim of leaving their concerns behind and focusing exclusively on God. "The Almighty cannot compete with cell phones," I said jokingly as Lavros was about to dial someone in Limassol. Somehow my caustic remarks made an impression and soon the atmosphere changed considerably. There was finally peace when everybody turned off their cell phones.

We all put on our winter coats and gathered at one of the balconies, chatting in the quiet night for another hour or so. The sky cleared up and the half moon appeared, crystal clear, illuminating the yard of the monastery. Antonis continued to play guide to his friends and he explained how the monastery, the largest on Mount Athos, regained its preeminence after decades of decline and neglect. "There was a time, believe it or not, when this monastery hosted over four thousand monks. But it went into decline and by the early seventies, only six or seven elderly monks lived here, barely making ends meet. The monastery was virtually abandoned. Those octogenarian monks simply could not maintain it. Things were falling apart, not only at Vatopedi but everywhere on Mount Athos," Antonis said gravely and went quiet.

"It's amazing how things turned around, leading to the current revival of Vatopedi and the whole of Mount Athos," Lavros marveled.

"It is certainly amazing," Antonis agreed. "It all got started fifty years ago with Joseph the Hesychast, a great elder and hermit. It was a period of depression and decline on the Holy Mountain. The general consensus was that it was only a matter of time before the entire Mountain would be empty of life and prayer. But this charismatic father managed to gather around him a group of young monks and he settled with them in a remote *skete* somewhere on Mount Athos. He trained them in the spiritual arts and carried on a struggle for their salvation, for *Theosis*. His fellow monks used to tease him: 'What are you planning to do with these youngsters, brother?' they would ask him. 'These youngsters' he replied, 'will bring about a revolution on the Holy Mountain one day.' And so it happened. Out of his companions there emerged several charismatic elders who turned the tide of decline and brought about this extraordinary monastic renaissance. Elder E—— of Arizona came out of that group. He has already created sixteen Athonite monasteries in North America. Out of that company of 'youngsters' there also emerged the late Elder Ephraim of Katounakia, famous for his prophetic *charisma* and Elder Joseph of Vatopedi, who in turn gathered around him another group of young monks. This is the group that moved from Nea Skete and took charge of Vatopedi during the 1980s."

Antonis paused as we gazed at the illumined yard below. "Vatopedi has by now about a hundred monks, and both its abbot, who just spoke to us, and Father Maximos were part of the original group of young monks that Elder Joseph, the disciple of Joseph the Hesychast, brought over from Nea Skete. Elder Joseph of Vatopedi, Elder Ephraim of Katounakia, and Elder E—— of Arizona as well as the late Elder Paisios were the elders of Father Maximos. They were the ones who trained and guided him. Then, as Kyriacos wrote in his book, Father Maximos was ordered by these elders to leave Mount Athos and return to Cyprus. He was accompanied in his 1993 return to Cyprus by three other monks, Father Isaac, Father Arsenios, and Father Nicholas, creating within ten years a monastic revival on the island. So as you see," Antonis concluded, "it all started fifty years ago with the work of an enlightened old hermit, Joseph the Hesychast."

"With the help of the *Theotokos*, the Mistress of the Holy Mountain, of course," Lavros interjected.

"Of course. That goes without saying."

All this information was new to Andreas and the other two novices, Paul and Nikos. They asked more questions about the history of the monastery that Antonis and Lavros were more than happy to answer. It was a casual way of getting acquainted with one another. The previous day many of us had been strangers to one another. Andreas began telling us about his thirty-five years as a diplomat, a rich repertoire of stories about the key historical events that marked the recent history of Cyprus and Greece. Paul narrated his adventurous life as a young man growing up in a prosperous and well-established Greek Cypriot family in Alexandria. With the rise of Arab nationalism in Egypt, he along with hundreds of thousands of other Greeks and all other foreign nationals were forced by the new Egyptian government to leave Alexandria, which was once a center of Greek learning and culture. After getting his medical education in Greece and London, Paul practiced medicine in England for a number of years. His nostalgia for the Mediterranean world, he claimed, brought him back to Athens, where he finished the last leg of his medical career. His diverse experiences opened him up to the possibility that there may be "something," as he put it, on Mount Athos. When the conversation moved in the direction of extraordinary healing phenomena, he seemed open to the possibility of "miraculous" healing and "alternative therapies."

Lavros told us stories from his life in Saudi Arabia. "Ibrahim was an engineer in my company and a very close friend. He was a devout Muslim who followed all the prescriptions in the Koran, praying five times a day, fasting during Ramadan, offering substantial amounts of money to charities, and so on. One day my late wife, who was a friend of his wife, said to me that Ibrahim was inconsolable. (His wife couldn't tell me this directly, since Muslims had a strict prohibition against men and women socializing

263

together.) Every night Ibrahim would shed bitter tears and he could not sleep. 'How can I go to paradise,' he told his wife, 'when my friend Lavros will end up in hell. He is not a Muslim!'" Lavros went on to describe how poor Ibrahim literally begged him to convert to Islam so that together they would enter paradise.

"It reminds me," I said, "of similar concerns among Christians. It is a universal problem. Only 'we' will inherit God's kingdom."

"Well listen to this," Lavros continued in an animated way, energized by our interest. "When I first came to Mount Athos I was introduced to Father Ignatios, a spiritual guide and confessor from another monastery. He was relatively young at the time and had a reputation, unlike Father Maximos, of being strict and austere during confessions. He was all too ready to assign penances to people for minor infractions. He was considered, in fact, as the toughest confessor on all of Mount Athos. In reality he was good-hearted, like my friend Ibrahim, and very devout. But he was very much a zealot when it came to religious questions. Incidentally, before becoming a monk, Father Ignatios had a thriving practice in Athens as a civil engineer.

"On a visit to his monastery," Lavros continued, "I decided to go for confession with him and tell him about my life in general. I mentioned in passing that while in Saudi Arabia, where there were no churches, I used to go on occasion to the mosque and pray next to my friend Ibrahim. He was praying to Allah and I was praying to Christ. 'This is very serious, very bad,' said Father Ignatios. 'You betrayed your religion and you will need to go through a special rite to reintroduce yourself back to Orthodoxy.' I protested that I did not feel I had betrayed my religion. I certainly did not become a Muslim. I tried to explain to him in vain that in Saudi Arabia there were no churches where Christians could go and pray. Father Ignatios was unmoved. 'You cannot take communion until we carry out the ritual tomorrow,' he insisted. Well, I had to abide by his rule. In that monastery they started services at two in the morning. So I went to church at that hour and sat in a corner, thinking and wondering about Father Ignatios's reaction. There was total darkness since there are no lights during services except a few candles to help the chanters read the verses. Father Ignatios was conducting the liturgy.

"At a certain moment," Lavros went on, "I saw him coming out of the sanctuary holding a lit candle. He walked around the church as if he was looking for someone. He eventually came to where I was sitting and holding the candle up to my face, he exclaimed, 'Ah, finally I found you. Listen, forget what I told you yesterday. I was wrong. When the time comes, go ahead and have communion.' 'What happened, Father?' I whispered with great surprise. He told me that while he was conducting the Eucharist, God spoke to him and enlightened his mind. God helped him realize, he said, that I had committed no sin by praying to Christ in a mosque! Therefore, there was no need to go through the special rite that Father Ignatios originally demanded as imperative before I could be allowed to get communion."

"Now this story, Kyriaco, deserves to enter your book," Antonis exclaimed.

I mentioned that this is an interesting aspect of Athonite spiritual culture. The elders teach that one should always be suspicious of personal opinions. This, of course, is an ideal that is very difficult to follow and, more often than not, is violated either within or outside of Athos. But when one practices such a habit, there is room left for God to occasionally intervene and offer a different course of action. Father Ignatios was a deeply spiritual person but limited in understanding the outside world. However, through his humility and prayer he had left room for God to voice advice that contradicted his own opinions and conclusions. In such cases an Athonite elder, as a rule, would be propelled to always follow the dictates of God rather than of his own logic.

"I know from personal experience as a doctor," Paul said, "that when your logic is contradicted by your intuition it is almost always wiser and safer to follow the dictates of your intuition."

"I have heard that Father Ignatios has mellowed over the years and he is no longer as austere a confessor as before," Lavros said.

"Years of ascetic practice and prayer apparently softened him up," added Antonis, who knew Father Ignatios personally.

Another reminiscence came to Lavros's mind regarding the controversial confessor and spiritual advisor. "Listen to this! During confession he asked me whether I'd ever had sex with animals, like goats, mares, even chickens! I protested. I said to him, 'Father Ignatie, what kind of a person do you think I am?' 'Sorry,' he said, 'but I had to ask.' Apparently he had heard confessions of this type and he wanted to make sure I was innocent of having sex with goats and sheep," Lavros said and burst out laughing. " 'In fact,' I said to him, 'your question reminded me of a case that I had to deal with myself.' And then I told him that in Saudi Arabia one of my workers, a poor Pakistani, was arrested by the police and accused of having intercourse with a camel. The poor man was going to be beheaded because according to their laws it is a grave sin to fornicate with animals. I had to go to court and testify on his behalf that he was a paragon of good character and that it was unthinkable that he would have slept with a camel. I believe my testimony saved him, poor fellow. He was trembling like a leaf."

"Maybe this is what Father Ignatius 'saw' intuitively in your past and confused him," I suggested. At that point we heard a knock at the door. It was Father Nyphon, who implored us to go to sleep because after eight there must be total silence in the monastery. The bells were to begin clanging at three thirty for the four-hour service and we needed to get our sleep.

Two days after our arrival the roads dried up and we decided to hire one of the few minibuses for an all-day excursion to the tip of the peninsula. Our destination was the monastery of the Great Lavra, the first monastery built on Mount Athos, about one thousand years ago. We all knew that even with motorized transportation the journey would not be easy.

Normally one travels to that part of the peninsula either on foot or by boat. Because of rough seas, travel by boat was not an option. Nor was hiking. It would have required several days to get there and as many to return. We wished to stop at various monasteries along the way and pay homage to famed miraculous icons of the Holy Virgin and other sacred relics. It was practical, therefore, to hire the minibus. We just hoped that the driver would be in a good mood. Mercifully, the driver was a different man, a retired grandfather who occasionally stopped his bus along the way to gather wild greens that had just popped up thanks to the abundance of rain of the previous days. "They are great with olive oil and lemon juice," he told us. He wanted to take them to Ouranoupolis to his wife, whom he planned to visit during the weekend.

Although there was no more mud, the road conditions were inappropriate for motorized transportation. However, after visiting various monasteries along the way we all felt energized and forgot the discomfort. "If travel on Mount Athos were made easy and comfortable it would no longer be Mount Athos," Lavros wisely pointed out as we got off the bus at the very tip of the peninsula. There was no more road beyond that point. A precipitous cliff dropped straight down nearly a thousand feet to the sea. It was where the fleet of the Persian king Xerxes got shipwrecked during his first military expedition against the Greeks. The tip of Mount Athos rose massively in the west. Covered with snow, it was an impressive sight and several in our company began taking pictures.

"Down there," our driver said as he pointed out at the cliff below, "is the cave of Saint Athanasios. Two hundred and twenty steps take you to it. If you choose to go there, keep your eyes on the rock. Don't look down at the sea. There are no railings and you may get dizzy. I will wait for you here."

I contemplated whether I should take the risk and walk down the steep precipice. The narrow steps were literally carved out of the granite rock. I was never a thrill seeker nor a fan of heights. But I would have felt that my trip was incomplete had I not ventured into the cave of the ninth-century saint who laid the foundations of the Athonite monastic community. We were ten on that excursion. Half of us decided to go ahead and walk down the steps.

Breathing heavily and reciting the Jesus Prayer, I focused my gaze on the side of the rock and very slowly walked down all 220 steps. At one point I looked down but realized the wisdom of the driver's advice. My heart raced faster and I felt my knees trembling slightly. I immediately turned my head toward the rock and away from that abyss below me. The others were already there, exploring the narrow cave, when I arrived. We found next to it not only a tiny chapel decorated with the icon of Saint Athanasios, but also a modern bathroom and a place where a pilgrim could wash his feet or even take a shower. Modernity had reached even the cave of Saint Athanasios. These amenities, however, did not detract from our wonder. How was it possible for a human being to live in a place fit for eagles and other birds of prey? Yet since the early years of Christianity, anchorites have been living in total isolation in such hermitages practicing an even more intense form of prayer and austere living than those in the monasteries.

I sat a few feet away from the edge of the cave and gazed at the blue Aegean below. I tried to imagine how it must have been to live in such isolation day after day year after year. I just couldn't. I remembered Father Maximos's words, that in the final analysis what is of importance for the spiritual life is to create a "desert" within our hearts, that is, to eradicate all traces of egotistical passions if we are to reach God. This is what the desert fathers tried to do in their own unique and inimitable way. This is what Saint Athanasios was practicing in that awesome hideout and this is what Elder E—— tried to introduce to America. In *Inner Christianity* Richard Smoley writes:

[margin handwriting: Spiritual life create a desert within our hearts eradicate egotistical passions]

When the turbulence of the mind and emotions has subsided, consciousness becomes still and clear, and the presence of God can be felt. Although, as we are constantly reminded, God is everywhere, we are rarely aware of this fact because our mental agitation makes it impossible to experience his presence. Practically all techniques of prayer and meditations are aimed at stilling the mind so that the Absolute can be made manifest in us.[2]

I pulled from my bag my notebook and wrote down a few observations as Lavros, who had just arrived, came and sat next to me, breathing heavily. I mentioned to him my thoughts on the subject of inner silence. "Look at it this way," he said. "Suppose you had just bought a CD of Beethoven's Ninth Symphony and you wanted to hear it. You place it on your player and push the button. It begins to play. But there are noises all around: the traffic in the street, the kids playing with drums, the neighbors screaming and fighting with one another, the dogs barking. Under such conditions you cannot hear anything from the symphony. All other noises must first be stopped before you can hear the 'Ode to Joy.' That's how I came to comprehend this incomprehensible retreat of people like Saint Athanasios. He came here so that he could clearly hear the voice of God, the symphony that goes on inside us but that we are unaware of because of all the noise around us."

On our way back to Vatopedi, we stopped at the monastery of Iviron in the hope of meeting with its abbot, Archimandrite Basilios. Stephanos, who knew him personally, urged me to do everything possible in order to meet him. One of the reasons that I joined the journey was the prospect of a contact with the elder. But as in the case of Elder E—— of Arizona, it was not to be. Father Basilios was out of Mount Athos that day and the best I could do was to buy a couple of his books that had just been published. During a quiet moment of rest next to a holy spring (considered to be miraculously discovered by Saint Athanasios with help from the Holy Virgin) while our driver was harvesting more wild greens, I opened one of the books. I then understood why Stephanos insisted that I meet Father Basilios. I read in Greek: "The entire life of humanity, of Creation and of History is a Divine Liturgy which leads towards a blissful *telos* [end] of all the universes. *'Ta epegia gegonen ouranos'* [the things of this world are transmuted into things of Heaven]."[3]

I reflected on this idea, one I found compatible with my own metaphysical understanding of Creation—that at the end everything is restored to its divine state. In the meantime, our driver was gathering his wild veggies at a furious pace. He soon called on us to get back on the bus for the remaining two hours of our bumpy trip so that we might get back in time to hear the chant of Cassiani. It was Holy Tuesday and once a year on that night, that magnificent, mournful chant is sung for close to half an hour. If the chanters are good it can be an aesthetic and spiritual experience of the highest order. If they are cacophonous, then it is a veritable torture. I was spoiled by having experienced the most superb chanting of that hymn by my friend Lambros. For the last thirty years he had been chanting that *troparion* of Saint Cassiani at our parish in Bangor. I was certain that the monks of Vatopedi would not disappoint us so we were eager to be in church on time.

I mentioned that a sentimental aunt of mine would weep every time she heard that *troparion*, and before we arrived Lavros narrated for us the story that led to its composition:

Cassiani was an exceptionally beautiful young aristocrat in Constantinople during the time of the Byzantine emperor Theophilus. Well educated and an accomplished poetess, Cassiani was the secret love of the new emperor, who planned to marry her. After his inauguration the emperor had to choose a wife and, according to the custom, the most beautiful and well-born prospective brides of Constantinople were paraded in front of him in a special ceremony during which the bachelor emperor would chose one as his wife and empress. According to the ritual the emperor would approach that assembly of maidens and hand a golden apple to the one he chose as his bride. Cassiani was, of course, among the group. The golden apple was for her. But when the emperor came in front of her he decided to tease her and declared: "Woman is the source of all evil because she persuaded Adam to eat from the forbidden fruit."

Cassiani was not a docile woman and shot back: "But it was through the womb of a woman that the Savior of the world was born." The proud emperor got angry at being outwitted by Cassiani and impulsively handed the apple to the woman standing next to her, to Theodora, who became the new empress of Byzantium.

Cassiani was inconsolable. In her grief and despair she withdrew from the world and joined a monastery, taking the vows of a nun. Inconsolable too was the emperor who found himself married to the wrong empress. Desperate, he climbed on his horse one night and frantically searched everywhere for Cassiani. He enquired at several monasteries until someone told him where he could find his beloved. When the abbess opened the door and recognized who the visitor was she ordered him to leave at once because Cassiani was no longer available and he should leave her in peace. But he pushed the abbess aside and ran up to her cell. In the meantime Cassiani got word of what was going on and ran off to hide. In her hurry she left on her desk a poem she had begun composing on the "woman of many sins" an allegory about her own life but based on the theme of the prostitute in the Gospel who wiped Jesus's feet with her hair. When the emperor rushed into her cell he found only the unfinished poem. He took Cassiani's pen and continued with his own words: "Those feet whose sound Eve heard at dusk in paradise, and hid herself for fear." He then got back on his horse and left the monastery without ever seeing his beloved

again. When Cassiani returned to her room she sat down and in tears fin- *what did she do to be declared a saint?*
ished the poem, leaving intact the lines written by her former lover and
now emperor. Cassiani was eventually declared a saint by the Church and
her poem was turned into a hymn, chanted and commemorated in church
every Holy Tuesday for over a thousand years. The poem stirred powerful
emotions in the hearts of people like my aunt, who became a widow very
early in her life.

The woman who had fallen into many sins,
Perceiving Thy divinity, O Lord,
Fulfilled the part of a myrrh-bearer;
And with lamentations
She brought sweet-smelling oil of myrrh to Thee before Thy burial.
"Woe is me," she said, "for night surrounds me, dark and moonless,
and stings my lustful passion with the love of sin.
Accept the fountain of my tears,
O Thou who drawest down from the clouds the waters of the sea.
Incline to the groanings of my heart,
O Thou who in Thine ineffable self-emptying has bowed down the heavens.
I shall kiss Thy most pure feet
And wipe them with the hairs of my head,
Those feet whose sound Eve heard at dusk in paradise,
And hid herself for fear.
Who can search out the multitude of my sins
And abyss of Thy judgments,
O Savior of my soul?
Despise me not, Thine handmaiden,
For Thou hast mercy without measure."[4]

271

FOURTEEN

SYNAXIS

henever I visit Mount Athos I always meet interesting pilgrims and journeymen from all over the world who enrich my experience. That is not surprising. It takes a certain idiosyncrasy to undergo the discomforts and tribulations of getting there to begin with, let alone to follow the demanding schedule of prolonged services and the ascetic lifestyle of the monastic community. Given the purpose of their sojourn at the Holy Mountain visitors are, as a rule, accommodative to one another. Discordant forms of behavior are rare, but they do happen.

The following morning we discovered that a Greek media mogul, notorious for his excessive ego, had settled into the cell next to ours. The heavy smell of cigars floated throughout the hallway of the monastery wing in which we were staying. Somebody was smoking profusely, in blatant violation of a strict rule forbidding such an act within the confines of Athonite monasteries. Flaunting his status as an "important" personality the newcomer ignored the monastic rule on smoking. When we were unavoidably introduced he made it clear, in case we did not know, how important he was. Wearing a three-piece suit, an oddity on Mount Athos, he showed an incessant need to impress us with his achievements, his connections, his influence among the political establishment and his extraordinary knowledge about everything.

Why, we wondered, would a person who was so vain in his external demeanor come to Mount Athos, where humility was the highest virtue to which one could aspire? Not only did the wealthy and extremely right wing pilgrim pollute the air we breathed but he interrupted the abbot on a few occasions in order to "correct" him when the elder was delivering a brief talk to his monks right after lunch. It was a gross violation of monastic protocol. The man of wealth and influence behaved as if he owned the monastery.

"Poor fellow," Lavros murmured as we walked to church. "I feel sorry for him. He must be suffering." I nodded in agreement, and my attitude toward our fellow pilgrim suddenly shifted dramatically. Sometimes a simple suggestion from a friend can point our hearts in the right direction. We then begin to see with greater clarity.

Mount Athos is not a place where only angels and holy men reside, I remember an elder from Mount Athos once telling me. It is a garden with great variety—flowers, weeds, and fruits, as well as poison ivy. One can encounter the very good as well as the very bad. And that includes the monks as well as the visiting pilgrims. Father Maximos never stopped reminding us that the *Ecclesia* is a spiritual hospital for the recuperation of troubled souls. Therefore, it welcomes everybody: saints and sinners, the humble and the vain, rich and poor.

Reflecting on these matters after Lavros's timely comment transmuted my attitude toward the man from disdain to compassion. As a result I felt better about myself.

We left Mount Athos a day earlier than planned, forfeiting another excursion to monasteries along the western coast on the opposite side of the peninsula. Nikos, the businessman, was complaining of heart pains, a chronic discomfort with him. Paul, the doctor in our group, as well as another internist who happened to be visiting the monastery, agreed that it would be safer for Nikos to leave Mount Athos as soon as possible and have a checkup at a hospital in Thessaloniki. In the event of an emergency there was no way of exiting Mount Athos except by sea and that was not always a reliable way out. In excellent weather we boarded the daily ferry at eleven in the morning right from Vatopedi itself. Our destination was Ierissos, a fishing town that also hosted pilgrims. It lay on the eastern side of the promontory, opposite to Ouranoupolis, which was the more customary port of entry to Mount Athos.

We loved the three-hour boat ride. The sky was clear and, with no wind blowing, the sea was perfectly serene, unusual on that unprotected side of Mount Athos. All of us congregated on the top deck and enjoyed the warmth of the April sun. Our doctor friend, while keeping a watchful eye on Nikos, went on to tell us more stories from his early years in Alexandria. Lavros added to his repertoire of tales from his life and adventures in the Arabian peninsula. They were the kind of stories, I mused, that could have provided the raw material for a skillful novelist.

As soon as I took my seat on the Cyprus Airways plane I pulled from my handbag Graham Speake's recently published work of Mount Athos, my companion during my pilgrimage. I read from it whenever I found some quiet moments. The two-hour flight was perfect for finishing this authoritative and detailed historical account of the Holy Mountain. I read and underlined the following:

> The exclusiveness of Athos is essential to its survival. If it were to be compromised, there is no doubt that within a very short space of time the sole surviving holy mountain would suffer the same fate as the others, like Meteora and countless other monasteries in Greece and the Middle East that are now either museums of Byzantine art or deserted ruins. Thirty years ago it seemed that this was the inevitable fate of Mount Athos. But the Mother of God was not willing to surrender her garden. Its soil has been

refertilized and has given birth to a new spring. The garden is blooming again as freshly as ever, welcoming newcomers to its groves, and exporting its fruits to the world. . . . The monks see their principal duty as being to pray for the world, a world of which they no longer form a part, a world to which they have died, but a world which they continue to cherish almost as if it were their creation. The world needs those prayers as never before. What could be more reassuring for us as we lie in our beds at night than to know that there are 1600 or so monks on Mount Athos praying now, *for us?*[1]

After some further reading I closed my eyes, thinking about my Athonite excursion and the works of the elder who had admonished me that I must visit the Holy Mountain at least once a year.

The opportunity to discuss my journey to Mount Athos with Father Maximos came up right after Easter when he casually asked me whether I wished to drive him to the Panagia monastery on Sunday. I, of course, cancelled my other plans.

The topic of our conversation during the drive, however, was mostly and unavoidably the extraordinary political developments on the island. The Turkish government, under pressure from the international community, particularly Europe, lifted the prohibition of travel between the occupied northern part of the island and the Republic of Cyprus. This allowed thousands of Greek and Turkish Cypriots to visit each other after thirty years of total separation. It was the beginning of hope for a possible solution to the Cyprus problem. What was particularly encouraging was the enthusiasm and open-hearted hospitality that Greek and Turkish Cypriots showed to each other. With such extraordinary developments it was difficult to talk about anything else and we left the subject of my visit to Mount Athos for some other time.

But just before I turned the ignition off at the gate of the Panagia monastery I hurriedly mentioned the episode with the media mogul and confessed my negative feelings toward him. Father Maximos found the whole episode more amusing than problematic and mentioned that it was just a spiritual exercise for me.

Father Arsenios, the new abbot and a close associate of Father Maximos, was waiting for us with several other young monks. As usual, they were joyous to see their elder. After the greetings, bows, and hand kissing, as is the custom among Orthodox monks when they meet one another, we headed straight to the kitchen for a late dinner. It was nine in the evening. Several young monks sat around watching us eat while in between mouthfuls Father Maximos told them jokes, generating uproarious laughter. Then we all went to sleep. My understanding was that I would drive Father Maximos back to Limassol late in the afternoon the next day.

It was seven o'clock, just after the *apodeipnon*, the short prayer service that always follows dinner. The sun had already disappeared behind the mountain peaks that encircle the Panagia monastery, leaving behind a reddish glow reminiscent of the mystic landscape paintings of my friend Michael Lewis. I was preparing to drive Father Maximos back to Limassol when I received a message that at the last moment he had decided to extend his stay for another evening and head back early the next morning. I did not ask what the reasons for his sudden decision were. I assumed he needed more time to complete his mission of offering counsel and confession to the monks under his supervision. Pleased that our stay in the monastery was extended, I went to the pay phone booth outside the monastery's gate and called Emily to tell her not to expect me back in Limassol before lunch on Tuesday.

Normally, after the *apodeipnon* all the monks would emerge from the church and spend a few minutes at the main courtyard before withdrawing to their cells. That was one of the few opportunities the monks had for socializing. But it was different that day.

"What's going on, Father Arsenie?" I asked, as everyone hurried toward the outside gate, forsaking the customary chitchat.

"There is going to be a *synaxis*," the forty-year-old abbot replied and waved his hand as he prepared to follow the others.

"Oh, I see," I said. "I assume it's only for monks, right?"

Father Arsenios turned back and nodded. With a sense of resignation he spread out his hands. By the expression on his face he seemed to be apologizing for being unable to extend an invitation to a layman like myself. The *synaxis*, the gathering of monks, was strictly for the members of the

276

monastic community. I presumed that Father Maximos planned to offer them lessons appropriate only for monks and novices. Now I understood the change of plans.

I walked up the steps, entered my temporary cell, and turned on the light. I prepared to spend the evening reading and taking notes while imagining the secret doctrines Father Maximos was about to unveil to his disciples. But as I took off my shoes and made myself comfortable on the bed I heard a knock at the door. It was Father Arsenios.

"The elder said that you can join us," he announced triumphantly. "Let's hurry."

I was pleasantly surprised and without delay I put on my shoes, shut the door, and followed him. It was the first time I had been given the opportunity to attend a *synaxis* at the Panagia monastery and I was naturally very curious. I knew that Father Maximos was making an exception for me and I felt privileged. Fortunately, it so happened that I was the only lay pilgrim in the monastery that Monday night. Weekend visitors had left by Sunday afternoon. Father Maximos, therefore, was able to bend his own rule without concern for possibly offending other pilgrims who could not be invited to the monks-only *synaxis*.

The gathering was taking place at a recently constructed wooden kiosk adjacent to the monastery. Until then I was not even aware of its existence. It was built at the edge of the cliff with a panoramic view of the mountains and the ravine below. All the thirty five or so monks were present. They sat silently next to each other, squeezed against one another on the long fixed bench that formed a square around the inside of the kiosk. It was an unusual sight and for an instant I felt out of place. I faced a sea of black: cassocks, beards, and *komboschinia*, which the fathers always held in their hands to facilitate their practice of ceaseless prayer.

I noticed several of the monks whom I had gotten to know over the years. I once mused to Stephanos that I suspected each of these monks had a life story that could provide the raw material for epic fiction. Stephanos knew them better than I since he had had connections to the monastery over many years and served as a sort of surrogate father figure to the younger monks. Through casual contacts with them Stephanos learned bits and pieces of their past, which as a rule they must avoid talking about except with their elder and for the sole purpose of their spiritual advancement.

My eyes caught those of Father Joachim, who nodded at me with a reserved smile. When I first met him in 1997 he was a beardless layman who used to spend a few days at a time at the monastery. I could not have suspected that he was exploring the possibility of joining the monastery. He was then a thirty-nine-year-old pediatrician with a well-established practice in Nicosia. During our long walks he would tell me of his adventures as a medical student in Italy and of his involvement with several mystical groups, both of Eastern and occidental vintage. A veteran of various methods of mental and spiritual practices, he was simply familiarizing himself, as he told me, with the ways of Christian monasticism. An avid reader, he was also a good conversationalist, a trait that often led me to seek his company. With a serene, quiet disposition he was now a transformed man. We could no longer spend those endless walks together talking of philosophical and spiritual matters, exchanging stories from our respective experiences in America and Italy. Now, in addition to various other assignments, Father Joachim supervised the nutritional needs of the monks and served as the resident physician. When I found him one day gathering herbs from the mountains I learned that he also specialized in alternative remedies and conducted ongoing experiments in an effort to invent natural ointments. I was present during the previous summer when he saved the life of Father Maximos's stepfather, who suffered a massive heart attack on a visit to the monastery. It took me some time to get used to the dramatic changes in Father Joachim's persona. He now had a long beard, he wore the black cassock, and instead of informally addressing me as "Kyriaco," he now used the more formal "Mister Markides." I, of course, had to address him not by his lay name of "Andreas" but as "Father Joachim."

Next to him sat Father Athanasios, another former layman I had first met at the monastery in 1997. At that time he was toying with whether to become a monk or get married, have a family, and continue managing one of the branches of the Cyprus Bank. His name at that time was Euripides. Three years later he was Father Athanasios. He gave up his well-paid managerial position, drove his white sedan to the monastery with everything he

owned in it, and joined the community of monks. After making the big decision to leave the world, he told me he had tired of spending his life in a
career as a banker, which now seemed like a meaningless pursuit. Now,
like Father Joachim, he looked radically different, serene and content with
his final decision. Wearing a bushy black beard and a long cassock, Father
Athanasios spent enormous amounts of time praying, prostrating himself
in front of the holy icons, and chanting. The banking skills he brought with
him were useful to the monastery. In addition to his other assignments, he
was in charge of keeping the accounts with the help of computers and of
Father Elias, who in his premonastic life was an economist, a graduate of
New York University.

On the opposite side of the kiosk, facing the others, were Father Abraham and Father Christodoulos. Father Abraham was a novice when I first
met him. A former elementary school teacher, he had a talent for music
and art. Taking that into consideration, Father Maximos assigned him the
task of learning iconography and Byzantine music. Likewise, Father
Christodoulous, which literally means "servant of God," was in charge of
the fields and the vegetable gardens. He had been a farmer most of his life
before he became a monk. After his wife died and his children got married,
Father Christodoulos abandoned the world and joined the monastery in a
full-time effort to attain his salvation. Over sixty, he was the oldest among
the fathers. In spite of his age, he was robust and healthy-looking, and
spent his time farming and praying. His hands looked rough and full of
muscular strength, befitting a lifelong farmer. Next to him sat Father
Chariton, once a manager of a Pizza Hut in Nicosia. Now he was managing
the monastery's library, and he eagerly sought my advice on what kind of
books to order.

Seeing all of them gathered together at the *synaxis*, I was struck by the
notion that the ideal Communist society as imagined by Karl Marx was
fully actualized in such communal monasteries. Here the motto of "from
each according to his abilities, to each according to his needs" is put into
practice. Every monk contributed to the common good in accordance with
his skills and talents, and every monk received whatever he needed to carry
on with the primary task of purifying his soul from egotistical passions in
an effort to unite with God. Their goal was not "self-actualization," as un-

derstood by Karl Marx and by contemporary humanistic psychologists, but God realization. Whatever self-actualization emerged from that effort in the form of personal creativity was secondary and subordinate to the supreme goal of *Theosis*, their union with God and their acquisition of the grace of the Holy Spirit. Real Communism, Father Maximos told me many years back, is found only in monasteries. The Communists failed because they believed they could bring about the good society through force and violence. It is only through spiritual growth and love, he went on to say, that such a society can be realized. I was told that an aging leading Greek Communist and member of parliament in Greece was so enthusiastic about the "real Communism" he found during a visit to Mount Athos that he voted in favor of a bill to finance the renovation and reconstruction of the monasteries, an important development in the history of Mount Athos.

Father Maximos eased my discomfort at being an oddity among the monks by signaling me to sit by his side. I felt like an honored guest. Emboldened by this reception, I asked and obtained permission to tape the talk. I placed my mini-recorder at a small table in front of Father Maximos. After reciting a short prayer, he started his talk.

"Being a monk, dear fathers," he began and looked around the kiosk, "is a great responsibility both toward the *Ecclesia* and toward ourselves. You must always keep in mind that there are grave dangers to monasticism today due to the overwhelming dominance of the worldly ethos all around us. It can enter into the life of the monastery without us even realizing it. In times past, there were deserts where hermits and monks could retreat and live alone. Today there are no such places. Take this monastery as an example. In earlier times it took three to four days for lay pilgrims to visit the monastery walking from Nicosia. The Panagia monastery for all practical purposes was a real desert where monks could pursue their goal of union with God without distractions. It is different today now that the monastery is accessible. We must, therefore, be extra vigilant to maintain the right atmosphere for spiritual work.

"So, is it possible to be a monk in today's world?" Father Maximos asked rhetorically. "You see, Fathers, being alone does not make one a monk. After all there are people in the surrounding villages who do live by themselves. Yet they are not monks. What is the difference? As you know very well, the difference is the way of life. The entire focus of the monk is his preoccupation with God. Everything else should be subordinated to this supreme goal, the goal of prayer. It is not the place that is important but the way of life, the way of prayer. Our responsibility as monks in these times of advancing worldliness and materialism is to preserve the way of monasticism for future generations. We must, therefore, be particularly attentive to detail. We must keep in mind that every time we begin to modernize and introduce innovations, even minor changes, we run the risk of undermining what we have inherited. If we do not pay attention to detail then we may set up a process of change that will distort monastic life and make it unrecognizable, affecting the prospects for spiritual work of future generations of monks.

"Dear Fathers, I must also point out that a monk has a different mission than that of a bishop. It would be impossible to incorporate monastic ways in the bishopric where I find myself now. It would simply not be appropriate. The role of someone in the bishopric is different from that of a monk living here at the Panagia monastery. That is why, my brothers, it is important that you must not be taken over by the worldly mind-set.

"To give you an example," Father Maximos continued, "not long ago, I visited another monastery and the abbot was eager to show me the great buildings they had constructed and the church's floor, which was an exact replication of the church floor of an Athonite monastery. But he was fixated on the externals. There was no monastic ethos in that monastery. The monks lived a worldly life. They had television sets in their cells, they smoked, played backgammon, and drank coffee at a nearby coffee shop. Their cells looked like luxury apartments and there was no elder to create a spiritual atmosphere. I am saying all this to emphasize the importance of vigilance. Buildings are necessary, constructing new cells and chapels is necessary. But these should not be a substitute for the way of prayer. Even minor innovations and changes can open Pandora's box and before you know it the worldly spirit will take over as in the case of that monastery that I recently visited."

Father Maximos stopped for a few seconds and looked thoughtful and focused. "We monks struggle for grace, which is none other than the uncreated energies of the Holy Spirit." He took a deep breath. "They sanctify

281

and assist each one of us and every human being to attain God realization, to attain *Theosis*.

"Given the fact that we are monks, we need to remind ourselves of the special way through which we must make room within our hearts so that the Holy Spirit, the *Parakletos* [Comforter], can take up permanent residence there. As you very well know, dear Fathers, it is only the Holy Spirit that can offer real comfort to the human heart, nothing else. It is for this reason that Abba Makarios defined a monk as a person who has nothing else in this life except Christ. These words are very important to keep in mind. Why? Because above everything else monasticism is a marital covenant between human beings and God. It is a mystery of love.

A monk has nothing else in this life except Christ

"Within the context of an authentic bond of love you cannot give your heart to anyone other than the beloved. You cannot have two wives or two husbands, for example. To do so is to betray the marital bond. It is considered adultery by the *Ecclesia* and it is legitimate grounds for divorce.

282

"Imagine how much more serious a commitment it is for the person who has vowed to dedicate his entire existence in spirit and in body to a marital bond with God, with Christ. We have not chosen to become monks because we wished to become better human beings, or because we wished to restrain ourselves from committing sinful acts, or because we wanted to spend secure, pleasant lives within a peaceful communal setting.

"No. It is not for such reasons that we became monks. We became monks precisely because through monasticism we labor to attain an eternal and absolutely loving relationship with God. It is not accidental that we are called *monachoi* [those who live alone], monks. We have chosen in this life to be alone, absolutely alone. We are not called to be with other things or other people. What do you think is the reason for this mystery, of being alone, which can be so painful?" Father Maximos remained pensive for a couple of seconds.

"You see, Fathers, when we first came here to become monks we took some actions that at that time, given our original enthusiasm, may not have appeared painful to us. We left behind us the world, abandoning parents, brothers, sisters, relatives, friends, careers, the entire familiar environment within which we grew up and lived all our lives. We came to this place where it is irrelevant who we were and what we did before. What matters now is whether we can achieve what we came here for, to develop spiritually and attain our goal of uniting with God. Otherwise monasticism has absolutely no meaning. Do you remember that monk who was once a Roman senator and boasted to Saint Basil about his former high worldly status? Saint Basil replied, 'Truly you gave up being a senator but you have failed as a monk.' In other words his loss was double. He abandoned his important worldly position but at the same time he remained emotionally attached to his previous status and sense of who he was.

"Being a real monk," Father Maximos continued, "means cutting off and ejecting from ourselves everything that connects us with the world: parents, friends, habits, places, ambitions for worldly success, a married life, and so forth. The only thing that we bring along to the monastery is ourselves. Everything else is left behind, be it wealth, honors, our country, our village, whatever. We come to the monastery and embark on this therapeutic pedagogy. It is not an easy path and it is not recommended for everybody."

Father Maximos took a brief rest as twilight began to cover the entire area. My tape recorder stood out against the advancing darkness with its feeble red light. "We are asked to commit ourselves," he continued, "to three most difficult monastic vows: *propertylessness, chastity,* and *obedience.* At first you may think of these as easy. Yet they are extremely difficult and of great importance. They have deep roots and great depths within human existence. Let us first examine the vow of propertylessness.

"It begins, of course, with the proscription against owning anything. We are asked to give up everything—money, wealth, or any object that we may feel connected with. I remember a prospective monk on Mount Athos who was rejected because he wished to bring along to the Holy Mountain his stamps. He was a collector. That was his passion and hobby. You cannot be a real monk and be attached to anything. You just can't be a monk and a stamp collector at the same time.

"What is important here is that we cut off any comfort that may originate from the ownership of things. In other words we literally own nothing in this world, not a penny. Absolutely nothing. Now when we are young, when we own very little we may not find this requirement particularly painful. But for an older person this is very difficult, very painful."

Father Maximos paused. "Let us say something happens and this monastery is destroyed. We may then ask ourselves, 'What do I do with nothing in the world? I have nothing material to stand on, nothing to offer me support.'

"Contemplating propertylessness, the holy elders concluded that avarice is a form of idolatry because the person afflicted by such a passion places his hopes in material objects. We may find comfort, let us say, in the fact that we may have a good job or a good pension or a nice house, so we feel a sense of security. When we have none of these, then we destroy a pillar of security that life in the world offers us. We may be comforted by the fact that we have a house and we praise God for that. Whether we realize this or not, such material possessions are forms of comfort for common people that can sustain them.

"But for the monastic life, you see, if we are deceived and we find comfort in objects that we may possess or in money or in whatever, we abandon our focus and hope in God and rely instead on the comforts of our possessions. It is for this reason that the holy elders made propertylessness a precondition for the monastic life."

As Father Maximos said those words I was reminded of the uncle of a friend of mine who fervently wished to live the life of a monk. But he was a man of means and when he was asked, before joining the monastery, to get rid of all of his wealth, he changed his mind. Several years back, while Father Maximos was still abbot of the Panagia monastery, my friend Stephanos gave him as a gift a good pair of sandals. Stephanos was pleased when he saw Father Maximos wearing them the next day. That was the first and the last time he put them on. When Stephanos asked him about the sandals Father Maximos replied that he loved them so much that he had to give them away. He said he feared that he would become too attached to them.

I once asked Father Maximos whether the kingdom of heaven is open only for the poor. No, he said and interpreted Jesus' words that 'it is easier for a camel to go through the eye of a needle than a rich man to reach heaven' in a radically different way than is commonly understood. He said that you cannot reach heaven so long as your heart is filled with attachments to objects of this world. You can own millions, he told me, but as long as your heart is free and is not a prisoner of your wealth, you can attain God realization. You can use your wealth to do much good in the world. On the other hand you can own very little, you can literally own only a nail, but if your heart is attached to that nail you cannot reach heaven. Reaching heaven implies liberation from all worldly passions and possessions. The rich man of the Bible is that person whose heart is filled with all sorts of obsessions about worldly objects.

"Now let's talk about the second monastic virtue, that of chastity," Father Maximos continued. "As monks we are asked to refrain from any physical relationship with other human beings. But not only physical. In reality, we are asked to have no special relationship with any other human being, period. We are asked to be totally alone. We don't have children, we don't have progeny. We are not to have another human being that we can direct and focus our love toward, and who can love us in return.

"We cannot share our lives with another human being," he said, "a human being who is with us day and night, partaking of our joys and sorrows. We as monks cannot say 'This is the person that I love.' And we must not have such a person. Chastity in its real monastic meaning implies the cutting off of all relationships with other human beings. We are asked to abstain from what the elders call 'particular friendships.' What does that mean? It means to avoid cultivating special relationships of sympathy with any other person. Now you may ask, 'Okay, is it bad to have a friend?' Of course not. But for the monk it is a disadvantage because it undermines his propensity and passion for the movement upwards toward God. It is like having a water turbine that pumps water over a distance. But if there are holes along the way and water is ejected here and there then the result is that the pressure of the water is bound to diminish.

"Shutting off all the holes of comfort, or in other words, placing our entire trust and hope in God, will help us achieve our objective. It will allow us to conserve all the love power that we as human beings carry within ourselves and redirect it completely toward God. So we shut the hole for material things. We also shut the comfort and support that comes from other human beings. We begin to do that by cutting off any natural, sexual contact. We do not marry. At the same time, as I said, we extend this abstinence toward a catholic withdrawal from any human source of comfort and

support, from any exclusive and particular friendships. All these depriva-
tions are not easy.

"The third monastic vow, which is also the most difficult, is obedience.
We are asked to cut off our very will. Cutting off our will or our desire does
not simply mean to obey our elder when he asks us to wash the floor of the
church or to do this or that errand. The essence of obedience is to learn to
deny our very self. We deny our opinions, our thoughts, our judgments, our
very mind. We are completely naked from human contact, from our parents, from our environment, from all the things we previously owned or
cherished, from any close friends that we can draw comfort from. One
would have thought that we can at least own our will. Yet we are asked to
give up even that.

"One can find comfort in his thoughts and points of view. As the holy
elders say, there are people who have as their children their opinions, their
words, the products of their minds. The philosophers or the intellectuals
are a good example. They could find joy, pleasure, a form of completeness
within themselves, by philosophizing or by producing ideas.

"Monasticism comes along and asks of us to cut off even that form of
comfort. We are asked to give up even the most simple and natural move-
ments of our mind. We are asked to completely deny ourselves. It is what
Christ urges us to do. Somewhere in the Gospel of Mark, Jesus says that we
must come to hate our very soul, anything that originates from within us.

"The sum total of this self denial that I have been talking about, Fathers, inadvertently leads a person to a state of psychic chaos. I don't know
how else to call it and I don't know how long it can last. Obviously we don't
have the strength to follow this path to perfection as some of the old desert
fathers did. But say we did. If we cut all these sources of support, then we
would experience a state of chaos within ourselves. It is a terrible void,
darkness, hell itself. This is what hell is all about, to reject everything and
to have nothing and no one to turn to for connection and sympathy. But at
that very moment when we arrive at this borderline point we must remember those important words that God revealed to Saint Silouan: 'Keep your
mind in hell but do not despair.' This is the darkness of hell, of despair, of
abandonment, a feeling that we are nothing, not seeing any hope anywhere
because there is no hope coming from anywhere. We have cut off every-

thing from which we could have gotten hope: material objects, human relations, parents, friends, our very self. Where would we draw hope from?
How can we be comforted? At that point of despair only God remains as a
source of hope and relief for us.

"The saints were precisely those people who followed this extremely
difficult path. They have tasted the despair of hell and anchored their
hopes only in God. They absolutely rejected any other source of comfort
and hope, just like Jesus did on the Cross.

"Naturally, under ordinary circumstances it is not desirable or advisable for a human being to be alone and therefore we neither recommend
nor encourage such a way of life. It is hell itself. In fact, normally, only the
devil is alone. Yet, in a paradoxical way we are asked as monks to live alone
in order to unite with Christ. What is even more onerous is that this does
not mean that from the first moment we enter into that hellish condition
we begin to experience and feel the living presence of Christ the way saints
experience Christ. However, because we are weak creatures, grace does
periodically provide us with temporary relief and sweetness so that we may
not be totally crushed. All these temporary interventions of grace take
place because of our weaknesses. But the ideal is to fearlessly enter into
that condition, to live through the hell of aloneness and refuse any kind of
compromise. We are asked to refuse consolation coming from all sources
except from God. This is the arduous struggle that we are asked as monks
to carry out.

"I confess, Fathers, that what I notice in myself and in all of us is that
somehow we have become comfortable being monks. We have become accustomed to the monastic way of life and we get distracted with a thousand things relating to our life as monks. We have, therefore, lost that
sense of mourning from the depths of our souls, that sense of effort by
which we must descend into hell through our own volition and stay there
utterly alone. This is the price we must pay and the precondition in accom-
plishing our mission. But instead of that, we begin to form special friendships that provide us with emotional support and comfort. We find all sorts
of outlets in the monastery that provide us with solace. I remember an old
hieromonk lamenting 'We have rejected everything else related to comfort
except a plate of food and a bed to sleep on.' We become forgetful of the

287

reasons that brought us into the monastery as we meet old friends who visit us, as we take walks with them, as we laugh together, as we reminisce about the past and about all sorts of things. That makes us feel good. It is a form of consolation, of comfort.

"Of course, for ordinary people, all these activities in themselves are human, very human and very good indeed, very healthy. They are innocent forms of passing time. But for us monks they may be an obstacle to our primary objective because they distract us from our *askesis*, from our supreme objective that only in God may we find rest. Some of the holy fathers would act in ways that appear really crazy from the point of view of an ordinary way of life. I am reminded of the case of that elder who lived for years at the edge of a beautiful gorge. But he refused to look down. Now, you may protest, what's wrong with looking down and saying 'Glory be to God for creating such magnificent beauty'? Is this bad? Of course it is not. But the elders knew that the more we cut off human comforts and consolations the more God comes to comfort us. Even for us monks such behavior is inconceivable, to refuse even to find solace in the beauty of nature. What can we say about Saint Neophytos who moved into a hole in a rock on his twenty-fourth birthday and remained there for sixty years!

"Elder Paisios refused a gift from a pilgrim, a sieve for making tea, because he said he would now have to worry about finding a nail to keep it on the wall. His hermitage was as barren of objects as it could be. That's how the desert fathers lived. In those terrible deserts of North Africa they set up their hermitages miles away from the nearest water source lest they make their lives easy. Isn't it reasonable that one should be near a water hole? Yet they preferred to be miles away in order to make their lives difficult. There was the case of a hermit who, upon deciding to move nearer to the water hole, was visited by an angel and counseled to stay where he was lest he become too comfortable and undermine his *askesis*.

"Of course I am not saying all these things to urge you to imitate those hermits. We are human beings and we must do only that which we can handle. But it is important to know about these matters, Fathers, so that we may protect ourselves from our natural tendency to seek human comforts and other distractions. From the moment that we decide to become monks we must know that to the degree to which we are able to reject human support and relief, to that degree we are consoled and comforted by the grace of God. That is why our great teachers are the desert fathers like the Great Antonios. That is why Elder Paisios spent two years in the Sinai Desert before coming to Mount Athos. We must not be afraid of that descent into Hades, which is indeed a very painful experience. It is a borderline point in our spiritual struggles. I have said this publicly: a monk can reach the same state of despair that ordinary people reach just before they are about to commit suicide.

"But we must keep reminding ourselves that sooner or later we must descend into that state of despair alone. And there alone, like Jonas inside the belly of the whale, we shall cry with all our might for God's mercy. Just think how it must feel to be inside the belly of a whale. You have no one to come to your rescue except God.

"Needless to say," Father Maximos went on, "such a state of aloneness, which is hell itself, will be a cause of insufferable grief because while we are in this state God remains silent, in hiding from us. God is not going to appear to us the moment we begin to weep with despair and cry out for him. He is not going to come to us like a mother who comes to comfort her baby the moment the baby utters a cry. We may be crying, we may be in a state of utter despair and grief, we may be calling God with all the power left in us, but God will be nowhere to be seen. God will let us be in that state of darkness for a while. Why? Because he does not wish to be unjust toward us. He does not wish to turn us into infants but wants to help us become mature adults, perfect human beings. He wants to offer us all the spiritual opportunities to actualize all the possibilities that exist within us. He will therefore leave us right there in hell to mourn and grieve and suffer while searching for our Savior.

"We must also know," Father Maximos continued, "that added to all this grief there will also be severe attacks by Satan. We will be subjected to the war of our passions. They come forward and swell within us at such critical moments. We will experience hell itself, and feel darkness everywhere. Yet nothing will happen, we will get no response from God. It is as if God does not exist. We will be in a position similar to David when he cried out, 'Where is your mercy, Oh God? I used to say a prayer and at that very moment I would feel your presence. Now you are nowhere to be found.'

"It is important to keep in mind what will happen later, once we reach the state of utter despair at the limits of our endurance. And I don't mean by that the false belief that we have reached our limits of endurance but rather our actual limits, objectively speaking, where there is no longer any room for further endurance. It is at that point, at that very moment that God begins to make his appearance in us. It is the point when the process of divine consolation begins to emerge in our hearts, yet not quite completely at first and not absolutely.

"It is a similar situation to that described in the Song of Songs. The bride searches for her beloved. She will find him briefly and then lose him again. She will frantically search here and there, asking one person and then another 'Have you seen him? Where can he be?' People will tell her go to this or that place. She will run there only to find out that the bridegroom has just left. She will smell his presence, so to speak, but lose him. She will reach out to grasp him but then he will disappear again and again. It is a continuous search of the soul for the Beloved, for God, who is hiding until the soul matures and reaches the utter depths of humility, the utter depths of being crushed, where nothing is left of the old person. Then finally God is offered to the human soul as the ultimate prize of this titanic struggle. God then comes as grace, as the real comforter who now permanently resides in the human soul. This happens because a human being refused to be comforted by anything else in this life except to await for the Great Beloved. The person becomes God realized and his existence is anchored entirely in God. This is *Theosis*, paradise, the state of saintliness.

"The last few days, Fathers, we have celebrated Pentecost, that momentous event, the descent of the Holy Spirit to the Apostles fifty days after the Resurrection. It is a special reminder for us monks that there must be no other comfort and consolation other than God so that we ourselves may experience the Pentecost. To repeat once again, the extent to which we accept human consolation is the extent to which we shall be deprived of divine consolation. Reflecting on this issue, we can easily recognize the mistakes that we commit today as monks.

"Sometimes I wonder. We modern monks and elders, and I include myself among the moderns, have changed our old ways of *askesis* to make life in the monastery less painful and demanding. Perhaps this is a mistake. The old-timers would ask, 'Abba, where should I go in order to save myself?' And the answer would be 'Go wherever there is dishonesty, grief, and hard work, a place where you cannot find comfort.' Another elder would go into a monastery and declare, 'I must leave this place. Everyone here is saintly and good. There isn't any hard work here, no toil. How am I going to work out my salvation? Let me go find a place where there is dishonor and hardship.'

"What I am trying to say, Fathers, is that today we often go to a monastery in order to find consolation and solace. We go to a good brotherhood, a good community. And we search for this solace. Yet, we often fail to find it. Our modern ways are unlike the ways of the old-timers who sought to find a place of grief and hardship so that they could engage in spiritual *askesis*. You see, when we search for a place of solace, it is in reality our desires that we are following.

"Of course, I am not suggesting that we resort to harsh pedagogical methods like those practiced by some of the old hermits that I met on Mount Athos. I simply tell you this in order to emphasize the importance of maintaining as much as humanly possible an ascetic ethos during our monastic career. We need to remind ourselves that we are monks. This is the road we have chosen. And if we truly wish to enjoy the ultimate consolation from God we must cut off all other sources of consolation, always remembering that 'Blessed are those who mourn, for they shall be comforted' [Matthew 5:4].

"Another point that I need to make is this: based on my own experiences with contemporary elders, and those of the past I read about, I have noticed that a major concern of theirs was not to make life comfortable for their disciples. To understand their concern I would like to offer you an analogy. Imagine a general who is trying to make soldiers out of young conscripts. But he is soft and concerned for the comfort of those young men. He makes their life in the army as easy and enjoyable as possible. Imagine me in such a position. Had I been a general I would have brought disaster to the army. I could see myself like a mother bringing those seventeen-year-old boys milk to their beds every morning."

There was an outburst of laughter as Father Maximos continued in his characteristic humorous way. "I would let the kids have their sleep and not trouble them with all those barbarous and strenuous military exercises. Fine. But that's not the way to make soldiers. I would have rendered those young men incapable of fighting a war, something that could have cost their lives.

"It is for similar reasons that Saint John Climacus advised an elder, 'Be careful to train your children regularly lest they unlearn their pedagogy.' To-day we are particularly cautious not to offend anyone, not to appear harsh, not to hurt the feelings of a novice. Again, I am not suggesting that we need to apply such excruciating methods as those of the desert fathers, nor is my own temperament compatible with harsh forms of *askesis*. I simply wish to remind you, Fathers, as well as remind myself, of what is at stake here and what is required of us in order to acquire the Holy Spirit.

"Old Paisios used to raise the question as to why so many rich and im-pious people have such easy and comfortable lives, beautiful lives, all paved with rose petals. He said, had God owed them something for any good works they might have done, they were repaid now. Any credit they may have accumulated was now all gone. There was nothing left for them to get.

"This brings to my mind the case of Saint Arsenios the Cappadocian. Every time he prayed with his *komboschini* and felt great solace in his heart, he worried whether God was paying him back right away for his ef-forts, leaving little for the future.

"Imagine! Some holy elders were even suspicious of the solace they were experiencing as a result of their spiritual work. Saint Arsenios would say, 'I don't want any comfort now. I want the comfort coming from the Holy Spirit later. What interests me now is toil, pain, hard work.' This is what the saints were seeking.

"We hope, therefore, that the grace of the Holy Spirit will provide us with strength so that each one of us can struggle according to our abilities and capacities for endurance. We will need this so that we can descend into hell by ourselves in order to acquire the scepter of our victory.

"We must realize and always remember, Fathers, that this is our path and we must be vigilant so that we may not get off it. We should learn to walk on solid ground and must not get distracted as we search for support through other means and pathways. Only God is our comforter and only in him must we rest all our hopes. Therefore, when we finally face our Maker we can say, 'Okay, my God, we have not done anything else in our lives except trust and hope in you. You have been our father, our brother, our friend, our teacher. You have been our only consolation. We sought no other comfort in our lives except you, our beloved. We, therefore, deserve your mercy and tender love.' Seeing that we have remained faithful in him, the Lord, as our only source of solace, will take up permanent residence within our hearts. This will happen in this life, not after we die. It is in this life and in this world that we will begin to experience the indescribable joy of the transformation of our hearts into a permanent chalice for the Holy Spirit. Amen!"

Father Maximos ended his talk in the total darkness of the night, symbolic, I thought, of the subject matter of his lesson. With no lights on and without any lit candles, we could barely recognize each other's faces. Only the brightness of the stars offered us any clues as to where we were.

With Father Maximos's last word everybody stood up. He recited a short prayer and then all thirty-five monks began chanting a hymn to the *Theotokos*. It was an experience I will never forget.

I had many questions that I wished to ask Father Maximos but it was not appropriate for me to do so right after his talk. We all silently walked to our cells. The opportunity to ask questions came during our journey back to Limassol on Tuesday. After the morning service and after a short communal breakfast we began the two-hour drive back to Limassol.

"What did you think of last night, Kyriaco?" Father Maximos asked as we walked toward the car. He must have seen the questions written all over my face.

"Now I know for certain that I can never be a monk. I understand, of course, that it was a lesson addressed strictly for monks and hermits and I am very grateful to you for letting me get a glimpse into that world." Father Maximos nodded. "I am beginning to appreciate the extraordinary difficulty of living such a life. I can see someone not fully familiar with the ways of the monastic life vehemently objecting to everything you said last night, particularly to the idea that if you give your heart to another human being such as a friend you will have less energy to climb toward God."

"As you very well know, Kyriaco, the monastic way of life is not for everybody," Father Maximos said softly as we got into the car and headed off. "That's why we do not try to recruit people into this lifestyle. It has to be a special calling that comes from within. Before you become a monk you must spend at least two years as a novice to see if you can indeed live this kind of life. Monastic life literally means cutting yourself off from all relationships in order to develop a perfect relationship with God. And once you establish such a perfect relationship with God then you automatically establish a perfect relationship with all other human beings. This is a law, a spiritual law discovered by holy elders throughout the ages. Since God is omnipresent and everywhere and you become one with God, then you become like God, *Kata Charin*, through grace. When you get to that point you begin to love the world like God loves the world, absolutely and unconditionally. Do you follow?"

294

"I think so, yes. You love totally and without discriminating."

"Definitely without discriminating. That's the whole point. God loves all his creatures. What people find difficult to understand is that God loves equally both good and bad people without special favors, absolutely, personally, and unconditionally. Sometimes people feel shocked when I tell them that God loves the devil as much as he loves the Holy Virgin."

"Otherwise he would not be God."

"But let me give you another example in regard to your concern. Suppose you are a surgeon and you are carrying on a very delicate operation to save the life of a patient. Under such circumstances you don't want visits from your parents, your friends, or your spouse. You wouldn't want any distractions would you? Likewise, a monk who is trying to focus exclusively on God in order to acquire the Holy Spirit needs this withdrawal from the world that I talked about."

Father Maximos continued. "When you are cut off from all sources that offer you your sense of self and identity, then sooner or later the person will experience the darkness and chaos that I talked about. Christ comes in at a certain point and reconstructs the self. The person then acquires a radically new sense of who he is. He develops an entirely new identity."

"I am just wondering," I said with some reluctance, "if in order to get to God you need to undergo such excruciating forms of *askesis*, then what chances do we have who live in the world? What chance has someone like me, a married person committed to wife, children, friends, to attain union with God? I know, of course, that we talked about this before. But that thought always crosses my mind."

"It is just as excruciating and difficult living in the world as it is being a monk," Father Maximos replied. "It only appears more difficult to be a monk because you are not a monk. In reality it is the same thing. You yourself are asked to transcend and forget yourself for the sake of the other. That is the deeper meaning of marriage and family life, an *askesis* of self-transcendence for the sake of the other. To raise a family means sacrifice and toil, no less demanding than living in a monastery. In fact I know of women who are real martyrs, their lives are much more challenging and difficult than the life of monks and hermits, believe me."

"Oh, I do believe you," I said, nodding. In fact, after learning of domestic abuse and violence through confessionals, Father Maximos had become so concerned with the status of women having problems from abusive husbands that, after creating a drug detoxification center, he placed as a top priority of his social outreach agenda the creation of a center for the support of abused women.

"What about others who live in the world and are not married?" I asked.

"Again, there are different paths toward God. Monasticism is one. Married family life is another. A single person has other opportunities for overcoming egotism. Every human being is being challenged in life in one form or another. What is important is to learn to take advantage of these challenges and progress spiritually."

It was close to noon when we arrived at the bishopric's offices in downtown Limassol. I thanked Father Maximos for the unique opportunity to be present at the *synaxis* and got ready to switch cars and enter my aging Honda.

"Tonight read from this book," Father Maximos said and handed me a book about Elder Porphyrios, an assemblage of homilies put together by his disciples after the legendary elder's repose several years back. "Perhaps you can find in it further clarification about these matters."

I thanked Father Maximos and drove off. In the evening I began reading the book passed on to me by Father Maximos. I read it nonstop until two in the morning, absorbed by the simple wisdom of Elder Porphyrios:

> There are two roads that lead towards God. One is the harsh and tiring way with the savage struggles and assaults of evil. The other is the smoother way, the one through the power of love. There are many who chose the tortuous, difficult road and, as the saying goes, they "shed blood in order to get spirit." Through that method they reached great heights of virtue and spiritual attainment. I personally prefer the second and easier method for I consider it the shortest and more direct way to God. That is the way I urge ordinary people to follow. . . . Struggle for the spiritual life with simplicity and without haste and force.[2]

Well, I am an ordinary person, I wrote in my journal, and as an ordinary person this "middle way" is more suitable to my temperament and situation. I liked what Elder Porphyrios had to say. I suspected this is what Father Maximos was saying also. At the same time, I admire the heroism of the monastic way. But like most mortals I am not made for it. I do believe that the monastic way that focuses on the "acquisition of the Holy Spirit," is necessary for the good of the world, for the benefit of the rest of us who cannot live like monks and nuns.

I switched the light off and slowly fell asleep, my heart and mind, my *nous* as the elders say, saturated with the tender and soothing words of this latter-day saint of Athonite spirituality.

FIFTEEN

PRIMAL PASSIONS

 no longer had to rely exclusively on Lavros's method of the "ambush" to continue my work, as more opportunities to spend time with Father Maximos arose. After we returned from the Panagia monastery he invited me to join him for a series of daily visits to elementary schools where he planned to meet and speak to children.

He made it a policy, he explained to me, to visit all the schools within his diocese at least once a year. This policy was based on his belief that children "should get exposed to the word of God from an early age so that they have a solid foundation in their lives as they grow up."

I promptly arrived at the bishopric just before seven thirty in the morn-ing the following Monday. I was not in the driver's seat during that formal excursion. I was simply an accompanying guest. Still, punctuality was es-sential and I was not so familiar with the area. I sat comfortably next to Father Maximos in the backseat of the bishopric's official but modest blue Volkswagen as Andreas, a happy and enthusiastic volunteer, drove us to our destination. We were to visit three elementary schools that Monday, one in a village by the sea and two in the foothills of the Troodos Mountains, a to-tal driving time of about three hours.

Our first visit was to be at a school by the sea, half an hour west of Li-massol. As we entered the car I mentioned to Father Maximos the sharp contrast between America and Cyprus. He listened with interest as I ex-plained to him that it would have been unthinkable for a bishop to visit a public school in America where children from various nationalities and re-ligious backgrounds were in attendance. It would have been considered a scandal, if not an illegal violation of the separation of church and state. But in Cyprus such an issue was irrelevant. Just about all the pupils and teach-ers were Greek Orthodox and the separation of church and state was not so clear. A bishop visiting their school was perfectly natural and a cause for celebration rather than legal action by irate parents of other denominations and faiths. But I warned that with Cyprus entering the European Union such visits by Father Maximos may become increasingly problematic. Al-ready Cyprus was becoming unavoidably a multicultural society with more and more people practicing religions other than Eastern Orthodoxy.

"I love to be with children," Father Maximos said as Andreas drove us through the agricultural Fasouri area of orange groves and cypress trees. "Their innocence fills me with good feelings and energy. I am not sure of course whether the teachers share my views." He then went on to confide that whereas adults often tire him during confessions, children always re-lax him. With their innocence they are even a source of entertainment.

"Children need spiritual pedagogy from an early age if they are to de-velop into healthy adults," Father Maximos said as he rested his eyes on the sea to our left. "They need to hold good images in their minds to serve as compasses during their lives."

As he spoke my mind traveled back to my own childhood growing up in Agioi Omologitai, a then suburb of Nicosia. I mentioned to Father Maximos how important it was for me as a child to have access to the late Father Paul and Father Vasili, the good-natured priests of our community. I think of them with fondness every time I reminisce about my early years. They would tell us extraordinary tales about the lives of saints. In fact it was perhaps these two elderly priests who first imprinted in my mind the reality of that minuscule category of human beings who have walked the earth gently and unobtrusively.

The entire school of about one hundred children between the ages of six and twelve, and their six teachers, assembled in the main hall and gave an enthusiastic reception to Father Maximos. The principal read a brief welcoming speech and then gave the floor to father Maximos to address his youthful audience. After expressing his happiness to be with them that morning and after cracking a few jokes that filled the auditorium with laughter, Father Maximos told the students of the reason for his visit—the need to build a good character before they grow up. "What is easier?" he asked. "To uproot a cypress tree when it is a small seedling or when it is a grown-up tree like that one?" The children looked outside the window at the tall cypress tree in the middle of the yard that Father Maximos was pointing at. All of them with one voice agreed that it would be easier to uproot a cypress seedling than a cypress tree.

"Good," Father Maximos exclaimed. "That is why you should uproot your bad habits now while you are young rather than wait until you grow up. Your bad habits will have such deep roots by then that it will be very difficult for you to extract them." He went on to explain to his unusually attentive audience the meaning of the word *morphosis* (education). "The verb *morphono* literally means in Greek 'to shape.' That means that real education first and foremost must aim at shaping your character. So my children, remember that as you go through your schooling the accumulation of knowledge must not be your only goal. After all, it is educated people who are making those bombs that are killing people today. These educated people are smart and know a lot of things, but they are not *morphomenoi*, they are not truly educated.

I told Father Maximos as we drove off to the next elementary school at a mountain village that what he told the children is what I tell my students at the university. If we destroy the earth in a nuclear cataclysm or if we make life unlivable because of industrial pollution, the primary responsibility will fall squarely on the shoulders of teachers, professors, and the highly trained business and scientific community, the "educated." We have learned how to uncover the secrets of nature but we woefully lack the wisdom to handle the power that we have unleashed in a nondestructive way.

Father Maximos listened attentively, nodding in silence as I made my points. Encouraged, I went on, elaborating on my notions about the education of the whole person, ideas that converged with those of Father Maximos. I was speaking to the converted, of course. In less than twenty minutes we reached our new destination.

In contrast to our arrival at the previous school, where both teachers and pupils stood at the gate with flowers in their hands, there was nobody around to welcome us except a frantic-looking and apologetic principal, who rushed out of her office to meet us. We learned that we were an hour early! Apparently there was a miscommunication between the school and the secretary of the bishopric as to the timing of our arrival. Father Maximos assured her that we did not mind waiting for an hour. The school was at the edge of the village, on the slopes of a beautiful mountain. At the top of the mountain, a twenty-minute walk from the school, was a newly constructed chapel of Prophet Elias, a popular saint in Greek Orthodoxy. Father Maximos considered the mishap a rare opportunity to take a mountain hike and pay homage to the prophet. While Andreas remained at the school, setting up some composition books that Father Maximos routinely offered as gifts to the children, I joined him for the hiking pilgrimage. The Greeks have left no mountain peak without a chapel in honor of the saint who, some would say, replaced Apollo in the Greek religious imagination. In fact, speaking for myself, Prophet Elias is always associated with the top of a mountain. The mountains were covered with a deep, lush green thanks to an unusually good rainfall during the winter months, a blessing for a rain-starved island. I could see that Father Maximos welcomed this unusual opportunity to walk without throngs of people following behind him or gathering around him trying to kiss his hand and get his blessing. I wasn't sure, however, whether he would have preferred to be totally alone.

After he lit a candle in the chapel and we paid homage to Prophet

Elias, we sat outside the church on a bench with a panoramic view of the valley below and the picturesque village on the side of the mountain. It was an opportunity to discuss further the ideas about education that Father Maximos's talk had triggered. Hardly had we gotten into our conversation, however, when Andreas came running up the hill to inform us that everybody was waiting at the school. We immediately hurried down the mountain. There was the usual enthusiastic reception by students and teachers. In addition there was a group of clergymen who arrived from surrounding villages to greet their bishop. In their midst, there was Lavros.

Father Maximos suggested to Lavros after the ceremonies were over that he join us for the journey to the remaining school. In order to ride with us, he hurriedly parked his car at a friend's house nearby while Father Maximos, Andreas, and I were treated to pastries and coffee.

As we were about to leave I offered Lavros the place next to Father Maximos. I settled myself in the front passenger seat, amidst several bouquets of flowers that the teachers and students had ceremoniously offered to Father Maximos. Lavros needed to discuss several issues with the bishop. On that particular day he had urgent business related to the planting of an olive garden at the bishopric's farm. It was a major undertaking that had given a major headache to poor Lavros, who had volunteered his services as acting manager of the property.

After going over some practical problems with the garden project, Lavros pulled out a newspaper reporting on the latest developments for the campaign to elect a new archbishop.

"Here is the official announcement of the Communist Party," Lavros said. He unfolded the newspaper and began reading. " 'The central committee of the Communist Party adopted the suggestion of the policy bureau of the party to support Bishop X——. The party decided that Bishop X—— is the most appropriate candidate. According to the official statement he is, among other things, *Polymehanos* [a man of many ways and means], worldly, well connected, and electable, whereas in the other camp'—meaning you," Lavros said in a joking tone while pointing his finger at Father Maximos, " 'one finds zealots, fanatics and medievalists.' "

We laughed with Father Maximos, who shook his head and sighed. It was not the first time that he had become a target of the local Commu-

301

nists. When he was about to be elected bishop, the party allegedly campaigned against his candidacy, spreading rumors that Athonite monks were like fanatical "ayatollahs." But the rank and file of the Communist Party, most of them churchgoers, disobeyed their leaders and voted "yes" for the then abbot of the Panagia monastery. Given the incapacity of the current archbishop to fulfill his duties due to Alzheimer's disease, there was a push to elect a new archbishop. Faced with this prospect, the hard-core among the Communists wished to make sure that Father Maximos's chances were slim. They were particularly alarmed by his growing popularity. Given the local tradition that both bishops and the archbishop are elected by popular vote, like sheriffs in American towns, the Communists wished to tilt the vote in favor of a bishop who was worldly and had little chance of bringing about a religious revival on the island.

The irony was that Father Maximos's parents were themselves former members of the Communist Party while he himself shied away from local politics, focusing exclusively on his spiritual mission. This is what apparently bothered the Soviet-trained leadership of the party. Father Maximos was redirecting the energy of the people, they feared, from potential membership in the party to spiritual gatherings and all-night vigils. Father Maximos represented for them the "opiate of the masses" par excellence. It was better, therefore, to have as the head of the church a businesslike archbishop who would exert no spiritual appeal to the young or to the older generation. Understandably, they did not want someone who would shift the attention of people from this world to the world beyond.

When we went on to discuss these developments, Father Maximos expressed feelings of deep discomfort. Just as he had had no felt desire to become bishop, he now dreaded the prospect of finding himself on the archiepiscopal seat. Certainly he was not campaigning for the position. However, as Lavros reminded him, the archbishop of Cyprus was in reality drafted by popular will and whatever happened would be beyond his own wishes and desires in the same way that it was beyond his wishes and desires to leave Mount Athos and come to Cyprus.

"Oh dear," Father Maximos exclaimed with marked despair in his voice. "What have I gotten myself into?" As bishop, he said, he had lost the freedom to walk down the street without people running after him. "Imagine what would happen if, God forbid, I became archbishop!"

Father Maximos went on to tell us how good he felt when he visited Athens recently and strolled alone around the city without anyone recognizing or following him. "I could enter a shop or a bookstore and browse without people approaching me. I felt great." Yet even in that megalopolis of five million he could not completely escape his growing fame. As he was about to take the underground a group of university students recognized who he was. They surrounded him, asking questions and requesting his blessing.

Father Maximos then reminisced about the "good old days" when he was an unknown monk on Mount Athos. It was then that Elder Paisios warned him: "Alas to the monk, Father, who becomes famous." At that time he could not understand the meaning of those prophetic words. But Father Maximos learned to graciously surrender to his providential fate. I had the feeling that, given his extroverted, sociable personality, he was beginning to enjoy his life and work "in the world." I could no longer imagine him as a recluse spending the rest of his life as a monk or a hermit in some Athonite cave.

We arrived at Pyrgos at about one o'clock. But instead of visiting the elementary school we went straight to the local church. "The appointment at the elementary school," Father Maximos said, "is at two thirty. I want you to see an icon of the Holy Virgin that has a story behind it."

There was nobody at the church except the local priest, who waited at the door. Apparently we had a prior agreement to meet there. A family man in his early fifties, the father, with his black cassock, priestly hat, and long gray beard, was greatly pleased to see his bishop. He was also happy to see Lavros, who was well known all over the Limassol district. He had represented Limassol in the Cyprus parliament when the island got its independence from England in 1960.

The friendly-looking priest escorted us inside the church and showed us the miraculous icon of the Holy Virgin. Father Maximos made a deep bow in front of the icon and after making the sign of the cross he kissed it. Then he said, "The father here will tell us later about why this icon is considered special."

303

Our host then invited us to his house where his wife had prepared lunch for the four of us. Right after lunch our host told us of the unusual phenomenon associated with the *Panagia Pyrgiotissa* (The Madonna of Pyrgos). According to the story, which had made national news, a woman from Athens had her right arm completely paralyzed. It was totally "gone," she felt no sensation whatsoever. One night she had a dream in which her deceased mother appeared and informed her that the Holy Virgin *Pyrgiotissa* would heal her. The woman could not understand what this meant. She searched all over Greece but could not find such an icon. She then tried Cyprus. She found out that there were two villages on the island called Pyrgos (Tower), one in the Paphos area and one near Limassol. She called up the priest of the Limassol Pyrgos, who said that the icon of the Holy Virgin in his church is not called *Pyrgiotissa* but *ChrysoPyrgiotissa* (The Golden Madonna of Pyrgos). Intrigued, the priest had experts check the icon and found out that the original name of the icon was just *Pyrgiotissa* and that the *Chryso* ("gold") part was a later addition as a result of popular usage.

The Athenian woman came to Cyprus to pay homage to the *Panagia Pyrgiotissa*. According to her own report, the moment she stood in front of the icon she sensed a hand grasping her sick arm. For the first time she felt a pain from her fingers all the way up through her entire arm. Overnight she began to feel her fingertips. The next morning when she went to church she remained fixated on the icon. She as well as her husband claimed that they saw a brilliant light moving from the icon toward her, enveloping her entire body. After that experience all feeling and movement came back to her arm. Skeptics, as was to be expected, had different explanations.

"Are you interested in such stories?" Father Maximos asked me as we left the priest's home and Andreas drove us toward the school, where students and teachers waited for us.

"Of course."

"Why?" Father Maximos asked.

His question took me by surprise. He rarely asked me questions. It was I who relentlessly played the role of the interrogator in our relationship.

"If real," I responded, "such experiences may be signs and ongoing confirmation of the interpenetration of other, higher realities on this material level. Let us say they are the hidden signatures of nonmaterial realities."

"Say more," Father Maximos asked again with an inquisitive smile, perhaps sensing a slight hesitation on my part.

Father Maximos's probing gave me the opportunity for the first time to outline for him some of my key conclusions about the nature of reality, the outcome of many years of exploration into the world of healers, mystics, and saints. I mentioned that the accumulated evidence in areas like extraordinary healing phenomena, the near-death experience, developments in modern quantum physics, and the reports of mystics throughout the ages leads to the conclusion that there is a need for a radical revision of the materialist metaphysic that has dominated modern culture during the last three hundred years. It so happened that Lavros and I had discussed such ideas at a seaside café only the other day, so this conversation had that déjà vu feeling about it.

Basically I paraphrased for Father Maximos what I had written in one of my previous books. There I proposed a new set of assumptions for guiding humanity's exploration into the nature of reality during the twenty-first century. In that earlier work I wrote:

Assumption number one: The world of the five senses is not the only world there is. . . . Assumption number two: Other worlds exist that interpenetrate our own. These worlds are layered—that means they relate to each other in a hierarchical manner. The world of the five senses is at the bottom of this spiritual totem pole. These layers are not only out there in nature, objectively speaking, but they are also part of the structure of human consciousness itself. . . . Three, the various worlds are in ongoing communication with one another. But most often the communication moves in a conscious way from top to bottom, rarely from bottom up. The higher realms constantly influence the lower realms in ways that the lower realms are not aware of. At all levels of this hierarchy there are conscious beings. Those above us are on a superior, more evolved vantage point in reference to consciousness and knowledge than ourselves. Some members of our own reality make contact with these higher realms. We have called them shamans, psychics, prophets, saints, and so on. Their reports of what they find always are couched within the language of the culture that these gifted people happen to live in. Therefore, knowledge of these higher worlds is always colored, filtered, and distorted in varying degrees through the cultural constructions of time and place. Even living saints are subjected to this law. . . .

Fourth, if the above assumptions are true . . . then it logically follows that we as a species and as individuals are never alone. The universe or, better, universes are peopled by higher intelligences than ourselves, and perhaps lower than ourselves. Fifth, contrary to Sartre, Camus, and Beckett the world is utterly meaningful. This meaning is derived from the fact that Creation is not an accident but the product of a Divine Plan. The project of Creation and the existence of all the hierarchy is for the sake of the unfoldment and evolution of consciousness. This consciousness has as its destiny the transcendence of the hierarchy itself and the conscious reunification with the Absolute spirit or the Personal God out of Whom we come and within Whom, like fish in the ocean, we constantly are. This means that history is not drifting aimlessly but is inherently purposeful like the individual lives that compose it. It is, as Hegel would have said, the autobiography of God. That means, also, that everything is related to everything else in the cosmos. It is for this reason that mystics have proposed the seemingly preposterous notion that a single thought disturbs the entire universe.[1]

Father Maximos listened with great interest in what I had to say. I, of course, had no idea how much of what I said was consonant with his Athonite way of thinking. My suggestions were addressed to a wider multicultural audience and the language I used was based on that understanding. Expressions like "evolution of consciousness" and "transcendence of hierarchy" are not phrases that Father Maximos would have used. I had a feeling, but only a feeling, that what I wrote then and what I had paraphrased for Father Maximos did not contradict the essential teachings of the Athonite elders.

Andreas parked the car in front of the school, where an army of pupils and teachers waited for us. Any further discussion with Father Maximos on the proposed set of assumptions or "paradigm" for the exploration of reality had to be postponed for another time.

On the way back to Limassol the story of the *Panagia Pyrgiotissa* came up again in conversation. This time instead of focusing on my ideas, I asked Father Maximos to explain why, in spite of miracles such as those he has witnessed on Mount Athos and in Cyprus, he had been reluctant to talk about the Holy Virgin when asked to do so the other night during a gathering in Limassol.

"It is very difficult to talk about the Holy Virgin," he said thoughtfully.

"But why?"

"We know very little about the Holy Virgin. There are no records. All we know are her miracles, which are endless, as in this particular case." He paused. "There is no way that any human being would ask for help from the Holy Virgin without getting it. It's true, you know. Yet there is very little to say about her." Father Maximos then laughed and described the case of a journalist who came to Mount Athos planning to write an article about the Holy Virgin and left empty-handed. The elders told him that there are no words to describe or explain the great mystery of the Holy Virgin.

We returned to Limassol in the late afternoon after visiting another elementary school. Upon our arrival, as Lavros and I were about to leave the bishopric, Father Maximos handed me a huge bouquet of red roses given to him at one of the schools. "Take it to Emily," he said with a smile. "She loves roses."

Lavros then asked whether Father Maximos would be willing to visit his humble home at the outskirts of Limassol for an evening of conversation with a small group of friends. To Lavros's and my delight, Father Maximos took out his calendar and chose a night that was still free.

"Let's do that in memory of Maroulla [Lavros's late wife]," Father Maximos said. The response touched Lavros deeply. Father Maximos had never visited my friend's home before. It was an opportunity to do so and fulfill a promise he made to Lavros's devout wife before her death.

The get-together was to be in the form of a potluck. In addition to Lavros, Emily, and I, Stephanos and Erato, as well as Helen and Patrick, a couple from California, would also be present. Helen was a forty-year-old art professor and Patrick a history professor. They were both fluent in

Greek because of extended stays on a Greek island. Along with her husband, Helen was a recent convert to Eastern Orthodoxy. She was eager to have the opportunity to speak with Father Maximos, whom she had never met in person but had heard so much about from Lavros, their close friend, and from my books.

By eight o'clock, when the red sun was just above the horizon, we had gathered at Lavros's home, which was surrounded by a lush green yard. Being an environmentalist he filled the space around his old house with a variety of local and exotic plants and trees, turning his yard into a small emerald forest at the edge of the city. Father Maximos expressed his appreciation of the ambiance as we sat on the veranda under a canopy of jasmine, which filled the air with its summery aroma. Cool breezes came as the sun disappeared into the sea.

After the introductions and a few humorous remarks by Father Maximos and Lavros, a specialist in multicultural jokes thanks to his many travels around the world, we gathered around the potluck dinner table. After Father Maximos recited the customary prayer we indulged. It was not a fasting period (when no meat, fish, poultry, or meat products are consumed) so we outdid each other in heaping up a cornucopia of gourmet food, particularly Stephanos, who once owned a posh restaurant in London where he worked as its chief chef.

Once we ate, Helen had several topics she wanted to discuss with Father Maximos, such as the presumed connection of Jesus with India. Before converting to Orthodoxy, Helen, as well as Patrick, had seriously investigated Buddhism and Hinduism, traveled to Nepal and India in search of spiritual wisdom, and even spent time at various ashrams including that of the famed Sai Baba. Father Maximos said that even though he was not a biblical scholar there seemed to be no reason to believe any other version of the early life of Jesus except whatever is said in the Gospels. He then proceeded to respond to further questions from his small audience, which were directly related to the spiritual life rather than to biblical history. For him the former were the most important questions, anyway.

"The struggle we carry on within the *Ecclesia*," Father Maximos responded to one of Helen's enquiries, "is to overcome our passions that like dark clouds hide the inner beauty of our being. When the clouds are gone we may discover who we truly are. Furthermore, when we accomplish this for ourselves we will then be able to apprehend the inner beauty in other human beings. That is, we will be able to perceive them as they truly are and not as they express themselves through their lowly, worldly passions."

"So someone who has the power to go beyond the clouds will be able to see the sun," Helen added with a nod. Being an artist she seemed to appreciate the images that Father Maximos employed in describing the inner state of the human soul.

"Exactly. That's why the pure at heart, that is, those who have healed themselves from egotism, are those who can also recognize in others that inner, yet hidden radiance."

"So human beings are in their innermost being good," I pointed out. In my mind flashed the ideas of eighteenth- and nineteenth-century romantics. Working primarily through secular channels of apprehending reality, they may have intuited, I reasoned, the mystical truths that Father Maximos was alluding to—that human beings are essentially good by nature.

"Absolutely," Father Maximos said. "There is no human being who is evil in their very essence. It is the passions that distort the basic goodness that resides in the very core of every person. And those who have cleansed themselves from their own passions, that is the saints, can also see in others their fundamental divinity."

"Can you tell us more about what you mean, what the Church means, by 'the passions,' Your Reverence?" Patrick asked, addressing Father Maximos in that formal honorific way, something the rest of us were unaccustomed to.

"Most of the passions," Father Maximos replied, "are simply distortions of divine gifts and virtues."

"For example?"

"As images of God we have within us the power of love, a divine passion. But it has become contaminated with egotism. Hatred is the absolute and total distortion of love."

"It means that hatred springs from the same power source as that of love," I suggested, a notion that I first encountered in the *Kybalion*, an ancient Hermetic classic.[2]

309

"Yes. Hatred is in reality love that has merged with egotism and been corrupted. It became transmuted into hatred."

"So love and hatred, as the ancient sages taught, form the opposite poles of the same frequency," I concluded. "That's why people who once loved each other passionately can become implacable enemies when that love is mixed up with their egotistical desires, or when their narcissism is wounded. At the same time hatred can also be transmuted into passionate love under certain circumstances. That leads me to further conclude that the opposite of love in reality is not hatred but apathy and indifference."

"Exactly," Father Maximos said and went on to point out that pride may be another example of this distortion in our very being. We are created, he claimed, with pride embedded in us insofar as we are "kings of creation" and "children of the living God." This divine pride has degenerated into a pathological form of pride that now torments us.

"How can one overcome these destructive passions, Father Maxime?" asked Helen. The rest of us remained silent to allow Helen and Patrick to raise their questions. "How can we recapture our original beauty?"

"The life of Christ is for us the archetype of our own lives. Through his example he has shown us how we can struggle to free ourselves from those passions that keep us enslaved to this world. We read in the Gospel that after Jesus was baptized by his cousin, the hermit John, he was guided by the Holy Spirit into the desert where for forty days he was alone. On the fortieth day he was visited by Satan, who tried to tempt him by mobilizing against Jesus three major human passions. The holy elders concluded that Jesus' experiences are a form of revelation. They are instructive insofar as they are the fundamental passions that plague human existence."

"What passions are you referring to, Your Reverence?" Patrick asked softly after a few seconds of silence.

"Satan confronted Jesus with three offers. They are known as the three temptations of Christ. Satan first urged him, starved as he was from his forty-day fast, to turn stones into bread so that he could satisfy the craving of his body. The second temptation was when Satan took Jesus to the top of the Temple's sanctuary and urged him to jump. Satan told him that no harm would come to him since he was the son of God. His heavenly father, after all, would dispatch all the angels of creation to rescue him. The last temptation was when Satan showed him all the kingdoms and wealth of the world and promised to offer them to him if Jesus would submit to Satan's authority. Jesus resisted all three temptations and was victorious over Satan.

"According to the holy elders," Father Maximos continued, "these three temptations are archetypal and instructive. They are the three fundamental passions that plague humanity, *hedonism, philodoxy* [love of glory], and *avarice*. The elders claimed further that these three principal passions form the womb out of which all other worldly passions are given birth."

"How is the first temptation of Christ suggestive of hedonism?" Helen asked.

"The elders felt that hedonism springs from our need to look after our bodily comforts and pleasures to survive in this world. So Satan tempts Christ to break his fast and turn stones into bread. According to the elders, the second temptation, that the angels will rush to the rescue of the son of God if he jumps from the edge of the Temple, is suggestive of our obsession with self-importance and self-glorification. And finally, the third temptation, the offer to own the world, is suggestive of the passion for avarice, of insatiable greed. Let me be more concrete. Let's look at hedonism first." Father Maximos took a deep breath in his characteristic way. "Again, this passion prior to the Fall functioned naturally within the individual, in accordance with God's wishes."

"Do you mean to say, Father," Helen asked, grinning broadly "that God created us for the sake of hedonism?"

"Absolutely so." Father Maximos spread his hands outwards as if it were a self-evident truth.

"It's hard to fathom what you are suggesting, Father Maxime," Lavros said in a joking tone.

"You know what I mean, Lavro. The greatest hedonism that a human being can attain is the love of God and our relationship with him. It is for this love and this pleasure that God has created us."

"This is what Saint Maximos the confessor calls *Eros Maniakos*, right?" I said.

"Exactly. The person who manages to overcome the lower passions and attain *Theosis* experiences this divine eros, this exquisite form of pleasure that is beyond all human description or comparison."

"God as an intoxicating lover," Patrick marveled. "Very interesting!"

"That's exactly what true hedonism is all about," Father Maximos added as if speaking from direct experience. "Every human being must strive to become a passionate lover of God. Believe me, it is the most potent, the most intoxicating form of pleasure."

"This is a new way of looking at hedonism," Helen commented.

"But that's why God originally placed us in paradise. He didn't place us in a world of suffering and torture but in paradise so that we could enjoy the experience of this indescribable joy and pleasure. That state of bliss was ruined by the Fall. So the power that we have within us to love God and through God to love other human beings and the whole of Creation got corrupted. God was forgotten and human beings redirected their love exclusively to the objects of the world and to themselves."

"Father, how is this distortion of hedonism expressed in concrete form?" Helen asked.

"When the *Ecclesia* speaks of hedonism it does not refer simply to the hedonism of the body, such as the desire for food and sex. These make up only a small portion of hedonism. There are people who are freed from the allurement of bodily pleasures but are plagued by other forms of hedonism. People may be enamored and delighted with their own cleverness and brilliance."

"How can we heal ourselves from hedonism, Father Maxime? It's very difficult," Lavros said.

"You heal yourself through hard work and diligence, through *philoponia*."

"But what does this mean in terms of one's salvation?"

"*Philoponia* means that a human being must cultivate an attitude of love for hard work and toil. As you have seen, Lavro, everything we do within the *Ecclesia*, particularly at the monasteries, is an expression of *philoponia*. One example is fasting. The *Ecclesia* instructs that during such and such days we must refrain from certain foods. For forty days before Easter we are not supposed to eat meat and meat products. The *Ecclesia* tells us that only on certain days we may eat fish. We are supposed to avoid oil on certain days, and so on. The *Ecclesia* puts us on a certain diet, telling us what we must eat and what not to eat—"

"The obvious question that an outsider could raise is why all these restrictions?" I interjected.

"But that's what I just said, to cultivate *philoponia*. To get accustomed to cutting off our wishes and desires. Cultivating *philoponia* also means working in the fields and spending long hours in liturgies and services and all-night vigils."

"Why the need to spend so many hours in an all-night vigil?" Helen wondered. Earlier on I had described to her my amazement at participating in an eleven-hour all-night vigil on Mount Athos without feeling bored or even tired.

"You see," Father Maximos replied, "the *Ecclesia* never compromised with the world. Why? Because it always acts therapeutically. It acts just like a physician who knows that a sick patient needs to take, let us say, ten very bitter pills of a certain medicine in order to get well. A conscientious doctor will never prescribe only four, because they won't be enough to restore the patient's health. The aim of the *Ecclesia* is to exercise human beings spiritually. We go to church and we stand there for hours. We have vespers, all-night vigils, liturgies, readings from the scriptures, and so on. Even here in the world a service will go on for three to four hours."

"This is a cause for incredulity in the West," I said.

"I am reminded of a German Lutheran minister who visited Mount Athos," Father Maximos said in a light tone. "He was staying at the monastery of the Great Lavra when they conducted an *agrypnia* lasting eighteen hours. Poor fellow, he was standing the whole time because there was nowhere to sit. It so happened that at that time there were three hundred monks and as many visitors."

"That's one way of keeping people from going to Mount Athos," Patrick joked.

"No. On the contrary. After the *agrypnia*, during *trapeza* (the communal meal), he announced that he had decided to become Orthodox. We were stunned and asked him why. His response was that the fact that he lasted for eighteen hours in a church service was a miracle in itself, an omen from God. He eventually became a monk and stayed there permanently."

"Hard to believe." Patrick shook his head in wonder.

"Such stories are routine on Mount Athos," explained Lavros, who had met that German monk.

"Do you see what is happening?" said Father Maximos. "*Philoponia*, which is part of the spiritual methodology of the *Ecclesia*, is offered as a form of healing and as an antidote to the illness of hedonism. After all it is this form of hedonism that ejected human beings from Eden. The most beloved child of hedonism is narcissism. That means that human beings love themselves excessively, they love themselves above everybody and everything else. This is pathological."

"Narcissism and extreme individualism are considered serious pathologies among many contemporary social thinkers,"[3] I said.

"Any reasonable person would consider such tendencies as serious maladies," Father Maximos added. "I should also mention that narcissism, this obsessive atomism, is the product of fear."

"Fear?" Patrick asked.

"Yes, fear. People are afraid to get sick, to be left alone, to lose their wealth, to have an accident, to lose respect, to be deprived of this or that. They are like the rich man in the Gospel that Jesus called 'foolish.' They are obsessed about having it good in this life rather than investing their hopes in eternal life within God. Foolish people invest their treasures in themselves, trying to feel secure in themselves."

"How do we stop being 'foolish' then? How can we heal ourselves from narcissism?" Patrick asked.

"Through *askesis*, of course."

"So far, Father Maxime, you spoke of hedonism as one of the key passions that obstruct our vision of God. What about philodoxy?" I asked.

"Oh yes, the love of glory. Ordinary human beings love to be admired and glorified. They love to feel superior to others. This is a form of human pathology. What we call pride, egotism, vanity, arrogance, rudeness, and the like are, according to Saint John Climacus, the children and grandchildren of the passion for glory, of philodoxy."

"But that's how God made us," Helen said.

"Yes. But God made us proud because we are made for heaven. He made us kings and queens of the created cosmos. God has given us a privileged position above all other creatures and objects of his creation. It was for us that both the earth and the heavens were made. At our deepest core we are created in such a way so that we may seek what is high and not desire what is low and transient and temporal," Father Maximos said. His eyes shone as he pointed out that this privileged status was shattered with the Fall, a theme that he repeated like a mantra.

Father Maximos's last words reminded me of the objections of the "deep ecologists" to such "anthropocentric" views about the nature of the world. They claim that such beliefs led to the ravaging of the planet and the destruction of other living forms. However, from the point of view of Orthodox spirituality this ravaging took place because of the alienation of humanity from its inner divine nature. Once *Theosis* is attained then peace is restored between the person and the created cosmos in that the person now becomes a custodian of nature rather than its destroyer. The lives of saints, as Father Maximos would often repeat, are the empirical validation of such an argument. Furthermore, one can interpret this anthropocentrism as implying that the cosmos is created for the sake of the development of consciousness itself within the eternal mind of God. It is as if the very act of creation had as its sole purpose self-consciousness, which in reality means created beings becoming aware of their Creator. This divine process leads automatically to a true knowledge of self. That means consciousness has a privileged status within creation.

"With the Fall," Father Maximos continued, "our divine pride degenerated into passion and sinfulness. It became vanity and hubris toward God. Human beings ended up believing in themselves, becoming autonomous, craving praise and glorification for their worldly achievements. They became content in this false image of themselves."

"If *philoponia* is the cure for hedonism then what is the cure for philodoxy?" Patrick asked.

"The cure is to stay alert and take advantage of those episodes in our lives that will subvert our propensity for self-glorification. Suppose somebody says something that you feel is unjust or humiliating. Or suppose that someone ignores you and makes you feel rejected and so on. Now, for the

315

average person this may be hard to take, but in reality these are golden opportunities for spiritual growth. They are sent to us by God as spiritual exercises. If we lash out and, let's say, win the argument, or whatever, in reality we are the losers. We have lost a great opportunity. A person who is serious about spiritual development will welcome such experiences as forms of exercise in the same way that an athlete subjects himself to rigorous training regardless of how painful such training might be. With such exercises you begin to cultivate the spirit of humility.

"I see people," Father Maximos continued, "who become devastated because they cannot tolerate making mistakes. Why? Because they have an exaggerated image of themselves, that somehow they are perfect, impeccable. They are incapable of seeing themselves as weak creatures in need of help. This is pride springing from this key passion of philodoxy. Do you understand now?"

Father Maximos continued. "Philodoxy is the product of human insecurity and faithlessness whereby one cannot offer glory to anyone else except to one's own self. Do you see why every time we conduct the liturgy we say '*Oti prepe si pasa doxa, time kai proskenisis to Patri kai to Yio kai to Agio Pnevmati*' [We offer glory and honor and worship only to the Father, Son and Holy Spirit]?

"If you are obsessed about your own glory," Father Maximos went on, "then you will be in continuous psychic turmoil, you will be in a constant state of self-defense and you will find yourself in a never-ending struggle to hold on to and control around you all those elements that support the foundations of your own glory. You will live in a constant state of fear and suspicion. You will believe that people are talking behind your back, that others are trying to destroy you. You will suspect that your enemies are ready to walk all over your corpse and so on. Well, let them. The liberated individual does not have such fears. It is a good thing to become a corpse and have others step all over you.

"Someone said to an elder, 'Father, they say bad things about you.' He laughed and his reply was 'Really? So they say bad things about a dead person?' You see, it is a blessing to be 'dead' as far as human passions are concerned. It is possible for people to say all sorts of terrible things about you but in so doing something paradoxical happens. Within the *Ecclesia* there is a kind of madness, a strange form of logic. As you descend, in reality you ascend. And as you ascend, in reality you descend. 'If you wish to ascend,' say the elders, 'then descend and you shall discover at the end that your descent is the real ascension.' This is real freedom."

We had a short break of pastries and tea. Then we sat back in our chairs and the conversation resumed. "How about avarice, Father Maxime?" I asked. "Why is avarice, along with hedonism and philodoxy, the mother of all passions?"

"Avarice has within itself a hidden microbe, a very dangerous virus," Father Maximos replied. "It steals hope in God because human beings invest all their hopes in their personal possessions. They don't believe that God is powerful enough to feed and protect them. They say to themselves, 'I feel secure if I have my investments, if I have money in the bank, if I have a good pension,' and so on. Do you see what happens here?" Father Maximos looked around to see our reaction. "Hope in God is given up and is replaced by our material possessions.

"Another form of avarice is obsessive self-reliance. I feel secure because I have a university degree. Or I have an important position in society. I have knowledge and skills. I am active and energetic. I can do things and have total trust in myself."

"But is it bad to be self-reliant?" Patrick probably had in mind the fact that self-reliance is a virtue celebrated from cradle to grave in American culture.

"From the perspective of our ultimate destiny it is pathological if it replaces faith in God and all trust is placed either in objects we possess or in our own abilities and talents. In fact I dare say it is a spiritual problem when our heart is stuck not only on material objects and on our own abilities but also on other people."

"Other people?" Helen asked with surprise.

"For example, 'I feel secure because my family is doing well.' Or as people often tell me 'My husband is everything for me. If I lose him I will be lost.' Or 'If I lose my girlfriend I will die because life will have no meaning for me.' I hear these things in confessions all the time and I pray that they may never, God forbid, lose each other!"

Father Maximos continued on a more serious tone. "I can understand feeling grief and pain for the loss of a loved one, but why lose yourself in the process?"

Father Maximos leaned back on his chair. "Again, the real tragedy is when people invest all their hopes in whatever is transient and not everlasting. It could be 'my husband,' 'my wife,' 'my children,' 'my work,' 'my wealth,' 'my career.' I hear such statements and say to myself, and what's going to happen to you, my dear, when those things you consider 'everything' are taken away from you? You may lose your job, sooner or later you will lose your wife or your husband. Nothing in this world is permanent. Nothing human can give us real rest and comfort. Only God, who is the base that cannot be shaken, can do that. Yet you ignore God and invest all your hopes in that which is finite. You are completely absorbed by your worldly pursuits.

"I will never forget when, several years ago, a man put an end to his life," Father Maximos said with sadness in his face. "He believed his wife had cheated on him and left behind a letter that she, heartbroken, brought to me during confession. He wrote, 'For me life has no meaning anymore. From the moment you betrayed me I could no longer bear this life.' I wept when I read that letter and realized how much unhappiness was in the heart of that tragic fellow. He based his entire existence on the love of his wife and on nothing else. What was even more tragic was that his poor wife didn't betray him in reality. But he believed that she did because of certain circumstances and the bad-mouthing of others. There was no meaning in his life outside of his relationship with his wife.

"Can you realize how asphyxiating such a mind-set is? And I asked myself, is it possible for a human being whose life is grounded in God to tell another human being 'For me you are everything' and 'If you cannot be with me then life is meaningless'? The answer of course must be a categorical no. Within our sojourn toward God everything is appraised within our prospect for union with God. No material or transient thing should interfere with that journey."

"But people do need material things, they need money in order to sustain themselves, Father Maxime," Lavros protested. "It is difficult for those of us who live in the world to have as our standard of measurement the way of life of monks and hermits. We wouldn't be able to function. To live in the world we need material things. We need to think of the future and have savings in the bank because we can't have the total faith of the saints who are given completely to God."

"I admit this is a very sensitive issue. But at least let's be humble about it and say 'Unfortunately I have this weakness. I need to have money on the side, something that will give me a sense of security. Yet I realize that ideally I should have all my hopes invested in God absolutely.' At least this attitude is better than ejecting God out of the picture completely, placing all hope in material possessions, or in our own powers, or in other human beings. You see, anything that steals our heart from being absolutely focused on God is symptomatic of our existential malaise, of being cut off from God. Consider this as an axiom and proceed accordingly."

"What you are suggesting, Father Maxime, requires extraordinary faith and gigantic spiritual strength," I pointed out.

"Well, yes! But those who manage to genuinely place their hopes totally in God will never be disappointed. God will be with them continuously. They will then be able to bear witness to the miraculous way Providence works in their lives, yet without recognizing it. All of us have such experiences if we pay attention."

"Can you give us some examples from your personal experience?" Helen asked, her voice betraying a certain trepidation for asking such a personal question.

"There are endless examples of Providential interventions. I remember when we were in *Nea Skete* [a cluster of hermitages on Mount Athos] and several of us were busy building a chapel. We used to carry sacks of cement brought by boat, as well as pebbles and sand from the beach and carry them on the backs of mules high up to our retreat. We walked up and down the mountain all day long. It was excruciating work. Ordinarily, we would eat well in order to have strength for such work. But it was the period of the Great Lent and we hardly ate. We just had one meal a day and no oil, except on weekends. On top of that we had to spend many hours in all-night vigils and long, tiring services and liturgies. We had few provisions and we were in the wilderness, in the 'desert' as we called it, of the Holy Mountain. There was nothing nearby, no grocery store, no monastery. Around us there were only a few *sketes* here and there where hermits lived.

"In our company," Father Maximos continued, "we had a new member, a novice who had finished medical school and, after a short period of practice as a physician, decided to leave the world and become a monk like us. He was in charge of the cuisine and was looking after our health, so to speak, by cooking for us as nutritiously as possible. I remember we had a jar of marmalade that someone sent us. But we ate it all up during the first week of Lent. Our elder was away that day when this brother approached me anxiously. 'Father,' he said, 'we must order some marmalade.' 'Marmalade in the *skete*?' I replied with incredulity. 'Do you realize where we are? We are not at Karyes [administrative center of Mount Athos] or in Thessaloniki. We are in the desert.' I told him that our elder never allowed us to buy marmalade.

"Marmalade was considered a luxury and we had very little money. It wasn't even a joke. Anyway, I said to him, 'Father we don't buy marmalade here at the *skete*.' 'But the fathers will get sick,' he complained and went on to tell me things about nutrition that I did not understand, such as the need to eat some sugar and so on. His knowledge of medicine was still fresh in his mind. 'Sit down, blessed one and don't be concerned,' I reassured him. 'The Holy Virgin is looking after us. If she thinks we have a need for marmalade she will send us marmalade. Just don't worry.' He shook his head and said, 'You must be joking, Father, to think that the Holy Virgin has nothing better to do than to be preoccupied with marmalade!'

"I advised him," Father Maximos went on, "that it was unwise to think that way. Those of us who had lived on Mount Athos for some time had repeatedly witnessed the providential interventions of the Holy Virgin. I say this in all sincerity," Father Maximos went on in a louder voice, "that I had hardly finished my sentence when the telephone rang—"

"Telephone?" I said surprised. It was hard to envision telephones in Athonite hermitages.

"Yes. An inventive brother had created a makeshift local telephone system connecting the various hermitages of the *Nea Skete*. So I asked our doctor novice to pick up the phone and see who the caller was. It was Old Tryfon, an elderly monk from another hermitage, farther down the mountain. 'Fathers,' he said, 'they sent me two huge cans of marmalade from my village but I have no use for them. I can't eat sugar. You are young and you can eat it. Do come and get it.' The doctor froze and turned pale from the shock. Then laughing I said to him, 'As a punishment for your disbelief you must now go down and fetch the marmalade.'

"You see, God is not dead. He is alive and shows his presence to those who deposit all their hopes and trust in him. It is for this reason that during the liturgy we chant 'Kai pasan ten zoen emon Christo to Theo parathometha' [And we place in front of Christ our entire life]. We don't say 'one part of our life' but our entire life. When you manage to attain this state of being then you acquire infinite freedom and you are liberated from all sorts of insecurities and from all the difficulties that may plague you at the moment. You witness in a tangible way God's Providence. But you can do that only at the point when you rest all your trust in God.

"You know, there are cases of saints who were so totally given to God that they would not even bother to search for food, or to cook. Believe me, extraordinary phenomena like that do take place. God would even set up a table full of food for them."

At a previous encounter Father Maximos had told me of an episode where apples had materialized on the holy altar in one of the hermitages in the middle of the winter. It was off-season for such a fruit and happened at a critical time when the elders faced starvation because an unusual heavy snowfall cut them off from the monasteries for more than two weeks. During my visits to Mount Athos I heard stories of how olive oil miraculously materialized in a monastery at a time when the monastery was going completely dry and the brothers had no way of getting new supplies in time for their needs. Even at Simonopetra, where the level of education of the monks was very high (several of them being former scientists who had held posts in American and European universities), we were told in all sincerity of how the Holy Virgin under mysterious circumstances had materialized for them olive oil reputed for its miraculous healing properties. When I would raise the usual skeptical questions the monks would reassure me that they themselves, as former scientists, had exhausted all alternative interpretations. The ongoing miraculous cures even of serious incurable illnesses through the use of that holy oil was a confirmation of their assessment of the origin of that oil and a further validation of their life of prayer.

Father Maximos saw traces of disbelief in some of the faces around him. "Yes, believe me there are cases of saints for whom God literally provided their daily bread. I am speaking of saints who lived not only during centuries past but during our own lifetime."

"You mean, Father Maxime," Helen asked skeptically, "God materialized food for them in the same way that it is written in the Bible that God fed the Israelites with manna during their exodus from Egypt?"

"This is exactly what I mean. And as in the case of Adam and Eve before the Fall. There are many such recorded stories in the lives of saints. But again, for such phenomena to take place the person must totally surrender to God's will. For us who lack the faith of saints it is understandable that we must provide for our sustenance, save money, provide for children, invest for old age and so on. What is important, given our state of imperfection, is to keep in mind that we must not allow our hearts to get stuck on our possessions or anything else worldly.

"We must also keep in mind," Father Maximos said after a few moments of reflection, "that what sacralizes material possessions is charity. I learned from personal experience that if you give a little you will get it back many times over. Here is what happened to me not long ago. One day while I was still abbot at the Panagia monastery a man pleaded for money that he claimed he urgently needed. He even alluded to the possibility of taking his own life out of desperation. We had no clue that in fact he was a swindler. Well, how could we possibly let him kill himself? I told Father Arsenios to just give this man eight hundred pounds that we had left in the safe. That was all we had. Poor Father Arsenios turned white," Father Maximos said with a chuckle.

"We had saved that money," he continued, "hoping to build a chapel for Saint Stephen. Well, the next day, on Monday, we got a message from Nicosia that this rogue had gambled all the money away. After that I was plagued by negative *logismoi* and feelings of guilt. 'Why did I give him that money? Why was I so naive? What kind of a fool am I? What right did I have to give the monastery's money away to that man?'

"The following Saturday morning I was getting ready to go to church. Before I left my cell I made a prostration in front of the icon of Saint Stephen that I had there and kissed it. 'Saint Stephen,' I said, 'if you wish that I build a chapel in your honor you must find me the money because I am totally hopeless.' "

When our laughter died down, Father Maximos continued. "I was even a bit angry at God, who said that when you give to charity he will give it back to you in multiple the amount. Well, many days had passed and I saw no evidence of it. After the liturgy I would always go to the confessional, serving pilgrims until late in the afternoon. One woman who came for confession placed an envelope on one of the chairs and as she walked out said, 'Father, this is for you.' I assumed it was a letter with names of relatives for a *paraklesis* [special prayer]. Perhaps someone was sick, I thought. Or perhaps she was requesting a memorial service for her departed loved ones. By the time I finished with confessions I had completely forgotten about the envelope. I just walked to my cell for a little rest and then went to church for vespers. During the service I remembered the envelope. I asked a novice to go fetch it. What do you think I found in there? Three thousand pounds!

"I have been a witness to such situations repeatedly. When I became bishop I felt desperate. The bishopric was plagued with debts because of what happened before. There were all sorts of loans that we inherited and we had no money. After all the scandals of mismanagement attributed to my predecessor, I could not possibly go around town trying to raise funds—"

"And yet things worked out," Lavros interjected with a satisfied look on his face.

"Thanks to a lot of prayer," Father Maximos stressed. "God has 'economized' us, as we say. All the work that needed to be done was done: youth centers, summer camps, churches, a radio station, and so on.

"You see," Father Maximos continued, "God will offer his assistance whenever we labor for spiritual goals and not for the sake of satisfying our egos. We still have economic problems and difficulties but we never stopped providing for charities. Consequently, God sent us back a hundredfold of what we gave. The charity of God comes in all its forms when people become charitable themselves. That's why the holy elders taught that avarice is identical with idolatry."

"How is that?" Patrick asked.

"As I said, avaricious people worship things that are not real. They invest their hopes, their love, their future, on things that are false and chimerical. Again, this is the reason why Jesus called the rich man in the Gospel *afron*, or foolish. This is an important point. He didn't call him something else, such as sinner, or evil, or criminal, or bad, or stupid, or whatever, but *afron*.

"Interestingly, only twice do we hear Jesus calling someone by such an epithet." Father Maximos brought forward two fingers. "He called the avaricious person *afron*, and the atheist, '*Afron en te kardia aftou ouk esti Theos*.' This is not coincidental. The atheist and the miser suffer from the same spiritual disease: foolishness."

"Father Maxime," Helen said, "it seems to me that overcoming the three passions of hedonism, love of glory, and avarice is much easier when one lives in a monastic community. How about us who live in the world? How could a married person cope with these three central passions? The passion for hedonism, for example."

"I think the answer is very simple," Father Maximos replied. "If you make hedonism the central purpose of your marriage, if you think of marriage as a way of gratifying your desires then unavoidably it will fail on earth as well as in heaven. The aim of marriage is to go beyond the satisfaction of personal desires. Forming a marital bond means to be ready to sacrifice for the sake of the other. Also, if you are obsessed with your personal status and glory and you cannot accept the view of the other, again you will fail. And if you are possessive about your property and the things you own and you are unwilling to be generous with the other members of your family, again you will fail.

"I will never forget a simple episode that I witnessed which forcefully made clear to me that a human being can attain saintliness not only through monasticism but also through ordinary, everyday life. One day I visited a summer camp of our diocese to offer confession to teenagers. A man arrived there with an old rusty pickup truck. He must have been a mason or a carpenter. The man was roughly built and dark complexioned from overexposure to the sun. He looked like a man of hard work and little means. He had two young teenage daughters staying at the camp. The moment they saw him they ran toward him. 'Papa, papa,' they cried with excitement, 'we need money.' The poor fellow took out his wallet and gave each twenty pounds. I have seen such scenes many times but only then did the thought come to my mind that this is an example of self-transcendence. That father earned those forty pounds working all day long and on top of that out in the open in the heat of the summer. Yet you could see in his face the great joy he felt as he gave that money to his two daughters, regardless of the fact that he earned it with his sweat and blood. This is an example, I thought, of how human beings can begin to transcend themselves on their way to reunification with God.

"So you see, Helen," Father Maximos concluded, "for you marriage and family may be the arena through which you must struggle to overcome your self-absorption. Your family and the special circumstances of your life are the equivalent to being in a monastery."

With that last remark Father Maximos excused himself as he had people, as usual, waiting for confession at the bishopric. It was ten thirty in the evening.

325

SIXTEEN

ROAD

TO

METANOIA

t was July and my sabbatical leave was soon coming to a close. For this reason, I planned to spend as much time with Father Maximos as possible. It was unclear how soon I would be able to return to Cyprus for further conversations with him. Father Maximos tried his best to accommodate me, and he would now take the initiative and call me up so that I could join him in his various outings and errands around the island, such as accompanying him to a conference of theologians in Nicosia.

I was particularly pleased, however, when he asked me to join him at the Panagia monastery, where he was to stay during the entire last week in July, a real luxury for him. It was the hottest period of the year and temperatures in the cities would often soar to over one hundred degrees Fahrenheit, rendering daily living unbearable for those without easy access to the sea or to the mountains, or to air-conditioning. Father Maximos, wearing a black cassock year round and unable to cool himself off by periodic splashes in the sea, suffered in the heat of the Cyprus summer. A few days' stay at the mountain monastery, confessing and counseling the monks, was Father Maximos's yearly escape from the inferno.

The days of his retreat matched Emily's visit to Greece, making my stay at the monastery more convenient. After vacillating for a while, Emily finally decided to follow Father Maximos's spontaneous suggestion to spend ten days at the women's monastery on the island of Patmos, no more and no less. Interestingly, when she made her decision to travel to the island of the Apocalypse, the only available two-way ticket was for ten days exactly.

The very afternoon of our arrival at the monastery for the weeklong retreat there were preparations for celebrating the name day of one of the young monks. The gathering took place at the large *archondariki*, which was reserved for such public occasions and receptions. All the monks and a few pilgrims sat around the room waiting for their brother to offer them the special sweet made of almonds covered with chocolate, compliments of a Nicosia confectionery. In addition, the monks were offered a small glass of liqueur produced locally by the monastery. Unlike the *synaxis*, in which Father Maximos gave a lesson to the monks, this gathering was more of a social event and, therefore, open to laymen who happened to be present.

At one point Father Maximos stood up, followed by everybody present. He gave the customary short prayer and then the forty or so monks in their strong voices chanted a hymn to the Holy Virgin and the *troparion* of the saint who was being celebrated that day. After everybody sat down, the monk who bore the name of the saint then walked to Father Maximos, carrying a tray full of the sweets. Another tray filled with small glasses of liqueur was carried behind him by an assistant. Father Maximos, after helping himself to the sweets and the liqueur, wished his disciple "Happy paradise." Then as they were offered their treat, monk after monk wished his brother the same fate, "Happy paradise."

When my turn came I had difficulty uttering that sentence. I found the statement dreary, a kind of death wish. Instead, I murmured, "To your health." I just did not find it relevant for a layperson like myself to wish anyone happiness in the afterlife.

Once everybody had a chance to wish the young monk "Happy paradise" Father Maximos gave a short talk on the necessity of deep states of humility and *metanoia* as a precondition for the attainment of paradise. This state, he said, has little to do with how educated or sophisticated a person is and a great deal to do with the purity of one's heart. To illustrate his point he narrated several anecdotes about simple, illiterate monks he had known who were nevertheless gifted by the Spirit.

"I met such a father once who asked me in all sincerity, 'Is it true that there is another life?'" After the laughter abated, Father Maximos went on to entertain his monks with more such humorous quips. "I asked Old Arsenios, 'Grandpa, what is the highest of virtues?' He replied 'Discernment.' Then I asked him 'But what about love?' 'Ah . . . ,' he mumbled, 'they did . . . say something about love.'

"Another grandpa," he went on in the midst of laughter, "was given as a gift a Swiss knife. He looked at it and then after making the sign of the cross he kissed it! Another one was taken out of Mount Athos unconscious. When he woke up in a hospital in Thessaloniki he covered his face with the bedsheet. He thought he was in heaven and the nurses were angels. Being humble he thought he was unworthy to look at angels.

"Yet," Father Maximos continued in a more serious tone after the laughter subsided, "some of these very simple old monks caused miracles to happen. You see, they had an unmediated, direct relationship with God regardless of their level of sophistication. This is what some people do not understand.

"By the way," Father Maximos said in excitement, "have I ever told you the story of Papa George?"

"No," several monks chanted, wishing to hear more stories.

"Now, that's an interesting case. He was a simple and humble priest from a remote mountain village in northern Greece. With a group of fellow villagers he arrived at our monastery on Mount Athos in order to confess and take communion. He approached me and requested that I become his confessor. I wasn't even thirty years old at the time. He was an old man, over sixty. I said to him, 'Father, please go and find an older confessor because I am too young for you.' He protested: 'But I came all the way to Mount Athos in order to confess. I came with my fellow villagers. They themselves went through confession. It would not be proper not to go through confession myself. They will think that I don't practice what I preach.' For some odd reason he insisted that I confess him and refused to go find someone else. I felt uncomfortable and I insisted that he should search elsewhere.

"The case reached our elder," Father Maximos went on. "Papa George insisted: 'I want Father Maximos to confess me. No one else.' I replied: 'No I will not.' Finally my elder requested that I confess Old Papa George. I had no choice but to obey. My elder explained to me that it did not matter that he was more than twice my age. He reminded me that in spiritual matters our physical age is of no consequence.

"Among other things," Father Maximos continued, "Papa George told me the following. Incidentally, what I am about to tell you is not in violation of confidentiality since he talked about these matters publicly before he died.

" 'Well,' he said to me, 'Father, forgive me for being an uneducated man. But one day something strange happened to me. It was Sunday when the bishop visited our village and conducted the liturgy. I was still a layman at that time without having any intentions of becoming a priest. But I noticed that while that bishop conducted the liturgy, the sanctuary was engulfed in flames. Really, he was covered from head to toe with these flames. The bishop looked at me and said, come and I will ordain you a deacon. I went and the moment he read some prayers over me a flame entered my head. Ever since that time, whenever I conduct the liturgy I see this flame. It appears to me either at the beginning or at the end or at any other time during the liturgy. One day,' he said and started crying, 'a terrible thing happened to me.' 'What happened to you Father?' I asked, surprised. He said, 'One day I was alone in the church, conducting the vespers. Suddenly I was lifted up one meter above the ground. I felt ashamed. I said to myself, what if a fellow villager walks into the church and sees me in this condition? What are they going to say? I'll become the laughingstock of the village. But at the same time,' Papa George said, 'I felt inside me such incredible joy. I have read somewhere in a book, I really don't remember which book, *Cherete kai agalliasthe oti o misthos sas einai ston Ouranon* [be happy and joyous for your reward is in heaven].' Of course, it is in the Gospel that these words are recorded but he didn't remember. In fact Papa George had very little knowledge and understanding of the Gospel.

"He was terrific, a real miracle worker," Father Maximos continued. "Old Papa George healed the sick and had the gift of prophetic vision. But he could hardly conduct the liturgy without making a thousand mistakes. Yet he was a saint with a very refined conscience and free of psychological complexes."

Father Maximos spent the rest of the evening telling further anecdotes of his life on Mount Athos while at the same time giving spiritual lessons on the importance of humbleness and *metanoia* as preconditions for the paradisiacal life.

The following afternoon I joined Father Maximos in a rare opportunity to hike with him to the *skete* of Saint John the Baptist, a hermitage that he himself set up while abbot at the Panagia monastery. It was about an hour's hike from the monastery and was built right at the edge of a cliff, overlooking a magnificent gorge. It was a perfect place for a spiritual retreat of contemplation, prayer, and meditation. The only sounds there were the soothing murmur of pine trees and the occasional song of a nightingale.

We sat on the balcony facing the gorge. I felt then that it was probably going to be my last opportunity to be alone with him before we departed from Cyprus. I began by mentioning my discomfort in wishing the young monk who celebrated his name day "Happy paradise."

Father Maximos burst into laughter. "When we wished him 'Happy paradise' we had in mind this life and not happiness after death." I immediately realized my gaffe. "We wish to attain paradise here during this present life, not when we are buried. This is a gross misunderstanding of the teachings of the *Ecclesia*."

"Father Maxime," I said after a while, "I will be leaving in a few days and I have some questions that you can help clarify in reference to what one could say to people who are not monks, who are not Orthodox, and who are not even Christian. These are the people that I spend most of my time with. What do you tell them about salvation and paradise? The surest and fastest way to put them off and have them dismiss you is to argue that they should first become converts to Orthodoxy. Some Christians and some Orthodox zealots say that much and the results are predictable, and embarrassing, I may add." As an example I mentioned the positions of some of the theologians and clergymen at the conference that I attended with him.

"The greatest miracle," Father Maximos responded warily after a sigh, "is that people still believe in God." After hesitating for a moment he continued. "We really have a serious manpower problem. Any other organization would have gone out of business long ago."

Then Father Maximos went on to say that the greatest proof of God's presence is that in spite of everything human beings still attain their salvation. "And they can do so even if they have never heard of the Gospel. Any human being can reestablish his or her relationship with God and become like Adam and Eve before the Fall because God and paradise are inside every human being. This is what some people in the *Ecclesia* simply cannot understand."

"It is an old problem, Father Maxime," I commented. "So, exactly what do the holy elders teach as the vehicle of everybody's salvation, irrespective of religious background or belief?"

"One's conscience, of course." Father Maximos shrugged his shoulders as if it were an obvious fact.

"But how does conscience work?"

"Look. Every person is endowed by God with conscience. When you do something bad or evil your conscience is going to let you know, it is going to react. It will tell you, 'What you do is not good.' 'What you have just said is not right.' 'The way you carry on is unconscionable.' Then if you learn to submit yourself to your conscience and say, 'Yes, indeed, what I have done is unacceptable,' you will notice that your conscience becomes more and more refined. It is like metal."

"Metal?"

"Yes. Just as a knife becomes razorlike as you work it through a knife sharpener, so too does conscience sharpen with use. Every time we listen to our conscience it becomes sharper, more refined, more alive. When we refuse to listen to our conscience, and when the yardstick of our actions and behavior is our egotistical desires, then our conscience becomes increasingly atrophied. Our criterion of conduct is then based on what 'I like,' not what my conscience dictates."

"From the point of view of the egotistical self, the 'good' is what is desired," I said. "On the other hand our conscience usually speaks to us about things that we don't like."

"Well, yes. Who in his right mind would like to be humbled? Who would like to remain silent when provoked? Are there a lot of idiots who would choose to restrain themselves when others do them an injustice? Turn the other cheek? Are you kidding? If someone slaps you on the face take out his jaws! That's normal," Father Maximos said, laughing.

"Whenever you violate your conscience," he went on, "it is as if instead of sharpening the knife you do exactly the opposite. After a while there won't be any sharp edges left and it will become a useless instrument. Likewise as you make it a habit of violating the dictates of your conscience there will be a time when its voice will become barely audible. On the other hand, a person who habitually listens to his conscience will gradually reach a point of real inner peace. He will be able to look inside himself and there will be nothing that would cause guilt or anxiety."

"What if the person makes errors and misreads his or her conscience?"

"Errors will always happen. It is different, however, when out of ignorance we make mistakes and it is another matter when we do wrong in full awareness that we are acting erroneously. But a person who habitually listens to his conscience will sooner or later be graced by the Holy Spirit."

"In spite of errors."

"Exactly. That person becomes a true child of God and acquires inner peace. In whatever condition a human being finds himself, he has conscience. With habitual submission to one's conscience, coarseness will fade away. God has his ways on how to commune with the hearts of all human beings regardless of religious background or beliefs."

"But isn't it possible, Father Maxime, that one's conscience may be distorted? People may think they are following their conscience when in fact they act on the basis of their lower passions and desires."

"That is also true. There is also the case of a person suffering from extreme forms of oversensitivity. These are people who are obsessively guilt-ridden and love to victimize themselves. As a result they have no inner peace. So there are two extremes. One is complete indifference to the voices of conscience and the other obsessive oversensitivity. These extremes are never of God. Satan has a way of intervening with the conscience of people, trying to push them toward the two extremes. He will either try to make a person who is insensitive more insensitive or make a hypersensitive person even more hypersensitive, leading him to despair and guilt, robbing him of inner peace, forcing him to resort to all sorts of tranquilizers, drugs, or even suicide.

"Elder Paisios," Father Maximos continued, "used to advise oversensitive young people to develop the 'good insensitivity,' the 'good indifference,' as he used to say. I believe that anything that generates inner turmoil and anxiety is not from God."

"The good is the midpoint between two equally undesirable and opposite extremes," I said, articulating the well-known Aristotelian axiom.

"Absolutely." We remained silent for a while. "The patriarchs are a good example of how to protect one's conscience," Father Maximos said.

"What do you mean?"

"I mean Abraham, Isaac, Jacob. They lived before the Mosaic law that set down rules on how humans should behave. Yet they were people who guarded their conscience. And these patriarchs had an immediate relationship with God. They were impeccable, faithful, and just. They were vigilant."

"Yet the question of how we can be certain that our conscience is on the right track remains," I said, not mentioning that I was never impressed with the story of Abraham being ready to sacrifice his son because he believed God told him so. It is certainly not a very good example for imitation. Today such behavior would be defined as a form of temporary insanity and the patriarch who would do such a thing would probably be locked up for life. But I kept those thoughts to myself and listened to what else Father Maximos had to say on the subject.

"If a human being," he continued, "is under the sway of his passions and has a history of repeatedly violating his conscience and mixing things up in his mind, he may not know exactly what gives solace to his conscience and what does not. His criteria of discernment may have been damaged. He may do things because of his passions, yet feel that this is in accordance with his conscience. That is why God, first through Moses and later through the incarnation of Christ the Logos, gave us objective commandments as criteria for our actions. That means these are criteria beyond our subjective feelings that spring from our conscience. We have the commandments that we can use as a yardstick to judge our actions. So if there is confusion inside us about what to do, we need to consult the Gospel and analyze our action based on God's objectively given commandments, independent of our subjectivity."

"What if you are not capable of carrying out such a research project?"

"Then ideally you should consult with someone who knows. Go find a spiritual counselor, a guide. Find yourself an elder."

I did not discuss the logistics of how over six billion people living in the world today could go find a spiritual guide but I asked a related question: "The other day, Father Maxime, you mentioned the necessity of 'mourning' as a step along the spiritual path. I wonder whether such a notion might alienate people who are neither monks nor ascetics."

"Perhaps so," Father Maximos replied. "We must bear in mind, however, that the way to God is not a picnic. It requires effort, tears, commitment, spiritual struggle. Christ told us of the key role of mourning in the second beatitude, 'Blessed be those who mourn for they shall be comforted.' By mourning of course he didn't mean those who lost their money in the stock market or experienced a personal tragedy but those who realized their estrangement from God. When you do that then mourning is unavoidable. In fact, the holy elders call it 'joyous mourning.' "

"Why?"

"Because we are not interested in mourning per se but in the divine comfort and healing that awaits us. We are interested in the Comforter, in Christ himself, not in mourning.

"Our therapy," he continued, "begins from the moment we become conscious that we have a problem. The moment we realize and mourn that we are far removed from God, our archetype, then we will marshal the energy and the effort to become like him. How? By becoming compassionate as the Gospel asks us to become. With such a realization we begin to experience that joyous mourning that the elders talk about. We become aware of the beauty of our true nature, of the way God made us and of the distortions we have caused because of our passions and worldly obsessions."

"It seems, then, that mourning is part of our very existence."

"And so is joy," Father Maximos hastened to add. "You cannot have one without the other. You cannot have real joy without first going through the process of mourning. That's why those who mourn are blessed. People who cannot mourn, who cannot cry, are people who cannot laugh and be joyous either."

"I presume that as far as the Orthodox way is concerned, this process of mourning must take place within the context of confession."

"Naturally. Confession plays a key role. It is an assault against the idol we created of ourselves. And that idol must be smashed. God is intolerant of idols. Confession is nothing but a method to help us take a good look at our real self. Like drug addicts who need their doses, we construct false images and idols of ourselves. Confession brings us to the truth about who we are, but in a philanthropic manner, for the sake of our salvation. Anyway, that is what I try to do when I offer confession to people."

"And our self idol is based on—?"

"On our knowledge, our gentility, our good works, good name, importance in society, and so on. You see, for this reason, religious people like the Pharisee of the Gospel parable can't get it right with God. It is easier for people like tax collectors, prostitutes, and sinners to find God than those considered to be moral and religiously correct. These people have no idols of themselves. They are a total failure and disaster to themselves and they know it. But God has the power to reassemble them once they have been torn apart. That can happen, of course, only if they marshal the power to hand over the pieces to God in order to allow him to put them back together. Believe me, the pieces of the tax collector and the prostitute are much more valuable than the idol of the individual who is proud of his religious virtues. Assuming that people like tax collectors and prostitutes reach genuine humility and *metanoia*, then redemption is attainable through God's grace. We see this clearly in the lives of many saints, like Maria the Egyptian, who was transformed from a prostitute into a leading saint of the *Ecclesia*."

We paused for a few minutes and listened to the sounds of the pine trees. Then Father Maximos reiterated what I had often heard him say. "Unlike the prideful individual, saints are humble. They do not believe in themselves or have faith in their own judgment. They seal their work, their opinions, by seeking consultation with others. The person who constantly says, 'I believe,' 'I know,' 'I found,' 'I discovered,' gives out a signal that something is not working right with him. Do you know how difficult it is to speak with someone who is in a state of delusion about his own knowledge and self-importance, what the holy elders call *plani*? It is better to converse with an immoral, an unethical person, than one who is overcome by such an affliction."

"Why so?"

"Because it is better for a person to be sinful than dominated by demonic energies."

"I just don't understand," I said, not hiding my discomfort about what Father Maximos said.

"The person who succumbs to sinful acts sooner or later will get disgusted," Father Maximos explained. "It is so programmed in the very nature of our soul. But when a person succumbs to delusion, to *plani*, it is much more difficult to be freed from it. It is terrible. Such a person absolutely does not listen to anyone else, only to his own opinions. People who are under such spells have ears but they cannot hear. They are under the influence of what the Gospel calls deaf and mute spirits."

"How do you help such persons, Father Maxime?"

"In my opinion only God can help them. Just pray for them because it is impossible to have a conversation with a person who is under the sway of *plani*."

"How then can one protect oneself from this condition?"

"As I have said many times, it is only through the cultivation of humility that we can protect ourselves from this most terrible of spiritual afflictions. In order to learn if you are on the right track, get into the habit of asking. Consult with a spiritual guide and check your own opinions. That's what you can do." Father Maximos suddenly chuckled. "I just thought of a story in the *Gerontikon*. A God-realized elder wished to explore some aspects of holy scripture. He said to himself, 'I will fast and through prayer God will reveal to me the truth about this issue—' "

"This approach to knowledge is something about which we academics have no clue," I mused. "In fact, most academics would find it ludicrous, a sort of *plani* in itself."

"But elders like him had knowledge of how God's energies work. However, no matter how fervently this elder prayed, nothing happened. God did not reveal his will to him. 'This is strange,' he said to himself as he tried repeatedly over a period of time but to no avail. God remained silent. Finally, he decided to go ask another elder nearby, another hermit like himself. The moment he shut the door behind him and placed the key into his pocket, God spoke to him, revealing the answer to his question. When the elder asked, 'Why now and not before?' God replied, 'Because now you have humbled yourself. You were ready to go and consult with your brother.' "

"Humility as a way to knowledge."

"Humility is a form of great security for a human being. There is a line somewhere in the scriptures which says that a man who refuses advice is an enemy to himself."

"You may ask someone's advice but it doesn't mean that you are willing to listen," I said.

"For sure. I remember how Old Paisios used to complain that many pilgrims would come to ask him questions about this and that but they lacked a willingness to listen to what he told them if it went contrary to their own opinions and preconceptions. 'My son,' he said with exasperation to one fellow, 'since you cannot abandon your *logismos* why do you come here to ask me these questions?' I find the same tendency on the part of some people during confessions. They come to talk about their problem. Then I offer my counsel but it is as if I am talking to the deaf. A person of such predisposition listens only to his *logismos*. It is virtually impossible to heal him or help him in any way."

"So what do you do in such cases?"

"As I said, just leave him alone and pray to God that he may enlighten his mind. It is for this reason that I believe it is less onerous and dangerous for a person to succumb to sinful acts than to enter into a state of *plani*.

337

From the point of view of Orthodox spirituality, *plani* is the worst evil that could happen to a person."

"This is a very strong statement, Father Maxime. I don't think it's easy for someone living in the world today to comprehend, let alone accept it."

"The elders consider *plani* a most serious problem because it can derail a person's path toward God."

"So *plani*, strictly speaking, is relevant only for spiritual matters?"

"No, not exactly. The elders speak of *plani* as a way of being in the world. It refers to all matters, be they spiritual, political, national, educational, or whatever. It is when a person is so certain of himself that he has no interest in seeking advice from anyone."

"This can be a problem with exceptionally intelligent people."

"Yes. We often meet highly educated people who are so proud of their own achievements that they are completely uninterested in and incapable of hearing what the other person has to say. They know it all. This is a serious spiritual affliction, a really demonic symptom, believe me. The devil does not accept any advice. He does not give up his own opinions and perceptions. He never doubts himself."

We walked back to the monastery, arriving there before vespers. Sitting on a bench at the outer gate was Father Chariton, a forty-year-old monk from South Africa. He was waiting for us, and held a letter out to Father Maximos. "It's from David," he announced with excitement.

I was surprised when I heard that name. Father Maximos asked Father Chariton to read the letter for him. Fluent in English, Father Chariton translated as he read the three-page handwritten letter.

"I'll respond to him tomorrow," Father Maximos promised. "I'll have the letter ready for you by the afternoon." It was understood that Father Chariton was to translate the letter into English and mail it to David, a death-row inmate in a maximum-security prison in Arizona.

I was directly involved with David's case. Several years back, David sent me a letter from his prison cell, asking whether I could connect him with a spiritual guide. I sent him Father Maximos's address. Since then they have corresponded on a regular basis. Through letters Father Maximos offered spiritual advice to David and sent him books related to the teachings of the holy elders. In addition, Father Maximos called up his friend and former colleague from Mount Athos, the abbot of Saint Anthony's monastery in Arizona, and asked him to visit David. After nine months of efforts, the prison authorities finally gave permission and a group of monks began paying regular visits to David. They placed him on a demanding ascetic program for repentance and *metanoia*, gave him instructions on the Jesus Prayer, showed him how to do prostrations, and offered him spiritual counseling.

This form of spiritual pedagogy had a dramatic effect on David's life, so much so that he decided to become an Orthodox monk himself. The brothers of Saint Anthony's monastery in Arizona carried on with the baptism and tonsure right in his maximum-security jail cell. Since then David has spent all his time praying like any hermit on Mount Athos.

One day I received a letter from him claiming that the only good thing to come from his past life was that he was arrested and sentenced to death. That was the way, he claimed, that led him to the discovery of God. In another letter he mentioned that he had never experienced greater love than what he felt through the letters of Father Maximos.

"The problem he faces now and which makes him sad," Father Chariton said as he placed the letter in his pocket, "is that David's relatives are very upset with his conversion to monasticism and they refuse to visit him. His only social contacts are with the monks of Saint Anthony's monastery."

"The story of David," Father Maximos said, "is a classic case of *metanoia*, this radical transformation of one's heart and mind. It is what we have been talking about today. His conscience was still alive. That is why he wrote that letter to you in the first place. Then with spiritual pedagogy and ascetic exercises and prayer he experienced mourning for his predicament, accompanied by deep repentance. His case is archetypal, similar to that of the robber who, as he was about to die on the cross, underwent a radical shift in his heart and mind. As a result he inherited paradise. An elder once joked that this robber in the Gospel spent all his life robbing people and at the end he even robbed paradise!"

"I assume you are certain that David's *metanoia* is genuine."

"Oh yes, as genuine and authentic as the *metanoia* of King David in the Old Testament. What King David felt and wrote in the Fifty-first Psalm, the psalm of *metanoia*, is what this death-row inmate in Arizona has

339

felt and experienced. I have no doubt about that. We have been communicating with him for several years now and I trust the discernment of the fathers in Arizona who have been helping him out and are in direct contact with him. This is an extraordinary story that shows God's infinite compassion and forgiveness. The state may execute him but in the eyes of God he is a saved soul. He has already entered paradise."

Father Maximos has said on several occasions that the "door of *metanoia*" never shuts and is always open for every human being. Even the most terrible criminals can attain their salvation if they undergo a genuine and deep *metanoia*.

Standing outside the gate of the monastery, awaiting for vespers to begin, I told Father Maximos that I found the Fifty-first Psalm extremely poignant, particularly the way it is set to Byzantine music of centuries past and chanted in church at the beginning of every service.

"Ah yes," he replied. "That's a very powerful prayer. King David wrote it after his great spiritual fall, after he committed the double sin of adultery and murder. His case is really instructive in many ways. He soon became aware of how low he had fallen and how he had become hostage to his passions. However, he did not stay there. That is the value of the Psalms. They show us how to come out of sin and out of despair and hopelessness. That's why we chant them every day: to remind us of God's infinite compassion and remind us that we must never despair but put our trust in God's mercy. The prophet, in a deep state of *metanoia* and sorrow, wrote those beautiful verses. 'Deliver me from blood guiltiness, O God, thou God of my salvation: and my tongue shall sing aloud of thy righteousness' [Psalms 51:14]. The guilt of bloodshed weighed heavily on his conscience."

"Such guilt could be psychologically devastating for any human being."

"Yes. But this is not just guilt feelings that follow the commitment of such sins."

"What do you mean?"

"Guilt feelings are just a psychological phenomenon springing from conscience that a human being may utilize for his own good. The awareness of sinfulness is deeper than simple psychological guilt. When a person commits such dreadful acts there is a fundamental distortion in the very depths of his nature, his human nature."

"And confession," I added, "is a way to rectify what he has done."

"It is not that simple."

"What do you mean?"

"Well, often when people confess their sins they come out of the confessional feeling great relief. They experience inner peace."

"That's how I felt when I would come out of confession when I was a kid."

"But this doesn't happen always. For example, you cannot kill someone and then go to confession and come out feeling happy, your guilt vanishing right then and there. Yes, you have confessed your sin in front of God but it requires an arduous struggle to reestablish your spiritual health. A sin like killing a human being is an act that traumatizes one's entire existence at its core, distorting both psyche and mind. A simple confession will not wash away guilt."

"What then needs to be done?"

"True *metanoia* requires persistent struggle, persistent *askesis* in order to reestablish your spiritual health, just like in the case of David, the death-row inmate."

"So struggle is needed to earn God's forgiveness," I concluded.

"No, no. That's not the way to look at it." Father Maximos's response surprised me. "God does not hold grudges against anyone. He is not vengeful. It is a popular misconception to assume that all you have to do to rectify a sinful act is to go to confession or to engage in spiritual struggles to get God's forgiveness. God's forgiveness is a given. God does not become resentful or angry as we commit sins. Then all we need to do is go to confession and do penances so that he will no longer be angry with us. This is a wrong understanding of sin and confession. We have the problem of sin within ourselves. It is not God's problem. That's why *metanoia* relates strictly to us, not to God. There is no need to expiate an angry God out there. God is next to us. He is the Good Samaritan who comes to our aid, to the aid of every human being. He takes us to the inn for our healing."

"And this is the road to *metanoia* according to the teachings of the holy elders."

"It is the only road. It begins the moment we are aware that we have a problem in our relationship with God and extends into eternity. We must struggle and toil and undergo a healing pedagogy like the one offered by the *Ecclesia* before we can restore our primordial beauty within ourselves, the state before our transgression. When we reach that state of deep *metanoia* then we experience an incredible sweetness, the recognition of the presence of the Holy Spirit within our heart's depths. It is not a matter of simply getting rid of guilt feelings but realizing the loving relationship between us and God. That is why the prophet says, further down, 'my tongue shall sing aloud of thy righteousness' [Psalms 51:14]. And that is how a human being eventually attains justice in his innermost being. From then on there is no trace of a blemish on the person's sinful past. Everything is erased. That is the ultimate power of *metanoia*."

The *symantron,* with its sharp metallic sound, announced the beginning of vespers. We proceeded through the outer gate toward the church. But I had one last question that came to my mind, a question related to the Psalms. I wanted to raise it before we stepped into the church.

"What does King David mean when he says, 'Do good in thy good pleasure unto Zion: build thou the walls of Jerusalem' [Psalms 51:18]?

"One can say that this expressed the desire of King David to see a particular place, Zion or Jerusalem, the City of God that was to be rebuilt," Father Maximos said as he stopped outside the church door. "But we can also assume that beyond that historical reference to Jerusalem, the city of God is our heart and our deepest desire is to reconstruct our heart the right way, so that we become the City of God where he will reign. It is the wish to feel God as permanent resident in our being once again. This is what Christ promised us: the heart of man becomes the temple of God and the residence of the Holy Spirit."

With these words Father Maximos stepped into the church, followed by Father Chariton and myself. Vespers, starting with the Psalms, had already begun.

SEVENTEEN

REFLECTIONS

mily's visit to Patmos, the island of the
Apocalypse, a visit spontaneously suggested
by Father Maximos, affected her profoundly.
She was radiant on her return to Cyprus after ten days with
the nuns of the Annunciation monastery. At Patmos she experienced a form of spirituality that, based on what she related to me, was as profound as the one I had encountered
twelve years earlier when I first set foot on Mount Athos.
Most important, she met Eldress Christonyphe (Christ's
Bride), with whom she established a deep spiritual connection.

The pilgrimage itself was a revelation for Emily as she

encountered a different face of the *Ecclesia* than the one she was accustomed to. As a Western-educated woman and a feminist she had an ambivalent and conflicting attitude toward the Church. Like most educated
women of today she felt excluded from its cultural life and treated like a
"second-class citizen." A trivial example that reflects the larger problem:
Constantine, our son, served as an altar boy. Our daughter Vasia, on the
other hand, could not play that role because there is a long-standing taboo
prohibiting women from entering the sanctuary. Most significantly, women
are on the margins of decisions that affect the life of the *Ecclesia*, not to
mention the tendency of clerical hierarchies to espouse, more often than
not, rigidly conservative social causes.

Yet, like myself, Emily was attracted to the spiritual wisdom of the elders as exemplified by Father Maximos and yes, she was enchanted with the
beauty of the worship services, but the issue of the noninclusiveness
toward women has remained a lingering shadow in her relationship to the
religious tradition within which she was born. This is the case with most
modern women today, who can no longer accept the traditional roles
imposed on them by an antiquated, male-dominated patriarchal world.
Emily's concern about the role of women seems to be the standard issue
that I am faced with every time I speak about Mount Athos, where traditionally not even female animals are allowed entry.

The Patmos experience softened significantly these feelings and concerns. She was exposed there to a more woman-centered Christianity. It
was clear that such a possible outcome was in the back of Father Maximos's mind when he had made the suggestion for her to visit Patmos. It
was helpful for Emily to connect with that monastery because many of the
nuns were sophisticated former professionals who came from diverse ethnic and cultural backgrounds.

Nevertheless, the wider problem of gender equality in the Eastern Orthodox Church waits to be addressed by its all-male bearded custodians.
To anyone attuned to the ways of the modern world it is self-evident that
the Church, particularly the Orthodox Church, is woefully out of touch
with contemporary social realities. There seems to be little understanding
of or sympathy toward the global demand on the part of women for equal
treatment and equal participation in every facet of their societies' institu-

tions, be it the state or the church. This is always hard for long-established traditional authorities to accept, regardless of their religious affiliation.

Ironically, as far as Orthodoxy is concerned, it is to a large extent women who keep it alive, who attend church more frequently, who practice the rites and rituals more diligently, who go to confession and communion, and who nurture religious participation in the younger generation. Furthermore, it is the Holy Virgin who, along with Christ, is at the center of worship. It is the Holy Virgin who causes healing miracles to happen and who appears in the visions of great elders like Paisios and Porphyrios. It is also to the Holy Virgin that both men and women instinctively appeal in times of crisis and it is the *Theotokos*, the Mother of God and "Queen of the Holy Mountain," who is celebrated in all the monasteries inside and outside of Athos. It is in front of her miraculous icon that the monks reverentially prostrate themselves and it is her icon that they carry around on their shoulders during litanies and special ceremonials. If we put aside the male-dominated church hierarchy, what is left, paradoxically, is a cultural arrangement that is women-friendly, more attuned to the temperament of women than of men. I remember, growing up in Cyprus, how many men often would opt to go to the coffee shop on Sunday morning to play backgammon, read the papers, and drink their cup of Turkish coffee while their women in church next door would be kneeling during the Eucharistic service. My aunts would attend vespers and burn incense at home while their husbands would play cards at their favorite soccer club or stay home and watch the evening news.

The contradictory status of women in the church was the issue that we reflected upon with our friends Stephanos and Erato before our departure from Cyprus at the end of the summer of 2003. We stayed with them for a few days at their mountain retreat near the Panagia monastery to escape from the continuous summer heat and to spend time together as Emily narrated with her usual electrifying enthusiasm the details of her Patmos epiphany. Erato, whom Emily considers not only one of her closest friends but also her spiritual guide for many years, reminded us that there are a large number of "desert mothers" and women saints who can serve as models for contemporary women who are attracted to the spiritual life. As a shining example she reminded us of the extraordinary case of the former podiatrist Eldress Gavrilia, a favorite of Emily's, who while a lay professional woman practiced her craft in London throughout the troubled years of the Second World War. She then spent many years in India serving lepers and the handicapped. It is there that she had a mystical experience during which God instructed her to return to her native Greece and become a nun. At the age of sixty she retired from her profession and joined a monastery. Soon after she was recognized as a charismatic eldress of exceptional spiritual force. Mother Gavrilia became a guide to women in the Athens area until her death in her late nineties. The magnificent homilies on love and compassion she left behind became spiritual nourishment to thousands of contemporary women as well as men.[1] "Patriarchy," Erato commented, "did not prevent her from becoming a God-realized soul, a liberated woman in the truest sense of the word."

Erato added that on balance there are more women's monasteries in Greece than men's and that the spirituality that men find on Mount Athos can also be found outside of the Holy Mountain in women's monasteries like the one in Patmos and in Ormylia, the large women's monastery south of Thessaloniki, which lies not far from Mount Athos.

Regardless of these considerations, however, and regardless of exceptional cases like that of Eldress Gavrilia, it was clear to us living in the West that the Eastern Orthodox Church, and perhaps the Christian churches in general, must come sooner or later to grips with the huge cultural gulf that exists between the way educated women think today and the way the contemporary fathers of the Church understand questions related to gender. I will never forget a particular incident that took place during one of the workshops that I offered several years ago. When the gender issue in Christianity came up a woman participant who was a former Catholic, sitting at the back of the audience, hollered: "That's why we are all becoming Hindus!"

During our flight back to Maine I had to agree with Emily when she pointed out that it is not a persuasive argument on the part of some conservative theologians and clergymen that men must always be dominant in the church because Jesus was a man and because his apostles were all men. For women of today such arguments add insult to injury and appear as nothing more than self-serving rationalizations and disingenuous myths for the continuation of male dominance and the maintenance of a historically outdated and discredited patriarchy. Jesus himself was anything but a patriarch, Emily reminded me. In fact he was close to women and it was to women that the news of the Resurrection was first revealed. It was in front of Maria Magdalene that Christ first appeared, bestowing upon her and her gender the honor to pass on the good news to the terror-stricken male disciples.

It was gratifying to discover that Bishop Kallistos Ware, during an interview given for a women's magazine, acknowledged that there is a need for a critical reexamination of customs and rules that are out of touch with contemporary realities, are alienating large numbers of women, and are not essential to the basic message and teachings of the *Ecclesia*. He suggested that the possibility of reintroducing the ordination of deaconesses, as was the custom among early Christians when women were full participants in the life of the Church, should be seriously examined.[2]

Such possible developments could lead the Church in a direction that would be more attuned to the social realities of the twenty-first century while at the same time guarding and preserving the power of its mystical pathways to God, the Threefold Way.

Upon our return to Maine the implications of the Threefold Way for contemporary men and women who are not necessarily Orthodox or even Christian were a theme that I discussed extensively with my artist friend and colleague Michael Lewis. He has followed my work closely over the years and has carefully read and critiqued this volume as well. As with Emily's concerns regarding gender issues, Michael challenged and helped me to keep focused on the need to maintain a broad-based and inclusive perspective as I processed the material I had gathered from my exploration of Orthodox spirituality.

Although not a practitioner of any specific religious tradition, Michael has developed a keen interest in spirituality, which is shown in the type of art he has been creating over the years and which I experienced through our conversations. Having his studio conveniently, and perhaps providentially, above my office was an arrangement conducive to frequent discussions about our work. During breaks while we walked through the university woods, he helped me identify those elements of Eastern Orthodoxy that would be of relevance to modern thought and to contemporary spiritual explorers irrespective of cultural or religious background. What can Orthodox spirituality, as practiced by the monks and nuns of Eastern Christianity, tell us about the nature of reality and our place in the universe? And what spiritual lessons could someone like him, who is not an Orthodox Christian, learn by delving into the Orthodox spiritual tradition? Those were the issues around which we focused our discussion during a late afternoon in August 2004, two days before school started. I was getting ready to submit my manuscript to my publisher while Michael had just completed a collection of paintings for an upcoming art exhibition in New York. We both needed a long break that afternoon.

Walking through our favorite footpaths in the university woods, which were the source of inspiration for many of Michael's paintings, we agreed that the Threefold Way of purification, illumination, and God realization (Catharsis, Fotisis, *Theosis*) may be an archetypal blueprint of human destiny. If the contemporary world were to acknowledge this process it could lead it to an understanding of the furthest reaches of human nature and perhaps to the deepest structure of reality itself. The notion that human beings are made in the image of God and the fact that they have the potential and ability to unite with God is a life-affirming theme that offers a map of existential orientation to help people navigate through life. The inner message that comes from the Christian East is that in spite of all the unavoidable tragedies and tribulations along the way, the end of the soul's journey is a joyous reunion with God. At the same time, we are constantly reminded by the saints that in order to attain this deification and return to our ultimate destination we must engage in a valiant and systematic spiritual struggle to overcome our egotistical passions. There are no shortcuts to get there.

Implicit in the Threefold Way is an evolutionary understanding of the self in relation to God. It is not, however, a blind, mechanistic, and automatic evolutionary movement toward deification. The self must wish intensely to attain godliness. The fulfillment of such a goal—the liberation from the stranglehold of the lower passions—requires effort and many sacrifices. It requires *metanoia*.

Another aspect of the evolutionary perspective implicit in the teachings of the holy elders is the theme of the three different stages in a person's relationship to God, namely the "slaves," the "employees," and the "lovers" of God (see chapter 7). This is the seed, I told Michael, of developmental theories in psychology. It is interesting, I said, that evolutionary theory in general may be at the core of how the Christian elders viewed the world. Naturally, they did not use the word *evolution* because such a concept did not exist during their times.

It may very well be that evolution is the story of creation at all levels of its manifestation: physical, biological, psychological, social, and spiritual. On the physical level, we learn that after the primordial "Big Bang" explosion, homogeneous dust particles joined, over billions of years, to create an infinitely complex and heterogeneous universe. Life evolved from simple homogeneous cells to more complex ones. Evolution is a movement, as Herbert Spencer pointed out in the nineteenth century, from homogeneity to heterogeneity, from simplicity to complexity, from lower integration to higher integration. On the biological level evolution is a fact accepted today by the overwhelming majority of biologists. Even the Vatican conceded recently that evolutionary theory in biology is more than just a theory.

We don't need to be hard scientists to notice the reality of evolutionary change at work. An acorn evolves into an oak tree; a spermatozoon joins an ovum and a human being begins its developmental trajectory into existent life. On the psychological level, developmentalists like Jean Piaget delineated stages of growth from the "sensorimotor" stage, at which human beings experience the world only through their senses, to the "formal operational" stage, at which the person is capable of thinking abstractly and critically. Sociologists have categorized in great detail the evolutionary stages that societies have gone through: from the simple food-gathering stage to the horticultural and pastoral stages, then on to the agricultural, industrial, and postindustrial stages. As communities, we have evolved from clans to tribes to ancient empires to modern states and on to superstates and global institutional arrangements like the European Union and the United Nations.

I mentioned to Michael during our walk that this evolutionary story has the signature of Providence, as the Jesuit priest and famous biologist and paleontologist Pierre Teilhard de Chardin (1881–1955) eloquently argued half a century ago in his classic work *The Phenomenon of Man*.[3] It seems that this is the way God works within creation. The mistake that most evolutionary biologists have made is to assume that evolution exists only on the biological level, when in fact what Darwin uncovered was only one facet of the total picture, misinterpreting the part for the whole. Most disastrously, God's hand in evolution has been tossed out by the materialists.

Developmental psychologists like Piaget also made the error of assuming that the evolution of the self stops at the "formal operational" stage at which human beings think abstractly and critically. Transpersonal psychologists, however, are beginning to tap realms of consciousness that transcend rational thought. They teach that there are transrational levels of awareness that mainstream psychology fails to acknowledge because of its materialist, reductionist assumptions about the world.[4]

Transpersonal psychologists, however, base their theories exclusively on Buddhism and Eastern practices like Yoga and Zen. They too have been unaware of the Threefold Way of the Christian elders, who also speak of stages of awareness that are beyond reason. These are stages that a purified soul can reach through *askesis*, realms that belong to the spirit world. This understanding has been an implicit and basic theme of the teachings of the saints of Eastern Christianity throughout the centuries.

The notion that there are spiritual stages of development is hardly known or understood by Western Christians, particularly by fundamentalists, who have waged a defensive and relentless war against "evolutionism." They have failed to see that the problem is not evolution but reductionism, the tendency of materialist scientists to reduce evolution and the whole of reality to the physical level and to conclude that human beings are nothing but animals, created not in the image of God but in the image of monkeys. This "nothing-butness" is the problem, not evolution as such. The Threefold Way of the Christian elders can bring clarity to this confusion and meaning to human existence, providing a vision of evolution as what sages like Pierre Teilhard de Chardin believe it to be: divine play within God's all-loving Providence.

Evolution, I mentioned to Michael that afternoon, may be a cosmic process for the unfolding purpose of created beings coming to know their

Creator through mystical union. I believe this is how the holy elders would have argued the case had they used the modern vocabulary of evolutionism. For them evolution would have had as its primary purpose the possibility for self-conscious beings like us to discover who we truly are. The ultimate aim is the deification or divinization of creation. It is as if creation becomes conscious of itself through the struggle of humanity to discover its true origins and destiny. Everything we do seems to lead in that direction. To quote once more the words of Father Basilios, abbot of the Athonite monastery Iveron: *"Ta epegia gegonen ouranos"*—the things of this world are transmuted into things of heaven.

"You speak of evolution as if it is an irreversible, one-way process," my friend pointed out. "But is it?"

In response to Michael's comment, I said that human freedom and human will can reverse or derange this evolutionary process. Our tampering with biological evolution could lead us to unforeseen and perhaps disastrous pathways. We can destroy life on earth through nuclear annihilation, or we can poison ourselves out of existence. We also know from history that great civilizations were destroyed. Athens was a glorious, highly "evolved" city in the fourth century B.C. but it degenerated into a simple peasant village by the nineteenth century, to be revived only after the Greek War of Independence in 1821.

Similarly, on the level of spiritual consciousness we can fall from grace. This is the primary fear of the great holy elders. There are many examples of highly spiritual people falling precipitously from great heights of attainment. That is why the desert fathers and mothers of Christianity were called *nyptic*, meaning vigilant, fully focused and conscious. They struggled to guard against sin, against a regression to lower stages. Persons who are highly evolved spiritually can degenerate into black magicians if they are not *nyptic* or spiritually alert.

"The other day you had mentioned that evolution takes place at two levels, the personal and the collective. Remember to comment on this in your epilogue," Michael suggested as he pulled out a piece of paper on which he had written some notes during our previous conversations.

I was trying to solve a paradox. I have often noticed a discrepancy between the state of development of culture and society in general and the stage of development of particular personalities. Some spiritually advanced elders seemed to be way out of tune with the stage of development or evolution that the general world culture and civilization has reached. For example, in my opinion, feminism on the whole is a positive development in history that is helping humanity to overcome the stifling shackles of patriarchal supremacy and violence. This global movement is analogous to the earlier struggles to abolish slavery, a leap forward in cultural evolution. It would be grotesque for anyone today to advise slaves to accommodate themselves to their slavery and to focus instead on the life to come. Similarly modern culture has advanced to a level of gender relations that a hermit on Mount Athos may not understand as he operates within a framework of gender relations that was relevant perhaps a thousand years earlier. Nevertheless, that very hermit who is innocent of gender issues may be a miracle worker, as his being is anchored in heaven. Unavoidably, such a spiritually advanced soul will have to speak through the vehicle of the culture within which he finds himself and that culture may be at a low level of development with reference to issues such as gender. A problem emerges when such an otherwise holy man absolutizes the relative, often relegating that which is outside his own cultural milieu to the workings of Satan. I cannot expect, for example, a hermit on Athos who has never left the insular, homogeneous, Orthodox, all-male world of the Holy Mountain to understand the complexities of gender issues in a city like New York or to get enthusiastic about the urgent necessity for interreligious dialogue for world peace in an increasingly multicultural and interdependent world.

At the same time, these very elders who are out of tune with the ways of modern culture have important things to teach us about the spiritual life, things that are crucial for our salvation and the survival of our species on this planet. The spiritual methods and practices of the Threefold Way and the homilies on love and compassion they left behind are guideposts for spiritual advancement for all human beings regardless of the culture from which they come and regardless of the level of the society within which they live. The opposite situation is also possible. A modern individual may be aligned in his way of thinking with the current collective stage of cultural evolution but at the same time low in terms of spiritual evolution. A professor of philosophy at an Ivy League university may be in tune with the level of cultural evolution in the society around him but way down at a low level of consciousness as a spiritual person. Such an individual may espouse all the right causes—gender equality, international justice and peace, human rights, and so on—but may be dominated by narcissism and egotism. On the other hand an illiterate peasant who lives in an undeveloped cultural milieu may be more advanced spiritually because he or she is "pure at heart."

After further probing into the theme of evolution and its paradoxes Michael and I shifted our focus to another important lesson that we agreed the Christian East could offer to the wider world. Knowledge of God and the attainment of information about higher realms of existence ideally necessitate training and counseling by an experienced guide as a safe way of proceeding on the spiritual path. In the same way that graduate students in astrophysics require mentoring by their professors and academic advisors in order to acquire knowledge of the physical heavens, so do spiritual seekers and explorers need guidance by experienced teachers in order to advance spiritually and to acquire knowledge of realities beyond this world. Of course, this argument is based on the presupposition that there are realities beyond this physical world that can be studied through appropriate spiritual methods. The problem in our university education is that all of our focus is on the accumulation of knowledge about the natural, sensate world. We have relegated the beyond to "mere faith" and virtually banished it from the classroom. In reality what we have done is to overemphasize the rational and problem-solving abilities of the mind. The intuitive, feeling side is neglected and remains atrophied since most of our efforts are so focused on enhancing our capacity to solve mental problems. Since the dominant belief is that the only real world is the physical world, there is little interest in or incentive for investing in the form of learning that transcends reason, the form of training and learning that we find in monasteries. The Christian elders challenge us to go beyond reason and beyond the limitations of our five senses. Michael and I agreed that the future of our species may in fact depend on how fast we move to incorporate some of the holy elders' perspectives on learning. It has become increasingly understood by pioneering thinkers of today that the single-minded pursuit of empirical, rational knowledge, by neglecting "inner" knowledge, is leading humanity to self-destruction. Our scientists have been unlocking the secrets of exter-

353

nal nature without balancing this advance, and the attendant accumulation of power in their hands, with an equal effort to acquire the wisdom that lies deeply buried within human consciousness. Our universities have failed to show an interest in, or devise a systematic strategy for, developing a psychology in the truest sense of the word that would tap into the hidden spiritual dimensions of our existence.

"Be careful what you are saying," Michael warned. "Are you suggesting bringing religion into the university?"

Given the multireligious nature of modern societies and the laws that keep a strict separation between church and state, such a suggestion would obviously be unacceptable, I told my friend. In my opinion it may not even be spiritually desirable to have one religion monopolizing God and becoming dominant to the exclusion of all others. It would be the equivalent of abolishing all languages except English. The infinite and ineffable God cannot be confined within specific cultural limits, within one historically created religion. It would be like confining the sun into a light bulb. Furthermore, we know from history that when one religion becomes dominant by merging with the state the outcome more often than not is religious intolerance and the violation of civil liberties, an ungodly development.

The cultural specifics of the Threefold Way were discovered and developed in a relatively homogeneous civilization, in which the overwhelming majority of people were Orthodox Christians and the imperial state offered its unremitting support to the religious establishment. It was, therefore, colored by the cultural characteristics of that particular civilization, the Byzantine civilization. Obviously, we cannot expect that Byzantium will be revived as the dominant religious culture of a modern multiethnic, multireligious America. I am not a prophet who can know how the Threefold Way, which I believe is transcultural and archetypal, will work itself out in an increasingly global, interdependent civilization during the next few centuries or even millennia. I do feel, however, that we need to frame our exploration of reality within the context of a wider vision that incorporates the Threefold Way. It will be based on the premise that reality is not confined within concrete, physical matter as our sciences have led us to believe. This is a lesson we can draw from the study of the lives of the great saints and their mystical experiences. This issue of bringing Spirit back into our educational sys-

354

tem will have to be negotiated by future generations. Current generations are burdened by heavy baggage related to rigid notions about the separation of church and state that, given our current level of cultural evolution, are perhaps needed in order to preserve our hard-won civil liberties. All we have to do here is point the way. We need to blend the relevant ways of the university with the relevant ways and methods of the monastery. Such a process may lead to the emergence of something entirely new. Unavoidably, it will be a complex and difficult process. It is too soon at the moment to know how it may unfold. But I am reminded of what André Malraux, a leading twentieth-century French author, once said: the twenty-first century will either be spiritual or it will not be. I would add that this spirituality must be based on what Father Maximos called that of the "lovers of God" rather than that of the "slaves" or the "employees," implying a mature and open relationship to the divine. One may also argue that the dominance of the type of faith that Father Maximos called the faith of "slaves" and to a lesser extent the faith of "employees" may be leading humanity to an ultimate catastrophe. These types of spirituality based on authoritarian social structures nurture the fundamentalist religiosity that tends to demonize the other, leading to the clash of civilizations and leaving no room for understanding, tolerance, compassion, and peaceful coexistence.

We need the vision of the "lovers of God" that presents us with a God who is loving, compassionate, and all-inclusive. I believe that the Christian elders in their desert struggles to reach *Theosis* opened up opportunities for the rest of us to gain insight into the nature of the heart of God, as much as that is possible by limited human minds.

It was easy to share and discuss these thoughts with Michael. He understood what I was suggesting. He himself uses intuition extensively in his artistic work. In so doing he has been trying through art to bridge the gulf separating the physical from the spiritual realms.

"Don't forget the power of thought," Michael reminded me once again as we walked back toward my office and his studio.

Based on the life and teachings of the holy elders of Eastern Christianity one can conclude that mind is not confined within the brain, that it is "nonlocal." Their "journeys out of the body" or, as they would call such experiences, "seeing through the Holy Spirit" (*en pneumati Agio*) challenge the dominant materialist worldview that mind and brain are identical and that mind cannot exist outside the physical brain. In fact, based on the teachings of the Christian elders, concentrated thought can have a profound impact not only on the spiritual level but also at the level of concrete, physical reality. Prayer in this sense can be seen also as concentrated thought energy that is sent out to heal body, mind, and soul. This is what some medical researchers, like Dr. Larry Dossey, claim today.[5]

Prayer and thought in general are not just abstractions but concrete energies that can have spiritual and practical implications on the praying person and on others for whom one is praying. On the basis of their personal experiences, the holy elders have known this fact all along. They are the masters and scientists par excellence not only of prayer but also of the laws that govern the supersensible, spiritual realms. Their legacy in the form of the Threefold Way is in reality a gift to humanity, a gift that they brought to life in places like the deserts of Egypt and Mount Athos. These "gifts of the desert" have remained dormant in our secularized civilization, the survival of which may depend on how quickly we make these gifts part of our everyday reality.

NOTES

All biblical quotations cited in
the text are taken from the
King James Version.

CHAPTER ONE: JOURNEY TO SEDONA

1. Kyriacos C. Markides, *Riding with the Lion: In Search of Mystical Christianity* (New York: Viking Penguin, 1995); *The Mountain of Silence: A Search for Orthodox Spirituality* (New York: Doubleday, 2001).

2. See Robert C. Fuller, *Spiritual but Not Religious: Understanding Unchurched America* (New York: Oxford University Press, 2001).

3. Paul Davis, "E.T. and God: Could Earthly Religions Survive the Discovery of Life Elsewhere in the Universe?" *Atlantic Monthly*, September, 2003, p. 112; see also Paul Davis, *The Mind of God: The Scientific Basis for a Rational World* (New York: Simon & Schuster, 1992).

4. Kyriacos C. Markides, *The Magus of Strovolos: The Extraordinary World of a Spiritual Healer* (New York: Penguin, 1985); *Homage to the Sun: The Wisdom of the Magus of Strovolos* (New York: Penguin, 1987); *Fire in the Heart: Healers, Sages and Mystics* (New York: Penguin, 1991).

5. John Chryssavgis, *Soul Mending: The Art of Spiritual Direction* (Brookline, MA: Holy Cross Orthodox Press, 2000), p. 1.

6. Jonathan Montaldo and Bernadette Dicker, eds., *Merton and Hesychasm: The Prayer of the Heart* (San Francisco: HarperSanFrancisco, 2003).

7. H. Middleton, *Precious Vessels of the Holy Spirit: The Lives and Counsels of Contemporary Elders of Greece* (Thessalonike, Greece: Protecting Veil Press, 2003); see also Markides, *Mountain of Silence*.

8. Paramahansa Yogananda, *Autobiography of a Yogi* (Los Angeles: Self-Realization Fellowship, 1987).

CHAPTER TWO: GIFT OF THE DESERT

1. See Jacob Needleman, *American Soul* (New York: Jeremy P. Tarcher, 2002).

2. Constantine Cavarnos, *Anchored in God: An Inside Account of Life, Art, and Thought on the Holy Mountain of Athos* (Athens: 1959), p. 183, quoted in Graham Speake, *Mount Athos: Renewal in Paradise* (New Haven, CT: Yale University Press, 2002), p. 206.

3. Peter France, *Hermits: The Insights of Solitude* (New York: St. Martin's Press, 1996), p. 31.

CHAPTER THREE: AEGEAN PILGRIMAGE

1. Keith A. Roberts, *Religion in Sociological Perspective* (Belmont, CA: Wadsworth, 1995), p. 169.

CHAPTER FIVE: A DIFFERENT HOSPITAL

1. N. Michael Vaporis and Evie Zachariades-Holmberg, trans., *The Akathist Hymn and Small Compline* (Needham, MA: Themely Publications, 1992).

2. See Markides, *Riding with the Lion*, pp. 327–332.

3. Joannes E. Chliaoutakis et al., "Greek Christian Orthodox Ecclesiastical Lifestyle: Could It Become a Pattern of Health-Related Behavior?" *Preventive Medicine* 34 (2002): 428–435.

4. Markides, *Mountain of Silence*, pp. 99–114.

CHAPTER SIX: ALTERATIONS OF THE SOUL

1. Michael Harner, *The Way of the Shaman: A Guide to Power and Healing* (New York: Bantam Books, 1982).

CHAPTER EIGHT: CONVERTS

1. Kallistos Ware, *The Orthodox Church* (New York: Penguin, 1964); *The Orthodox Way* (London: Mowbray, 1979).
2. Sophrony (Sakharov), *The Monk of Mount Athos: Staretz Silouan, 1866–1938* (Crestwood, NY: St. Vladimir's Seminary Press, 1975). Trans. from the Russian by Rosemary Edmonds.
3. Robert Thurman suggested something similar about Tibetan Buddhism and the Western Enlightenment. Robert Thurman, *Inner Revolution: Life, Liberty, and the Pursuit of Real Happiness* (New York: Riverhead Books, 1998).
4. Kallistos Ware, *The Inner Kingdom* (Crestwood, NY: St. Vladimir's Seminary Press, 2000).
5. For an elaboration on the Jesus Prayer see the Russian nineteenth-century classic written by an anonymous author: *The Way of the Pilgrim and the Pilgrim Continues His Way* (New York: Ballantine Books, 1974).
6. Kallistos Ware himself along with Philip Sherrard and G. E. H. Palmer translated the *Philokalia* into English. See Kallistos Ware, ed., *Philokalia: The Complete Text, Compiled by St. Nikodimos of the Holy Mountain and St. Makarios of Corinth*, Vol. 4 (London: Faber & Faber, 1999).

CHAPTER NINE: CUNNINGNESS

1. Kyriacos C. Markides and Joseph S. Joseph, "The Cypriots," in Jean S. Forward, ed., *Endangered Peoples of Europe* (Westport, CT: Greenwood Press, 2001), pp. 49–69.
2. Saint John Climacus, *The Ladder of Divine Ascent* (Boston: Holy Transfiguration Monastery, 1991).

359

CHAPTER ELEVEN: FAITH OF SAINTS

1. John Shelby Spong, *A New Christianity for a New World* (New York: HarperCollins, 2001).

CHAPTER TWELVE: DEATH AND NEAR-DEATH

1. Raymond Moody, *Life After Life* (St. Simons Island, GA: Mockingbird Books, 1975).

2. Seraphim Rose, *The Soul After Death: Contemporary "After-Death" Experiences in the Light of the Orthodox Teaching on the Afterlife* (Platina, CA: Saint Herman of Alaska Brotherhood, 1980).

3. Sophrony, *Monk of Mount Athos*, pp. 100–101.

4. For an examination of the teachings of Saint Silouan, see the website "Saint Silouan the Athonite," devoted to this contemporary Russian saint, http://silouan.narod.ru/linksil2.htm, http://silouan.narod.ru/indexe.html.

5. Joseph the Hesychast, *Monastic Wisdom: The Letters of Elder Joseph the Hesychast* (Florence, AZ: 1998). Quoted in Graham Speake, *Mount Athos: Renewal in Paradise* (New Haven, CT: Yale University Press, 2002), p. 202.

6. Huston Smith, *Why Religion Matters* (San Francisco: HarperSanFransisco, 2001), pp. 269–270.

7. One of the best sources in English of Saint Silouan's wisdom is Rosemary Edmonds's translation of Archimandrite Sophrony's *Saint Silouan the Athonite* (New York: St. Vladimir's Seminary Press, 1999). For Greek readers I recommend the excellent translation from the Russian by Father Zacharias of Essex, *O Agios Sylouanos Oh Athonites* (Essex, UK: Monastery of Saint John the Baptist, 1990).

CHAPTER THIRTEEN: REMEMBRANCE OF GOD

1. Robin Amis, *A Different Christianity: Early Christian Esotericism and Modern Thought* (Albany: State University of New York Press, 1995).

2. Richard Smoley, *Inner Christianity: A Guide to the Esoteric Tradition* (Boston: Shambhala, 2002), p. 165.

3. Basilios Gontikakis, *Fos Christou Fainei Pasi* [The Light of Christ Enlightens Everyone] (Athens: Armos Press, 2002), p. 25.

4. When I was writing this chapter I tried to find a good translation of the poem written in Byzantine Greek. On the day of my search I found in my e-mail, dated April 6, 2003, a message sent by an Orthodox bishop from the state of New York named Father Christodoulos (a person I have never met) reminding his parishioners of the upcoming celebration of Holy Tuesday. In that reminder he included the *troparion* of Cassiani translated in beautiful English. For this uncanny synchronicity I am very grateful.

CHAPTER FOURTEEN: SYNAXIS

1. Graham Speake, *Mount Athos: Renewal in Paradise* (New Haven, CT: Yale University Press, 2002), p. 265. For a magnificent pictorial presentation of Mount Athos see Douglas Demetrios Lyttle, *Miracle on the Monastery Mountain* (Pittsford, NY: Greenleaf Book Group, 2002). Professor Lyttle, a photographer, has collected rare color photos related to life on Mount Athos during more than twenty visits over the last thirty years. In his dazzling presentation he also provides a narrative of his experiences over the years.

2. Gerontos Porphyriou Kavsokalyvetou, *Vios kai Logoi* [Life and Words] (Chania, Crete: Holy Monastery of Chrysopege, 2003), pp. 282–283.

CHAPTER FIFTEEN: PRIMAL PASSIONS

1. Markides, *Riding with the Lion*, pp. 336–338.

2. Three Initiates, *The Kybalion: A Study of the Hermetic Philosophy of Ancient Egypt and Greece* (Chicago: Yogi Publication Society, 1912).

3. Robert Bellah et al., *Habits of the Heart* (Berkeley: University of California Press, 1985).

CHAPTER SEVENTEEN: REFLECTIONS

1. Gabrilia, *Mother Gavrilia: The Ascetic of Love* (Thessaloniki, Greece: Series Talanton, 1999).

2. Teva Regule, "An Interview with Bishop Kallistos Ware," *Saint Nina Quarterly* (June 11, 1997), http://www.stnina.org/97s/97s-ware-interview.htm.

3. Pierre Teilhard de Chardin, *The Phenomenon of Man* (New York: Harper, 1959).

4. Ken Wilber, *A Brief History of Everything* (Boston: Shambhala, 2001).

5. Larry Dossey, *Prayer Is Good Medicine: How to Reap the Healing Benefits of Prayer* (HarperSanFrancisco, 1997).

GLOSSARY

AGRYPNIA All-night prayer vigil.

AMARTIA The state of being cut off from God, commonly known as sin. Alienation from God.

ARCHONDARIKI Refectory. The guest room where pilgrims at the monastery are treated to refreshments.

ASKESIS Spiritual exercises, such as fasting, ceaseless prayer, all-night vigils, confession, communion, studying sacred texts and the lives and teachings of saints, and charity. Life's trials and temptations are considered an ongoing form of askesis.

CATHARSIS Purification of the heart and mind from egotistical passions and addictions. The first stage in the development of the soul as it moves toward God.

CHARISMA Divine gift. A charismatic is someone considered to be endowed with gifts of the spirit such as prophecy, healing, clairvoyance, and other psychic abilities. Such gifts are natural to the self and emerge when the soul is cleansed of egotistical passions.

CHRISTOS LOGOS The Christ that resides in the heart of every human being. It is beyond time and space. Jesus as the historical manifestation of the Logos.

DIAKONIA Assignment to a particular task in a monastery. It also means providentially assigned life's task.

ECCLESIA   The sum total of Church practices, methods, and sacred texts, as well as the testimony of saints and their teachings on how to know God. It includes the organizational structure of the Church. The *Ecclesia* is seen as a spiritual hospital for the cure of the maladies of the heart that obstruct our vision of God.

EFCHE   The Jesus Prayer. The repetition of "Lord Jesus Christ, Son of God, have mercy on me."

ELDER (ELDRESS)   Spiritual guide.

EROS MANIAKOS   A term used by Saint Maximos the Confessor expressing the "maniacal eros" of the lover of God. State of ecstatic love of God.

FOTISIS   The enlightenment of the soul. The gift of the Holy Spirit after the soul has undergone its purification, when it becomes endowed with divine charisma.

GERONTIKON   Multivolume compilation of biographical stories about the lives of holy elders.

HESYCHASM   Quietude. The silent and ceaseless form of meditative prayer, the hallmark of Athonite spirituality.

HESYCHAST   The practitioner of hesychasm, or quietude. A Christian hermit.

HIEROMONK   A monk who is ordained as a priest. A hieromonk can perform the sacraments such as confession and communion.

ICONOSTASIS   The icon screen separating the sanctuary from the rest of the church.

KOMBOSCHINI   Prayer knots made of wool used during the recital of the Jesus Prayer. See *Efche*.

LOGISMOS (LOGISMOI)   Thought form(s). Negative *logismoi* obstruct our vision of God. Catharsis involves cleansing our hearts and minds of such *logismoi*.

METANOIA   A fundamental transformation of mind and heart that takes the form of profound repentance. The beginning of the process, and a necessary stage, of the soul's reunification with God.

NOUS   The heart and mind of a human being. The center and totality of the mental and psychic powers of the self.

ORTHROS   Very early morning service preceding the liturgy and the Eucharist.

PANAGIA The Most Holy One (Mother of God).

PARAKLESIS Prayer invocation to the Holy Virgin or Christ for healing. A set of prayers for such purposes.

PHILODOXY Obsessive love for fame and glory.

PHILOPONIA Love for work and toil.

PLANI Delusion. An error of perception and cognition related to spiritual matters that undermines one's ascent to God. A product of human imperfection.

PNEUMATIKOS Spiritual guide and confessor. See also *elder*.

SKETE A hermitage attached to a monastery for more intense spiritual work. A *skete* may be home to a single hermit or a few monks with their spiritual elder.

THEORIA The vision of God while in a state of ecstasy. It follows the purification of the heart from egotism.

THEOSIS Union with God. The final destination and ultimate home of the human soul.

THEOTOKOS Mother of God. One of the names of the *Panagia*, the Most Holy One.

THREEFOLD WAY The stages that a soul must go through in order to reach God. See Catharsis, Fotisis, *Theosis*.

TRAPEZA The communal meal in monasteries.

TROPARION Hymn.

TYPIKON The prescribed program followed by monks and nuns.

UNCREATED LIGHT God's divine light. Mystical illumination.

BIBLIOGRAPHY

Amis, Robin. 1995. *A Different Christianity: Early Christian Esotericism and Modern Thought*. Albany: State University of New York Press.

Anonymous. 1974. *The Way of the Pilgrim and the Pilgrim Continues His Way*. New York: Ballantine Books.

Bellah, Robert N., Richard Madsen, William M. Sullivan, Ann Swidler, and Steven M. Tipton. 1985. *Habits of the Heart*. Berkeley: University of California Press.

Cavarnos, Constantine. 1959. *Anchored in God: An Inside Account of Life, Art, and Thought on the Holy Mountain of Athos*. Athens: np.

Chardin, Pierre Teilhard de. 1959. *The Phenomenon of Man*. New York: Harper.

Chliaoutakis, Joannes E.; Drakou I.; Gnardellis C.; Galariotou S.; Carra H.; Chliaoutaki M. 2002. "Greek Christian Orthodox Ecclesiastical Lifestyle: Could It Become a Pattern of Health-Related Behavior?" *Preventive Medicine*. 34: 428–435.

Chryssavgis, John. 2000. *Soul Mending: The Art of Spiritual Direction*. Brookline, MA: Holy Cross Orthodox Press.

Climacus, John. 1991. *The Ladder of Divine Ascent*. Boston: Holy Transfiguration Monastery.

Davis, Paul. 1992. *The Mind of God: The Scientific Basis for a Rational World*. New York: Simon & Schuster.

———. September, 2003. "E.T. and God: Could Earthly Religions Survive the Discovery of Life Elsewhere in the Universe?" *Atlantic Monthly*.

Dossey, Larry. 1997. *Prayer Is Good Medicine: How to Reap the Healing Benefits of Prayer*. San Francisco: HarperSanFrancisco.

France, Peter. 1996. *Hermits: The Insights of Solitude*. New York: St. Martin's Press.

Fuller, Robert C. 2001. *Spiritual but Not Religious: Understanding Unchurched America*. New York: Oxford University Press.

Gabrilia. 1999. *Mother Gavrilia: The Ascetic of Love*. Thessaloniki, Greece: Series Talanton.

Gontikakis, Basilios. 2002. *Fos Christou Fainei Pasi* [The Light of Christ Enlightens Everyone]. Athens: Armos Press.

Goritschewa, Tatiana. 1987. *Die Kraft der Ohnmächtigen*. Wuppertal, Germany: R. Brockhaus Verlag. Translated in Greek as *E Atheate Plevra tes Rossias*. [The Invisible Phase of Russia]. Athens: Akritas Press.

Greeley, Andrew M. 1975. *The Sociology of the Paranormal: A Reconnaissance*. Beverly Hills, CA: Sage Publications.

Harner, Michael. 1982. *The Way of the Shaman*. New York: Bantam.

Joseph the Hesychast. 1998. *Monastic Wisdom: The Letters of Elder Joseph the Hesychast*. Florence, AZ: Monastery of Saint Anthony Press.

Lyttle, Douglas Demetrios. 2002. *Miracle on the Monastery Mountain*. Pittsford, NY: Greenleaf Book Group.

Markides, Kyriacos C. 1985. *The Magus of Strovolos: The Extraordinary World of a Spiritual Healer*. New York: Penguin Arkana.

———. 1987. *Homage to the Sun: The Wisdom of the Magus of Strovolos*. New York: Penguin Arkana.

———. 1991. *Fire in the Heart: Healers, Sages, and Mystics*. New York: Penguin Arkana.

———. 1996. *Riding with the Lion: In Search of Mystical Christianity*. New York: Penguin Arkana.

———. 2001. *The Mountain of Silence: A Search for Orthodox Spirituality*. New York: Doubleday.

——— and Joseph S. Joseph. 2001. "The Cypriots." In Jean S. Forward, ed., *Endangered Peoples of Europe*, 49–69. Westport, CT: Greenwood Press.

Middleton, H. 2003. *Precious Vessels of the Holy Spirit: The Lives and Counsels of Contemporary Elders of Greece*. Thessaloniki, Greece: Protecting Veil Press.

Montaldo, Jonathan, and Bernadette Dicker, eds. 2003. *Merton and Hesychasm: The Prayer of the Heart*. San Francisco: HarperSanFrancisco.

Moody, Raymond. 1975. *Life After Life*. St. Simons Island, GA: Mockingbird Books.

Needleman, Jacob. 2002. *American Soul*. New York: Jeremy P. Tarcher.

Porphyriou, Gerontos Kavsokalyvetou. 2003. *Vios kai Logoi* [Life and Words]. Chania, Crete: Holy Monastery of Chrysopege.

Regule, Teva. June 11, 1997. "An Interview with Bishop Kallistos Ware." *Saint Nina Quarterly.* http://www.stnina.org/97s/97s-ware-interview.htm.

Roberts, Keith A. 1995. *Religion in Sociological Perspective*. Belmont, CA: Wadsworth.

Rose, Seraphim. 1980. *The Soul After Death: Contemporary "After-Death" Experiences in the Light of the Orthodox Teaching on the Afterlife*. Platina, CA: Saint Herman of Alaska Brotherhood.

"Saint Silouan the Athonite," website with links to Web pages, icons, and photographs, http://silouan.narod.ru/linksil2.htm, http://silouan.narod.ru/indexe.html.

Smith, Huston. 2001. *Why Religion Matters*. San Francisco: HarperSanFransisco.

Smoley, Richard. 2002. *Inner Christianity: A Guide to the Esoteric Tradition* Boston: Shambhala.

Sophrony (Sakharov). 1975. *The Monk of Mount Athos: Staretz Silouan, 1866–1938*. Crestwood, NY: St. Vladimir's Seminary Press.

———. 1999. *Saint Silouan the Athonite*. Translated by Rosemary Edmonds. New York: St. Vladimir's Seminary Press.

Speake, Graham. 2002. *Mount Athos: Renewal in Paradise*. New Haven: Yale University Press.

Spong, John Shelby. 2001. *A New Christianity for a New World*. New York: HarperCollins.

Three Initiates. 1912. *The Kybalion: A Study of the Hermetic Philosophy of Ancient Egypt and Greece*. Chicago: Yogi Publication Society.

Thurman, Robert. 1998. *Inner Revolution: Life, Liberty and the Pursuit of Real Happiness*. New York: Riverhead Books.

Vaporis, N. Michael, and Evie Zachariades-Holmberg, trans. 1992. *The Akathist Hymn and Small Compline*. Needham, MA: Themely Publications.

Ware, Kallistos. 1964. *The Orthodox Church*. New York: Penguin.

———. 1979. *The Orthodox Way*. London: Mowbray.

———. 2000. *The Inner Kingdom*. Crestwood, NY: St. Vladimir's Seminary Press.

———, ed. 1999. *Philokalia: The Complete Text, Compiled by St. Nikodimos of the Holy Mountain and St. Makarios of Corinth*, Vol. 4. Translated by Kallistos Ware, Philip Sherrard, and G. E. H. Palmer. London: Faber & Faber.

Wilber, Ken. 1983. *Eye to Eye: The Quest for the New Paradigm*. Garden City, NY: Anchor.

———. 2001. *A Brief History of Everything*. Boston: Shambhala.

Yogananda, Paramahansa. 1987. *Autobiography of a Yogi*. Los Angeles: Self-Realization Fellowship.